# Science and Racket Sports III

Racket sports such as badminton, tennis, table tennis and squash pose many challenges to sports scientists, sports physicians, therapists and coaches.

*Science and Racket Sports III* contains the peer-reviewed papers and keynote addresses presented at the combined Third World Congress of Science and Racket Sports and Eighth International Table Tennis Federation Sports Science Congress.

Speakers at the conference presented cutting edge research in racket sports science along the five key themes of:

- Notational match analysis
- Sports medicine
- Biomechanics
- Sports psychology
- Sports physiology

The collection embraces a broad spectrum of the issues being examined by contemporary sports scientists.

# Third World Congress of Science and Racket Sports and the Eighth International Table Tennis Federation Sports Science Congress 17–19 May 2003

held at the National Institute of Sport and Physical Education, Paris, France

**Organizing Committee**
Michel Jacquet
Jean-Francois Kahn (Chair)
Adrian Lees
Didier Lehenaff
Gilbert Liegeois
Christian Palierne

**Scientific Committee**
Jeff Chandler
Jean-Francois Kahn
Adrian Lees (Chair)
Gilbert Liegeois
Bernard Maton
Ian Maynard
Carole Seve

# Science and Racket Sports III

The Proceedings of the Eighth International Table Tennis Federation Sports Science Congress and the Third World Congress of Science and Racket Sports

**Edited by**

## A. Lees

*Research Institute for Sport and Exercise Sciences,*
*Liverpool John Moores University, UK*

## J.-F. Kahn

*Faculty of Medicine, Pitié-Salpêtrière,*
*Pierre and Marie Curie University, Paris, France*

and

## I.W. Maynard

*Centre for Sport and Exercise Sciences,*
*Sheffield Hallam University, Sheffield, UK*

Routledge
Taylor & Francis Group

LONDON AND NEW YORK

First published 2004
by Routledge
2 Park Square, Milton Park, Abingdon, Oxon OX14 4RN

Simultaneously published in the USA and Canada
by Taylor & Francis Inc
270 Madison Avenue, New York, NY 10016

*Routledge is an imprint of the Taylor & Francis Group*

Transferred to Digital Printing 2005

*Publisher's Note*
This book has been produced from camera-ready copy supplied
by the authors

Every effort has been made to ensure that the advice and information in
this book is true and accurate at the time of going to press. However,
neither the publisher nor the authors can accept any legal responsibility or
liability for any errors or omissions that may be made. In the case of drug
administration, any medical procedure or the use of technical equipment
mentioned within this book, you are strongly advised to consult the
manufacturer's guidelines.

*British Library Cataloguing in Publication Data*
A catalogue record for this book is available
from the British Library

*Library of Congress Cataloging in Publication Data*
A catalog record for this book has been requested

ISBN 0–415–33840–9

Printed and bound by Antony Rowe Ltd, Eastbourne

# CONTENTS

# Preface

The meeting incorporating both the Third World Congress of Science and Racket Sports and the Eighth International Table Tennis Federation Sports Science Congress was held at the National Institute for Sport and Physical Education, Paris France from May 17$^{th}$–19$^{th}$ 2003.

The World Congress of Science and Racket Sports was the third in its series (the first being held at Runcorn, UK in 1993 and the second at Lilleshall, UK in 1997) and this volume represents the third published book of proceedings of this congress. It is a part of the academic programmes initiated by the World Commission of Science and Sports which, over the last three decades, has promoted applied sports science congresses on swimming, football, golf, and winter sports. The broad aim of these congresses is to bring together scientists whose research work is concerned with particular sports and practitioners in these sports who are interested in obtaining current information about scientific aspects.

The International Table Tennis Federation (ITTF) holds its Sports Science Congress biannually and this was the eighth in its now well established series. It has the aim of promoting and disseminating scientific research specifically within the game of table tennis.

The aims of each congress are thus broadly similar and so when the opportunity arose to combine the two congresses again (they were also amalgamated at Lilleshall in 1997) this was welcomed by both groups. Joint organising and scientific committees were established and their members worked together to promote the aims of both organisations. The scientific programme consisted of a series of keynote lectures, podium communications, poster presentations and workshops. The result was a well attended congress with participants from every continent who were able to interact across the scientific disciplines and across the various racket sports.

The organisers are indebted to the ITTF whose sponsorship of the combined event ensured its success. The organisers are also grateful for the co-operation and support given by the French Table Tennis Association.

# Introduction

This volume is the third in the Science and Racket Sport series and contains papers presented at the Third World Congress of Science and Racket Sports and the Eighth International Table Tennis Federation Sports Science Congress which was held at the National Institute for Sport and Physical Education, Paris France from May 17th–19th 2003.

Each manuscript has been subject to peer review by at least two expert referees and editorial judgement before being accepted for publication. This review process has ensured that there is consistency and a high level of scientific quality across all papers. We are particularly indebted to those anonymous reviewers without whose help this volume could never have been completed on time.

The volume contains 44 papers covering all four racket sports, although several address issues which have application across all racket disciplines. The papers are organised into seven scientific parts, each part representing a theme of the congress and in most cases introduced by one of the keynote lectures. The choice of location of papers in a section was at the discretion of the editors and it is acknowledged that some papers could fit happily into more than one section. A choice had to be made and it should be remembered that this choice was an attempt to aid the reader rather than to categorise work, which in many cases represents the best of interdisciplinary research.

The sections and papers indicate current research in the racket sports and provide markers for the topics that researchers are currently addressing. Less than half of the papers presented at the Congress are included due to non-submission or rejection due to lateness or inadequate scientific merit. Nevertheless those contained within are a reasonable reflection of the topics covered within the Congress programme.

The editors are grateful to the contributors for their painstaking preparation of the manuscript and their willingness to comply with the publisher's guidelines and deadlines. We are also indebted to them for rapid and helpful responses to queries raised in the editing process.

It is our aim that the papers in this volume should function as an up-to-date reference for researchers in the racket sports and yield important current information for racket sport practitioners. The material may motivate others to embark on research programmes prior to the Fourth World congress of Science and Racket Sports which hopefully will be held in Madrid, Spain in 2007.

**Adrian Lees (Chair)**
**Jean-Francois Kahn**
**Ian Maynard**

# Part One

# Physiology of Racket Sports

# 1 An on-court, ghosting protocol to replicate physiological demands of a competitive squash match

R.A. Sherman, T.J. Creasey and A.M. Batterham
*Applied Physiology Research Group, Department of Sport and Exercise Science, University of Bath, Claverton Down, Bath, BA2 7AY, UK.*

## 1 Introduction

Squash is an intermittent, high-intensity sport which places demand on both the aerobic and anaerobic energy systems (Montpetit, 1990). A normal match consists of a minimum of three and a maximum of five games and can last anywhere from 40 min to over 120 min, depending on skill standard (Graydon et al., 1998). Each game of squash can require as much as 82 rallies and 1722 shots, with only 7 s rest between each rally (Sharp, 1998). As a result of the restricted environment and specific movement patterns, squash match play results in a large physiological and thermoregulatory strain (Blanksby et al., 1980).

An on-court squash protocol has been published (Steininger and Wodick, 1987), but this was primarily for maximal fitness testing and was not designed to simulate match play demands, although it could be adapted for this purpose. To our knowledge, only one previous paper has been published that attempts to recreate the demands of normal match play. Using two common training drills, Todd and co-workers (1998) suggested that short boast & drive and boast, drop & drive routines closely replicated the physiological demands, indicated using heart rate (HR) and oxygen uptake ($\dot{V}O_2$), of a time limited match. Heart rate responses during competitive match play and boast & drive shuttles (Todd et al., 1998) compared favourably to competitive match play (Blanksby et al., 1973; Gillam et al., 1990; Brown and Winter, 1996). More recently, the advent of reliable portable gas analysers has enabled $\dot{V}O_2$ to be measured accurately during squash matches. Results have suggested an average $\dot{V}O_2$ of 42 ml·kg·min$^{-1}$ (Gillam et al., 1990; Todd et al., 1998) and a relative intensity of 74% $\dot{V}O_2$max (Todd et al., 1998).

The investigation of the physiological changes that occur during, and as a result of exercise, can be performed in the laboratory setting or in a field-based setting. Both of these environments have unique advantages; the laboratory allows tight control of influencing variables and test adherence and field-testing provides an ecologically valid environment for both the test and participant. The ability to combine laboratory control with field validity has allowed research findings to be applied to the activity used in the testing. Utilising appropriate sporting activities as the model for investigating changes in physiology is an established procedure, with soccer being a popular, recent focus (Drust et al., 2000; Nicholas et al., 2000). Only a limited number of published studies have used squash as the model and none have used a controlled field test. In order to fill this gap, an on-court, simulated match-play (sMP) protocol was designed to allow ecologically valid testing of squash match play, yet at the same time allowing maintenance of a high degree of control. Furthermore, the sMP protocol was designed to allow comparison of whole match demands, rather than short duration demands.

Accordingly, the aim of the present study was to validate the physiological demands of a newly designed, on-court, sMP protocol against previous published physiological data from competitive match play.

## 2 Methods

### 2.1 Participants

Seven male squash players (age $22.3 \pm 5.0$ years, height $1.79 \pm 0.03$ m, body mass $72.2 \pm 4.9$ kg, $\dot{V}O_2max$ $62.0 \pm 7.8$ ml·kg·min$^{-1}$; mean $\pm$ SD) volunteered and gave written informed consent to participate in this study, which had local ethics committee approval.

### 2.2 Preliminary testing

Maximal oxygen uptake ($\dot{V}O_2max$) was measured using a progressive incline treadmill protocol adapted from a previous study (Chin et al., 1995). The incline started at 0 % for the first 2 min and increased by 2.5 % every further 2 min, with the speed set at 12 km·h$^{-1}$ throughout the test. Body mass was recorded using a beam scale (Weylux Model 424, H Fereday & Sons Limited, London, England) to the nearest 50 g and height was measured using a wall mounted Harpenden stadiometer (Holtain Limited, Crymych, Wales) to the nearest 1 mm. To minimise any training and learning effect prior to the study, participants completed two runs of the simulated match play before completing the experimental trial.

### 2.3 Experimental testing

Participants completed four games of simulated match play, each game followed by 90 s rest in accordance with normal match rules (World Squash Federation, 2001). Each game of simulated match play lasted 11 min 22 s and contained blocks of 'fast' and 'slow' ghosting lasting 3 s and 3.5 s, respectively. The duration of each ghosting block was three, five, nine or 15 shuttles and at the end of each ghosting block there was an 8 s rest period. Participants were instructed that during all the ghosting blocks their front foot must reach the taped markers on the court floor (located 1.2 m away from each corner) and that they must always pass through a 0.25 m square box located over the 'T' between shots. Furthermore, they were instructed that the first shuttle in every block had to be to a front corner and the experimenters ensured that all the corners were used. Auditory cues, from a CD, indicated the start and end of each game and ghosting block and acted as a pacer back to the 'T' during each ghosting block.

All experimental tests were completed on the University of Bath squash courts. On-court air temperature ($T_a$) and relative humidity (RH) were recorded at the end of each game of simulated match play using a digital thermohygrometer (Testo 625, Testo Ltd., Alton, England). Participants were able to drink *ad libitum* during each 90 s rest period.

### 2.4 Physiological measurements

Heart rate was monitored every 5 s during exercise using a short-range telemetry system (Polar Vantage NV, Polar Electro, Kempele, Finland). Mean HR and maximum HR (HRmax) data were expressed in absolute terms (beats·min$^{-1}$) and mean HR was also expressed relative to age-predicted maximum (age-predicted max = 220 - age) and HR at $\dot{V}O_2$max (HR @ $\dot{V}O_2$max). A subjective rating of perceived exertion (RPE) was recorded using a 15-point scale (Borg, 1973) at the end of each game of simulated match play.

### 2.5 Statistics

One-way, repeated measures analysis of variance (ANOVA) was performed on the HR data to identify any differences between the four games of simulated match play. Significance was accepted at $P < 0.05$ and all results are reported as mean ± standard deviation (SD).

### 3 Results

### 3.1 Heart rate

Mean HR during the simulated match play was 170 ± 12 beats·min$^{-1}$ and mean HRmax was 182 ± 12 beats·min$^{-1}$. The non-significant ($P = 0.15$) changes in mean HR across the four games can be seen in Figure 1. Participation in the simulated match play resulted in the participants attaining an age-predicted max HR of 86 ± 8 % and HR @ $\dot{V}O_2$max of 87 ± 6 %.

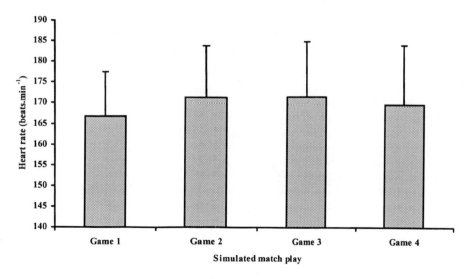

Figure 1. Mean HR changes during the simulated match play (Error bars = 1 SD).

### 3.2 Ratings of perceived exertion

The subjective RPE rose steadily throughout the simulated match play, from $14 \pm 3$ at the end of the first game, reaching a peak of $16 \pm 3$ at the end of the fourth game.

### 3.3 Environmental conditions

The $T_a$ rose by 0.7 °C from the pre-trial measurement of $22.5 \pm 0.1$ °C to the post-trial measurement of $23.2 \pm 1.0$ °C and the relative humidity rose from $43.4 \pm 4.0$ % at the start of the first game to $47.3 \pm 2.7$ % at the end of the fourth game.

## 4 Discussion

The results from this study indicated that participation in the simulated match play resulted in a large physiological demand being placed on the participant, with a mean HR of 170 beats·min$^{-1}$ and a relative intensity of 86 % and 87 % of age-predicted max HR and HR @ $\dot{V}O_2$max, respectively. There were no significant differences in physiological demand and intensity between the games of simulated match play, as measured by HR. As the HR rose, so there was a concomitant rise in subjective exertion.

The mean HR resulting from the simulated match play was higher than previous match play findings (Blanksby et al., 1973; Beaudin et al., 1978; Blanksby et al., 1980; Graydon et al., 1998), although the participants' training status must be taken into account, as highly trained squash players have been shown to have similar HR during match play (Gillam et al., 1990). Intermittent exercise imparts an increased physiological strain on the participant in both a cool (Nevill et al., 1995) and hot environment (Kraning and Gonzalez, 1991) and may be an interaction between the pulses of intermittent activity and heat exposure and short recovery periods (Belding et al., 1966). Superimposed upon the physiological strain, thermoregulatory responses are overloaded during squash match play (Blanksby et al., 1980; Locke et al., 1997) and can lead to increased cardiovascular strain, mediated via increased vasodilation, cardiac output and stroke volume. Elevated mean HR during the simulated match play could be due to the crouched position (Reilly and Seaton, 1990) frequently adopted and also a combination of the unique environmental conditions on-court and use of the arms (Graydon et al., 1998). Interestingly, the inclusion of one participant who had a high HR response to exercise, with mean HR of 192 beats·min$^{-1}$ and age-predicted max HR of 104 % during simulated match play, may have exaggerated the mean HR response.

The RPE increase throughout the duration of the simulated match play is in agreement with a previous squash match play study (Graydon et al., 1998), although their findings also showed a concomitant increase in HR across the three games of squash match play. Our HR findings, of an early rise followed by maintenance throughout the remainder of the match, contradict Graydon and colleagues (1998) but support Blanksby and co-workers (1973) who found a rapid increase in HR during the first 7 min followed by a plateau for the remainder of the match. It must be noted that Graydon and co-workers (1998) questioned the validity of their own protocol thus raising doubts about their HR and RPE data. The increasing mean HR in their placebo trial even though the length of each game was decreasing, possibly suggests that the participants, although being club standard, were not well trained and could not match the demands of the protocol.

The relative intensity of the simulated match play, as indicated by the age-predicted max HR and HR @ $\dot{V}O_2$max data, clearly showed that the protocol represented a high-intensity exercise challenge, as would be expected from squash match play (Montpetit, 1990). Furthermore, although the intensity of this protocol was higher than that in earlier work conducted on competitive squash players (Blanksby et al., 1973; Beaudin et al., 1978; Blanksby et al., 1980), it was consistent with the trend of increasing intensity in the modern game (Brown and Winter, 1996) and recent match analysis (Todd et al., 1998). The HR @ $\dot{V}O_2$max data were included due to the limitation of using age-predicted max HR with participants with low resting HR (Whaley et al., 1992) and clearly supported the findings that the simulated match play resulted in a high-intensity exercise challenge.

## 5 Conclusions

It is clear that the simulated match play replicated the physiological demands of squash match play, as indicated by HR response. As the HR response indicated an overloaded cardiovascular system, the simulated match play could be utilised as a training tool for competitive squash players, as it may result in beneficial adaptations. Furthermore, the simulated match play provided a suitable field-based testing protocol and could be used for future research investigating the physiological consequences of competitive squash.

## 6 References

Beaudin, P., Zapiec, C. and Montgomery, D. (1978). Heart rate response and lactic acid concentration in squash players. **Research Quarterly**, 49, 406-412.

Belding, H.S., Hertig, B.A. and Kraning, K.K. (1966). Comparison of man's responses to pulsed and unpulsed environmental heat and exercise. **Journal of Applied Physiology**, 21, 138-142.

Blanksby, B.A., Elliott, B.C. and Bloomfield, J. (1973). Telemetered heart rate responses of middle-aged sedentary males, middle-aged active males and 'A' grade male squash players. **Medical Journal of Australia**, 2, 477-481.

Blanksby, B.A., Elliott, B.C., Davis, K.H. and Mercer, M.D. (1980). Blood pressure and rectal temperature responses of middle-aged sedentary, middle-aged active and "A" grade competitive male squash players. **British Journal of Sports Medicine**, 14, 133-138.

Borg, G.A. (1973). Perceived exertion: a note on history and methods. **Medicine and Science in Sports**, 5, 90-93.

Brown, D. and Winter, E.M. (1996). Heart rate responses in squash during competitive match-play. **Journal of Sports Sciences**, 14, 68-69.

Chin, M.-K., Steininger, K., So, R.C.H., Clark, C.R. and Wong, A.S.K. (1995). Physiological profile and sport specific fitness of Asian elite squash players. **British Journal of Sports Medicine**, 29, 158-164.

Drust, B., Reilly, T. and Cable, N.T. (2000). Physiological responses to laboratory-based soccer-specific intermittent and continuous exercise. **Journal of Sports Sciences**, 18, 885-892.

Gillam, I., Siviour, C., Ellis, L. and Brown, P. (1990). The on-court energy demands of squash on elite level players. In **Third Report on National Sport Research Program** (edited by J. Draper), Australian Sports Commission, Canberra, pp. 35.

Graydon, J., Taylor, S. and Smith, M. (1998). The effect of carbohydrate ingestion on shot accuracy during a conditioned squash match. In **Science and Racket Sports II** (edited by A. Lees, I. Maynard and T. Reilly), London: E & FN Spon, pp. 68-74.

Kraning, K.K. and Gonzalez, R.R. (1991). Physiological consequences of intermittent exercise during compensable and uncompensable heat stress. **Journal of Applied Physiology**, 71, 2138-2145.

Locke, S., Colquhoun, D., Briner, M., Ellis, L., O'Brien, M., Wollstein, J. and Allen, G. (1997). Squash racquets: a review of physiology and medicine. **Sports Medicine**, 23, 130-138.

Montpetit, R.R. (1990). Applied physiology of squash. **Sports Medicine**, 10, 31-41.

Nevill, M.E., Garrett, A., Maxwell, N., Parsons, K.C. and Norwitz, A. (1995). Thermal strain of intermittent and continuous exercise at 10 and 35 °C in man. **Journal of Physiology**, 483, 124P-125P.

Nicholas, C.W., Nuttall, F.E. and Williams, C. (2000). The Loughborough Intermittent Shuttle Test: A field test that simulates the activity pattern of soccer. **Journal of Sports Sciences**, 18, 97-104.

Reilly, T. and Seaton, A. (1990). Physiological strain unique to field hockey. **Journal of Sports Medicine and Physical Fitness**, 30, 142-146.

Sharp, N.C.C. (1998). Physiological demands and fitness for squash. In **Science and Racket Sports II** (edited by A. Lees, I. Maynard and T. Reilly), London: E & FN Spon, pp. 3-13.

Steininger, K. and Wodick, R.E. (1987). Sports-specific fitness testing in squash. **British Journal of Sports Medicine**, 21, 23-26.

Todd, M.K., Mahoney, C.A. and Wallace, W.F.M. (1998). The efficacy of training routines as a preparation for competitive squash. In **Science and Racket Sports II** (edited by. A. Lees, I. Maynard and T. Reilly), London: E & FN Spon, pp. 91-96.

Whaley, M.H., Kaminsky, L.A., Dwyer, G.B., Getchell, L.H. and Norton, J.A. (1992). Predictors of over- and underachievement of age-predicted maximal heart rate. **Medicine and Science in Sports and Exercise**, 24, 1173-1179.

World Squash Federation (2001). **World Squash Singles Rules Booklet**. World Squash Federation, London.

# 2 The effect of a new sports drink on fatigue factors in competitive tennis athletes

B.L. Marks, T.J. Angelopoulos, E. Shields, L.M. Katz, T. Moore, S. Hylton, R. Larson and J. Wingo

*Department of Exercise and Sport Science and Department of Emergency Medicine, University of North Carolina at Chapel Hill, NC, 27599-8700 and Department of Child, Family and Community Sciences, University of Central Florida, Orlando, FL 32816-1250, USA.*

## 1 Introduction

Competitive tennis is an intermittent moderate to high intensity endurance sport with bursts of anaerobic activity which may be aggravated by heat and dehydration. In college matches, as well as some futures professional matches, it is common for players to compete in both doubles and single matches on the same day, sometimes with less than an hour of rest between matches. When matches approach or exceed 2 hours, it is not unusual to see performance deteriorate rapidly in the third set. Past sport nutrition research has shown that supplementing with a 6-8% carbohydrate (CHO)-electrolyte sports substantially reduces fatigue and assists re-hydration (Coleman, 1988). Furthermore, studies have determined that CHO supplementation may also reduce the sensation of effort and improve motivation (Davis, 2001). Tennis-specific sport nutrition research has reported that CHO-electrolyte beverage supplementation during match play maintains blood glucose levels, reduces dehydration, improves alertness and coordination, decreases unforced errors, and reduces fatigue (Burke and Ekblom, 1982; Keul et al., 1995; Vergauwen et al., 1998).

A new sports drink, Accelerad™, suggests its formula can deliver more energy to the muscles faster than the traditional CHO-electrolyte sport drinks available. The manufacturer's research has suggested that adding 1.9% protein (PRO; less than 7 g) to a 7.5% CHO-electrolyte sport drink will delay fatigue by boosting insulin levels, thereby sparing muscle glycogen stores and improving endurance capacity. Research with beverages designed to enhance recovery has shown that the addition of PRO to a CHO drink in a 4:1 ratio increased insulin levels, glucose uptake, and glycogen loading following exercise (Willliams et al., 2003). When this ratio of protein was added to a 7.75% CHO drink and consumed during an intermittent intensity cycle ride in a laboratory setting, the researchers found a 24% improvement in endurance compared to the same 7.75% CHO drink without protein and a 54% improvement compared to water (Burke, 2001).

The purpose of this study was to investigate whether ingestion of the sports drink Accelerad™ at regular intervals during a routine hard tennis practice in the heat reduces fatigue in male college tennis players when compared to a placebo.

## 2 Methods

### 2.1 Design
The study was approved by the university's Institutional Human Use Review Boards. The design was double-blind with the subjects randomly assigned to a counterbalanced treatment sequence comparing the effectiveness of a CHO-PRO drink to a placebo drink for delaying the onset of fatigue (Accelerade™ and placebo, Pacific Health Laboratories, Woodbridge, NJ). The study required three visits, of which the first was a pilot and not included in the data analyses. Full participation and analyses details are described later. The independent variables were the sport drink conditions: Accelerad™ (AC) versus Placebo (PL) and "spider test" trials (10 repeated effort agility tests with 25 seconds rest between trials). For each trial, the dependent variables were measures of performance time in seconds (s), heart rate (beats·min$^{-1}$), and ratings of perceived exertion (RPE, Borg, 1973). The spider test trials immediately followed a 2-hour 'hard' practice session. Additionally, the dependent variables of body mass (kg) , blood glucose (mmol·L$^{-1}$), and urine specific gravity (Usg) were measured pre-practice and post-practice.

### 2.2 Participants
Eighteen male tennis athletes from two U.S. Division I university tennis teams volunteered to participate in the study, although only 9 players completed both experimental conditions. The high rate of attrition was attributed to poor palatability of the product, inability to comply with nutritional requirements, and athletic injury/fatigue unrelated to the study. Both teams were ranked in the top 50 by the United States Intercollegiate Tennis Association. The means (± s) for age, body mass, and height were: 20 years (± 1.4), 76.5 kg (± 2.4), and 1.8 m (± 0.1), respectively.

### 2.3 Materials
The AC sport drink contained 586 kJ, 26 g CHO, 6.5 g PRO, 1 g Fat, 190 mg Na, and 64 mg K per 354 ml. Players had a choice of either orange or lemon-lime. The PL drink was similar in taste, texture, and electrolytes but was void of PRO and CHO. An artificial non-caloric sweetener was used in the PL. The volume load given to each subject was in accordance with current National Athletic Training Association (NATA) guidelines, 230 ml approximately every 15 minutes throughout the 2-hour practice session (Casa et al., 2000). Body mass and height were measured with a digital scale and height board. Urine specific gravity (Usg) was determined using Multistix® Reagent Chem Dip Sticks (Bayer Corp., Elkhart, IN) immersed in a 5 ml urine sample. Blood glucose was measured using the One-Touch Ultra Blood Glucose Meter Kit (LifeScan Inc., Johnson and Johnson, Milpitas, CA) which required 1 μl of blood and provided an analysis in 5 seconds. Heart rate monitoring was conducted using Polar A1 heart rate monitors (Polar Ectro Inc., Woodbury, NY). At the conclusion of practice, the players immediately began the maximum effort 5-directional pattern spider test trials. The test pattern consisted of forward, backward, lateral, and diagonal sprinting to and from the baseline "center T" to the net or right and left sidelines.

## 2.4 Procedures

One week prior to the experimental trials, the players participated in a pilot session. The coaches were instructed to standardize each practice session with an RPE of "15" (hard) as rated by the players (Borg, 1973). To reduce a performance-related learning effect for the spider tests, players completed 10 spider test trials immediately following practice. Seven days after the pilot testing, the players underwent the two experimental treatments (AC or PL) separated by 7 days each. On test days, the players' food intakes were standardized. In lieu of their regular meals, 3-4 hours prior to practice they were instructed to consume a 354 ml liquid meal (Slim Fast Ultra: 921 kJ, 70 % CHO, 12% FAT, 18% PRO) plus one-half of a sport nutrition bar (Harvest Power Bar: 460 kJ, 75% CHO, 15% FAT, 11% PRO) totaling 1381 kJ. They were asked to refrain from eating/drinking anything else other than water and were given sugarless non-caloric gum to discourage additional food intake. Upon arrival to the training room, players were weighed and urine and blood samples were obtained. They then participated in an outdoor practice consisting of a 20-minute warm-up, 30 minutes of drills, approximately one hour of match play, and 10 minutes of serve practice. The heat stress index for both days at both sites were considered "moderate risk", with the average thermal conditions being 31°C, 44% RH (Powers and Howley, 2002). For all test days, pre-measured personal fluid containers were prepared. The research assistants gave the players 230 ml of chilled fluid every 15 minutes from their individual bottles. Any fluid not consumed was returned to their container. Total fluid consumption was determined at the end of each practice. Immediately after practice but before the spider test trials began, the player gave an overall RPE rating for the intensity of the 2-hour practice. At the end of practice, the players began the spider test trials. After each trial, the time to complete the spider test, the RPE, and heart rate were recorded. The spider test was repeated 10 times with 25 s rest given between trials. No food/fluids were permitted to be taken during this testing period. Afterwards, the players participated in a food recall interview for that day to verify food intake compliance as well as to check to see if they could determine the type of drink they consumed. Nutritional compliance was 90% (one site reported 100% compliance and the other 80%); none were able to determine the type of drink consumed. The players reported back to the training room for a post-practice weigh-in and to give a urine and blood sample after which they were fed.

## 3 Results

### 3.1 Statistical analyses

Two-tailed paired t-tests with Bonferonni adjustments were used to determine significant differences pre-practice to post-practice for the participants' body mass, fluid volume intake, urine specific gravity (Usg), and blood glucose. All three dependent variables for the spider test trials (performance time, heart rate, RPE) were analyzed using 2 x 10 (Group x Trial) within subjects repeated measures analysis of variance with planned contrasts. For all analyses, the alpha level was set at the $P < 0.05$ level of confidence.

### 3.2 Body mass, volume load, urine specific gravity, and blood glucose measures

Body mass (kg) remained stable for all practice conditions (AC: pre = 76.3 ± 8, post = 75.9 ± 7.6; PL: pre = 75.8 ± 7.8, post = 76.3 ± 8.2; $P \geq 0.901$). Total and hourly fluid intake were not significantly different between groups (Total (ml): AC =1557 ± 553 vs. PL = 1740 ± 551; P = 0.407; Hourly (ml·hr⁻¹): AC = 856 ± 322 vs. PL = 868 ± 368; P = 0.937). For both groups, Usg increased significantly (P ≤ 0.002) by the end of practice (AC pre =1.014 ± 0.007, AC post =1.026 ± 0.009; PL pre = 1.012 ± 0.006, PL post = 1.023 ± 0.009). Blood glucose values (mmol·L⁻¹) were also similar pre-practice to post- practice (PL pre = 0.98 ± 0.15, PL post = 1.01 ± 0.18; AC pre = 0.99 ± 0.15, AC post = 1.03 ± 0.14; P > 0.634). None of these dependent measures differed significantly between groups (P ≥ 0.231).

### 3.3 Performance times for spider trials
Sprint times (s) for the spider test trials did not differ significantly between groups and there were no significant interaction effects. Actual trial times ranged from 20.3- 23.7 (± 1.1-1.8). There was a significant main effect of Trial (T) where T1 was significantly faster than T2 for both groups (AC: T1 = 22.8 ± 1.1 vs. T2 = 23.4 ± 2.3; PL: T1 = 22.4 ± 1.2 vs. T2 = 23.1 ± 1.2; P ≤ 0.03). Although T1 of the PL condition (22.4 ± 1.2) was significantly faster than T10 (23.2 ± 1.8; P = 0.018), this was not true for the AC condition (T1 = 22.8 ± 1.1 vs. T10 = 23.6 + 1.8; P = 0.085). Mean sprint time for the AC trials was 23.4 ± 1.6 while mean sprint time for the PL trials was 23.1 ± 0.7 (P = 0.613).

### 3.4 Heart rate responses
Heart rates (beats·min⁻¹) taken immediately after each spider test trial were not significantly different between experimental groups nor were there any significant Group x Trial interactions. There was a significant main effect of Trial (T) where heart rates for T1 (AC=155 ±13; PL = 161 ± 11) were always significantly lower (P < 0.001) than T2 (AC = 173 ± 7; PL = 174 ± 12) and T10 (AC, PL = 187 ± 8). Heart rates increased linearly from 155 to 187 (± 2.0 - 4.5). The mean heart rate response for the AC trials was 180 ±10 and the mean heart rate response for the PL trials was 179 ± 8 (P = 0.818).

### 3.5 RPE responses
A One-Sample statistics test established that the RPE for the 2-hour practices were not significantly different from the "goal" rating of 15 = 'hard' (p = 0.183). Paired t- tests confirmed that the overall perception of intensity of the practice sessions were similar between experimental conditions (AC Practice RPE = 13.7 ±1.2 vs. PL Practice RPE = 14.3 ± 1.2; P = 0.423). For the spider test trials, although the RPE were slightly higher for the AC group, the responses were not statistically different from the PL (P > 0.05). There was a significant main effect of Trial (T) as the RPE scores rose significantly in a linear fashion from T1 through T10 regardless of the experimental group (P < 0.04). In sum, the RPE scores increased from 13.6 to 18.2 (± 1.5). The mean RPE for the AC trials was 16.2 ± 1.5 and the mean RPE for the PL trials was 15.9 ± 1.4 (P = 0.667).

### 4 Discussion

This is the first report on the use of Accelerade™ (AC) in a field study involving tennis. The only other field study using AC involved female collegiate soccer players

(Seifert and Burke, 2002). In that study, the soccer players consumed approximately 888 ml over a 75 min practice. Equating this to an hourly basis, the soccer players consumed about 20% less than our tennis players. This may help to account for the lack of adverse affects reported by the soccer team. Contrary to our lack of finding a performance enhancing effect between the AC vs. PL groups, the soccer study indicated an improved 'last sprint' time (91.5 s for AC versus 95.5 s for PL, P < 0.05) with AC times slightly faster than the PL in the first 3 sprint trials (0.1 s, 0.1 s, 1.1 s, respectively). It is possible there was a confounding effect of learning and motivation in the soccer trials as their reported performance improvement occurred in sequential trial order. This was not the case in our tennis study. Another important factor to consider is the work:recovery ratio. The soccer players completed 4 sprints in approximately 1.5 min separated by a 5 min recovery period. This anaerobic/aerobic interval utilizing a 1:3 work:recovery ratio enabled a full recovery between sprint events and emphasized the aerobic system. Conversely, we used a short anaerobic interval utilizing a 1:1 work:recovery ratio (10 spider tests lasting 20-24 s/trial with 25 s recovery) which required tapping into phosphocreatine stores as well as anaerobic glycolysis (Powers and Howley, 2002). Hence the deterioration in spider test performance by the tennis players (as evidenced in all three dependent variable results) may have been due to inexperience with short anaerobic training leading to a lack of full recovery between trials. Allowing a 1:3 ratio would have enabled fuller recovery, however, the anaerobic emphasis with the 1:1 work:recovery ratio and trial number was chosen to best replicate tennis-specific performance demands that tend to fatigue an otherwise aerobically conditioned player.

For all measured variables under both treatment conditions, the first trial was the "best" trial followed by a steep and significant performance decrement in Trial 2. This was most likely a factor of initial motivation. As the trials continued, performance times, heart rates, and RPE deteriorated. Interestingly, the first and last AC trial times were not statistically different and there was also a slight improvement in the AC trial times midway, between trials 4 through 7. There was a corresponding brief stabilization of heart rate in the AC trials (AC HR=182, 183, 182, 185 beats·min$^{-1}$). In contrast, in the PL trials' performance leveled off while the heart rate continued to increase (PL HR =177, 180, 183, 185 beats·min$^{-1}$). Although these values were not statistically different, they suggest that perhaps AC did give the athletes a slight performance benefit, even though they did not perceive this difference as evidenced by their higher RPE ratings. The importance of this slight difference in tennis might translate to a player getting to a critical shot that would otherwise have been missed. The fact that this happened in the middle of the trials, when fatigue would presumably be accumulating, further suggests that AC may have attenuated the mounting fatigue for a brief period of time. At the elite level, inability to get to the ball towards the end of a long arduous match could influence the outcome of the match. A larger study is needed to ascertain if the "fatigue stalling" observed midway through the trials in this study is statistically or clinically relevant. Our limited study design and small subject number (n=9) lacked sufficient power to determine if these trends would be pertinent for tennis. Studies investigating the use of AC during actual tennis competition, rather than practice, may be useful. Product palatability created the greatest limitation in this study. The fluid intake goal of 1840 ml during practice was not achieved. This limited fluid intake could have predisposed players to dehydration. Fortunately, the players' weight did not change significantly pre- to post-practice nor did their Usg results suggest significant dehydration.

## 5 Conclusions

Accelerade™ did not significantly delay fatigue in tennis players, although there was a non-significant trend observed for a brief attenuation of mounting fatigue midway through the test trials. The product may benefit from a modification of the current formula in order to have greater acceptance by college tennis players. A more palatable product could have influenced the outcome of this study.

## 6 Acknowledgements

This study was funded in part by the International Tennis Federation and the sports drink products were supplied by Pacific Health Laboratories, Inc., Woodbridge, NJ.

## 7 References

Borg, G. (1973). Perceived exertion: A note on history and methods. **Medicine and Science in Sports**, 5, 90-93.

Burke, E.R. and Ekblom B. (1982). Influence of fluid ingestion and dehydration on precision and endurance performance in tennis. **Athletic Training**, 17, 275-277.

Burke, E.R. (2001). A new generation sports drink delivering more energy to the muscles faster. Clinical Trial. www.accelerade.com.

Casa, D.J., Armstrong, L.E., Hillman, S.K., Montain, S.J., Reiff, R.V., Rich, B., Roberts, W.O., and Stone, J.A. (2000). National Athletic Trainers' Association Position Statement: Fluid replacement for athletes. **Journal of Athletic Training**, 35, 212-224.

Coleman, E. (1988). Sports drink update. In **Sports Science Exchange**, Gatorade Sports Science Institute, Sports Nutrition, Volume 1, Number 5, pp. 1-4.

Davis, M.J. (2001). Carbohydrates, hormones, and endurance performance, in **Sports Science Exchange**, Gatorade Sports Science Institute, Volume 14, No.1, pp. 1-4.

Keul, J., Berg, A., Konig, D., Huonker, M., and Halle, M. (1995). Nutrition in tennis. In **TENNIS: Sports Medicine and Science** (edited by W. Hollmann, K. Struder, A. Ferrauti, and K. Weber). Dusseldorf: Rau publishers, pp. 219-226.

Powers, S.K. and Howley, E.T. (2004). **Exercise Physiology Theory and Application to Fitness and Performance**. 5th Edition, McGraw-Hill, New York.

Seifert, J.G. and Burke, E.R. (2002). The influence of a carbohydrate/protein sports drink on soccer sprint performance. Unpublished Abstract, PacificHealth Laboratories, Woodbury, N.J.

Vergauwen, L., Brouns, F. and Hespel, P. (1998). Carbohydrate supplementation improves stroke performance in tennis. **Medicine and Science in Sports and Exercise**, 30, 1289-1295.

Williams, M.B., Raven, P.B., Fogt, D.L., and Ivy, J.L. (2003). Effects of recovery beverages on glycogen restoration and endurance exercise performance. **Journal of Strength and Conditioning Research**, 17, 12-19.

# 3 Dehydration during table tennis in a hot, humid environment

Y. Kobayashi, T. Takeuchi, T. Hosoi and S. Takaba
*Laboratory for Health and Human Performance, Chukyo University and School of Pharmacy, Meijo University, Japan.*

## 1 Introduction

High ambient temperature and humidity reduce the capacity to perform prolonged exercise because of dehydration and thermoregulatory stress contributing to fatigue. Thermoregulatory sweating causes a reduction in plasma volume and elevated heart rate and core temperature. If no fluid is ingested during work, the plasma $Na^+$ concentration and osmolality will increase (Armstrong et al., 1985). Fluid intake is important to maintain plasma osmolality in activities where dehydration and thermoregulation are of primary concern because reduced central blood volume reduces skin blood flow.

If the prolonged exercise in high temperature and humidity is of moderate intensity then the exercise duration may not be affected, but the physiological homeostasis and motor performance might be more subtly altered. In Asia, attention has recently been focused on table tennis as a preferred leisure-time sport that can combat inactivity and the risk of related chronic diseases because of its convenience, popularity and moderate intensity. Facilities where table tennis is played are often inadequate to prevent heat stress during hot weather because the game is played in small rooms with insufficient ventilation to prevent air movement from affecting the ball. The heat and humidity generated by the players and lack of fluid intake may contribute to the heat stress.

Apparently, no information is available about thermoregulatory stress during table tennis in a hot and humid environment and how performance may be altered. Therefore, the primary purpose of this study was to compare thermoregulatory stress and performance scores during controlled, simulated table tennis matches in high and moderate temperature and humidity; secondly, to determine the effects of drinking a carbohydrate-electrolyte beverage before and during the matches on these measures.

## 2 Materials and methods

### 2.1 Participants
Eight male college level table tennis players volunteered for the study and informed consent was obtained. The mean ($\pm$ s) values for age, height, body mass, %body fat (body impedance method) and body mass index (BMI) were 19.5 ($\pm 0.2$) years, 168 ($\pm 1$) cm, 61.7 ($\pm 2.0$) kg, 18.8 ($\pm 2.6$) % and 21.8 $\pm 0.9$) $kg \cdot m^{-2}$, respectively.

A maximal treadmill exercise test was given prior to experiments using the Bruce protocol. The mean ($\pm$ s) values for maximal heart rate (HR), $O_2$ uptake and respiratory exchange ratio were: 194 ($\pm$4) bpm, 59 ($\pm$2) ml·(kg·min)$^{-1}$ and 1.19 ($\pm$0.02), respectively.

## 2.2 Experimental protocol

The test trials consisted of three sets of table tennis bouts for each participant. The first trial without fluid replacement was conducted at moderate ambient temperature and humidity ($M_0$) in April. Two trials at high ambient temperature and humidity were repeated in August, one with ($H_F$) and one without fluid intake ($H_0$). The $H_0$ and $H_F$ trials were at least 10 days apart and given at the same time of day with the order of the trials randomized. Ambient temperature and humidity near the table were measured every 10 min during trials. During $H_0$ and $H_F$ the means ($\pm$ s) were 30 ($\pm$0)°C and 70 ($\pm$1)%. The corresponding values during $M_0$ were 17 ($\pm$1)°C and 50 ($\pm$0)%.

For each test trial the participants were matched against a standardized table tennis robot (Newgy 5000, Nihon Takkyu Inc., Tokyo) that was programmed to deliver 60 balls·min$^{-1}$ with slight topspin. For each trial the participants played eight bouts for 10 min continuously with a three min rest period between each bout, totaling 101 min. The performance task was to return the ball to the far side of the table to an area 1/8 the table size. The number of errors was subtracted from 600 to obtain the total score.

For the $H_F$ trial, the participants consumed 500 ml of Pokarisweat® (6 % glucose, 18 mEq·l$^{-1}$ Na$^+$) 30 min prior to testing and drank *ad libitum* during each rest period.

Each participant reported to the laboratory eight hour post-prandial. Upon arrival they performed an anaerobic power test. This consisted of 20 s of maximal vertical jumping performed on the Jump Meter (VMJ-023, Vine Ltd., Tokyo). The test was performed following a 5 min standardized warm-up before the first test bout and again 5 min after the last (eighth) bout. After the first jumping test the participants were given the same snack and then rested sitting before beginning the test bouts.

## 2.3 Measurements

Before and after each test, nude body mass was measured after voiding urine. Sweat rate (l·h$^{-1}$) was calculated as change in mass corrected for fluid intake during $H_F$. Rectal temperature ($T_{re}$) was measured by thermocouple (Yellow Springs Instrument Co., Yellow Springs, OH) and $T_{re}$ and HR were continuously recorded.

Ten ml of venous blood were drawn from an arm vein at rest before the bouts, after the 4th exercise bout (mid-trial) and immediately after the last bout (post-trial). Haematocrit (Hct) and haemoglobin (Hb) concentration (cyanmethaemoglobin method) were measured and % changes in plasma volume ($\Delta$%PV) were calculated as described by Dill and Costill (1974). Whole blood lactate concentration was measured immediately after sampling (1500 Sport, Yellow Springs Instrument Co.). Remaining blood was centrifuged and plasma stored at 4°C for analyses within two hour for osmolality (freezing point depression), total proteins (Biuret) and glucose and free fatty acids (FFA) by enzymatic assay.

## 2.4 Statistical analysis

A two-way repeated measures analysis of variance was used with post-hocTukey tests. Paired t-tests were used to test pre-post differences. Significance was set at $P<0.05$.

# 3 Results

## 3.1 Heart rate, temperature and body fluid responses

Body mass declined during $H_0$ and $H_F$ by 1.47 (±0.09) and 1.43 (±0.13) kg, respectively, after correcting the latter for fluid replacement of 1.94 (±0.18) l, indicating a sweat loss of 0.86 l·h$^{-1}$. The sweat rate for $M_0$ was 0.34 l·h$^{-1}$, significantly below $H_0$ and $H_F$.

There was no significant difference in baseline HR in Figure 1. The HR at the end of each bout was always lower, by an average of 12 beats.min$^{-1}$, for $H_F$ than for $H_0$ and significantly lower for all but the 3rd and 6th bout. Figure 1 also shows that HR during $M_0$ was significantly lower than during $H_0$ at all time points, by an average of 15 beats.min$^{-1}$. During $H_F$ the HR was insignificantly (3 beats.min$^{-1}$) higher than for $M_0$.

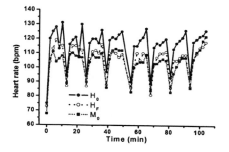   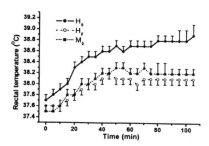

Figure 1. Mean HR during table tennis trials.   Figure 2. $T_{re}$ during table tennis trials.

During $H_F$ and $M_0$ the $T_{re}$ gradually rose during the first 45 min (Figure 2) and then stabilized at 38.1-38.2 °C with no significant differences between $H_F$ and $M_0$. During $H_0$ the $T_{re}$ rose throughout the trial. During H trials the ANOVA and post hoc analyses indicated significantly lower $T_{re}$ during $H_F$ than during $H_0$ at all times after 20 min.

Most of the Δ%PV changes calculated from Hb and Hct occurred by the mid-way point of the trials (Figure 3). After four and eight bouts the PV loss during $H_0$ was significantly greater by 3.4% than during $H_F$ and $M_0$. The difference calculated from protein concentrations was similar, at 3.5%. The changes in PV were mirrored by inverse changes in plasma osmolality, which increased significantly above baseline in $H_0$ and $H_F$ by the mid-point, but only continued upward during $H_0$. No significant changes in osmolality were noted in $M_0$. Overall, the plasma osmolality was significantly higher during $H_0$ than during $H_F$ and $M_0$.

Lactate levels remained below 2 mmol·l$^{-1}$, but increased significantly by the mid-point during the two H trials, by 1.3 mmol·l$^{-1}$ during $H_0$ and 0.8 mmol·l$^{-1}$ during $H_F$, and then declined to baseline by the end. Resting plasma glucose was significantly higher for $H_F$ than $H_0$ (Table 1) and increased insignificantly by mid-point and then significantly declined by the end. The glucose levels in both $H_0$ and $M_0$ did not change significantly over the trials. The mean plasma concentration of FFA rose significantly between the mid-point and the end of the trials for $H_0$ and $M_0$, but during $H_F$ it declined significantly by the mid-point, in contrast to the glucose elevation, and then remained depressed.

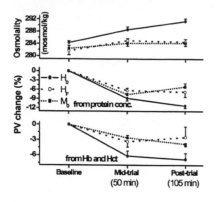 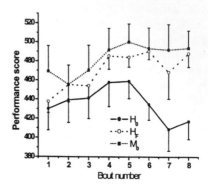

Figure 3.  PV changes and plasma osmolality.    Figure 4. Mean performance
scores.

## 3.2 Anaerobic test and performance scores

Following $H_0$ trials the anaerobic power was reduced by 14%, but only by 2% after
$H_F$ and $M_0$, with the difference being highly significant ($P=0.002$).

Figure 4 shows that the performance score increased over the first four bouts.  The
scores then leveled off for $M_0$ and $H_F$, but declined significantly over the last four
bouts in $H_0$ compared with $H_F$ and $M_0$.  The average score of 436 during all bouts for
$H_0$ was significantly lower than the means of 469 for $H_F$ and 484 for $M_0$.

**Table 1.** Mean (±SE) plasma glucose and free fatty acid levels

|  | Condition | Pre | Mid | Post |
|---|---|---|---|---|
| **Glucose** | $H_0$ | 4.02 (0.21) | 3.92 (0.29) | 4.41 (0.24) |
| (mmol·l⁻¹) | $H_F$ | 4.70 (0.12)& | 5.14 (0.28)& | 4.17 (0.24)# |
|  | $M_0$ | 4.56 (0.11)& | 4.22 (0.17) | 4.57 (0.15) |
| **FFA** | $H_0$ | 0.41 (0.08) | 0.30 (0.05) | 0.82 (0.11)*# |
| (mmol·l⁻¹) | $H_F$ | 0.35 (0.08) | 0.11 (0.01)* | 0.09 (0.01)* |
|  | $M_0$ | 0.30 (0.04) | 0.27 (0.05)$ | 0.66 (0.11)*#$ |

*: significant difference ($P<0.05$) vs. Pre   #: significant difference vs. Mid
&: significant difference ($P<0.05$) vs. $H_0$  $: significant difference vs. $H_F$

## 4 Discussion

Many studies have determined the efficacy of fluid replacement during activity at
elevated temperatures (Morris et al., 2000), but none in table tennis in the heat.

Body temperature appeared to be a limiting factor in the performance ability of this
prolonged, moderate intensity activity.  The $T_{re}$ stabilized during the second half of
the bouts in $M_0$, as well as in humid heat when fluid was ingested (Figure 2).  Body
water loss during the prolonged exercise in $H_0$ was associated with a decrease in PV
and an increase in plasma osmolality.  These results indicate that intake of a particular
drink can prevent changes in PV and osmolality during exercise in a hot and humid
environment.  Fluid intake may serve to prevent circulatory stress during exercise at
high temperatures by increasing the volume of blood contained in the dilated

cutaneous veins (Montain and Coyle, 1992). However, sweat losses during this moderate exercise in a hot environment were unaffected by fluid intake, in accordance with other findings (Daries et al., 2000).

The mechanism of the relationship between increased $T_{re}$ and performance decrements during $H_0$ is unclear. Nielsen et al. (1990) suggested that detrimental effects on performance resulted from elevated body temperature acting on the central nervous system to reduce mental drive for activity. Hancock (1982) concluded that decrements in mental and cognitive skills were associated with ambient temperatures above 29.4°C. Bergeron et al. (1995) found a direct association between body temperature and performance decrements in outdoor tennis players in the absence of adequate fluid intake.

Less physiological heat stress was evident in the participants prior to and during this exercise when ingesting the drink with carbohydrates and electrolytes. The drink prior to exercise in $H_F$ elevated blood glucose early during the exercise and subsequently repressed FFA levels, as glucose is the preferred energy source when available. The optimal formulation of beverages designed to enhance performance and minimize homeostatic perturbations is controversial. Millard-Stafford (1992) concluded that a 4 to 8% carbohydrate beverage was optimal for fluid and energy delivery during prolonged exercise and caused no adverse effects. Daries et al. (2000) observed that serum $Na^+$ concentration could be maintained with a drink containing 16 $mEq \cdot l^{-1}$ of $Na^+$. However, some studies have reported that the addition of electrolytes to a carbohydrate drink had no clear benefits (Levine et al., 1991; Meyer et al., 1995). Precipitous reductions in plasma $Na^+$ concentration may occur when only pure water is ingested during work in a hot environment (Vrijens and Rehrer, 1999). Blood lactate levels may be elevated during exercise in the heat compared to exercise in thermoneutral environments (Yaspelkis et al., 1993). Lactate concentrations were higher in $H_0$ than $M_0$, but not significantly. Fluid intake did not appreciably influence lactate concentration, but reduced it during the mid-point of the trial. The low lactate concentrations indicate that table tennis exercise depends primarily on aerobic energy production, especially because the aerobic power of these participants was relatively high.

The reduction of anaerobic power after $H_0$ may reflect the cumulative fatigue of prolonged exercise and thermoregulatory stress impairing precise muscle function. This finding is supported by a previous study that found fluid restriction to be detrimental to performance of a short, high intensity exercise (Hoffman et al., 1995).

## 5 Conclusions

High ambient temperatures and humidity detrimentally affected the simulated match performance in experienced table tennis players. Fluid ingestion during this exercise in the heat prevented the significant performance decrement. The performance decrements and premature fatigue were associated with high body temperatures and circulatory stress caused by a plasma volume loss. For recreational players, playing for enjoyment and fitness, or for skilled players wishing to maximize performance, frequent and adequate intake of carbohydrate-electrolyte beverages is recommended under these conditions.

## 6 Acknowledgements

The authors are grateful to Ms. T. Oohashi, RN, The Health Center at Chukyo University. This study was supported by a Research Promotion Grant from Chukyo University.

## 7 References

Armstrong, E.L., Costill, D.L. and Fink, W.J. (1985). Influence of diuretic-induced dehydration on competitive running performance. **Medicine and Science in Sports and Exercise**, 17, 456-461.

Bergeron, M.F., Armstrong, L.E. and Maresh, C.M. (1995). Fluid and electrolyte losses during tennis in the heat. **Clinical Sports Medicine**, 14, 23-32.

Daries, H.N., Noakes, T.D. and Dennis, D.C. (2000). Effect of fluid intake volume on 2-h running performance in a 25°C environment. **Medicine and Science in Sports and Exercise**, 32, 1783-1789.

Dill, D.B. and Costill, D.L (1974). Calculation of percentage change in volumes of blood, plasma and red cells in dehydration. **Journal of Applied Physiology**, 37, 247-248.

Hancock, P.A. (1982). Task categorization and the limits of human performance in extreme heat. **Aviation, Space and Environmental Medicine**, 53, 778-784.

Hoffman, J.R., Stavsky, H. and Falk, B. (1995). The effect of water restriction on anaerobic power and vertical jumping height in basketball players. **International Journal of Sports Medicine**, 16, 214-218.

Levine, L., Rose, M.S., Francesconi, P., Neufer, P.D. and Sawka, M.N. (1991). Fluid replacement during sustained activity in the heat: nutrient solution vs water. **Aviation, Space and Environmental Medicine**, 62, 559-564.

Meyer, F., Bar-o, O., MacDougall, D. and Heigenhauser, G.J. (1995). Drink composition and the electrolyte balance of children exercising in the heat. **Medicine and Science in Sports and Exercise**, 27, 882-887.

Millard-Stafford, M. (1992). Fluid replacement during exercise in the heat. **Sports Medicine**, 13, 223-233.

Montain, S.J. and Coyle, E.F. (1992). Fluid ingestion during exercise increases skin blood flow independent of increases in blood volume. **Journal of Applied Physiology**, 73, 903-910.

Morris, J.G., Nevill, M.E. and Williams, C. (2000). Physiological and metabolic responses of female games and endurance athletes to prolonged, intermittent, high-intensity running at 30 degrees and 16 degrees C ambient temperatures. **European Journal of Applied Physiology**, 81, 84-92.

Nielsen, B., Savard, G., Richter, E.A., Hargreaves, M. and Saltin, B. (1990). Muscle blood flow and muscle metabolism during exercise and heat stress. **Journal of Applied Physiology**, 69, 1040-1046.

Vrijens, D.M. and Rehrer, J. (1999). Sodium free fluid ingestion decreases plasma sodium during exercise in the heat. **Journal of Applied Physiology**, 86, 1847-1851.

Yaspelkis, B.B., Scroop, G.C., Wilmore, K.M. and Ivy, J.L. (1993). Carbohydrate metabolism during exercise in hot and thermoneutral environments. **International Journal of Sports Medicine**, 14, 13-19.

# 4 Heart rate monitoring of table tennis players

Z. Djokic

*Faculty of Physical Education and Sport, University of Novi Sad, Serbia & Montenegro.*

## 1 Introduction

Heart rate during competition, and also during training can be a sign of the quality of effort made by players, the condition of players, and a useful indicator for the further planning of the training process. It is very hard to get an opportunity to check this data during a match situation, especially in the area of top table tennis. A knowledge of heart rate during play would enable better programming of the intensity and the volume of training, with the aim of achieving the best possible results. The aim of this study was to collect data during various table tennis activities including match-play and physical training.

## 2 Methods

Participants were senior Yugoslav Team members who played during the 2002/2003 season in top form (second position in European Super Division). Most data were taken from one good world ranked player, and others younger senior players. Data were collected with a POLAR S-710 heart rate monitor with memory (Polar Electro Oy, Kempele, Finland) and all the data were analyzed by Polar Precision Performance SW 3.0 software.

## 3 Results

### 3.1 Heart rate changes during competition
During a table tennis match the heart rate increased as the game continued. The average values of the heart rate during 6 official competition matches were from 162 to 172 beats.min$^{-1}$.

### 3.2 Heart rate changes during table tennis training
During table tennis training the approximate value of the heart rate was 142 beats.min$^{-1}$. The lowest value of the heart rate was 98 beats.min$^{-1}$, found at the beginning of training, and at the end of the first part of the training (the beginning of the rest period). In purely tactical training when stress is placed on the precision of performing and returning the serve, the average values of the heart rate were 152-156 beats.min$^{-1}$.

During interval training – where many balls are played – the values of the heart rate were between 98 to 115 beats.min$^{-1}$ at the beginning, and between 144 to 192 beats.min$^{-1}$ at the end of an interval. Heart rate depended on the type of interval training but the more demanding training yielded heart rates in excess of that found in competition.

In aerobic training (moderate intensity) where the exercise typically consisted of forehand topspin with backhand counter strokes for 10 minutes with a ball rate of about 50 balls per minute the average values of the heart rate at the beginning were 98-110 beats.min$^{-1}$ while at the end were 144-168 beats.min$^{-1}$.

In aerobic endurance training (high intensity) where the ball rate increased to 65-67 balls per minute the heart rate at the beginning were 105-120 beats.min$^{-1}$ while at the end were 175-185 beats.min$^{-1}$.

In speed training (maximum intensity) where a series of 4-5 balls were projected rapidly followed by a short rest of 1-1.25 min, the heart rate at the beginning was 110-115 beats.min$^{-1}$ while at the end were 168-192 beats.min$^{-1}$.

### 3.3 Heart rate changes during physical training

During aerobic endurance training which consisted of continual slow running, with a little change in rhythm and speed for about 10 min the average value of the heart rate was 140 beats.min$^{-1}$. The minimum value of the heart rate was 119 beats.min$^{-1}$ while the maximum was 186 beats.min$^{-1}$, but this was measured at the end of fast running.

During anaerobic endurance training, which consisted of combination of slow and fast running (about 70-80% of maximum speed) in the time intervals of 3 min, the average of the measured value during the whole training was 152 beats.min$^{-1}$ .The average value during slow running was 137 beats.min$^{-1}$ while the average value during fast running was 172 beats.min$^{-1}$.

During strength training – which involved a series of exercises for the legs, arms, back and abdomen of duration 45 min - the measured value of the heart rate was 154-162 beats.min$^{-1}$.

During speed training in which multiple sprints were undertaken the average values of the heart rate ranged from 110-201 beats.min$^{-1}$ and depended on the intensity of the run with the higher values associated with the maximum intensity running.

### 4 Discussion and conclusion

Observation of heart rates during training, and especially in competition, are valuable as they illustrate the nature and intensity of the pressure on the player. The data represent a qualitative basis for planning and programming of the rational and efficient training process.

From the analysis of the heart rate values in competition conditions, for a sample of top players, we can conclude that modern table tennis is a sport which requires both sub-maximal and maximal work and this puts pressure on both anaerobic and aerobic energy systems. Approximately the same pressures should be applied to the player during the most part of training, to increase the efficiency and relevance of training.

**Part Two**

# Ergonomics of Racket Sports

# 5 Influence of exercise intensity on physiological parameters and on the drive execution in table tennis

V. Fayt, G. Quignon and S. Lazzari
*Laboratoire d'Analyse Multidisciplinaire des Pratiques Sportives*
*UFR STAPS de Liévin, Université d'Artois, France.*

## 1 Introduction

Facing a game situation or a prolonged exercise in table tennis, the player has to adapt as much to the energy requirements as to the level of motion performance. A player wanting to win the rally will have to keep up a high level of precision, a stable movement execution and a quality of footwork, despite fatigue which increases with the number of strokes. These constraints are increased by the new rules in table tennis: as the new ball is bigger (40 mm) and heavier (4.2 g), it moves forward more slowly and thus, tends to increase the duration of rallies (Sève, 2001; Yquel, 2001). These alterations should influence the energetic cost and require technical and tactical adjustments from the player (Durand, 1992). Since adaptation processes depend on practice level (Abernethy et al., 1994), a difference between national level and regional level players might be expected.

In this study, factors limiting the performance of a table tennis player are investigated. From this point of view the change in drive execution (accuracy and hitting speed) and physiological effort (heart rate, HR) related to the intensity of the exercise were analysed. Heart rate was considered as a relevant indicator of the exercise intensity. The aim of this study was to study the effects of the exercise intensity on drive performance according to playing level.

## 2 Method

### 2.1 Participants

Nine right-handed table tennis players (1 female and 8 males) students from the LIEVIN UFR STAPS took part in the experiment having given their informed consent. On average they had been practising club table tennis for nine years. They were divided in two groups according to their ranking: the 1st group involved 4 players ranked at French national level and the 2nd group consisted of 5 players ranked at French regional level.

Anthropometric characteristics such as age (20.2 ±1.6 years), height (179.4 ±5.1 cm), mass (71.9 ±10.2 kg), maximum heart rate (204 beats.min$^{-1}$, ±10.6) and heart rate at rest (63 beats.min$^{-1}$, ±7.6) were collected from the players. Heart rates (HR) were measured whilst lying supine for 15 min for heart rate at rest (HRrest), and during a progressive, continuous and maximum test running around a track for maximum heart rate (HRmax, Léger-Boucher, 1980). The mean (± s) data in each group are reported (Table 3).

## 2.2 Task

Players were confronted with a simple to achieve exercise but increasing in intensity. This exercise let the player move and quickly take up his/her position again in order to hit the ball under the favourable conditions necessary to maintain precision despite the increasing exercise intensity and resulting muscle stiffness.

The players had to achieve a forehand topspin using a chop stroke. The balls were propelled by a coach from a basket at a rate given by a metronome and a built-in metronome earphone. The balls were sent alternately on the right and middle hand side of the player's half court in order to lead to lateral footwork (see Figure 1). The player had to achieve his/her stroke aiming at a target area materialized on the opponent's court (42 x 29.7 cm).

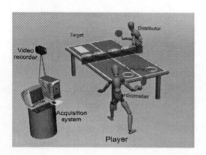 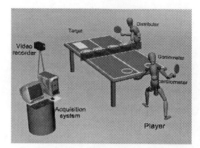

Figure 1:    A view from behind the experimental set up where the player had to hit balls propelled by a coach alternately on the middle (Fig. 1a) and on the right (Fig. 1b) towards a target (white square) placed on the opponent's half court with his forehand. Ball projection rate increased every 30 s.

The initial ball projection rate was 42 balls.min$^{-1}$ with increases every 30 s. The rate increased by 6 balls.min$^{-1}$ until stage 6 (72 balls.min$^{-1}$) was reached, then the increment was 4 balls.min$^{-1}$ (Table 1). The exercise stopped when the participant was systematically late and unable to hit the ball back.

Table 1. The successive 30 s steps of balls projection rate

|  | Stage 1 | Stage 2 | Stage 3 | Stage 4 | Stage 5 | Stage 6 | Stage 7 | Stage 8 |
|---|---|---|---|---|---|---|---|---|
| balls.min$^{-1}$ | 42 | 48 | 54 | 60 | 66 | 72 | 76 | 80 |

## 2.3 Collecting and analysing data

The participant was equipped with a heart rate monitor (Accurex plus, Polar, Kempele, Finland) including a polar coded transmitter, an elastic belt and a receiver wristband. These data were analysed using Training Advisor Polar WINDOWS software. A goniometer placed on the elbow joint and connected to the data logging system MP100 and to the Acknowledge v 3.7.1 software (MP100, Biopac Systems, Goleta, CA, USA), recorded positions during the exercise at 100 Hz. These data were filtered with a recursive, second-order Butterworth filter, with a cut-off frequency of

60 Hz, and normalized. A Sony digital camcorder (25 Hz) was used in filming the players.

Data analysis dealt with the percentage of achievements (ratio between the number of balls reaching the target and the number of balls played), the heart rate during the exercise and the peaks of movement velocity during driving and during backward swing. Student's *t*-test and correlation analysis were performed on the data. The level of significance for the *t*-test was set at $P < 0.05$.

# 3 Results

## 3.1 Performance

Whatever the practice level, performance gradually decreased with increasing stages ($r^2 = 0.91$): players shifted from $57.1 \pm 17.4$ % achievement at the first stage to $32.1 \pm 16.0$ % at the last stage accomplished by all the participants (Table 2). Only one national level player kept up with the exercise until stage 8. A *t*-test revealed a significant difference between the two groups ($P = 0.006$).

Table 2. Average achievement percentage ($\pm s$) from players according to their practice level and the number of players going through the exercise at different increased intensity stages

| Stage | 1 | 2 | 3 | 4 | 5 | 6 | 7 | 8 |
|---|---|---|---|---|---|---|---|---|
| National | 67.8 ±20.0 | 54.1 ±15.6 | 55.5 ±10.9 | 45.8 ±4.2 | 40.9 ±10.1 | 46.3 ±9.8 | 30.3 ±16.7 | 22.5 |
| Regional | 52.3 ±12.1 | 43.3 ±17.3 | 29.6 ±3.7 | 29.3 ±9.2 | 23.0 ±9.7 | 16.6 ±2.8 | | |
| Whole group | 57.1 ±17.4 | 46.2 ±16.7 | 40.7 ±14.6 | 36.0 ±10.7 | 32.1 ±12.9 | 32.1 ±16.0 | 30.3 ±16.7 | 22.5 |
| Number of players | 9 | 9 | 9 | 9 | 9 | 6 | 2 | 1 |

## 3.2 Heart rate

Players had a maximum heart rate of 204 beats.min$^{-1}$ (range between groups 195-211 beats.min$^{-1}$). The groups showed a significant difference ($P = 0.011$) as far as average maximum heart rate is concerned and this significant difference could also be noticed during the exercise (Hrexo, $P = 0.013$, Table 3).

Table 3. Heart rates (beats.min$^{-1}$, mean $\pm s$) recorded during exercise with incrementing intensity

| | Regional level | National level | Whole group | Student's t-test between levels (P value) |
|---|---|---|---|---|
| HRrest | 64 ±9.3 | 60 ±6.0 | 63 ±7.6 | 0.49 (ns.) |
| HRmax | 211 ±6.9 | 195 ±7.1 | 204 ±10.6 | 0.011 (*) |
| HRexo | 201 ±9.2 | 184 ±5.4 | 194 ±11.0 | 0.013 (*) |
| Time (s) | 179 ±16.4 | 210 ±28.6 | 192 ±25.2 | 0.078 (ns.) |

Results concerning changes of accuracy and heart rate are presented in Figure 2. As duration and intensity of the exercise increased, accuracy decreased inversely compared with the heart rate curve (r=-0.99, Figure 2a).  A negative correlation was observed among seven out of nine participants.  An analysis of variance (ANOVA) with the factors Level (National vs. Regional) and Stage with repeated measures on the last factor was carried out on the ratio between performance and HR.  Significant main effects were found for the factors Level ($F_{1,44}$=36.04, P<0.001) and Stage ($F_{4,44}$=5.6, P=0.001).  A gap between the practice level was observed, the national level players having a greater ratio (performance/heart rate, Figure 2b), whatever the stage studied.

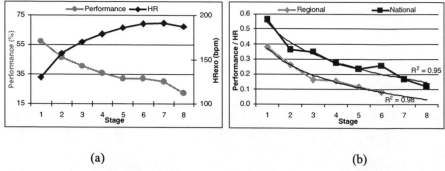

(a)                                                    (b)

Figure 2:   (a) Interaction between heart rate and accuracy level during the drive execution exercise with stage of ball projection frequency; (b) ratio of accuracy/heart rate during the exercise according to playing level.

### 3.3 Drive execution speed
The peak angular speed recorded at the elbow level showed that the execution speed increased during the different intensity stages.

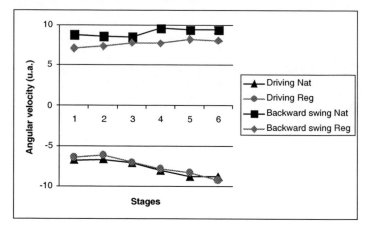

Figure 3:   Change in elbow peak angular velocity with stage according to playing level during driving or backward swing. (u.a. = arbitary units).

The ANOVA on the mean values of peak velocity during backward swing revealed a significant main effect of the factor Level: The national level players had a greater drive execution speed at all stages ($F_{1,44}=7.11$, $P<0.05$). The ANOVA on the mean values of peak velocity during driving revealed a significant main effect of the factor Stage ($F_{4,39}=3.23$, $P<0.05$). Comparison between backward swing and driving phase showed that the main adaptation occurs during the backward swing (Figure 3).

## 4 Discussion and conclusion

When the exercise intensity was increased by stages, a fall in performance (57% versus 22%), a greater execution speed (7.2 units at the first stage versus 8.9 units at stage 6) and heart rate (130 beats.min$^{-1}$ at the first stage versus 190 beats.min$^{-1}$ at stage 6) were noticed for table tennis players taking part in the study. In this type of extreme situation, it can be seen that drive speed (Fayt et al., 1997) and physiological responses were altered. This adaptation processes depend on the playing level (as noticed by the recurrent main effect of the factor Level for performance, HR and peak of velocity). The existing differences during the first exercise stages became all the more obvious as the exercise intensity increased. The national level players showed a better adaptation (accuracy level, execution speed, heart rate progression) to the demands of the activity (increase in ball frequency; Abernethy et al., 1994).

It can be assumed that national level players had, from the start, a better level of physical preparation which made adaptation to the demands of the exercise easier (confirmed by a significant lower maximum heart rate; $P<0.05$). This facility allows them to carry on with the exercise for a longer period of time (Allen, 1991; Orfeuil, 1982).

As the duration of rallies becomes longer, the increase in energy cost due to the new ball diameter may somehow alter the profile of rallies: players may tend to use energy sources other than aerobic. It could be interesting to determine more precisely the maximum aerobic speed and explore more thoroughly the physiological responses (Cazorla and Léger, 1993; Blondel et al., 2000).

These results allow us to suggest some guidelines in order to set up a training method which would take these variables into account. The coach could then determine a threshold of intensity and a duration at which the player is no longer able to maintain precision. Finally, we are able to tackle the problem of acquisition of motor skill by comparing durations and intensities of an exercise for which the player will be more efficient and will learn more thoroughly.

## 5 Acknowledgements

This study was supported by the Fédération Française de Tennis de Table.

## 6 References

Abernethy, B., Kippers, V., Mackinnon, L.T., Neal, R.J. and Hanrahan, S. (1997). **The Biophysical Foundations of Human Movement**. Champaign, IL: Human Kinetics.

Allen, G.-D. (1991). Physiology characteristics of elite Australian table tennis athletes and their responses to high level competition. **Journal of Human Movement Studies**, 3, 133-147.

Blondel, N., Billat, V. and Berthoin, S. (2000). Relation entre le temps limite de course et l'intensité relative de l'exercice, exprimée en fonction de la vitesse critique et de la vitesse maximale. (Relation between running time to exhaustion and relative intensity of exercise expressed in function of the critical speed and the maximal speed). **Science et Sport**, 15, 242-244.

Cazorla, G. and Léger, L. (1993). Comment évaluer et développer vos capacités aérobies (How to evaluate and develop aerobic capacities). **Epreuves de course navette et épreuve Vam-éval**. AREAPS Cestas.

Durand, M. (1992). L'optimisation de la performance. Etude dans des tâches constituant une sollicitation non optimale (2ème partie). (The optimization of performance. A study of tasks constituted by a non optimal solicitation (2nd part)) **Revue STAPS**, 28, 41-57.

Fayt, V., Bootsma, R.J., Marteniuk, R.G., MacKenzie, C.L. and Laurent, M. (1997). The effects of task constraints on the organization of interception movements. **Journal of Sport Sciences**, 15, 581-586.

Léger, L. and Boucher, R. (1980). An indirect continuous running multistage field test, the Université de Montréal Track Test. **Canadian Journal of Applied Sports Sciences**, 5, 77-84.

Orfeuil, F. (1982). **Le Tennis de Table: physiologie et entraînement**. (Table tennis : Physiology and training). Paris, INSEP France, 78.

Sève, C. (2001). A propos de la balle de 40mm. (About the 40 mm ball). **France Tennis de Table Magazine**, 758, 12-13.

Yquel, R. (2001). La balle de 40 millimètres : plus visible, plus physique. (The 40mm ball : more visible, more physical). **France Tennis de Table Magazine**, 758, 10.

# 6 Monitoring effort during increasing levels of training exercises in table tennis

L. Jospin and V. Fayt
*Laboratoire d'Analyse Multidisciplinaire des Pratiques Sportives*
*UFR STAPS de Lievin, Université d'Artois, France.*

## 1 Introduction

Observing an elite table tennis player during matches gives an impression of ease; this means that all difficulties inherent in his/her sport (biomechanical, bio-energetic, bio-informational and psychological constraints) seem to disappear. Skilful behaviour (Guthrie, 1952), deriving from a long and particularly hard training is defined by a high level of performance (the player is sure to reach his goal) and of efficiency (i.e., the relation between the obtained level of performance and what it costs to get it). Despite this, a review of texts published on motor learning leads to an astonishing remark "*leaving aside research works on automatic behaviour, there are very few data at the moment, combining efficiency, absence of effort, optimisation, etc., with progress in training*" (Famose, 1990, p.181).

Table tennis is defined as a "speed sport" requiring precision and skill; it is highly technical and strategic, appealing for anticipation qualities, adaptability, emotions control and concentration. The qualities make it a complex sport activity requiring the player to learn very sharp motion skills.

If, as Famose (1990) stressed it "*a similar performance will be achieved with less resources when training improves*" then, three activities with variable constraints carried out by table tennis players with different playing level (national, regional level, non-ranked players) should generate a performance (represented by % of successful achievement) and an efficiency (represented by the maximum HR at the end of the exercise) according to playing level. In a basic situation, the participant knows about placing, nature and speed of the balls sent towards him or her. Making tasks more complex will deal with spatial constraints (uncertainty about ball placing) and/or precision constraints (size of target).

In this study, we deal with the interaction between energetic cost (inferred from physiological indicators), corresponding mainly to muscle involvement required for achieving motion, and a sustained level of performance as a function of task complexity and playing level.

## 2 Method

### 2.1 Participants
Twenty one students (4 girls and 17 boys, average age : 20.9 years) from Lievin UFR STAPS took part in the experiment having given their informed consent. They were divided into three groups according to their ranking: Group 1 (5 National level players), Group 2 (8 Regional level players) and Group 3 (8 non-ranked players).

Anthropometric characteristics such as age, height, mass, the number of years of practice, maximum heart rate (HR max), and heart rate at rest (HR rest) have been collected from the players (Table 1). Heart rates were measured whilst lying supine for 15 min for heart rate at rest (HR rest), and by means of a progressive, continuous and maximum test running around a track for maximum heart rate (Léger and Boucher, 1980). Only average data in each group are mentioned.

Table 1. Anthropometric characteristics (mean ± s) from the 3 groups of participants (national, regional and non-ranked players)

| Participants | Age | Height | Mass | Number of years of practice | HR rest | HR max |
|---|---|---|---|---|---|---|
| | (years) | (cm) | (kg) | (years) | (beats.min$^{-1}$) | (beats.min$^{-1}$) |
| Group 1 | 22.0 ±2.1 | 181.0 ±6.3 | 77.0 ±11.8 | 12.2 ±2.0 | 61.2 ±5.7 | 194.2 ±6.3 |
| Group 2 | 20.2 ±2.0 | 180.5 ±6.0 | 73.1 ±10.0 | 8.3 ±3.0 | 64.3 ±5.3 | 209.7 ±9.8 |
| Group 3 | 20.5 ±1.6 | 175.9 ±7.1 | 63.7 ±5.7 | 1.7 ±1.8 | 67.4 ±4.1 | 203.7 ±8.7 |
| Total | 20.9 ±1.0 | 179.1 ±2.8 | 71.3 ±6.8 | 7.4 ±5.3 | 64.3 ±3.1 | 202.5 ±7.8 |

## 2.2 Design

Each player carried out three exercises of increasing difficulty : (a) a series of forehand drives on balls without spin, sent straight into the player's forehand, with a free return to the opponent's half court; (b) a series of forehand or backhand drives on balls without spin sent anywhere on the table (spatial uncertainty), the return of the ball is free; (c) same exercise as (b) but the ball must be returned hitting a target represented by a 45 mm diameter circle drawn on the forehand side of the opponent's half court. The choice of these three activities was the result of a survey carried out among 1st degree graduates in sports from the Nord-Pas-De-Calais regional table tennis association.

During these three exercises, the trainer propelled balls from a basket at a rate of 60 balls.min$^{-1}$ for 60 s. Participants were requested to be as precise as possible.

At the beginning of each exercise, the participant ignored the first three balls, when the fourth came, he triggered the heart rate monitor to start the exercise on the fifth ball, then the test was conducted for 60 s. A single test was carried out per session and there was a week between each test. The ball projection rate (60 balls.min$^{-1}$) was determined by a metronome and a built-in metronome earphone. This choice of distribution technique was done while most coaches prefer to use this projection technique perfected by the Chinese in the 1980's, which brings into light the notion of open skill defining table tennis.

## 2.3 Collecting and analysing data

Each participant was equipped with a heart rate monitor (Accurex plus, Polar, Kempele, Finland) including a polar coded transmitter, an elastic belt and a receiver wristband. These data were analysed using the *Training Advisor Polar* software. A Sony digital camcorder was employed in filming the players.

Data analysis was conducted on the percentage of return success (ratio between the number of balls reaching the target and the number of balls projected), and on the heart rate during these three exercises of increasing difficulty.

Analysis of variance (ANOVA) was carried out to determine the success rate (%) and the maximum heart rate at the end of the exercises (HRexo) with factors such as Playing Level (national, regional and non-ranked players) and Test (Exercise 1, 2 and 3) with repeated measurements on the last factor. The level of significance was fixed at P<0.05.

## 3 Results

### 3.1 Performance
A significant main effect was found for Playing Level ($F_{2,36}$=12.84, P<0.001) and Test factors ($F_{2,36}$=73.97, P<0.001). It was noticeable that national level players achieved the three tasks in a better way than regional level and non-ranked players (a 66 % success average in favour of national players against 52% and 46% respectively in favour of regional players and non-ranked players). The difference between regional players and non-ranked players was not significant. A significant decrease in the success percentage, whatever the practice level, was noticed according to the constraint of the activity (Figure 1, with 61% for exercises 1 and 2, and 37% for exercise 3). A post-hoc Newman-Keuls test indicated that the third test significantly differed from the other two.

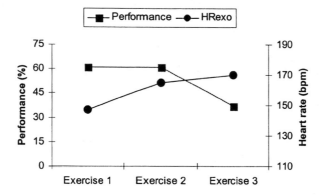

Figure 1:   Changes in performance (success %) and heart
            rate at the end of the activity during three
            exercises of increasing difficulty.

### 3.2 Heart rate
A significant main effect was found for heart rate at the end of the exercise (HR exo) for the Test factor ($F_{2,36}$=31.96, P<0.001). A post-hoc Newman-Keuls test indicated that the first test significantly differed from the others (HR exo : exercise 1 = 147 beats.min$^{-1}$, exercise 2 = 165 beats.min$^{-1}$, exercise 3 = 170 beats.min$^{-1}$ ; Figure 1).

   The results obtained during the analysis of the average heart rate and of the exercise relative intensity did not generate any additional information.

## 4 Discussion

Results obtained are in agreement with classical results from published works (Schmidt, et al., 1990). Whatever the exercise and its constraints, we systematically noticed that national level players achieved better results than the other two playing levels. It seems that through experience, as years, training sessions and exercises go by, players become more able to achieve motor actions at a high level of performance (Fitts and Posner, 1967).

During the second exercise, if players want to be efficient in that sort of situation, they have to maintain an optimal distance which Arzel (1994, pp. **) defined as "the optimal distance separating the vertical plane of the ball trajectory from the vertical axis of the player in position". Therefore they have to use appropriate footwork to find this optimal distance again in order to be efficient. Thus, a player is required to make two complex activities compatible: There are an anticipation-coincidence activity in order to achieve the ball-bat contact and a trajectory producing activity when using a racket. Many studies show that the efficiency of the response will mainly depend on the quality of information processing (Arnold, 1985; Ripoll et al., 1986 ; Ripoll, 1987 ; Véronèse, 1988). The third exercise presented contradictory demands on the player (Durand, 1992) since participants had to be accurate and fast at the same time. The results from this conflicting situation are in agreement with published work (Fitts, 1964; Schmidt, 1982; Durand, 1992) since increasing precision constraints bring about a significant decrease in achievement percentage among players, whatever their practice level. Yet national players remained superior to those at other levels. It seems that given the same task, the degree of difficulty varies according to the participant's skill level and that the efficiency of the response will depend on the quality of information processing.

Analysis of maximum heart rate, Relative Intensity and average heart rate all indicated that exercise 1 significantly differed from exercises 2 and 3. This result confirms that the energetic cost rises with an increase in activity constraints (Durand, 1992). Footwork which players are compelled to achieve in order to protect their playing area, though quite restricted (Parlebas, 1986), represents a non-negligible energetic cost since HR rises in a linear way ($r^2=0.90$) during the exercises.

The increase in accuracy constraint, as far as placing the ball on the opponent's half court rather than on a small target, does not lead to an additional energetic cost (HR exo from exercises 2 and 3, $P>0.05$), whatever the practice level. An effect was expected because the increasing accuracy demand made motor adjustments necessary, with more important work done at shoulder level or at foot level. Yet the analysis revealed that participants used their distal segment (hand-racket) to compensate for potential weakness in footwork. These compensatory movements very frequently noticed among non-ranked players have consequences for their efficiency (28% success). In fact, video analysis revealed that non-ranked players simplified exercise 3 by not playing all the balls. These players would have considered that some balls did not deserve to be played because their distance and speed would lead to energy-consuming footwork and the probability of reaching the target on the opponent's half court was extremely low. This attitude meant a lower energetic cost than expected. These players complied with a lesser effort logic. This strategy could explain that the heart rate, indicating the level of commitment in the activity and by inference the efficiency level, did not significantly differ with regard to the playing level. Of course, these "diverted" behaviors have consequences on the players' efficiency since regional level players, given a similar energetic cost, achieved a lower success level.

## 5 Conclusion

It would appear that during learning and training sessions table tennis players increase their efficiency, which is closely akin to previous studies on that topic. However, the implemented experimental method (HR chosen as an indicator to rate energetic cost) was unable to confirm clearly an effect on efficiency improvement. Players, except for experts, adopted strategies termed "diverted" when subjected to speed and accuracy constraints. So they may have simplified the exercises by using compensatory movements or by limiting footwork.

These results can be of interest for coaches using the "balls basket" distribution technique as a tool. If the purpose is to improve the players' efficiency, it seems appropriate firstly to adapt the ball projection rate to their information processing ability and to the quality of their footwork, and then, secondly to increase the projection rate progressively. This approach would avoid "diverted" behaviours and the different compensatory movements observed among non-ranked players. Above all, it will force the players to seek systematically an optimal distance.

## 6 Acknowledgements

This study was supported by the Fédération Française de Tennis de Table.

## 7 References

Arnold, R.K.S. (1985). **Le développement des habiletés sportives**. (Sport abilities development). Adaptation Française, Dossier EPS, 3. Paris: INSEP.

Arzel, G. (1994). Pour une pédagogie du développement des potentialités d'adaptation (approche clinique d'une pratique d'apprentissage). (For a pedagogy to develop the potentialities of adaptation (a clinical approach of a learning practice)). In **Dossier E.P.S**, 22, 20-27.

Durand, M. (1992). L'optimisation de la performance. Etude dans des tâches constituant une sollicitation non optimale ($2^{ème}$ partie). (The optimization of performance. A study of tasks constituted by a non optimal solicitation ($2^{nd}$ part)). **Revue S.T.A.P.S.**, 28, 41-57.

Famose, J.P. (1990). **Apprentissage moteur et difficulté de la tâche**. (Motor learning and task difficulty). Collection Recherche. Paris: INSEP.

Fitts, P.M. (1964). Perceptual motor-skill learning. In A.W. Melton (ed.), **Categories of Human Learning**. New York: Academic Press.

Fitts, P.M. and Posner, M.I. (1967). **Human Performance**. Belmont, C.A.: Brooks and Cole.

Guthrie, E.R. (1952). **The Psychology of Learning**. New York: Harper and Row.

Léger, L. and Boucher, R. (1980). An indirect continuous running multistage field test, the Université de Montréal Track Test, **Canadian Journal of Applied Sports Sciences**, 5, 77-84.

Parlebas, P. (1986). **Eléments de sociologie du sport**. (Elements of sport sociology). Paris: PUF.

Ripoll, H. (1987). La résolution du conflit sémantique-sensorimoteur en sport. (The resolution of semantic-sensory motor trade-off in sport). In **Neurosciences du Sport** (edited by H. Ripoll and G. Azemar), Paris: INSEP. pp. 126-136.

Ripoll, H., Fleurance, P. and Cazeneuve, D. (1986). **Analyse des comportements exploratoires visuels des pongistes de haut niveau**, (Analysis of exploratory visual comportments in high level table tennis players). Paris: INSEP. pp. 100-120.

Schmidt, R.A. (1982). **Motor Control and Learning : A Behavioral Emphasis**. Champaign, IL: Human Kinetics.

Schmidt, R.A., Lange, C.A. and Young, D.E. (1990). Optimizing summary knowledge of results for skill learning. **Human Movement Science**, 9, 325-348.

Véronèse, C. (1988). Les fonctions anticipatrices et de préparation à l'action en tennis de table. (Anticipatory and preparatory functions for action in table tennis). **Mémoire de Brevet d'Etat d'Educateur Sportif 3ᵉ degré**. Paris: INSEP.

# 7 Effect of the Type 3 (oversize, slow speed) tennis ball on heart rate, activity level and shots per point during tennis play

J.R. Blackwell[1], E.M. Heath[2] and C.J. Thompson[1]
[1]University of San Francisco, 2130 Fulton Street, San Francisco, CA 94117.   [2]Utah State University, 7000 Old Main Hill, Logan, UT 84322, USA.

## 1 Introduction

The International Tennis Federation (ITF) has officially amended the Rules of Tennis in order to approve the use of two new types of balls in tournament play. The aim of introducing the new balls is to increase the speed of the game (fast-speed, Type 1 ball), or decrease the speed of the game (slow-speed, Type 3 ball), compared to the speed of the game when using the regular (medium-speed, Type 2) ball. The Type 1 ball is the same size as the Type 2 ball, but is harder and has a lower coefficient of restitution (i.e., bounces less), thereby allowing for a lower rebound angle after contacting the court surface (Blackwell and Heath, 1997). This ball is meant for play on a slow pace (Category 1) court surface (e.g., clay). The Type 3 ball has the same bounce and mass as the Type 2 ball, but is 6% larger in diameter. The larger size of the Type 3 ball allows for a greater amount of drag due to air resistance as well as a greater Magnus effect (i.e., the ball's path tends to curve more due to the ball's rotation), when compared to the Type 2 ball. The Type 3 ball, therefore, moves through the air more slowly, has a shorter horizontal distance through the air, and topspin tends to allow the ball to clear the net and still land in the court boundary more easily than the Type 2 ball (Blackwell and Heath, 1997). The Type 3 ball is meant for play on a fast pace (Category 3) court surface (e.g., grass), and was the focus of this study.

The physics associated with the balls is predictable, and has been confirmed using the Type 3 ball (Brody, 1987; Haake et al., 2000; Blackwell and Knudson, 2002). The effect of the Type 3 ball versus the Type 2 ball on the players' movement activity and physiological responses, however, is in question. During point play, Mitchell and Caine (2000) reported similar games per match and that any differences found between the number of points and number of shots depended to some extent on the play format. They also reported that fatigue rates and muscle activation patterns are independent of ball type. Davey (Personal Communication, March, 2003), found increased time to volitional fatigue as well as improved accuracy and consistency (with fewer balls hit out). They also report reduced blood lactate, perceived exertion and heart rate responses to using the Type 3 ball during the Loughborough Intermittent Tennis Test (LITT), devised by Davey et al. (2002). Anecdotal evidence received from players who participated in tournaments that used the Type 3 ball suggests that senior players tend to default (quit) during match play at a higher rate than when playing with the Type 2 ball. The evidence regarding the effects of the

Type 3 ball on tennis play and the player seemed to be inconclusive. Therefore, the purpose of this study was to investigate differences in heart rate, activity level and the number of shots per point using the Type 3 ball compared to the Type 2 ball.


## 2 Methods

### 2.1 Design
The independent variable for this study was the comparison of Type 2 and Type 3 ball types. The dependent measures were heart rate (HR), vector magnitude of activity levels (VM), and the average number of good shots per point. Each of these comparisons was tested with a dependent groups (paired) t-test. Significance was determined when $p < 0.05$.

### 2.2 Participants
A sample of twenty participants (M = 16, F = 4) was recruited from a local tennis facility (San Francisco Tennis Club) to play in ten 1-hour matches. The participants' mean ($\pm$s) descriptive statistics were; age = 41.9 ($\pm$10.5) years, height = 1.75 ($\pm$0.08) m, mass = 72.8 ($\pm$11.5) kg. The average number of years of tennis experience was 20.9 ($\pm$ 10.5) and the average United States Tennis Association National Tennis Rating (NTRP) was 4.2 ($\pm$ 0.4), where a rating of 1.5 indicates a beginner and a rating of 6.0 indicates a player with a sectional/national ranking. All players were free from injury, exercised an average of 5.6 ($\pm$2.3) times/week and gave informed consent.

### 2.3 Instrumentation
In order to measure HR, players wore a heart rate transmitter (Vantage NV, Polar, New Bedford) that was strapped around the chest and a receiver, worn around the wrist, that stored the data. Heart rate was averaged over 5 s time periods throughout each 30 min period of play for both the Type 2 and Type 3 balls. To measure the VM of a player's activity level, an activity monitor that utilizes 3-dimensional accelerometer technology (RT3, Stay Healthy, Monrovia) was worn on the waistband at the middle of the back. The VM data (arbitrary units) were collected every second and averaged for each 30-min play period. All matches were videotaped to allow for match play analysis at a later date. Type 2 balls were Wilson, Regular Duty Championship balls and Type 3 balls were Wilson Rally balls. Matches were played on an indoor court.

### 2.4 Procedure
All participants completed a survey and resting HR values were measured prior to play after the participant had been sitting quietly for at least 5 minutes. The HR transmitter and receiver were worn during a 10 min warm-up period to allow the participants an opportunity to get used to the instrumentation. Participants were matched as playing opponents according to their NTRP rating. At the end of the warm-up period, just prior to the match play, the activity monitors were clipped on. Participants began the match playing no-add scoring and they kept a running total of games won. That is, they did not play sets. This change in scoring was made in order to reduce the possibility of an abrupt emotional change due to the outcome of a set, which might affect a player's style of play. They changed sides of the court after each odd game, but were not allowed to rest during the changeovers. However, at a changeover close to the 15 min mark, players were asked to sit down for only a short

time while their blood pressure was measured. At the 30-min mark, a different ball type was given to the players. Near the 45 min mark, during a convenient changeover, blood pressure was again measured. The decision to start with a particular type of ball was randomized. However, an equal number of matches started with each ball type. At the end of the match, players were given the opportunity to make comments about the balls.

## 3 Results

Overall, 10 matches were analyzed. These amounted to 5 hours of play with each type of ball that included 1134 points.

### 3.1 Heart rate (HR)
Heart rates while playing with the Type 3 ball were 157 ($\pm$ 18) beats min$^{-1}$ and significantly greater (t $_{1,19}$ = 3.04; P = 0.007) than the heart rates of 153 ($\pm$ 17) beats.min$^{-1}$, measured while playing with the Type 2 ball.

### 3.2 Vector magnitude (VM) activity level
Statistical significance was also demonstrated (t $_{1,19}$ = 3.09; P = 0.006) for the VM activity levels. Type 3 ball play resulted in 2024.8 ($\pm$ 314.7) units, a higher value than the Type 2 ball result of 1919.7 ($\pm$ 267.1) units.

### 3.3 Good shots per point
Additional to HR and VM, a significant difference was revealed when looking at the number of good shots per point. The average was significantly higher (t $_{1,19}$ = 2.58; P = 0.022) while using the Type 3 ball (4.3 $\pm$ 1.1), compared to the average while using the Type 2 ball (3.6 $\pm$ 1.0).

## 4 Discussion

The development of the Type 3 ball was aimed at reducing the speed of the professional game and making tennis easier and more enjoyable to play at the recreational level. The ball's slightly (6%) larger diameter causes additional drag and allows for a greater Magnus effect than when using the Type 2 ball. This should translate into more accuracy and a greater number of balls that stay in the court of play compared to the regular ball. This was, in fact, confirmed by our results as the number of good shots per point increased significantly with the Type 3 ball. This also confirms earlier work by Mitchell and Caine (2000). Given the fact that the points lasted longer when using the Type 3 ball, it is logical that players' heart rates and activity levels would increase as well during Type 3 ball play. The predicted increase in HR and VM while playing with the Type 3 ball was apparent, and supports the subjective reports that players fatigue more while using the Type 3 ball than when playing with the Type 2 ball. However, these results seem to contradict the work by Davey (Personal Communication, March, 2003) and an ITF (2003) statement posted on its web site which states players can play 35% longer while using the Type 3 ball. The LITT (Davey et al., 2002) that was used in the ITF study used intermittent hitting bouts of 4 min interspersed with 40 s of recovery. Players performed to the point of volitional fatigue in order that direct controlled comparisons could be made between the two ball types. The differentiating factor between Davey's results and our results may lie in the different work:rest ratios observed and the intensity of play. Two hypotheses seem apparent: 1) players play longer points with the Type 3 ball (as observed in our study) and therefore fatigue sooner, or 2) due to the increased time that is available to react to an opponent's shot, when using the Type 3 ball, the player in turn moves with a slower velocity (Li and Laurent, 1995). The players are then able to play for a longer time by playing at a lower intensity than with the Type 2 ball, as observed by Davey. The extra time gained for a return of service is estimated at only 10-16 ms for serves between 145-195 km.h$^{-1}$ (Haake et al., 2000). Therefore, we favor the first hypothesis not only as a result of our data, but because the extra time gained and the hypothesized lower intensity used when using the Type 3 ball are most likely insignificant when considering the effect the Type 3 ball has on tennis play. That is, the Type 3 ball can create more opportunities for shots that utilize more severe angles as well as more effective drop shots. As a result, the players may be allowed to use a larger percentage of the court and consequently be forced to cover a greater distance during the course of a point.

Davey's study relied to some extent on a player's subjective evaluation of volitional fatigue and so this may be a differentiating factor between Davey's results and our results. Also, the point of volitional fatigue was measured in time (minutes). In tennis, a point of fatigue is most important relative to the progress of the match, not time. Given our results that points last longer using the Type 3 ball, it would be possible to fatigue (quit) faster, relative to the progress of the match, than when using the Type 2 ball, even if the actual times to fatigue were the same. Finally, participants in Davey's tests were asked to hit at maximum effort, something our participants probably never did during the course of actual match play.

The effort with which a player hits the ball is an interesting topic and was the concern of earlier work (Knudson and Blackwell, 2001; Blackwell and Knudson, 2002) in which peak racket acceleration and electrical muscle activity (EMG) were measured during tennis performance. The concern stems from the idea that if a player knows the Type 3 ball will travel slower than the Type 2 ball, then a greater effort is needed in order to create the same ball velocity after ball-racket impact. Some participants were found to have increased peak racket accelerations and EMG, but the results were not overwhelming. This should, nevertheless, be a concern when investigating the etiology of tennis injuries and fatigue during tennis play. It would be an unfortunate consequence if the Type 3 ball was to lead to a greater incidence of injury in players, when an intended goal of adopting the ball is to increase enjoyment and participation of the game.

Another issue to consider when regarding the use of balls that change the speed of the game is the effect these balls have on training. Players who consistently use the Type 2 ball during practice and then play a tournament with the Type 3 ball might be at a disadvantage compared to players who practice with the Type 3 ball. Given the results in this study, (HR and VM increase during Type 3 ball play), it could be that playing a match with the Type 3 ball allows for an increased exercise bout. This would be comparable to training continuously for a set distance running race, and then discovering that the race is actually longer than anticipated. Looking at the other side of this issue, using the Type 3 ball during practice might actually benefit the player when the tournament match is played. Londeree (1997) stated that exercising at or near the "lactate threshold" allows for the improvement (increase) of the threshold in sedentary participants, and suggests that a higher intensity may be required to increase the threshold for trained participants. In addition, Londeree concluded that overall, the higher the intensity of training, the greater the benefit in terms of lactate threshold.. Although there was no measure of lactate threshold in the present study, the intensity most likely reached the lactate threshold for some of our participants, given the participant's age-predicted target heart rate zone (THRZ) (American College of Sports Medicine, 2000). That is, 35% of participants exhibited average HR values that exceeded the upper limit of the THRZ with both balls or with the Type 3 ball only. The Type 3 ball also showed greater aerobic training benefit for 60% of our participants as evidenced by the 4 beats.min$^{-1}$ higher average HR within the THRZ (i.e., above the lower limit and under the upper limit) versus the Type 2 ball. Therefore, even though the observed differences in HR may, at first glance, appear small, the increased training effect for the Type 3 ball may be as important as the statistical significance. Of course, the player has to consider the specificity of the practice task versus the performance task. After all, the flight characteristics of the Types 2 and 3 balls are different and this could affect player performance during match play if the practice conditions are not similar to the match-play conditions.

## 5 Conclusions

In middle aged players the use of the Type 3 ball resulted in longer rallies than when using the Type 2 ball. In turn, the players' levels of 3-dimensional activity and their heart rates increased when playing with the Type 3 ball.

## 6 Acknowledgements

We wish to acknowledge the helpful e-mail discussions with Dr. Polly Davey, Faculty of Engineering Science and Technology, School of Applied Sciences, Sport and Exercise Science Research Centre, South Bank University, 103 Borough Road, London, SE1 0AA, UK and the hospitality extended by the San Francisco Tennis club. This study was supported by a University of San Francisco Faculty Development Fund Grant.

## 7 References

American College of Sports Medicine. (2000). **ACSM's Guidelines for Exercise Testing and Prescription**. Philadelphia: Lippincott Williams & Wilkins.

Blackwell, J.R., and Heath, E.M. (1997). Mechanical and strategic considerations of the approach shot in tennis. **International Sports Journal, 11**, 30-38.

Blackwell, J.R., and Knudson, D.V. (2002). Effect of Type 3 (Oversize) tennis ball on serve performance and upper extremity muscle activity. **Sports Biomechanics, 1**(2), 187-191.

Brody, H. (1987). **Tennis Science for Tennis Players**. Philadelphia: University of Philadelphia Press.

Davey, P.R., Thorpe, R.D., and Williams, C. (2002). Fatigue decreases skilled tennis performance. **Journal of Sports Sciences, 20**, 311-318.

Haake, S.J., Chadwick, S.G., Dignall, R.J., Goodwill, S., and Rose, P. (2000). Engineering tennis-slowing the game down. **Sports Engineering, 3**, 131-143.

International Tennis Federation. (2003). **Rules and regulations: Rules of tennis**.

http://www.itftennis.com/html/rule/rules_ball_ruling.html.

Knudson, D.V., and Blackwell, J.R. (2001). Effect of Type 3 ball on upper extremity EMG and acceleration in the tennis forehand. In **Proceedings of Oral Sessions: XIX International Symposium on Biomechanics in Sports**, (edited by J.R. Blackwell), San Francisco: University of San Francisco, pp. 32-34.

Li, F., and Laurent, M. (1995). Intensity coupling in interceptive tasks. In **Studies in Perception and Action III** (edited by B.G. Bardy, R.J. Bootsma and Y. Guiard), New Jersey: Lawrence Erlbaum Associates,  pp. 195-198.

Londeree, B.R. (1997). Effects of training on lactate/ventilatory thresholds: a meta-analysis. **Medicine and Science in Sports and Exercise, 29,** 837-843.

Mitchell, S.R., and Caine, M. (2000). Playing with a larger tennis ball: a comparative study of the effects on point play, player perception, muscle fatigue and soreness. **ITF Technical Report**: Loughborough University.

# 8 Effects of the ground surface on the physiological and technical responses in young tennis players

## O. Girard and G.P. Millet

*Faculté des Sciences du Sport, Université de Montpellier 1, 700 Avenue du Pic Saint Loup, 34090 Montpellier, France.*

### 1 Introduction

The type of the tennis court's ground surface determines the rebound angle and velocity of the ball, and also influences the displacements of the player (Roetert and Groppel, 2001). Quality of a ground surface may be evaluated by its stiffness and its slipperiness, and these are different between slow surfaces (*i.e.*, clay) and fast surfaces (*i.e.*, Greenset®). Slow surfaces, named rugged surfaces, reduce the speed of the ball and induce a higher and slower rebound, in contrast to fast surfaces.

Technical and physical characteristics of a player, defining his/her game style, are widely influenced by the characteristics of the ground surface. Generally, net-rushers would prefer fast surfaces, giving them the ability to move forward to the net whereas aggressive baseliners would appreciate long rallies from behind the baseline and tend to be more effective on slow surfaces. Thus, one could suggest that different metabolic ways may be required on different ground surfaces. Technical characteristics [*i.e.*, duration of rallies (DOR); effective playing time (EPT); distance ran (DR); shots played consecutively (SPC)] constitute indirect indicators of the energy demands according to Smekal et al. (2001). Currently, knowledge of the physiology of tennis is improving, mainly due to the analyses on court of physiological parameters reflective of metabolic adaptations.

Tennis match play is characterized by intermittent exercise, alternating short (4-10 s) bouts of high-intensity play and short (10-20 s) recovery bouts, but interrupted by several periods of longer duration (60-90 s) (Dansou, 1998). However, one aspect of this sport relates to the great variability in duration of active and resting periods, leading to a difficulty in characterising the energy consumption. To date, it has been reported that singles tennis required both anaerobic and aerobic pathways, with different relative contributions (Bergeron et al., 1991; Chrismass et al., 1998; Smekal et al., 2001). The intensity of the game and DOR are considered as the two main variables influencing the contribution of the energy systems. However, on the one hand, Bergeron et al. (1991) reported that the oxidative metabolism was the most important pathway for the ATP resynthesis. On the other hand, Elliott et al. (1985) showed that the energy production was principally anaerobic.

In fact, environmental factors (*e.g.*, wind, spectators,...), but, more importantly the characteristics of the opponent (gender, rhythm, level and game style) influence the energy consumption in tennis players. Moreover, the influence of ground surface has been reported in relation to the game style of the player or the frequency of injuries, but rarely on metabolic responses. König et al. (2001) suggested that the type of

ground surface determines DOR.  Similarly, Richers (1995) showed that rallies were
~2 s longer on clay than on Greenset® in professional male tennis players.  However,
to the best of our knowledge, the effects of the type of ground surface on the
physiological and technical characteristics in young tennis players has not yet been
investigated.

Therefore, the purpose of the present study was to test the hypothesis that rallies
were longer and related to a higher contribution of the aerobic pathway on clay than
on Greenset®.

## 2 Methods

### 2.1 Participants
Seven good club standard male players of approximately equal playing ability,
volunteered as participants for this study. The study was approved by the institutional
ethics committee (University of Montpellier). Participants provided written,
voluntary, informed consent prior to participation. All were regular players and
accustomed to high levels of exertion.  The age, height and body mass were 15.1 ±
2.4 years, 167.0 ± 11.6 cm and 56.9 ± 15.0 kg, respectively.

### 2.2 Design
Players performed firstly a maximal treadmill test to exhaustion and secondly two
randomised 30 min trials on clay and on Greenset® outdoor courts, respectively.
Ground surface was the independent variable.  The dependent variables were
measures of technical and physiological parameters of oxygen uptake ($\dot{V}O_2$); heart
rate (HR); pulmonary ventilation (VE); respiratory exchange ratio (RER) and blood
lactate concentration (LA).

### 2.3 Materials
The $\dot{V}O_2$, HR, VE and RER were measured by a portable breath-by-breath gaz-
exchange analysis system (K4b², Cosmed, Rome, Italy) and averaged over 5 s. Post-
exercice blood lactate concentration was measured by the Lactate Pro (Arkray,
Kyoto, Japan).  Video analysis allowed to quantify DR, DOR and SPC with digital
video camera (JVC, Ottawa, Ontario).

### 2.4 Procedure

#### 2.4.1 Incremental test
All participants performed a maximal 3% grade treadmill running test (Powerjog®
GX 100, Sport Engineering Ltd, Birmingham, UK) consisting in an initial workload
of 9 km.h⁻¹ and stages of 2 km.h⁻¹ increment every 4 min. During both exercise tests,
HR was measured during a 30 s break between each stage. The test ended with the
voluntary exhaustion of the participants or when participants reached their $HR_{max}$
value, expressed by the following relationship: 220 - age. HR values at the end of
each stage were monitored with a heart rate monitor (S610, Polar, Kempele, Finland).
The $\dot{V}O_{2max}$ evaluation was based on the HR - velocity relationship.

#### 2.4.2 On-court test
Before each match, participants performed a 10 min standardized warm-up on court,
followed by 5 min recovery with the K4b². For each participant, the two trials were

undertaken against the same opponent, deemed to be of equal ability. Players were limited to 20 s between points. The trials did not include change-overs. Participants were encouraged to play at their best level as in an official tournament.

### 2.5 Statistics

The results were expressed as mean ± SD. Paired t-tests determined the significance of differences in technical and physiological parameters between clay and Greenset® values measured during the 30 min trials. Pearson correlation coefficients between the technical and physiological parameters were also determined (Statistica 5.5, Statsoft, Tulsa, OK, USA). A value of P<0.05 was accepted as the level of statistical significance.

## 3 Results

### 3.1 Physiological parameters

The estimated $\dot{V}O_{2max}$ and $HR_{max}$ during the incremental test were 50.3 ± 3.9 $ml \cdot kg^{-1} \cdot min^{-1}$ and 201.1 ± 8.5 beats.min$^{-1}$, respectively.

Mean physiological parameters were higher (P < 0.05) on clay than on Greenset® : $\dot{V}O_2$ (40.3 ± 5.7 vs. 35.9 ± 7.5 ml.kg$^{-1}$.min$^{-1}$), estimated % $\dot{V}O_{2max}$ (80.1 ± 10.8 vs. 71.6 ± 15.3), %HR$_{max}$ (90.4 ± 4.5 vs. 85.8 ± 5.9), HR (181.8 ± 11.9 vs. 172.8 ± 17.2 bpm), VE (58.9 ± 15.6 vs. 50.7 ± 12.3 l.min$^{-1}$), RER (1.04 ± 0.07 vs. 0.98 ± 0.07) ; but lactate concentration was not different (2.36 ± 0.47 vs. 3.08 ± 1.12 mmol.l$^{-1}$, P > 0.05).

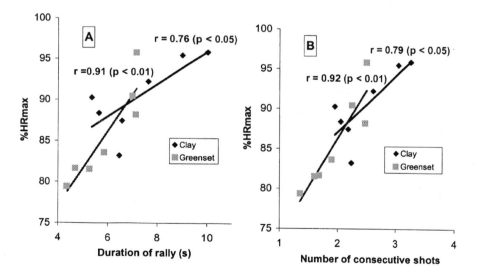

Figure 1. Correlations between duration of rallies (A), number of consecutive shots (B) and percentage of maximal heart rate (%HR$_{max}$) on clay and on Greenset® (N =7).

### 3.2 Technical characteristics

Similarly, the technical characteristics were higher (P < 0.01) on clay than on Greenset[®] : DOR (7.2 ± 1.7  *vs.*  5.9 ± 1.2 s), DR (9.8 ± 2.5 *vs.*  7.7 ± 1.7 m) and SPC (2.5 ± 0.5 *vs.* 1.9  ± 0.4).  High correlations were found between several physiological and technical characteristics on Greenset[®] ; % $\dot{V}O_{2max}$ and SPC (r = 0.99 ; P < 0.001), % $\dot{V}O_{2max}$ and DOR (r = 0.97 ; P < 0.001)  and %HR$_{max}$ and DR (r = 0.92 ; P < 0.01). Correlations obtained between DOR, DR and %HR on clay and Greenset[®] are shown in Figure 1.


### 4 Discussion

The main results of the present study are : 1. There are differences in metabolic responses between clay and Greenset[®]; the aerobic metabolism being more important on clay. 2. Technical characteristics of the game explain to a great extent the metabolic differences observed when playing on two surfaces. These observations support the initial hypothesis.

Continuous measurement of $\dot{V}O_2$ allowing the determination of  average and peak intensities during tennis matches is of interest to researchers (Smekal et al., 2001). Oxygen uptake values were higher in the present study than in previous ones (60-70 % $\dot{V}O_{2max}$) (Dansou, 1998; Smekal et al., 2000).  The fact that players were young and that change-overs were excluded may explain the relatively higher intensity. Moreover, Docherty (1982) showed that a match with opponents of equal ability would induce an increase in cardiac activity and therefore in exercise intensity.  In the present study, trials were sustained at a mean intensity of ~80% and ~70% of the estimated $\dot{V}O_{2max}$ on clay and Greenset[®], respectively; slightly above the ventilatory threshold.  Dansou (1998) and Smekal et al. (2001) reported the ventilatory threshold at ~80 % $\dot{V}O_{2max}$ and ~90 %HR$_{max}$. Therefore, the elevation of blood lactate at the end of the test was moderate, in agreement with Reilly and Palmer (1994) during singles tennis played on Greenset[®].  Blood lactate is considered as a reflection of anaerobic glycolysis.  The intermittent nature of tennis with numerous rest intervals explains why the mean value of blood lactate do not exceed 4 mmol.l$^{-1}$ (Bergeron et al., 1991). Blood lactate measurements were performed at the end of the 30 min trials. Therefore, any potential change in blood lactate during the trials  could not have been detected.  The participation of anaerobic glycolysis may have been  underestimated because lactate can be oxidized locally or transported from production sites to oxidative muscle fibres for subsequent oxidation during exercise and recovery periods (Brooks, 1986).

Ground surface appears to have a major influence on cardiorespiratory load since $\dot{V}O_{2max}$, VE and RER are greater on clay than on Greenset[®]. To our knowledge, the present study is the first one showing that the differences in the technical characteristics explain to a great extent the physiological differences observed between clay and Greenset[®].

The present results showed that DOR were more important on clay than on Greenset[®], in line with  Richers (1995) who reported DOR to be 2 to 4 s  longer on clay.  Smekal et al. (2001) reported  that DOR influenced the physiological responses on Greenset[®], explaining ~30% of $\dot{V}O_2$ differences between players. High correlations between several physiological (estimated % $\dot{V}O_{2max}$ and %HR$_{max}$) and technical characteristics suggested previously (Reilly and Palmer, 1994 ; Smekal et al., 2001) could provide a rationale for the present results in terms of differences between ground surfaces. Reilly and Palmer (1994) reported significantly higher HR and blood lactate concentration in singles tennis with longer rallies and EPT. On clay, the ball rebounding higher gives the player longer response time (*i.e.*, the time that a tennis player has to make a judgment about the speed, angle and trajectory of the ball). The difference in response time between "slow" and "fast" surfaces was shown to be a result of the interaction between ball and surface and is ~10% longer on clay (Roetert and Groppel, 2001). Moreover, the reduced speed of the ball on clay allows players to be active during a longer period and then to increase DR and SPC. Technical and tactical considerations explain these differences: on clay, the required racket speed is lower, inducing the need of more spin effect on the ball and a higher and deeper rebound than on Greenset®.

## 5 Conclusions

Mean intensity of singles tennis varies widely. Even though it is difficult to quantify exactly the contribution of the metabolic pathways, the present study showed clearly that ground surface has a large influence on it. Although the anaerobic contribution does not seem different, the aerobic pathway is more required on clay due to the longer duration of the rallies allowing a greater increase in $\dot{V}O_{2max}$ and HR. So, the present results which show physiological and technical differences between clay and Greenset® suggest that the young players may benefit from practice on different ground surfaces; on clay in order to increase their endurance, and on faster surfaces to enhance their technical skills.

## 6 References

Bergeron, M.F., Maresh, C.M., Kraemer, W.J., Abraham, A., Conroy, B., and Gabaree, C. (1991). Tennis: A physiological profile during match play. **International Journal of Sports Medicine**, 12, 474-479.

Brooks, G.A. (1986). The lactate shuttle during exercise and recovery. **Medicine and Science in Sports and Exercise**, 18, 360-368.

Chrismass, M.A., Richmond, S.E., Cable, N.T., Arthur, P.G., and Hartmann, P.E. (1998). Exercise intensity and metabolic response in singles tennis. **Journal of Sports Sciences**, 16, 739-747.

Dansou, P. (1998). *Adaptations cardiorespiratoires, métaboliques et hormonales au cours d'un match de tennis. Du laboratoire au terrain.* (Cardiorespiratory, metabolic and hormonal adaptations during a tennis match : From laboratory to court) **Ph. D. thesis, Université Grenoble 1, France.**

Docherty, D. (1982). A comparison of heart rate response in racket games. **British Journal of Sports Medicine**, 16 , 96-100.

Elliott, B.C., Dawson, B., and Pyke, F. (1985). The energetics of singles tennis. **Journal of Human Movement Studies**, 11, 11-20.

Groppel, J.L., and Roetert, E.P. (1992). Applied physiology of tennis. **Sports Medicine**, 14, 260-268.

König, D., Huonker, M., Schmitz, A., Halk, M., Berg, A., and Keul, J. (2001). Cardiovascular, metabolic and hormonal parameters in professional tennis players. **Medicine and Science in Sports and Exercise**, 33, 654-658.

Reilly, T., and Palmer, J. (1994). Investigation of exercise intensity in male singles lawn tennis. In **Science and Racket Sports** (edited by T. Reilly, M. Hughes and A. Lees) London: E & FN Spon, pp 10-13.

Richers, T.A. (1995). Time-motion analysis of the energy systems in elite and competitive singles tennis. **Journal of Human Movement Studies**, 28, 73-86.

Roetert, P., and Groppel, J. (2001). World-class Tennis Technique. Champaign, Il., **Human Kinetics Publishers**, 41-59.

Smekal, G., Pokan, R., Von Duvillard, S.P., Baron, R., Tschan, H., and Bachl, N. (2000). Comparison of Laboratory and "on court" endurance testing in tennis. **International Journal of Sports Medicine**, 21 (4), 242-249.

Smekal, G., Von Duvillard, S.P., Rihacek, C., Pokan, R., Hofmann, P., Baron, R., Tschan, H., and Bachl, N. (2001). A physiological profile of tennis match play. **Medicine and Science in Sports and Exercise**, 33 (6), 999-1005.

# 9 Influence of table tennis ball diameter on precision, organization of movement and heart rate

V. Fayt, G. Quignon and B. Catoire
*Laboratoire d'Analyse Multidisciplinaire des Pratiques Sportives LAMAPS, UFR STAPS Liévin, University of Artois, France.*

## 1 Introduction

In January 2001, modified table tennis rules, previously introduced in September 2000 in international competitions, were introduced in French competitions. This specifically affected the ball diameter which was increased by 2 mm from 38 mm to 40 mm.

Table tennis is a whole-body activity requiring continuous footwork and accurate hitting of the ball, and where precision in task performance is extremely important. If the player cannot reach the ball still maintaining a good posture and a correct timing, his performance will inevitably deteriorate causing less accurate shots.

Changing from 38 mm to 40 mm diameter decreased ball speed (Meichel and Labrune, 2000) and consequently increased rally duration, introducing a conflict with the player's goal of ending the rally as soon as possible (Sève, 2001). These changes could therefore be identified as causing a change in effort production and movements (Wilmore and Costill, 1994), leading to a change in performance. The awareness of these implications could be used in programming training and playing strategies (Yquel, 2001; Jégouzo, 2001).

The aim of this study was to examine the effects of the increase in diameter of the table tennis ball on performance, as assessed by the level of accuracy, on movement execution (experiment 1) and also on heart rate and subjective feelings of exertion (experiment 2).

## 2 Methods: Experiment 1

The goal of this first experiment was to analyse the effects of table tennis ball diameter on precision and on execution of the drive movements.

### 2.1 Design

A repeated measures design with all the participants completing the two levels of the factor "ball diameter" was adopted. Independent variables were the level of practice (experts versus beginners), and the ball diameter conditions (38 and 40 mm diameters). Dependent variables were performance (% of balls hitting a target) and movement amplitude (recorded with a camera at 25 Hz).

## 2.2 Participants
Eighteen male students of the Sports University of Liévin participated in the study. Two groups were set up: Group 1 consisted of high level participants (n=9, National level) and Group 2 involved beginners (n=9, participants who had acquired fundamentals of activity). The average (± s) age was 20.13 ±1.55 years.

## 2.3 Equipment
Players were required to perform a forehand drive towards a target of 21 cm diameter, placed in the opponent's half-court. A robot (TT Matic 500B, Tibhar, Horb-Ihlingen, Germany), adapted for different balls diameters (38 and 40 mm), ejected balls at a rate of 60 per minute toward the right side of the player half-court. Each session of testing consisted of 20 hits, in one of the two diameter conditions. A camera (25 Hz) placed on the right side of the table filmed movements of the participants in the sagittal plane.

After some practice trials, the participants returned 20 balls towards the target. The accuracy was measured as the percentage of balls hitting the target. Movement amplitude was analyzed on a screen of 17" with Photo Express 2, and it was calculated as the distance between the high dead point - position where the hand stopped to change his movement direction - and the low dead point - drive movement finish (the palm of the hand was taken as the reference point). This measure was chosen as a uni-dimensional indicator of the amplitude of participant's movement.

## 2.4 Procedure
Before the test began, participants were allowed a 5 min warm up period at the table (to simulate match conditions). All scores were recorded by the experimenter. Different test conditions were separated by a 20 min rest period. To minimize order effects, participants were submitted to different tests in a random sequence. Analysis of variance (ANOVA) tests were performed on data with a level of significance fixed at $P<0.05$.

## 3  Results: Experiment 1

### 3.1 Accuracy
An ANOVA was conducted on the accuracy data for factor "Level of Practice" (beginners and experts) and for factor "Ball Diameter", with repeated measures on the last factor. A significant main effect was found on "Level of Practice" ($F_{1,16}=37.80$, $P<0.05$), and on "Ball Diameter" ($F_{1,16}=6.81$, $P<0.05$). The interaction effect failed to reach significance. This indicates that experts were more accurate than beginners (as could be predicted) and that performance, for both participants categories, was lower with 40 mm balls. Results are shown in Figure 1. Changing from 38 to 40 mm balls caused a relative decrease in performance of 7.5% for beginners and of 5% for experts.

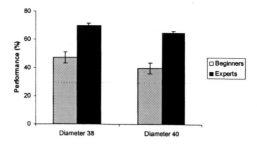

Figure 1.  Performance of experts and beginners in a hitting
task with balls of 38 and 40 mm diameter.


## 3.2 Amplitude

An ANOVA was conducted on the movement amplitude data for the factor "Level of Practice" (beginners and experts) and for the factor "Ball Diameter" with repeated measures on the last factor.  There was no significant main effect for the factor "Level of Practice".  A main effect for "Ball Diameter" ($F_{1,16}$=5.95, P<0.05) and an interaction effect between "Level of Practice" and "Ball Diameter" ($F_{1,16}$=7.37, P<0.05) were found (Figure 2).

Movement amplitude was wider on average with expert players (10.6 cm versus 9.90 cm) than with beginners.  A meaningful difference was observed between 38 mm and 40 mm balls with the experts, while movement amplitude did not vary with beginners (Figure 2).

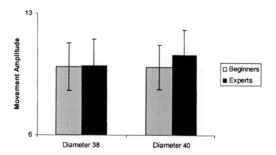

Figure 2. Amplitude of the movement according to the practice
level of the participants and diameter of the ball.

## 4  Methods: Experiment 2

The goal of this second experiment was to analyze the effects of the diameter of table tennis balls on performance, heart rate and perceived exertion.

### 4.1 Participants
Eleven students (1 female, 10 males) from the Sports University of Liévin participated in the study. All were regular players, with an average experience of 10.27 ±3.04 years in table tennis activity. The average (± s) age was 20.91 ±2.21 years and mass was 73.82 ±11.67 kg.

### 4.2 Design, equipment and procedure
Balls were ejected without spin by robot (TT Matic 500B, Tibhar, Horb-Ihlingen, Germany), adapted for both 38 mm and 40 mm balls. The robot allowed a standardization of the exercise and guaranteed identical conditions for all the participants.

Participants were asked to perform a drive (forehand or backhand according to the placement of the ball), hitting balls towards the imposed target which was the opponent's half-court. The duration of the task was set for 1 min, with a rate of 60 balls.min$^{-1}$. To minimize order effects, participants were submitted to different tests in a random sequence.

All the participants were involved in both situations (38 mm and 40 mm balls). The independent variable was the ball diameter (38 mm and 40 mm), while dependent variables were accuracy, heart rate (beats.min$^{-1}$) and perceived exertion.

The performance was evaluated directly by an experimenter counting the number of balls hitting the target. Heart rate was measured with a heart rate monitor (Accurex plus, Polar, Kempele, Finland) and perceived exertion was rated using the Perceived Exertion Scale (Borg, 1973). Maximum heart rates (Table 1) were measured by means of a progressive maximum test running around a track (Léger and Boucher, 1980).

## 5  Results

### 5.1 Performance test
Performance data obtained in the two experimental conditions (38 mm vs 40 mm balls) were analyzed using Student's $t$-test. There was a significant difference between performance with 38 mm and 40 mm balls (t = 2.55, P = 0.029). This observation suggests that participants could maintain a higher level of performance with the 38 mm ball than with the 40 mm ball (73% ±10.1 vs 67.73% ±8.22).

### 5.2 Heart rate changes
Heart rate was measured four times during and during the last 5 s of each task. The average values of the five measures were used in data analysis presented in Table 1.

The analysis did not show significant difference between the average heart rate obtained with 38 mm balls and that obtained with 40 mm balls, during the execution of the task (t = 2.072; P = 0.065).

Table 1. Mean (± s) heart rates (beats.min⁻¹) obtained with 38 mm and 40 mm balls

| | HR max Léger-Boucher | HR max Test 38 mm | HR max Test 40 mm | HR mean Test 38 mm | HR mean Test 40 mm |
|---|---|---|---|---|---|
| Mean | 203 | 170 | 170 | 144 | 147 |
| Standard Deviation | ± 10.6 | ± 12.2 | ± 13.3 | ± 12.1 | ± 13.5 |

## 5.3 Rating of perceived exertion

At the conclusion of each task participants were asked to rate their perceptions of exertion on the Borg RPE-Scale (Borg, 1973). The average rating of perceived exertion with 38 mm balls was 14.4 ±1.3 and the score with 40 mm balls was 14.9 ±1.6. Data analysis was carried out through a Student's t-test and did not show any significant difference for perceived exertion between the two types of balls ($t = 0.545$, $P = 0.1399$).

## 6 Discussion

The aim of this study was to examine the effects of increased ball diameter on accuracy, on movement amplitude (Experiment 1), on heart rate and perception of exertion (Experiment 2).

A decline in performance was observed as the ball diameter increased for both participants groups (beginners and experts) in both experimental conditions (more accurate or less accurate). The first experiment showed that changes in movement amplitude appeared only for experts, while beginners maintained a constant amplitude when changing from 38 mm to 40 mm balls. The second experiment, proposing a standard task for experienced players, did not reveal a significant influence of ball diameter on heart rate or on perceived exertion measured on the Borg RPE-Scale.

In order to maintain a high ball speed during rallies, an increase in heart rate and perceived exertion could be expected for ball diameter modification, but no changes were observed in our study. Probably the limited duration of the exercise (1 min) can be an explanation for these results. Exercise duration was chosen in order to replicated activity characteristics of table tennis, without engaging the anaerobic system (Lundin, 1973; Orfeuil, 1982). During the tasks, participants maintained an average heart rate at 85% of their maximal heart rate (estimated with a progressive, continuous and maximum test around a track, Léger and Boucher, 1980), as observed during table tennis rallies.

Increasing the ball diameter led to an overall performance decrease: average accuracy was higher with 38 mm than 40 mm balls. This change in performance and the movement modifications emphasize the significance of diameter change in influencing players' actions. These results seem to be opposed to the original goal of diameter increase: i.e. decrease the ball speed and increase the response time of the player (decreasing the difficulty of the task and increasing the duration of rallies). There was also evidence of a re-organization of movement execution, experts having wider movement with 40 mm than with 38mm balls, probably due to a lower ball speed.

A more coherent interpretation of all the results could be found in the experienced players' attempts to perform movements with the highest level of ease, using the longer time response interval, and limiting their energy expenditure.  In fact, a longer time response interval, keeping arm movement speed and amplitude constant, would introduce a rest period in arm movement, causing an increase in energy requirements . Expert participants seemed to prefer a wider and continuous movement and a constant arm speed, securing a lower exertion level.


## 7 Conclusions

The first objective for increasing the diameter of the ball was to decrease rally speed and to increase duration.  Adaptation from the player was expected in terms of movement change and effort production to thwart these modifications.  Our results show an adaptation in terms of movement amplitude (only for experts), but a constant level of effort (at heart level and perceived exertion).  These results seem to suggest that adaptations in movements are adopted to keep a constant energetic level and not to keep ball speed constant during rallies (in contrast to expectations).  Further investigations should be made to explore the influence on these parameters of players experienced in using 38 mm balls, against the relatively recent introduction of 40 mm balls.


## 8 References

Borg, G. (1973). Perceived exertion: A note on history and methods. **Medicine and Science in Sports**, 5, 90-93.

Jégouzo, M. (2001). Le monde en bref. (The world in short). **France Tennis de Table Magazine**, 750, 16-17.

Léger, L. and Boucher, R. (1980). An indirect continuous running multistage field test, the Université de Montréal Track Test, **Canadian Journal of Applied Sports Sciences**, 5, 77-84.

Lundin, A. (1973). Bordtennis (Table Tennis. Sports physiology). **Idrottsfysiologi**, Rapport No.12, Trygg-Hansa, Stockholm.

Meichel, R. and Labrune, E. (2000). Pour 2 millimètres de plus. (For 2 mm more). **Var info Tennis de Table**, 23-25.

Orfeuil, F. (1982). **Le Tennis de Table: Physiologie et entraînement**. (Table tennis: Physiology and training). Paris, INSEP France, 78.

Sève, C. (2001). A propos de la balle de 40mm. (About the 40 mm ball). **France Tennis de Table Magazine**, 758, 12-13.

Wilmore, J.H. and Costill, D.L. (1994). **Physiology of Sport and Exercise**. Champaign, IL, Human Kinetics.

Yquel, R. (2001). La balle de 40 millimètres: plus visible, plus physique. (The 40 mm ball: more visible, more physical). **France Tennis de Table Magazine**, 758, 10.

# 10 Does practising on clay affect the level of motor abilities of tennis players?

P. Unierzyski and E. Hurnik
*University School of Physical Education, Tennis Department, Poznan, Poland.*

## 1 Introduction

Previous research (Elliott et al., 1989, 1990; Muller, 1989; Schönborn, 1984) indicates that the most important factors affecting sports results in tennis performance are coordination, agility, dynamic power and speed, tennis technique, footwork and a group of mental features. It is also well established that agility and footwork as well as speed and power are important components of performance level among tennis players (Elliot et al., 1989, 1990; Królak, 1990; Muller, 1989; Schönborn, 1984, 1993; Unierzyski, 1996). There are also many publications (Higger, 1993, 2002; Pluim, 1999; Snelleman, 1993; Unierzyski et al., 1998; van Aken, 1998) describing training methods for improving these abilities.

Based on this information many coaches focus on developing major abilities affecting performance during the training process from the beginning of a player's career. Besides training methods, there have been many concerns about which surface is the most helpful to a players' development. From one point of view, fast courts help to create an aggressive, "all court" or serve and volley game while clay encourages players to rally from a baseline and is safer than the harder surface.

Based on the success of Spanish players, many coaches believe that players who practise and compete predominantly on clay courts should be fitter, faster and more agile. Until now this belief has not been verified.

The characteristics of a clay court game include long rallies and matches and therefore more spurts, changes of directions than on hard courts (Collette, 1992; Crespo, 1993; Królak 1996; Schönborn, 1999). Therefore it can be suggested that practising on this surface might indeed help to develop motor abilities and footwork skills better than practising on other surfaces. The purpose of this research was to verify this suggestion.

## 2 Method

The research was conducted during 9 seasons (1993 to 2001) of "La Raquette de Corail", one of the most prestigious tournaments for players under 12 years of age. A total of 253 of Europe's top players, 12 years of age (at the time of testing), took part in the project. The possibility of simultaneous comparison of the results with the current competitive performance of a player was a reason for carrying out this study during tournaments.

Investigations consisted of simple anthropometric measurements, and data for playing age, tennis training load (in hours per week), number of matches played during previous season were recorded (Table1) and motor ability tests (Table 2). As the study was conducted during tournaments the motor abilities tests had to be relatively simple and not tiring for the players. The battery of motor ability tests consisted of:

1. Grip strength (dominant hand) was measured with an electronic hand dynamometer (kg),
2. Arm dynamic (explosive) power was measured by 2kg medicine ball throw (both hands, service motion) (m),
3. Dynamic (explosive) power was indicated by performance in a standing broad jump (cm),
4. 20 m run (s),
5. Figure of "8" shuttle run (s),
6. Flexibility was measured using a sit-and-reach test (cm),

The players had three attempts at each test except the shuttle run which was executed once only (repeating was possible only when the player was eliminated from the event). The participants had an opportunity to rest between trials. The tests were performed on a hard court, always on the same morning of the week, to enable comparisons to be made from year to year. All players were ranked and the ranking was based on the results in the above-mentioned tournament.

For the purpose of the study the players who claimed to have spent at least 70% of training and competitions either on hard or on clay courts, were put into "hard" (n= 22) and "clay" (n= 44) groups, while the remainder constituted the 'other' group. The significance of differences between groups was measured by Student's t-test.

## 3 Results and Discussion

Generally "hard" and "clay" groups were quite homogeneous and also did not differ much from the rest of the players taking part in the research (Table 1). The "clay" and "hard" groups were similar with regards to body build, sports results (average ranking in tournament), playing age and training load.

Table 1. Player characteristics: "hard" those who practised mostly on hard courts, and "clay" those who spent at least 70% of training time on clay courts compared to the rest of players (all non-significant at P<0.05)

| GROUP | Other players n=187 | "clay" n=44 | "hard" n=22 |
|---|---|---|---|
| Playing age (years) | 6.2 ± 1.3 | 6.1 ± 1.5 | 6.3 ± 1.2 |
| Tennis training(h.wk$^{-1}$) | 9.8 ± 3.6 | 11.3 ± 3.2 | 10.1 ± 4.1 |
| Physical training(h.wk$^{-1}$) | 4.1 ± 2.5 | 4.4 ± 2.5 | 3.5 ± 2.5 |
| Number of matches per year | 72.5 ± 26.1 | 81.7 ± 27.8 | 86.1 ± 36.0 |
| Place in tournament | 15.9 ± 8.2 | 11.9 ± 8.7 | 11.5 ± 8.5 |
| Body height (cm) | 154.0 ± 6.9 | 154.9 ± 6.9 | 153.8 ± 6.6 |
| Body mass (kg) | 40.3 ± 5.1 | 40.8 ± 5.8 | 40.0 ± 5.6 |

Players also did not differ significantly from the control group in all motor ability trials (Table 2), except that the "clay" group achieved better results than the hard group in the standing broad jump (P<0.05) and in the shuttle run (P<0.01).

Table 2. Results of motor abilities tests and comparison between investigated groups of players. (* differences between groups significant at P<0,05; **,++ differences between groups significant at P<0.01)

| GROUP | Other players<br>n=187 | "clay"<br>n=44 | "hard"<br>n=22 |
|---|---|---|---|
| Grip strength (kg) | 25.6 ± 4.7 | 26.9 ± 4.6 | 25.9 ± 5.3 |
| Med. Ball Th. (m) | 6.5 ± 1.2 | 6.7 ± 1.3 | 6.1 ± 1.2 |
| SB Jump (cm) | 183.4 ± 16.7 | 187.9 ± 16.1* | 177.6 ± 17.9* |
| 20 m run (s) | 3.5 ± 0.2 | 3.4 ± 0.2 | 3.5 ± 0.2 |
| "8" Shuttle run(s) | 12.5 ± 0.5 ++ | 12.1 ± 0.4**,++ | 12.6 ± 0.4** |
| Flexibility (cm) | 24.0 ± 5.6 | 24.0 ± 5.8 | 24.0 ± 3.7 |

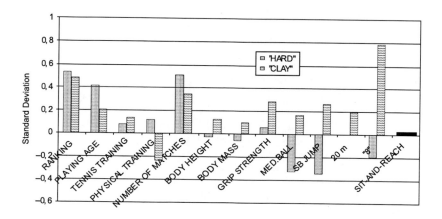

Figure 1. Mean profiles of two groups investigated (standardized data).

The standardised (Z) score in relation to the other players for each measure taken is presented in Figure 1. There was also no evidence that practising on clay courts helps to develop speed better than training on other surfaces. The difference in agility/footwork (shuttle run) and explosive power of the legs (broad jump) suggest that practising on clay might support the development of power in the lower extremities. It is still unknown if this difference is because of longer rallies (i.e. higher number of repetitions) or rather due to the characteristics of the surface.

Although there is no evidence from other research it is quite probable that demands of a clay court game (many stops, changing directions etc. executed in more repetitions than it occurs on hard courts) favour developing these important abilities. Certainly, there is an area for further investigation.

## 4  Acknowledgements

The authors would like to thank the ITF Development Fund and personally Dave Miley, Marcel Ferrari and Jean-Pierre Stefani for supporting this research.

## 5  References

Crespo, M. (1993). Duration de los puntos en un partido de tennis (duration of rallies in a game of tennis). **Communications to ETA Symposium Rome; ETA.**

Collette, D. (1992). Problem solving as pedagogical tool. **Proceedings of 3rd National Tennis Seminar,** Melbourne, Tennis Australia, 1-13.

Elliott, B.C., Ackland, T.R., Blanksby, B.A., Hood, K.P. and Bloomfield, J. (1989). Profiling junior tennis players part 1: morphological, physiological and psychological normative data. **Australian Journal of Science and Medicine in Sport,** Canberra Sept. 21(3), 14-21.

Elliott, B., Ackland T.R., Blanskby, B.A. and Bloomfield, J. (1990). A prospective study of physiological and kinanthropometric indicators of junior tennis performance. **Australian Journal of Science and Medicine in Sport,** 22, 87-92.

Higger, Y. (1993). Physical Training for Tennis, An Integrating Approach. A presentation from **8th ITF Worldwide Coaches Workshop.** Key Biscayne.

Higger, Y. (2002). Physical training for tennis – the need for better integration. **ITF Coaching and Sport Science Review,** 26, 13-14.

Królak, A. (1990). **Introduction to modern tennis** (in Polish). AWF Warszawa.

Müller, E. (1989). Sportmotorische Testverfahren zur Talentauswahl im Tennis (Motor ability tests for talent identification in tennis). **Leistungsport,** 2, 8-13.

Pluim, B. (1999). Conditioning and medical aspects on the female tennis players. **ITF Coaching and Sport Science Review,** 18, 13-14.

Schönborn, R. (1984). Leistungslimitierende und Leistungsbestimmende Faktoren (Factors limiting and determining performance in tennis). In **Talentsuche und Talent Förderung im Tennis** (Talent search and talent promotion in tennis) (edited by H. Gabler and B. Zein), Beitraege vom 1. Symposium des Sportwissenschaftlichen Beirats des DTB 1983, Ahrensburg bei Hamburg, Czwalina, pp. 51-75.

Schönborn, R. (1993). Players' performance and development. **ITF Coaches Review** 2, 1.

Schönborn, R. (1999). **Advanced techniques for competitive tennis.** Meyer & Meyer, Aachen.

Snelleman, L. (1993). Speed training related to co-ordination, anticipation, footwork and concentration. **ITF Coaching and Sport Science Review,** 1, 8-9.

Unierzyski, P. (1996). A retrospective analysis of junior Grand Slam winners. **ITF Coaching and Sport Science Review,** 9, 2.

Unierzyski, P., Szczepanowska E. and Schefke T. (1998). Training methods for improving endurance. **ITF Coaching and Sport Science Review,** 15, 6-8.

Van Aken, I. (1998). Maintaining fitness during tournaments. **ITF Coaching and Sport Science Review,** 15, 8-11.

# Part Three

# Medical Aspects of Racket Sports

# 11 Physiological demands and injury in racket sports: Differences and similarities

B. Pluim
*Royal Netherlands Lawn Tennis Association, Displayweg 4, 3821 BT Amersfoort, The Netherlands.*

## 1 Introduction

This paper compares physiological and physical demands and injuries in squash, tennis, badminton and table tennis. In some ways, these four racket sports are very similar, involving bursts of high intensity exercise, followed by rest periods between points and games. There are also considerable differences, however. A table tennis match generally lasts only 20 min, for example, whereas a tennis match may take up to five hours to complete. The physiological demands of the various racket sports are compared in terms of the effective playing time and mean heart rate and lactate levels. Physical demands are compared by studying the various injury rates, injury locations and causative mechanisms of the most common injuries.

## 2 Physiological demands

Squash is generally considered the most demanding of the four racket sports. The mean rally duration in squash is around 8-12 s, followed by rest periods of approximately 7-8 s, resulting in an effective playing time of 50-70% (Locke et al., 1997). However, individual rally duration may show considerable variation, with rallies lasting anything between one stroke and 1.5 s, or 400 strokes and 10 min! (Sharp, 1998). Medium and highly skilled players tend to have longer rallies than those of a lower level of skill. Mean heart rate levels in squash are 80-90% of maximum, with lactate levels ranging from 3.5 to over 10 mmol·$L^{-1}$ (Sharp, 1998). Average rally duration in badminton is around 4-5 s, with rest periods of approximately 10 s, resulting in an effective playing time of some 35% (Majumdar et al., 1997). Mean heart rate levels in badminton range from 75-85 % of maximal heart rate, with highest values found in those players with highest skill levels (Majumdar et al., 1997). Maximum lactate reported in the literature during match play varies from 3-6 mmol·$L^{-1}$, but much higher values of 8-10.5 mmol·$L^{-1}$ have been recorded during on-court training (Majumdar et al., 1997).

In tennis, average rally duration varies from 4-8 s, depending on the surface, gender and playing style (O'Donoghue and Ingram, 2001). The rest periods between the points range from 15-25 seconds with a maximum permitted rest period of 25 seconds. This results in an effective playing time ranging from 10 to 30%. The average heart rate is 70-85% of maximum heart rate in singles tennis, compared to 60-70% of maximum in doubles (Christmass et al., 1998). Mean lactate levels in singles tennis vary from 2-3 mmol·L$^{-1}$, with maximum recorded values of 6 mmol·L$^{-1}$, (Smekal et al., 2001; Ferrauti et al., 2002).

In table tennis, the average rally duration is 3-4 s, with rest periods twice as long, resulting in an effective playing time of 35% (Weber, 1987). In table tennis, average heart rate is 80-85% of maximum (Baron et al., 1992). This is surprisingly high, reflecting the high sympathetic arousal in addition to the physical demands. Lactate levels, however, are more consistent with the physiological demand (2 mmol·L$^{-1}$).

## 3 Epidemiology of injuries

The varying physiological demands are also reflected in player injury, which is highest in the most demanding sport (squash), and lowest in the least demanding (table tennis).

One has to be cautious when comparing injury data from the four racket sports from different studies, because differences in injury definition, study design, methods of data collection, population under study and observation period may lead to substantial variations. Thus, for a valid statement regarding the relative injury risk, it is advisable to consider studies that include all four racket sports simultaneously. Two such studies were recently performed in the Netherlands.

In the study by Schmikli et al. (2001), telephone surveys were conducted in 1986/1987, 1992/1993 and 1997/1998 regarding sports participation and sports injuries in the general population. Injuries were defined as accidents or afflictions that occurred during and/or as a result of sports participation. The interviewees decided what they regarded as an injury. Unfortunately, there was a change in methodology, with a recall period of 4 weeks in the first two surveys, and a recall period of 3 months in the last period. This may have led to over-reporting of more serious and acute injuries, and under-reporting of the less serious injuries in the last survey. However, it is still possible to compare the four sports. Injury risk was calculated as the number of injuries per 1,000 hours of play. Over the years, it was consistently shown that injury risk is slightly higher in squash (3.6, 3.1 and 2.0 injuries per 1,000 hours of play in 86-87, 92-93, and 97-98 respectively). This was followed by indoor tennis (1.8, 2.9, and 1.0), badminton (2.7, 1.2 and 1.9), and outdoor tennis (1.2, 1.2. and <0.5). The injury risk in table tennis was so low that it was not reported. When all sports are ranked according to injury risk, squash ranks 11, indoor tennis 14, badminton 15, and outdoor tennis 19. Injury risk in downhill skiing and indoor soccer is about 2-3 times as high as injury risk in squash.

Table 1. Yearly number of casualty ward treatments after a tennis, squash, badminton or table tennis injury per 1000 participants with respect to age and gender

| | Number | Number per 1,000 | Number | Number per 1,000 | Number | Number per 1,000 | Number | Number per 1,000 |
|---|---|---|---|---|---|---|---|---|
| Age | 6 to 80 years | | 16 years and older | | | | | |
| | Total | | Total | | Males | | Females | |
| Tennis | 5,300 | 4.4 | 4,900 | 4.7 | 2,700 | 4.5 | 2,200 | 4.9 |
| Badminton | 1,500 | 2.1 | 1,350 | 2.8 | 750 | 2.9 | 600 | 2.6 |
| Squash | 2,200 | 4.8 | 2,160 | 4.8 | 1,800 | 6.0 | 360 | 2.7 |
| Table Tennis | 260 | 0.56 | 170 | 0.67 | 130 | 0.69 | 40 | 0.52 |

In the LIS study (LIS, 2003), all patients that received treatment on the casualty ward of a selection of hospitals in the Netherlands during 1998-2001 were registered. These hospitals form a representative sample of all the teaching and general hospitals in the Netherlands with a casualty ward. In this study, it was primarily acute and more serious injuries that were registered, while chronic and/or less serious injuries would have been reported less often. Injury risk was calculated as the number of injuries per 1,000 participants per year. Sports injuries were all afflictions that occurred during or as a result of sports participation. Again, injury risk in squash was highest (4.8 per 1,000 participants), especially among adult male players (6.0 per 1,000 participants: see Table 2). In tennis, badminton and squash, injury risk is fairly similar for males and females (Table 2). In tennis and table tennis, the older age groups are affected most often, whereas in squash and badminton, the injury risk is higher among younger players.

Table 2. Yearly number of casualty ward treatments after a tennis, squash, badminton or table tennis injury per 1000 participants with respect to age

| | Number | Number per 1,000 | Number | Number per 1000 | Number | Number per 1000 | Number | Number per 1000 |
|---|---|---|---|---|---|---|---|---|
| Age | 16 to 35 | | 35 to 50 | | 50 to 65 | | 65 years and older | |
| Tennis | 1,400 | 3.3 | 1,800 | 5.3 | 1,400 | 6.5 | 280 | 5.3 |
| Badminton | 660 | 3.1 | 570 | 3.1 | 110 | 1.6 | 20 | 1.4 |
| Squash | 1,500 | 4.9 | 560 | 5.9 | 30 | 2.1 | <10 | 2.8 |
| Table Tennis | 80 | 0.50 | 60 | 0.93 | 30 | 0.91 | <10 | 0.68 |

## 4 Injury location

In squash, badminton, and table tennis, musculo-skeletal injuries to the lower extremities predominate in most studies (Locke et al., 1997). In tennis, a fairly even distribution of injuries over the upper and lower extremities is generally found, with a minority of injuries located in the trunk (Chard and Lachman, 1987; Winge et al., 1989). However, tennis studies that focus on either juniors (Hutchinson et al., 1995) or on acute injuries (LIS, 2003; Steinbrück, 1999), also report a predominance of lower extremity injuries.

## 5 Lower extremity injuries

Three common injuries are the ankle sprain, the partial rupture of the gastronemius muscle ('tennis leg') and the Achilles tendon rupture.

### 5.1 Ankle sprain

The ankle sprain is generally considered the most common injury in all four racket sports, accounting for 20-30% of all injuries (Fahlström, 1998b). An ankle sprain typically occurs during a backhand stroke or when landing after a jump, rupturing one or more ligaments on the lateral side of the ankle. The risk of an ankle sprain is increased after a previous injury, so adequate protection with a tape, brace, or stabilising exercises is warranted, since this has been shown to reduce the injury risk (Handoll et al., 2001).

## 5.2 Achilles tendon injuries

Typical for badminton is the high number of Achilles tendon injuries and acute
Achilles tendon ruptures. In a study of elite and recreational badminton players,
10.5% of all injuries were classified as achillodynia (Jörgensen, 1987). Pain in the
Achilles tendon was reported by 32% of young Swedish elite badminton players and
44% of middle-aged badminton players, either presently or during the last five years
(Fahlström et al., 2002). Most injuries (87-94%) seem to occur in the middle or late
part of the game (Fahlström et al., 1998a). It has been suggested that an important
causative factor is fatigue, with impaired neuromuscular function and co-ordination
of the triceps surae muscle, as a result of the many plyometric movements and jumps
in badminton. Eccentric muscle training of the gastrocnemius and supplements are
recommended as preventative measures. Long-term results favour surgery over
conservative treatment, because of shorter sick leave absence, fewer remaining
symptoms, and a lower risk of re-rupture (Fahlström et al., 1998b).

## 5.3 Tennis leg

As the name suggests, tennis leg (a partial rupture of the medial head of the
gastrocnemius muscle) is typical of tennis. This injury is seen most commonly as a
result of a sudden eccentric contraction of the calf muscles with the foot in dorsal
flexion and the knee in extension, such as during jumping, lunging or a sprint to the
ball (Figure 1). Treatment is conservative, with rest and functional exercises (cycling,
toe raises and gentle stretching).

Figure 1. Position of leg at the onset of rupture.

## 5.4 Upper extremity injuries
Upper extremity injuries are most common in tennis. This is (1) because of the higher weight of the racket and ball compared to the other sports, resulting in a higher load on the muscles and tendons, e.g. when hitting a backhand, and (2) the overhead movements in tennis (service, overhead smash). In badminton, the overhead smash is hit the same way as in tennis, but the serve is hit from the level of the waist. In squash and table tennis, most balls are hit below shoulder level.

## 5.5 Superior labrum anterior posterior (SLAP) lesions
The 'dead arm' syndrome has been defined as any pathologic condition in which the player is unable to serve the ball with pre-injury velocity and control because of a combination of pain and subjective unease in the shoulder (Burkhart et al., 2003). Tennis players, in particular, are susceptible to this problem, due to overuse of the shoulder in hitting the ball, particularly when serving and hitting overheads. In squash, badminton and table tennis, the ball can be brought into play without bringing the arm in an overhead position.

Until recently, micro-instability was considered the universal cause of the disabled shoulder in overhead athletes, but this view has been challenged (Burkhart et al., 2003). It has been hypothesised that SLAP lesions are the most common pathologic entities associated with this problem.

After the wind up of the serve, the arm accelerates in a fraction of a second. Speeds of more than 1500 deg.s$^{-1}$ have been measured during the acceleration phase, with high forces at the end of the cocking and the deceleration phase (Kibler et al., 1995). The rotator cuff muscles and biceps support and guide this motion, but failure of the muscle tendon unit may eventually occur from fatigue, repetitive activity and/or acute injury. Failure will prevent the humeral head from being centred during elevation, thus stressing the associated tendons, labrum, and biceps. The humeral head will migrate superiorly, which will lead to increased cuff compression ('impingement'). This impingement will be aggravated when there is postero-inferior capsular contracture, resulting in loss of internal rotation. The upper and posterior parts of the rotator cuff run the highest risk of failure, because they are stressed the most by the high forces of the follow-through. Important preventative measures include strengthening of the scapular stabilisers (upper and lower trapezius, serratus) and posterior rotator cuff muscles (infraspinatus, teres minor), and stretching of the posterior inferior capsule.

## 5.6 Vascular injuries
Although musculo-skeletal injuries are most common and best known, upper extremity symptoms are seldom caused by vascular injury. Digital ischaemia may result from occlusion of the distal ulnar artery at the level of the hamate bone. This is known as hypothenar-hammer syndrome (Noel and Hayoz, 2000). Endothelial injury due to repeated microtrauma of the hand is responsible for the activation of blood coagulation and arterial thrombosis. The usual manifestations are pain in the hypothenar eminence, with cold intolerance and Raynaud's phenomenon. A cushioned grip tape can increase racket damping by up to 100%, reduce the grip reaction force by 20%, and may help prevent this affliction (Wilson and Davies, 1995). Mechanical compression of the subclavian or axillary arteries and veins may occur during the wind up phase of the serve, when the arm is in hyperabduction and external rotation (thoracic outlet). The compression may be accentuated by

hypertrophy of the muscles, subluxation of the shoulder and bone anomalies such as cervical ribs. This may lead to yenous thrombosis and/or and spasm and aneurysm of the arteries. The player should be referred to a vascular surgeon.

### 5.7 Tennis elbow

Tennis elbow is characterised by pain, tenderness, and degeneration of the tendon attachment of the extensor muscles (most commonly the m. extensor carpi radialis brevis) at the lateral side of the elbow. There is pain and/or weakness when hitting the backhand, and in daily life with lifting, gripping, and twisting motions of the wrist. This affliction occurs frequently in tennis due to the repetitive wrist movements when hitting the backhand, resulting in stress and strain of the muscles and tendons that attach the forearm muscles to the elbow. Blackwell and Cole (1994) showed that expert tennis players have their wrist extended an average 23 degrees just prior to ball impact and that they extend their wrist further at impact when hitting a one-handed backhand. In contrast, novice players strike the ball with their wrist in 13 degrees of flexion, moving the wrist into further flexion on impact. In a computer simulation model, Riek et al. (1999) demonstrated that these wrist joint angles in novice players indicate conditions that promote wrist extensor injury. In the novice group, the stretch due to ball impact lengthened a muscle that was already beyond the plateau of its length-tension relationship, with an increased risk of muscle damage. In the advanced group, however, the muscle length was below the optimal length, and therefore any sudden stretch would push the muscle to a more advantageous position on its length-tension relationship. In order to prevent tennis elbow, therefore, it is important to keep the wrist firm and straight at ball impact and to strengthen the forearm muscles. Also, the shoulder muscles should be strengthened, so they help propel the arm and racquet, decreasing the load on the elbow and wrist. In squash, badminton, and table tennis, the forces on the wrist are much lower, because of the lower weight of racket and ball, so excessive wrist movements are less likely to lead to injury.

### 5.8 Stress fractures

Stress fractures may occur as a result of repeated loading over a long period of time, when the resorption of bone exceeds that of repair. Stress fractures of the lower extremities are well known in sports that involve running and jumping, but stress fractures of the upper extremities are less common and more typical of throwing sports. They are caused by the repeated impact loading of the arm during the ball strike. There is stress distribution in the bone during continued activity with diminishing muscle dampening secondary to fatigue. Torsional stress and shearing forces have been cited as important factors with stress fractures of the humerus and ulna (Fragnière et al., 2001). The repetitive impact force of the racket against the hand may give rise to stress factors for the hook of the hamate, carpals, and metacarpals (Guha et al., 2002). Other risk factors include a previous stress fracture, nutritional deficiencies and disorders, especially when there are menstrual irregularities, and bone abnormalities (osteoporosis). Treatment is generally conservative (rest, training and equipment modification and correction of dietary and/or hormonal deficiencies).

### 5.9 Back injuries

The trunk is placed under high stress during racket sports, because they involve a great deal of flexion, extension, and rotatory movements. The general feeling is that racket sports increase the risk of back injuries. However, this has not been confirmed by epidemiological studies.

MacFarlane and Shanks (1998) investigated the prevalence of back injuries in competitive squash players in New Zealand. The observation that 51.9% of the competitive players reported suffering some form of back injury (56.5% of males and 46.4% of females) is similar to the prevalence of back injury in New Zealand, where 55% (57% of males and 54% of females) reported the occurrence of back pain at some time in their lives. The frequency was seen to increase with playing ability and frequency of play, but not with playing duration. It thus appears that squash players may not suffer a greater frequency of back injury compared to the general population.

The same results are found in tennis. Although intense tennis practice is generally held to be a risk factor for low back pain, Saraux et al. (1999) did not find evidence for a higher risk of low back pain with or without sciatica in tennis players compared to age and gender-matched controls.

However, these data should be interpreted with caution, because intense practice at a young age with a lot of rotation and hyperextension does seem to be associated with an increased risk of spondylolysis and spondylolisthesis. The strength of the growth plate against anterior shearing forces depends on skeletal maturity (Kajiura et al., 2001). Furthermore, at higher loads or larger extended postures, muscles play a more crucial role in stabilizing the spine. When muscles become fatigued, higher loads have to be absorbed by the discs and ligaments. An emphasis on exercises to improve core stability for the prevention of injuries in junior and elite athletes is therefore still warranted.


## 6 Conclusion

Average rally duration and the length of the rest periods varies considerably between the four sports, resulting in the highest effective playing time, heart rate, and lactate levels in squash, and the lowest in table tennis. Injury risk is also highest in squash and lowest in table tennis. Tennis and badminton are in between, both with respect to intensity of play and injury risk.

All four sports involve many lateral movements, jumps and lunges, resulting in a predominance of injuries to the lower extremities. The most common injuries are the ankle sprain (especially badminton), tennis leg (tennis), knee problems (squash), and Achilles tendon injuries (badminton). Most upper extremity injuries are encountered in tennis players, mainly because of the repetitive overhead motion during serving (rotator cuff injury) and high loads on the elbow during the one-handed backhand stroke (tennis elbow). The risk of a lower back injury, although generally thought to be higher, does not in fact seem to be increased among racket players.


## 7 References

Baron, R., Petschnig, R., Bachl, N., Raberger, G., Smekal, G., and Kastner, P. (1992). Catecholamine excretion and heart rate as factors of psychophysical stress in table tennis. **International Journal of Sports Medicine,** 13, 501-505.

Blackwell, J.R. and Cole, K.J. (1994). Wrist kinematics differ in expert and novice tennis players performing the backhand stroke: implications for tennis elbow. **Journal of Biomechanics,** 27, 509-516.

Burkhart, S.S., Morgan, C.D., and Kibler, W.B. (2003). The disabled throwing shoulder: spectrum of pathology. Part 1: Pathoanatomy and biomechanics. Arthroscopy: **The Journal of Arthroscopy and Related Surgery**, 19, 404-420.

Chard, M.D. and Lachmann, S.M. (1987). Racquet sports-patterns of injury presenting to a sports injury clinic. **British Journal of Sports Medicine**, 21, 150-153.

Christmass, M.A., Richmond, S.E., Cable, N.T., Arthur, P.G., and Hartmann, P.E. (1998). Exercise intensity and metabolic response in singles tennis. **Journal of Sport Sciences**, 16, 739-747.

Dufek, P., Ostendorf, U., and Thormählen, F. (1999). Streßfraktur der Ulna beim Tischtennisspieler. **Sportverletzungen und Sportschaden**, 13, 62-64.

Fahlström, M., Lorentzon, R., and Alfredson, H. (2002). Painful conditions in the Achilles tendon region in elite badminton players. **American Journal of Sports Medicine**, 30, 51-54.

Fahlström, M, Björnstig, U., and Lorentzon, R. (1998a). Acute Achilles tendon rupture in badminton players. **American Journal of Sports Medicine**, 26, 467-470.

Fahlström, M., Björnstig, U., and Lorentzon, R. (1998b). Acute badminton injuries. **Scandinavian Journal of Medicine and Science in Sports**, 8, 145-148.

Ferrauti, A., Bergeron, M.F., Pluim, B.M, and Weber, K. (2001). Physiological responses in tennis and running with similar oxygen uptake. **European Journal of Applied Physiology**, 85, 27-33.

Fragnière, B., Landry, M., and Siegrist, O. (2001). Stress fracture of the ulna in a professional tennis player using a double-handed backhand stroke. **Knee Surgery Sports Traumatology Arthroscopy**, 9, 239-241.

Guha, A.R. and Marynissen, H. (2002). Stress fracture of the hook of the hamate. **British Journal of Sports Medicine**, 36, 224-225.

Handoll, H.H., Rowe, B.H., Quinn, K.M. and de Bie., R. (2001). Interventions for preventing ankle ligament injuries. **Cochrane Database Systematic Review**, 3, CD000018.

Hutchinson, M.R., Laprade, R.F., Burnett, Q.M., Moss, R., and Terpstra, J. (1995). Injury surveillance at the USTA Boys'Tennis Championships: a 6-yr study. **Medicine and Science in Sports and Exercise**, 27, 826-830.

Jörgensen, U. and Winge, S. (1987). Epidemiology of badminton injuries. **International Journal of Sports Medicine**, 8, 379-382.

Kajiura, K., Katoh, S., Sairyo, K., Ikata, T., Goel, V.K., and Murakamı, R.I. (2001). Slippage mechanism of pediatric spondylolysis: biomechanical study using immature calf spines. **Spine**, 26, 2208-2212.

Kibler,W.B., Livingston, B., and Bruce, R. (1995). **Advances in Operative Orthopaedics**, 3, 249-300.

Letsel Informatie Systeem 1998-2001 (2003). **Ongevallen tijdens racketsporten.** Amsterdam: Consument en Veiligheid.

Locke, S., Colquhoun, D., Briner, M., Ellis, L., O'Brien, M., Wolstein, J., and Allen, G. (1997). Squash racquets: a review of physiology and medicine. **Sports Medicine**, 23, 130-138.

MacFarlane, D.J. and Shanks, A. (1998). Back injuries in competitive squash players. **Journal of Sports Medicine and Physical Fitness**, 38, 337-343.

Majumdar, P., Khanna, G.L., Malik, V., Sachdeva, S., Arif, M., and Mandal, M. (1997). Physiological analysis to quantify training load in badminton. **British Journal of Sports Medicine**, 31, 342-435.

Noel, B. and Hayoz, D. (2000). A tennis player with hand claudication. **Vasa**, 29, 151-153.

O'Donoghue, P. and Ingram, B. (2001). A no ational analysis of elite tennis strategy. **Journal of Sport Sciences**, 19, 107-115.

Riek, S., Chapman, A.E. and Milner, T. (1999). A simulation of muscle force and internal kinematics of extensor carpi radialis brevis during backhand tennis stroke: implications for injury. **Clinical Biomechanics**, 14, 477-483.

Saraux, A., Guillodo, Y., Davauchelle, V., Allain, J., Guedes, C., and Le Goff, P. (1999). Are tennis players at increased risk for low back pain and sciatica? **Reviews of Rhumatism**, 66, 143-145.

Schmikli, S.L., De Wit, M.J.P., and Backx, F.J.G. (2001). **Sportblessures drie maal geteld** (Sports Injuries Counted Three Times). Arnhem: NOC*NSF,.

Schmikli, S.L., Backx, F.J.G., and Bol, E. (1995). **Sportblessures nader uitgediept**. (Sport Injuries Further analysed) Houten/Diegem: Bohn Stafleu Van Loghum.

Sharp, N.C.C. (1998). Physiological demands and fitness for squash. In **Science and Racket Sports II** (edited by A. Lees, I. Maynard, M. Hughes and T. Reilly), London: E & FN Spon, pp. 3-13.

Smekal, G., Pokan, R., Duvillard, van S.P., Baron, R., Tschan, H., and Bachl, N. (2000). Comparison of laboratory and on-court endurance testing in tennis. **International Journal of Sports Medicine**, 21, 242-249.

Steinbrück, K. (1999). Epidemiologie von Sportverletzungen-25-Jahres-Analyse einer sportorthopädisch-traumatologisches Ambulanz. (Epidemiology of sports injuries - A 25 year analysis of a sports outpatient clinic) **Sportverletzungen und Sportschaden**, 13, 38-51.

Weber, K. (1987). **Der Tennissport aus internistisch-medizinischen Sicht**. (Tennnis from an internal medicine point of view) Sankt Augustin: Verlag Hans Richartz.

Wilson, J.F. and Davis, J.S. (1995). Tennis racket shock mitigation experiments. **Journal of Biomechanical Engineering**, 117, 479-484.

Winge, S., Jorgensen, U., and Lassen Nielsen, A. (1989). Epidemiology of injuries in Danish championship tennis. **International Journal of Sports Medicine**, 10, 368-371.

# 12 Glenohumeral arthrokinematics of two test-cases with internal impingement at the end of late cocking

J.-P. Baeyens, P. Van Roy, G. Declercq and J.-P. Clarys
*Dep. Experimental Anatomy, Vrije Universiteit Brussel,*
*Laarbeeklaan 109, 1030 Brussels, Belgium.*

## 1 Introduction

Warren (1983) and Garth et al. (1987) described throwers with symptoms of posterior shoulder pain by means of application of an external rotation force at 90° of abduction, but found no signs of instability. Walch et al. (1994) reported on arthroscopic cases with impaction of the deep surface of the supraspinatus tendon on the posterior-superior glenoid rim. Cadaveric research performed by Jobe and Sidles (1994) has shown that the rotator cuff pinched against the posterior-superior glenoid rim when the shoulder is positioned in maximum external rotation and abduction. Transection of specimens fixed in this position demonstrated the greater tuberosity forcing the rotator cuff and labrum against the glenoid rim. Davidson et al. (1995) termed this finding "internal impingement" relating it to a rotator cuff impingement mechanism. Jobe (1996) demonstrated that besides rotator cuff tendon, posterior glenoid impingement also may injure the superior labrum and/or the greater tuberosity.

This paper compares the arthrokinematic results obtained from two test-cases suffering from posterior shoulder pain at the end of late cocking with non-symptomatic throwers. Initially, these two throwers presented neither instability nor subacromial impingement signs. Within two years, these two symptomatic shouders had evolved into an articular side rotator cuff lesion (as confirmed by MRI) without instability signs. The experiment comprised an early stage measurement of the relationships of the glenohumeral joint in two poses. Related to the anatomical planes, the shoulder was first set in 90° abduction and 90° external rotation (pose 1). Subsequently, the late cocking position with the arm maximally externally rotated was assessed (pose 2). Helical CT-data of these discrete shoulder positions were three dimensionally reconstructed. Based on humeral and scapular sets of skeletal landmarks, rotation matrices and translation vectors were estimated and processed in a glenohumeral Euler convention and finite helical axes.

## 2 Methods

Methodologically, to fully assess glenohumeral joint kinematics, the following points of view are of interest:
i) The variability in glenoid tilt and glenoid version (Matsen et al., 1998) necessitates the use of a co-ordinate system embedded on the articular surface of the glenoid to

which the kinematics of the humerus and the scapula can be referred. To quantify *in vivo* the 3D translation of the humeral head on the glenoid, 3D reconstructions based on magnetic resonance imaging have been used in asymptomatic volunteers during active internal and external rotation of the 0° abducted arm (Rhoad et al. 1998)) and during passive and active abduction (Graichen et al., 2000). No in vivo studies were found in which quantitative assessment of the 3D rotations of the humeral head was performed relative to the glenoid.

ii) Also of interest are the displacements between the articular surfaces at the contact area.

In this study, these two points of view are assessed by processing helical CT data of discrete joint poses into finite helical axes.

The experiment comprised the measurement of the relationships of the glenohumeral joint in two poses. Related to the anatomical planes, the shoulder was first set in 90° abduction and 90° external rotation (pose 1). Subsequently, from a clinical point of view, the late cocking position with the arm maximally externally rotated was assessed on an individual basis (pose 2). It has been suggested that these positions cannot be investigated in the narrow CT gantry (Graichen et al., 2000). This problem was solved by positioning the subjects in the gantry in an oblique angle and with a body roll in the opposite direction of the examined shoulder.

## 2.1 Medical imaging data and 3D skeletal reconstruction
Fast helical CT-scanning (HiSpeed CT/I, General Electric) enabled the subjects to maintain the uncomfortable late cocking position throughout the entire scanning procedure. Using Advantage Windows, these helical CT data were 3D reconstructed into skeletal configurations of the shoulder joint.

## 2.2 Osteokinematics analysis
At least four humeral and four scapular landmarks were measured on the 3D skeletal reconstructions, three times each. Their co-ordinates were used in the algorithms of Veldpaus et al. (1988) to estimate the rotation matrix R and the translation vector of the humeral set of landmarks related to the scapular set. Veldpaus et al.'s approach involved the estimation of a matrix of the form d.R with a scalar d (>0), which emphasized that R is a rotation matrix. These estimates were then processed into finite helical axis parameters (shift **t**, rotation θ, direction vector **n** and position vector **s**).

## 2.3 Arthrokinematics analysis
(i) After virtual disarticulation of the glenohumeral joint, a co-ordinate system was embedded on the glenoid cavity (Figure 1). This co-ordinate system was built on three landmarks on the glenoid rim: $P_i$ (superior) with position vector **i**, $P_j$ (inferior) with position vector **j** and $P_k$ (anterior) with position vector **k**. The position vector **m** was the intersection $P_m$ of the trace connecting $P_i$ and $P_j$ with its perpendicular through $P_k$. The deduced right-handed co-ordinate system consisted of a superiorly directed vector $I_G$ ($I_G=(m-j)/|m-j|$), an anteriorly directed unity vector $J_G$ ($J_G=(m-k)/|m-k|$) and a laterally directed unity vector $K_G$ ($K_G=J_G \times I_G$) (Figure 1). Due to the variability in shape of the glenoid cavity, we did not use the centre of mass as centre for the co-ordinate system (Rhoad et al., 1998; Graichen et al., 2000), but $P_0$ with position vector $(i+j)/2$.

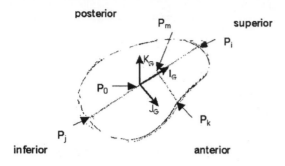

Figure 1.   Co-ordinate system embedded on the glenoid cavity.

Legend        $P_i$, $P_j$, $P_k$ : bony landmarks at the glenoid margin.
              $I_G$, $J_G$, $K_G$ : unit vectors of the co-ordinate system embedded on the
              glenoid , with $I_G=(m-j)/|m-j|$ , $J_G=(k-m)/|k-m|$ and $K_G=J_G \times I_G$
              in which **m** is the position vector is the intersection $P_m$ of
              **i-j** with its perpendicular through Pk.

Subsequently, the glenohumeral finite helical axis vectors **n**, $\theta(=\theta.n)$ and $t(=t.n)$ were
decomposed on this co-ordinate system, with:
$n = n_{IG}I_G + n_{JG}J_G+ n_{KG}K_G$  ;  $\theta =\theta_{IG}I_G + \theta_{JG}J_G+ \theta_{KG}K_G$  ; $t = t_{IG}I_G + t_{JG}J_G+ t_{KG}K_G$
The rotation angle components were termed as follows: $\theta_I$ as glenohumeral intra-
articular horizontal abduction (-)/ adduction (+), $\theta_J$ as glenohumeral intra-articular
abduction (-)/adduction (+), and $\theta_K$ as intra-articular glenohumeral external (+)/
internal (-) rotation. The shift components were termed as follows: $t_I$ as glenohumeral
intra-articular superor (+)/inferior (-) translation, $t_J$ as glenohumeral intra-articular
anterior (+)/posterior (-) translation, and $t_K$ as glenohumeral intra-articular lateral
(+)/medial (-) translation. Although the use of the term 'intra-articular' can be
theoretically questioned, specifically in this context it points out that these glenoid
referenced motions are not the same as motions that are referred to the traditional
anatomical planes of the body.
(ii) In addition, the translation of the centre point of the humeral head on the glenoid
was measured (cf. Euler/Cardan approach). In the axial and sagittal planes, the centre
point of the humeral head was estimated by circles that were fitted to the central part
of the articular surface of the humeral head. This relates to Graichen et al.'s (2000)
approach that computationally matched a sphere to the central part of the articular
surface of the humeral head.

**2.4 Error sensitivity analysis**

**2.4.1 Intra-positional detection accuracy**
For each of the bones, no significant differences between the measurement errors for
the x, y and z coordinates ($\sigma_x$, $\sigma_y$, and $\sigma_z$ respectively) of the humeral and scapular

landmarks were found using paired t-test. Consequently, the measurement error distribution may be considered isotropic. Using a t-test, no significant differences in measurement accuracy between the landmarks on the different bones were found. Altogether, the intrapositional detection errors had an average of $0.37(s = 0.02)$ mm per co-ordinate.

### 2.4.2 Inter-positional deformation sensitivity

The difference from 1 of the positive scalar d (in the estimated matrix) d.R gives information about the quality of the inter-positional stability of the measurement. The averaged $|1- d|$ value of $6.90 \pm 1.53$ pro mille demonstrates neglibible expansion/implosion of the (rigid) bones between the different poses. A better indicator for the inter-positional measurement error is the variation of the distance between two bony landmarks on the same bone. The distance $d_{12}$ between two landmarks $P_1(x_1, y_1, z_1)$ and $P_2(x_2, y_2, z_2)$ is a non-linear function of the co-ordinates of each landmark: $d_{12}=\sqrt{(x_2-x_1)^2+(y_2-y_1)^2+(z_2-z_1)^2}$. The standard deviation of $d_{12}$ ($\sigma_{d12}$) is a function of the standard errors of the co-ordinates of each landmark. With isotropic distribution of the variance of the co-ordinates, approximation in a first-order Taylor expansion gives: $\sigma_{d12} = \sqrt{\sigma_{x1}^2 + \sigma_{y1}^2 + \sigma_{z1}^2 + \sigma_{x2}^2 + \sigma_{y2}^2 + \sigma_{z2}^2}$ (Woltring et al., 1985) With $\sigma_x = \sigma_y = \sigma_z = 0.37$ (S = 0.02 mm), the estimated $\sigma_{d12}$ is 0.91 (S = 0.05 mm). The absolute values of the interpositional differences of the distances between the landmarks were 0.91 (SD = 0.67 mm).

### 2.4.3 Errors in the estimation of the finite helical axis parameters

The errors on the parameters of the glenohumeral finite helical axis were estimated by the sum of the absolute errors on the parameters of the humeral and scapular finite helical axes as estimated by Woltring et al.'s (1985) error propagation model. Comparing their experimental data with error predictions based on Woltring's model, de Lange et al. (1990) concluded that even for anisotropic landmark distributions, Woltring's model maintains its approximate predictive value. The averages for the errors ($\underline{\sigma}$) of the glenohumeral finite helical axis parameters were: $\underline{\sigma}_\theta$ 0.425° (S = 0.07°), $\underline{\sigma}_n$ 2.79° (S = 1.71°), $\underline{\sigma}_s$ 0.94mm (S = 0.61mm), $\underline{\sigma}_t$ 0.43 mm (S = 0.19 mm).

## 3 Results

The arthrokinematic data between pose 1 and pose 2 (see Table 1) demonstrated the following differences:

- For the normal shoulders, the relative and absolute contribution of intra-articular external/internal rotation ($n_{KG}$ (+/-): external/internal rotation component of the direction vector; $\theta_{KG}$ (+/-): external/internal rotation magnitude) was minimal ($n_{KG}$ 0.05, -0.01 and –0.21 with $\theta_{KG}$ 0.27°, -0.18° and –1.67°). In contrast, a large external rotation component ($n_{KG}$ 0.83 and 0.85) together with a significantly different large external rotation magnitude ($\theta_{KG}$ 28.43° and 27.22°) were found in the symptomatic shoulders with internal impingement.
- In the late cocking pose, the centre point of the humeral head of both the internal impingers and the normal shoulders translated into a posteriorly localized position on the glenoid cavity (related to the centre of the glenoid -7.54 and –7.73mm for the internal impingers; respectively -7.63, -8.51 and –6.42mm for the normal shoulders).

Table 1.  Decomposed values of the rotation angle (θ), the direction vector (n), and the shift (t) of the humeral motion on the glenoid from pose 1 to pose 2

|  | $\theta_{IG}$ (°) | $\theta_{JG}$ (°) | $\theta_{KG}$ (°) | $n_{IG}$ | $n_{JG}$ | $n_{KG}$ | $t_{IG}$ (mm) | $t_{JG}$ (mm) | $t_{KG}$ (mm) |
|---|---|---|---|---|---|---|---|---|---|
| asymtomatic shoulders | | | | | | | | | |
| DB | -2.51 | -5.2 | 0.27 | -0.43 | -0.90 | 0.05 | -3.14 | -6.50 | 0.34 |
| DH | -4.67 | 19.20 | -0.18 | -0.23 | 0.97 | -0.01 | 3.00 | -12.51 | 0.11 |
| JS | -1.02 | -7.82 | -1.67 | -0.13 | -0.97 | -0.21 | -0.68 | -5.22 | -1.12 |
| internal impingers | | | | | | | | | |
| FT | -16.44 | -9.24 | 28.43 | -0.48 | -0.27 | 0.83 | -1.45 | -1.87 | 2.98 |
| MG | 8.00 | -14.73 | 27.22 | 0.25 | -0.46 | 0.85 | 3.01 | -2.98 | 5.11 |

## 4 Discussion and conclusion

Internal impingement has been hypothetically related in the literature to excessive external rotation with or without anterior-inferior glenohumeral instability (Davidson et al., 1995). The arthrokinematic data in this study support the influence of excessive intra articular external rotation without anterior instability in the development of an internal impingement syndrome. Fleisig et al. (1995) pointed out a critical moment of shoulder kinetics shortly before the arm reached maximum external rotation during the late preparatory phase. Large loads were produced at the shoulder including 67 ±11Nm of internal rotation torque. Theoretically, control of the excessive intra articular external rotation in internal impingement at the end of the late preparatory phase could be obtained by increasing the internal rotation torque with the internal rotators in combination with good stabilization of the scapula as fulcrum, or by an earlier beginning of the acceleration phase. Experimental work on these possibilities still has to be done.

## 5 References

Davidson P.A., El Attrache N.S., Jobe C.M. and Jobe F.W. (1995). Rotator cuff and posterior-superior glenoid labrum injury associated with increased glenohumeral motion: A new site of impingement. **Journal of Shoulder and Elbow Surgery**, 4, 384-390.

de Lange A., Huiskes R. and Kauer J.M.G. (1990). Measurement errors in roentgen-stereophotogrammetric joint-motion analysis. **Journal of Biomechanics**, 23, 259-269.

Fleisig G.S., Andrews J.R., Dillman C.J. and Escamilla R.F. (1995). Kinetics of baseball pitching with implications about injury mechanisms. **American Journal of Sports Medicine**, 23, 233-239.

Garth W.P. jr., Allman F.L. and Armstrong W.S. (1987). Occult anterior subluxations of the shoulder in noncontact sports. **American Journal of Sports Medicine**, 15, 579-585.

Graichen H., Stammberger T., Bonel H., Englmeier K.-H., Reiser M. and Eckstein F. (2000). Glenohumeral translation during active and passive elevation of the shoulder – a 3D open-MRI study. **Journal of Biomechanics,** 33, 605-613.

Jobe C.M. and Sidles J. (1994). Evidence for a superior glenoid impingement upon the rotator cuff. **Journal of Shoulder and Elbow Surgery,** 2(1), Part 2, S19 (abstract).

Jobe C.M. (1996) Posterior superior glenoid impingement: Expended spectrum. **Journal of Shoulder and Elbow Surgery,** 5(2), Part 2, S45/120 (abstract).

Matsen F.A., Thomas S.C., Rockwood C.A. and Wirth M.A. (1998). Glenohumeral instability. In **The Shoulder** (edited by C.A. Rockwood and F.A. Matsen) Philadelphia: W.B. Saunders Company: pp. 611-754.

Rhoad R.C., Klimkiewicz J.J., Williams G.R., Kesmodel S.B., Udupa J.K., Kneeland J.B. and Iannotti J.P. (1998). A new in vivo technique for three-dimensional shoulder kinematics analysis. **Skeletal Radiology,** 27, 92-97.

Veldpaus F.E., Woltring H.J. and Dortmans L.M. (1988). A least squares algorithm for equiform transformation from spatial marker coordinates. **Journal of Biomechanics,** 21, 45-54.

Walch G., Nove-Nosserand L. and Levigne C. (1994). Tears of the supraspinatus tendon associated with 'hidden' lesions of the rotator interval. **Journal of Shoulder and Elbow Surgery** 3, 353-360.

Warren R.F.(1983) Subluxation of the shoulder in athletes. **Clinics Sports Medicine,** 2, 339-354.

Woltring H.J., Huiskes R. and De Lange A. (1985). Finite centroid and helical axis estimation from noisy landmark measurements in the study of human joint kinematics. **Journal of Biomechanics,** 18, 379-389.

# 13 The effect of tennis participation on bone mass is better retained in male than female master tennis players

J. Sanchis Moysi, G. Vicente-Rodríguez, J.A. Serrano,
J.A.L. Calbet and C. Dorado
*Departamento de Educación Física, Universidad de Las Palmas de Gran Canaria, Campus Universitario de Tafira, 35017, Las Palmas de Gran Canaria, Spain.*

## 1 Introduction

Osteoporosis is a skeletal disease defined by low bone mass, reduced bone mineral density, and altered bone geometry, whose prevalence is attaining epidemic dimensions in developed countries. Between the age of 20 and 30 years, a peak in bone mass and density is attained, after both mass and density decline with age. This process is accelerated after the menopause, leading in many cases to osteoporosis. The rate and magnitude of bone loss may differ markedly from one skeletal site to another, depending, among other factors, on local mechanical stress. Several investigations have shown that sports eliciting high impact forces, at elevated strain rates, in varied directions, are the most osteogenic (Burr et al., 2002). However, the benefit from a mechanically appropriate sport, depends also on the duration of sport participation, as we have recently observed (Dorado et al., 2003). Adherence to physical activity in aged people declines when the exercise requires the development of high strength levels which have proved to be the most effective in increasing bone mineral density, (Suominen, 1993; Humphries et al., 2000). Moderate or low intensity activities have positive effects in muscular strength, but variable effect in bone (Kerr et al., 1996); and unfortunately, daily activities such as walking, are the less effective (Suominen, 1993; Humphries et al., 2000).

Tennis imposes a high mechanical loads thereby promoting a marked increase of muscle and bone mass in men (Calbet et al., 1998; Sanchis Moysi et al., 1998) and young women (Kontulainen et al., 2002). In this regard, tennis may be proposed an osteogenic sport to prevent or attenuate osteoporosis later in life. The extent to which master tennis players have greater bone mineral content (BMC) and density (BMD) in clinically relevant areas than their sedentary counterparts remains unknown. It has been reported that tennis players who started their career after the menarche do not benefit as much as those who begun at a prepubertal age (Kannus et al., 1995). Whether participation in tennis starting before the menopause could attenuate bone loss in the following years is not known.

The aim of this study was, therefore, to examine the effect of tennis participation on bone mass and density in postmenopausal women, as well as in men of similar age. Special attention was given to describing the longitudinal effects of tennis participation on lumbar spine and femoral neck bone mass and density in post-menopauseal tennis players.

## 2 Methods

### 2.1 Participants

This study was carried out according to the Declaration of Helsinski and all participants provided a written informed consent. Seventeen male tennis players (55±2 years, 79±2 kg body mass, 1.73±0.02 m height, and 26±2% body fat) and 9 female tennis players (61±1.3 years, 60±2 kg body mass, 1.61±0.02 m height, and 39±2% body fat) volunteered as experimental participants. The mean participation in tennis was 26.8±6.8 years, while the actual time devoted to tennis training and competition was 3 hours per week in both groups. As a control group, 15 men (56±3 years, 78±3 kg body mass, 1.68±0.02 m height, and 29±2% body fat) and 20 women (62±2 years, 69±2 kg body mass, 1.60±0.01 m height, and 43±2% body fat) non-exercisers from the same population were included in the study. The non-active participants had a sedentary life style over their life. Additionally, 7 postmenopausal tennis players and 10 female controls from the same population were examined two years later in order to obtain longitudinal data.

### 2.2 Materials

Total and regional composition was measured by dual-energy X-ray absorptiometry (DXA) (QDR-1500, Hologic Corp., Waltham, MA). From the whole body scans, the lean body mass (g), body fat (g), total bone area (cm$^2$) and BMC (g) was determined (Sanchis Moysi et al. 1998). Bone mineral density (g.cm$^{-2}$) was calculated from these measures using the formula BMD = BMC · total bone area$^{-1}$. The following sub-regions were also obtained from the analysis of the whole body scans: left and right legs and arms, and trunk (pelvis, neck, thoracic and abdominal regions). Fat-free lean mass was assumed to be equivalent to limb muscle mass. A further examination was conducted to determine bone mass in the lumbar spine and the proximal region of the femur. To save time and reduced X-ray exposure only the left femur, which was the non-dominant femur for most of the participants, was scanned. The femoral neck, inter-trochanteric and greater trochanter sub-regions were analysed. These sub-regions were determined automatically by the software program of the DXA scanner. Values reported for the lumbar vertebrae L2-L4 were obtained from an anteroposterior lumbar scan and expressed as the mean BMC and BMD of the three vertebrae.

### 2.3 Statistical analysis

Data were analysed using the SPSS mainframe statistical program and statistical significance was set at $P<0.05$ level. Results are presented as means ± standard error of the mean. The influence of gender and tennis participation on BMC and BMD, was determined using ANCOVA analysis with the age, height and body mass as covariates. In the female group an additional analysis was performed using the time elapsed from the menopause as covariate. The effect of tennis participation on the increment/decrement of BMC and BMD after two years follow up, was assessed by comparing the changes observed using Student's unpaired t-test.

## 3  Results

Male tennis players showed 16 % and 10% greater BMC and BMD in the legs than the control participants (P<0.01). In addition, 10-30% greater BMC and BMD were also observed at the hip regions (femoral neck, greater trochanter and inter-trochanteric area) and lumbar spine (L2-L4) in tennis players compared with the controls (Figure 1).

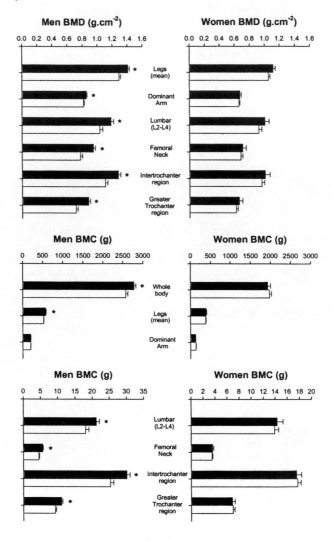

Figure 1. Bone mineral content (BMC) and bone mineral density (BMD) in male and female tennis players (black bars) and non-active control participants (white bars). Male values adjusted for age, height and body mass. Female values adjusted for time elapsed from menopause, height and body mass (*P<0.05 tennis players compared with control participants).

Female tennis players showed, in general, similar BMC and BMD values to their sedentary counterparts in all these regions, except a trend to a greater leg BMC in the tennis players (P=0.06) (Figure 1). This apparently lower osteogenic value of long-term tennis participation in women was confirmed in the two years follow up study. The follow up data, corroborated this picture, i.e. post-menopauseal tennis players did not benefit, in terms of BMC and BMD gain (or attenuation of losses) in all regions studied. An exception was the inter-trochanteric femoral BMD which increased by $3.7 \pm 1.4\%$ in the tennis players while it decreased by $1.7 \pm 1.1\%$ in the controls region (P<0.05).

Leg muscle mass was 11% greater in the male tennis players that in their sedentary counterparts (P<0.05). In contrast, female tennis players had a similar leg muscle mass to the sedentary women. After accounting for differences in age and body size, the male tennis players showed 24% more muscle mass in the legs than the female players (P<0.05). In contrast, the age and body size-adjusted gender difference in leg muscle mass was only 13% in the control group (P<0.05), being also greater in the males than in the females (P< 0.05).

## 4 Discussion

The most important finding of this study was that middle-aged male tennis players showed markedly higher BMC and BMD at the lumbar spine, femoral neck, legs, and dominant-arm than the control participants. The magnitude of bone adaptation observed in these middle-age tennis players is similar to that previously observed in young tennis players from the same population, studied with the same equipment (Calbet et al., 1998). In contrast, women tennis players have similar lumbar spine BMC and BMD to their sedentary counterparts. Furthermore, the lack of relevant changes in neither BMC nor BMD after a two-year follow up confirmed these results in postmenopausal women who play tennis three times a week.

The present findings indicate that there is a sexual dimorphism in bone adaptability to mechanical loading which is accentuated in middle-aged men and women, such that mechanical stress appears to be less efficient in maintaining or increasing bone mass in postmenopausal women than in men of similar age. Before puberty there is no consistent gender-related difference in bone mass nor density (Bonjour et al., 1991; Gilsanz et al., 1991; Glastre et al., 1990). During puberty bone mineral mass accrual is accelerated such that, at the end of this period, bone mass and areal bone mineral density become higher in males than in females (Bonjour et al., 1991; Theintz et al., 1992). It has been suggested that this sexual dimorphism appears as a consequence of a longer period of bone mass gain in males than females (approximately two years more), resulting in a larger increase in bone size and cortical thickness in the males (Seeman, 1997). Despite these differences in BMC and areal BMD, volumetric bone density $(g.cm^{-3})$ is similar in both genders at the end of puberty (Gilsanz et al., 1998).

Several reasons could explain why tennis appears to be less osteogenic in older women than in men, but the most likely is that the quantity and/or magnitude of mechanical impacts elicited during tennis is lower in women than in men. Women have less strength than men due to lower muscle mass (Gallagher et al., 1997; Miller et al., 1993), inasmuch as muscle strength per cross-sectional area is almost similar in older men and women (Ford et al., 2000). Muscle mass declines with age, but men lose more muscle mass than women (Gallagher et al., 1997). The current investigation suggests that tennis participation may attenuate the loss of muscle mass in middle-aged men, but in women may be less efficient. However, neither age nor gender affects muscle volume response to whole-body strength training (Roth et al., 2002). A possible explanation for the lack of increase of leg muscle mass with tennis participation in our female players could be that women practice tennis in a more recreational, less competitive way than men, so they develop less muscle hypertrophy. Muscles are responsible for generating forces which acting on the bones provide the mechanical stimuli necessary to maintain or increase bone mass and density. Therefore, with a lower muscle mass, women will not be able to provide mechanical stimuli of sufficient magnitude as to elicit clinically relevant changes in bone mass, at least the kind of changes that can be detected with DEXA.

## 5  Conclusions

Tennis participation contributes to the preservation of muscle and bone mass in middle-aged male players, such that lumbar spine, femoral neck, legs and dominant arm bone mineral content and bone mineral density values are markedly enhanced, compared to a control group from the same population matched for age and body size. In contrast, women tennis players have similar muscle mass and bone mass than their sedentary counterparts. These results have been confirmed through a two-year long survey conducted with postmenopausal women who played tennis three times a week.

## 6  Acknowledgements

The authors wish to thanks José Navarro de Tuero for his technical assistance. This study has been granted by the University of Las Palmas de Gran Canaria and Gobierno de Canarias PI200/067.

## 7  References

Bonjour, J.P., Theintz, G., Buchs, B., Slosman, D. and Rizzoli, R. (1991). Critical years and stages of puberty for spinal and femoral bone mass accumulation during adolescence. **Journal of Clinical Endocrinology and Metabolism**, 73, 555-563.

Burr, D.B., Robling, A.G. and Turner, C.H. (2002). Effects of biomechanical stress on bones in animals. **Bone**, 30, 781-786.

Calbet, J.A., Moysi, J.S., Dorado, C. and Rodriguez, L.P. (1998). Bone mineral content and density in professional tennis players. **Calcified Tissue International**, 62, 491-496.

Dorado, C., Moysi, J., Vicente, G., Milutinovic, L., Garcés, G. and Calbet, J. (2003). Isokinetic strength and arm bone mass in postmenopausal tennis players. In **Tennis Science and Technology** (edited by S. Miller) International Tennis Federation, London, 237-242.

Ford, L.E., Detterline, A.J., Ho, K.K. and Cao, W. (2000). Gender- and height-related limits of muscle strength in world weightlifting champions. **Journal of Applied Physiology**, 89, 1061-1064.

Gallagher, D., Visser, M., De Meersman, R.E., Sepulveda, D., Baumgartner, R.N., Pierson, R.N., Harris, T. and Heymsfield, S.B. (1997). Appendicular skeletal muscle mass: effects of age, gender, and ethnicity. **Journal of Applied Physiology**, 83, 229-239.

Gilsanz, V., Roe, T.F., Mora, S., Costin, G. and Goodman, W.G. (1991). Changes in vertebral bone density in black girls and white girls during childhood and puberty. **New England Journal of Medicine**, 325, 1597-1600.

Gilsanz, V., Skaggs, D.L., Kovanlikaya, A., Sayre, J., Loro, M.L., Kaufman, F. and Korenman, S.G. (1998). Differential effect of race on the axial and appendicular skeletons of children. **Journal of Clinical Endocrinology and Metabolism**, 83, 1420-1427.

Glastre, C., Braillon, P., David, L., Cochat, P., Meunier, P.J. and Delmas, P.D. (1990). Measurement of bone mineral content of the lumbar spine by dual energy x-ray absorptiometry in normal children: correlations with growth parameters. **Journal of Clinical Endocrinology and Metabolism**, 70, 1330-1333.

Humphries, B., Newton, R.U., Bronks, R., Marshall, S., McBride, J., Triplett-McBride, T., Hakkinen, K., Kraemer, W.J. and Humphries, N. (2000). Effect of exercise intensity on bone density, strength, and calcium turnover in older women. **Medicine and Science in Sports and Exercise**, 32, 1043-1050.

Kannus, P., Haapasalo, H., Sankelo, M., Sievanen, H., Pasanen, M., Heinonen, A., Oja, P. and Vuori, I. (1995). Effect of starting age of physical activity on bone mass in the dominant arm of tennis and squash players. **Annals of Internal Medicine**, 123, 27-31.

Kerr, D., Morton, A., Dick, I. and Prince, R. (1996). Exercise effects on bone mass in postmenopausal women are site-specific and load-dependent. **Journal of Bone Mineral Research**, 11, 218-225.

Kontulainen, S., Sievanen, H., Kannus, P., Pasanen, M. and Vuori, I. (2002). Effect of long-term impact-loading on mass, size, and estimated strength of humerus and radius of female racquet-sports players: a peripheral quantitative computed tomography study between young and old starters and controls. **Journal of Bone Mineral Research**, 17, 2281-2289.

Miller, A.E., MacDougall, J.D., Tarnopolsky, M.A. and Sale, D.G. (1993). Gender differences in strength and muscle fiber characteristics. **European Journal of Applied Physiology and Occupational Physiology**, 66, 254-262.

Roth, S.M., Ferrell, R.E., Peters, D.G., Metter, E.J., Hurley, B.F. and Rogers, M.A. (2002). Influence of age, sex, and strength training on human muscle gene expression determined by microarray. **Physiological Genomics**, 10, 181-190.

Sanchis Moysi, J., Dorado Garcia, C. and Calbet, J.A.L. (1998). Regional body composition in professional tennis players. In **Science and Racket Sports II** (edited by A. Less, A. Maynard, M. Hughes and T. Reilly) London: E & FN Spon, pp. 34-39.

Seeman, E. (1997). From density to structure: growing up and growing old on the surfaces of bone. **Journal of Bone Mineral Research**, 12, 509-521.

Suominen, H. (1993). Bone mineral density and long term exercise. An overview of cross- sectional athlete studies. **Sports Medicine**, 16, 316-330.

Theintz, G., Buchs, B., Rizzoli, R., Slosman, D., Clavien, H., Sizonenko, P.C. and Bonjour, J.P. (1992). Longitudinal monitoring of bone mass accumulation in healthy adolescents: evidence for a marked reduction after 16 years of age at the levels of lumbar spine and femoral neck in female subjects. **Journal of Clinical Endocrinology and Metabolism**, 75, 1060-1065.

# 14 Strength training maintains muscle mass and improves maximal dynamic strength in two professional tennis players

J. Sanchis Moysi

*Departamento de Educación Física, Universidad de Las Palmas de Gran Canaria, Campus Universitario de Tafira, 35017 Las palmas de Gran Canaria Spain, and El Cortijo Club de Campo, Gran Canaria, Spain.*

## 1 Introduction

Given the speed of the games in tennis, the duration of the tournaments and the length of the matches, the outcome of competitions is increasingly determined by the degree of physical fitness, due to the similar abilities of most professional tennis players (Konig et al., 2001). It appears that explosive strength is becoming an important aspect in tennis performance (Roetert et al., 1996). During a tennis match, the players carry out high-speed movements executed within very short periods of time. The time available to execute each hit depends not only on the velocity of the ball, but also on the resistance or the load that the player has to overcome (the racket and the body weight), as well as on the distribution of the movement acceleration. These aspects determine the characteristics of force production in tennis: low resistance high-speed movements. Thus, tennis is an intermittent sport, in which there is a requirement to move quickly in varied directions, to stop and start with an explosive first step (Bergeron and Keul, 2002). It has been estimated that during a tennis match, 300-500 high-speed movements are performed (Deutsch et al., 1988). The mean displacement of a tennis player is 3 m per shot and 8-12 m per point in a mean time period of 3-8 s each rally (Ferrauti et al., 2001a). Modern tennis also demands high power generation in every tennis stroke. Moreover, in professional tennis players, a close correlation between the velocity of the ball and performance has been recently reported (Vergauwen et al., 1998).

Neuromuscular activation can be improved with explosive strength training programme (Häkkinen, 2002). The maximal dynamic strength (MDS) indicates the resistance that a subject has to overcome to displace a load one time (1 repetition maximum or 1 RM) and is expressed in Newtons (N). Further, the peak dynamic strength is the maximal voluntary strength applied to displace a certain load. When measuring the force developed during movements executed at maximal speed, but with lower loads than that corresponding to 1 RM, one value of peak force is obtained for every speed of movement. In such a way, each subject has just one value of MDS but as many values of relative MDS as loads have been used to measure it, as determined by the force-velocity relationship (Häkkinen, 2002). Thus, appropriate peaks of strength are required for each specific task depending on the characteristics of the movement (load or weight to be displaced and velocity of movement). Therefore, the main purpose of a strength training programme designed for tennis players should be to enhance the peak force developed during ball strokes, particularly during the serve (Konig et al., 2001). In so doing, one option could be to aim at improving, or at least at maintaining the MDS during the whole season and, somehow, adjust it to the specific tennis demands before the competition. The MDS can be enhanced or, at least maintained, during the overall competitive season by means of a well designed strength training programme, while currently little information is available in regard to more specific strength training programme for tennis.

The influence of muscle hypertrophy on tennis performance still remains unknown. Recent studies show that tennis practice is not associated with a significant increment in total lean mass in professional tennis players (Calbet et al., 1998; Sanchis Moysi et al., 1998). However, tennis produces marked increases of muscle mass in the dominant-arm (between 10-20% compared with the contralateral arm) (Calbet et al., 1998; Sanchis Moysi et al., 1998). These studies suggest that specific muscle hypertrophy of the dominant arm could contribute to enhance power in tennis strokes.

The main purpose of this study was to analyse the effects of tennis competition on the MDS in two female professional tennis players. We present the improvements of MDS after a weight-lifting strength training programme (STP), as well as the evolution of MDS during the competitive phase of the season (in-season) in two different tennis players who either performed or eschewed a single session of MDS training per week.

## 2 Methods

Two professional female tennis players (P1 and P2) who participated in the World Tennis Association circuit (WTA) competitions were studied (P1: 22 years, 75.6 kg, 1.65 m, top 50 WTA ranking; P2: 16 years, 61.6 kg, 1.71 m, top 100 WTA ranking). Both players were right handed and from the same caucasian population. Player 2 (P2) had no previous experience of strength training with weight-lifting exercises. The mean time spent in tennis training or competitions was 22 ± 8 hours per week.

### 2.1 Strength training programme (STP)

Both P1 and P2 followed a 4- and 12-week STP to improve the MDS, respectively. The two subjects carried out the same lower body and upper body strengthening exercises (Table 1). Before the STP, P2 trained for 3 months with light loads to familiarise herself with the exercises (Delavier, 2001). Then, the STP programme was organised in microcycles, each lasting for 1 week. During the week, P1 and P2 alternated sessions of upper body or lower body exercises, with a frequency of 4 sessions/week .The day after the last training session of the week both subjects carried out a 3 RM test to adjust the training weight for the next week. The upper body exercises were selected according to the involvement of muscular groups during the acceleration and impact phases of most tennis strokes. In turn, general lower body exercises were carried out. During the training session, the subjects performed 3 series of 8 repetitions each, executed at maximal speed, at 70-80% of 1 RM, with a 5 m rest period between series. During the STP, P1 did not participate in any competition, while P2 participated in 3 preparatory tournaments (3 weeks), during which the same STP was performed. Except in the latter case, both subjects always executed the exercises with the same training machines and dumbbells.

## 2.2 Strength training during the competitive phase of the season (in-season)

The in-season phase had a duration of 39 weeks for P1 and 31 weeks for P2. During this phase, P1 performed 1 session/week of strength training while P2 did not add any weight-lifting exercises to her training routine. During the training session, P1 executed one series of 3 RM per exercise. From week 14 until the end of the in-season phase, to prevent staleness and to avoid monotony, some upper body and lower body exercises of P1 were replace by new exercises performed applying the same training routine than the substituted (once a week, 1 series of 3 RM per exercise). The main criterion for substitution was that the new exercises worked-out approximately the same muscle groups to those of the STP (Delavier, 2001).

Table 1. Pre-season and in-season strength training programme (STP). P1 and P2 represent the two subjects studied

| UPPER BODY EXERCISES | | | | | |
|---|---|---|---|---|---|
| **DURING THE STP (P1 and P2)** | | Inclined Bench Press (dumbbell) | Lateral Pulldown Behind Neck | Concentrate Biceps Curl (dumbbell) | Seated Lateral raise (dumbbell) |
| **DURING IN-SEASON (P1)** | Before week 14 | x | x | x | x |
| | After week 14 | Inclined Dumbbell Fly | x | Seated Dumbbell Curls - Alternative | x |
| LOWER BODY EXERCISES | | | | | |
| **DURING THE STP (P1 and P2)** | | Back Half Squat | | Leg (knee) Extension | |
| **DURING IN-SEASON (P1)** | Before week 14 | x | | x | |
| | After week 14 | x | | x | |

## 2.3 Maximal dynamic strength test

The MDS was measured before (T1) and after (T2) the STP, as well as at the end of the in-season ($T_{END}$) using a test of maximal repetitions (between 3 and 12 maximal repetitions, with 3 different load levels), in all the upper body and lower body exercises. Additional tests were carried out by P1 during the 14th week (T3) and at $T_{END}$ to measure the MDS when she performed replacing exercise. Before T1 both players were instructed about the correct execution of the exercises, according to Delavier (2001).

During the MDS test the initial load was calculated in a manner that the subject could execute 12 RM, in the subsequent series the loads were progressively increased until the subject could perform only 3 RM in the last series. The load corresponding to 1 RM was then estimated from the logarithmic relationship between load and number of repetitions, as previously reported (Sanchis Moysi, 1998).

## 2.4 Body composition

Body composition was measured at T2 and at $T_{END}$ by dual energy X-ray absorptiometry (DXA)(QDR-1500, Hologic Corp., Waltham, MA) in both players. The principle of DXA, as well as its validity and reliability have been described previously (see Calbet et al., 1998). From the whole body scans, the lean body mass and fat mass were measured. The software of this instrument allows regional body composition to be determined. Of particular interest was the assessment of the tissue composition of the limbs, since fat-free lean body mass in the limbs is equivalent to muscle mass. The laboratory precision error as defined by the coefficient of variation of repeated measurements for young volunteers (n=9) was less than 3% for all the DXA variables (Calbet et al., 1998).

## 3 Results

### 3.1 MDS during the STP
Both players improved the MDS in all the upper body and lower body exercises at the end of the STP. This improvement was higher in P2 than in P1 (126% vs 34% and 79% vs 36% for upper body and lower body exercises, respectively).

### 3.2 MDS during the in-season
The MDS increased in P1 in all the exercises from T2 until $T_{END}$ (upper body by 16% and lower body by 21%). In contrast, during the same period the MDS decreased in P2 in all the exercises, 18% and 22%, respectively. Further, MDS of P1 also increased in all the new exercises performed from T3 until $T_{END}$ (from 12.5 kg up to 19.2 kg and from 20.3 kg up to 28.3 kg for alternative seated dumbbell curls and inclined dumbbell fly, respectively). The substituted exercises showed similar values of MDS in $T_{END}$ compared with T2 (from 17.4 kg to 16.9 kg and from 30.0 kg to 27.1 kg for concentrate biceps curl and inclined bench press, respectively).

### 3.3 Body composition
During the in-season, P1 maintained the muscle mass of the upper and lower limbs. In contrast, P2 lost some muscle mass from T2 until $T_{END}$.

## 4 Discussion

This study suggests that these for two female professional tennis players the gains in maximal dynamic strength obtained during the preparation phase of the season can be maintained, and even slightly increased, if one session/week of explosive strength training is performed during the competitive phase of the season. This improvement of strength was likely mediated via neuromuscular mechanisms, inasmuch as the muscle mass remained unchanged during the competitive season.

The improvement of MDS was higher in P2 than in P1. The greater increase in MDS of P2 could be explained by her inexperience in strength training with weight lifting exercises, her age and longer duration of the STP. This improvement in muscular strength has been associated with an increased muscle activation and a higher co-ordination of the neuromuscular system, more than with muscle hypertrophy (Gardiner, 2001). Although the improvements of MDS observed for P2 in some exercises in which the estimated values of 1 RM were duplicated are really spectacular, these results can be obtained in muscle groups that have not previously been subjected to strength training (Campos et al., 2002).

Hypertrophy of the dominant arm muscle is a relevant adaptation to tennis participation (Calbet et al., 1998; Sanchis Moysi et al., 1998; Sanchis Moysi et al., 2000). However, dominant arm muscle mass did not change much in these tennis players. Thus, it is likely that the STP performed by the players elicited neuromuscular adaptations, which increased the rate of force development (RFD). It is possible to improve the neuronal activation with low muscle hypertrophy. This should allow for better exploitation of the muscular potential with minimal effects on body mass (Häkkinen, 2002). The mean power generated during a dynamic contraction can only be improved by increasing the mechanical impulse in the same period of time or generating the same mechanic impulse in a shorter time (in both cases greater RFD is required). Theoretically, the increase in MDS observed in P1 and P2 should have contributed to improving the capacity of the players to generate maximal strength in a shorter period of time and, therefore, to increasing power in every stroke. Recently, (Kraemer et al., 2000) analysed the effects of 9 months of three different types of strength training on the ball velocity, in mid level young female tennis players. These authors observed moderate correlation between the increase in the velocity of the ball and the weight lifting exercises performed at the end of the training period.

Several studies using specific fitness tests have found moderate to high correlations between speed and power tests on the one hand, and tennis performance on the other hand. Further, Vergauwen et al., (1998) using a field test, found a close correlation between the velocity of the ball and performance in tennis. In addition to these important findings, other data indirectly support the importance of explosive strength in tennis. For example, the velocity of the ball ranges from 95 to 115 $km.h^{-1}$ in baseline forehand and backhand strokes (Vergauwen et al., 1998) and increases to 105-125 $km.h^{-1}$ for passing shots in high level male tennis players (Ferrauti et al., 2001b). Due to these elevated ball velocities the time period between one stroke and another diminishes. In an interesting study, Smekal et al. (2001) reported an average stroke frequency of 30-50 $shots.min^{-1}$ during effective playing time (calculated from the duration of all the rallies). This stroke frequency demands very fast accelerations of the body to allow the player to drive in the direction of the next stroke. Our data suggest that tennis players would have more chances to accomplish appropriately with these requirements if they maintain or increase their MDS during the in-season or competition period.

## 5 Conclusions

In summary, the results achieved in these two outstanding tennis players indicate that the gains of maximal dynamic strength obtained during the preparation phase of the season can be maintained, and even slightly increased, if one session/week of explosive strength training is performed during the competitive phase of the season. This improvement of strength was likely mediated via neural mechanisms, inasmuch as the muscle mass remained unchanged during the competitive season. In contrast, the total elimination of strength training was accompanied by some loss of muscle mass and muscular strength, which negatively affected performance during the rest of the season. Although this report may be of some help to tennis coaches, who have to deal with the challenge of maintaining and/or improving in-season strength in top tennis players, these results have to be confirmed on larger and more homogeneous groups of tennis players.

## 6 References

Bergeron, M.F. and Keul, J. (2002). The physiological demands of tennis. In **Tennis** (edited by R.A.F.H.) Blackwell Science, Oxford, pp. 46-53.

Calbet, J.A., Moysi, J.S., Dorado, C. and Rodriguez, L.P. (1998). Bone mineral content and density in professional tennis players. **Calcified Tissue International,** 62, 491-496.

Campos, G.E., Luecke, T.J., Wendeln, H.K., Toma, K., Hagerman, F.C., Murray, T.F., Ragg, K.E., Ratamess, N.A., Kraemer, W.J. and Staron, R.S. (2002). Muscular adaptations in response to three different resistance-training regimens: specificity of repetition maximum training zones. **European Journal of Applied Physiology,** 88, 50-60.

Delavier, F. (2001). Strength Training Anatomy. Champaign, IL: Human Kinetics.

Deutsch, E., Deutsch, S.L. and Douglas, P.S. (1988). Exercise training for competitive tennis. **Clinics in Sports Medicine,** 7, 417-427.

Ferrauti, A., Bergeron, M.F., Pluim, B.M. and Weber, K. (2001a). Physiological responses in tennis and running with similar oxygen uptake. **European Journal of Applied Physiology,** 85, 27-33.

Ferrauti, A., Pluim, B.M. and Weber, K. (2001b). The effect of recovery duration on running speed and stroke quality during intermittent training drills in elite tennis players. **Journal of Sports Sciences,** 19, 235-242.

Gardiner, F. (2001). Neuromuscular Aspects of Physical Activity. Champaign, IL: Human Kinetics.

Häkkinen, K. (2002). Training-specific characteristics of neuromuscular performance. In **Strength Training for Sport** (edited by W. J. Kraemer and K. Häkkinen) Blackwell Science, Oxford, pp. 20-37.

Konig, D., Huonker, M., Schmid, A., Halle, M., Berg, A. and Keul, J. (2001). Cardiovascular, metabolic, and hormonal parameters in professional tennis players. **Medicine and Science in Sports and Exercise,** 33, 654-658.

Kraemer, W.J., Ratamess, N., Fry, A.C., Triplett-McBride, T., Koziris, L.P., Bauer, J.A., Lynch, J.M. and Fleck, S.J. (2000). Influence of resistance training volume and periodization on physiological and performance adaptations in collegiate women tennis players. **American Journal of Sports Medicine,** 28, 626-633.

Roetert, P.E., Brown, S.W., Piorkowski, A.P. and Woods, R.B. (1996). Fitness comparisons among three different levels of elite tennis players. **Journal of Strength and Conditioning Research,** 10, 139-143.

Sanchis Moysi, J. (1998). Muscular fatigue and energy efficiency in humans. Unpublished Doctoral Thesis: University of Las Palmas de Gran Canaria, pp. 212.

Sanchis Moysi, J., Dorado García, C. and Calbet, J.A.L. (1998). Regional body composition in professional tennis players. In **Science and Racket Sports II** (edited by A. Lees, I. Maynard, M. Hughes and T. Reilly) E. & F.N. Spon, London, pp. 34-39.

Sanchis Moysi, J., Dorado García, C. and Calbet, J.A.L. (2000). High femoral neck bone mass and density in master tennis players. **Medicine and Science in Tennis,** 1, 7.

Smekal, G., von Duvillard, S.P., Rihacek, C., Pokan, R., Hofmann, P., Baron, R., Tschan, H. and Bachl, N. (2001). A physiological profile of tennis match play. **Medicine and Science in Sports and Exercise,** 33, 999-1005.

Vergauwen, L., Spaepen, A.J., Lefevre, J. and Hespel, P. (1998). Evaluation of stroke performance in tennis. **Medicine and Science in Sports and Exercise,** 30, 1281-1288.

# Part Four

# Biomechanics of Racket Sports

# 15 An overview of the application of biomechanics to racket sports

A. Lees

*Research Institute for Sport and Exercise Sciences, Liverpool John Moores University, Liverpool L3 2ET, UK.*

## 1 Introduction

Biomechanical analysis of racket sports (badminton, squash, table tennis and tennis) is undertaken to identify those mechanical characteristics that affect both performance and risk of injury. One of the main areas of application is the technique used by players while playing shots. The advance of technology in recent years has enabled detailed three-dimensional kinematic and kinetic characteristics of racket skills to be established and has enabled biomechanists to investigate the underlying mechanisms used in performing racket skills. Although there are interacting factors that are more related to the mechanical behaviour of the racket, ball, surface and environment, these are beyond the scope of this overview, which will be restricted to the application of biomechanics to the understanding of technique in racket sports and the implications for performance and injury prevention.

## 2 Motion analysis studies - kinematics

Kinematics is the description or measurement of motion. Documenting the movements in racket sports has been based on qualitative observations and quantitative measurements of varying levels of sophistication. The most notable early qualitative and quantitative research in several racket sports was by Plagenhoef (1970, 1971). Plagenhoef's studies enabled players and coaches for the first time to understand the complexity of movement associated with fast powerful actions like the tennis serve. Analysis has shown that these actions are characterised by trunk and upper limb rotations. The trunk rotates initially away from the direction of the stroke (retraction phase) and then towards the direction of the stroke (action phase). During retraction, the upper arm at the shoulder is abducted and external rotated, the lower arm at the elbow flexed and supinated, and the hand at the wrist extended and radially flexed. During the action phase these joint motions are reversed. This description of events has been helpful to coaches to understand the sequential nature of rotations involved in skills of this type and to clinicians who have appreciated the importance of joint flexibility and ranges of motion demanded by the performance of these skills.

Many of these important joint motions involve rotation about a segment's longitudinal axes and were first analysed qualitatively. Gowitzke and Waddle (1979 and 1986) used cine film at 400 Hz to analyse fast overhead and underarm strokes in badminton. By placing tape along the length of the forearm they were able to establish that racket-head speed in the power strokes was derived substantially from rotation (pronation) of the forearm about its longitudinal axis. Further, their qualitative analyses were able to establish the specific technique used in many badminton strokes, and in several cases they were able to show that the way in which players actually performed contradicted coaching descriptions found in the literature. Specifically these were to do with the importance of wrist flexion, pronation of the forearm and internal rotation of the upper arm.

Quantitative technique analysis has developed along with technological advances in high-speed imaging. The most recent and important developments have been in three-dimensional (3D) kinematic analyses. The first studies that applied 3D analyses to racket sports established some basic data for joint flexion angles, joint flexion-extension angular velocities, linear joint velocities and racket and ball speeds for a number of tennis skills. It is not possible to detail all of this information but some of the skills analysed are the tennis serve (Elliott et al., 1986; Papadopoulis et al., 2000; van Gheluwe et al. 1987), the tennis backhand drive (Elliott et al., 1989a), the tennis forehand drive (Elliott et al., 1989b; Knudson 1990), and the tennis volley (Elliott et al., 1988). There are limited 3D data on skills in other racket sports like badminton, squash, or table tennis.

More recently, Chow et al. (2003) investigated the detailed kinematic characteristics of ball placement and racket head velocities in the first and second serve for professional tennis players. Compared to the first serve, the players in their second serve tossed the ball closer to the body and imparted sidespin and topspin on the ball by increasing the vertical and lateral velocities of the racket head at impact. The resultant velocity of the ball after impact was reduced by 24% in the second serve even though the pre-impact speed and orientation of the racket face remained unchanged between the two serves, an interesting finding from the point of view of the consistency required in the general serving technique.

The 3D kinematic methods referred to above have been developed to analyse rotations about the longitudinal axis of the forearm and upper arm during fast shots like the serve in tennis and the smash in badminton. In order to investigate these more complex 3D characteristics of movement, a specialised marker system and analysis method are required. The first attempt to do this was reported by van Gheluwe et al. (1987) who attached several markers to the wrist, elbow and upper arm and from the reconstructed 3D location of these markers they were able to quantify the magnitude of rotation of the upper arm and forearm. Using a similar approach, Tang et al. (1995) investigated the kinematics of the badminton forehand smash. They reported on forearm pronation, wrist flexion-extension and ulnar and radial deviation, and found that although there was considerable wrist joint motion about its two axes of rotation, the most important in this shot was pronation of the forearm.

A method for obtaining the contribution of all rotations of the arm segments to racket speed was presented by Sprigings et al. (1994). A series of markers were used to define segment positions and orientations which allowed a full 3D description of segment rotations including flexion-extension, abduction-adduction and internal-external rotation of the upper arm, lower arm and hand. This method showed that in the tennis serve the greatest contribution to final speed of the racket head was upper arm internal rotation (29%), followed by wrist flexion (25%), upper arm horizontal adduction (23%), forearm pronation (14%) and forward movement of the shoulder (9%). These results, though, contradict the earlier reports with regard to the importance of forearm pronation. This method was used by Elliott et al. (1995) to investigate the tennis serve in more detail. They reported the same order of importance as above although the percentages differed slightly. They also reported that the elbow extension played a negative role (-14%) by reducing the forward velocity of the centre of the racket at impact. A similar approach by Wang et al. (2000) led to a rather different conclusion. For the flat serve in tennis they concluded that the power of the serve (presumably racket head velocity) comes from the rotation and bending of the trunk and elbow extension. Clearly there are some issues of interpretation that need further attention. Since kinematics are motion descriptions and the contributions change throughout the movement, joint motions that appear to contribute little kinematically may be making substantive kinetic contributions to generating racket speed. The method of Sprigings et al. (1994) has been used to investigate the effects of upper limb contributions to velocity of the racket head in the forehand drive in squash (Elliott et al., 1996) but appears to date not to have been applied to other shots in tennis or squash or other racket sports.

Based on these results, Marshall and Elliott (2000) commented that the traditional concepts of proximal-to-distal sequencing are inadequate to describe the complexity of racket shots and that the contribution that specific segments make to end-point velocity, including the role of forearm pronation, should be taken into account when coaching racket skills, and developing training or injury prevention programmes.

### 3 Motion analysis studies - kinetics

The 3D kinematic studies reviewed above have recently been recently extended to estimate the net joint forces and torques acting at the shoulder and elbow during the performance of racket skills. This technique is referred to as inverse dynamics and provides the overall pattern of joint kinetics but cannot provide accurate estimates of individual muscular forces contributing to movement. The kinetics of powerful racket shots, such as the tennis serve and badminton smash, have indicated that joint torques related to the motions of ab/adduction, horizontal ab/adduction and internal/external rotation at the shoulder and flexion/extension, varus/valgus and pronation/supination at the elbow are important for the understanding of the way technique may influence injury.

An analysis of joint torques at the shoulder have only recently been reported for racket sports. Elliott et al. (2003) have presented shoulder and joint torque data for the tennis serve from male and female Olympic competitors with respect to two aspects of technique - the extent of backswing and the level of knee flexion. These latter two technique factors have been implicated in injury. They reported highest torque levels in male players for shoulder horizontal adduction (107.8 Nm). The next highest value was in elbow varus (78.3 Nm) and shoulder internal rotation (71.2 Nm). At the position of maximal internal rotation, all of these joint torques were close to maximum tolerances suggesting that the joints are at their greatest risk of injury close to this position. They found that the joint torques were lower (by between 30-50 %) in female players. They also reported that there was no difference in joint torques between players who used a full, as opposed to an abbreviated, backswing although the data suggested that the joint forces may be lower in the full swing. It is apparent that aspects of technique are related to the way in which the body experiences load and their advice to players was to undertake a strengthening programme incorporating both eccentric and concentric exercises, to use a technique which incorporates a support leg knee flexion enabling them to produce a 'leg-drive' during the action phase of the serve, and preferably to use a full backswing.

A second recent study (Bahamonde and Knudson, 2003) has investigated joint torques in the open and square forehand drive in tennis. The rationale for this study was the fact that as the modern game has increased in speed, players are tending to use an open stance rather that the traditional square or side on stance as the drive is made. The open stance is now being routinely taught to players but there is some concern that as the open stance does not optimally use the base, rotations and kinetic chain of the lower body. If so, some overstressing of the player's upper limb may result and this may lead to greater risk of overuse injury. They reported the highest torque levels in shoulder horizontal adduction (91 Nm) with the next highest value being in elbow varus (62 Nm) and shoulder internal rotation (52 Nm). Interestingly these peak torques were similar to those reported by Elliott et al. (2003), but were a little lower suggesting less risk of overuse injury in the forehand than in the serve. The conclusions reached by Bahamonde and Knudson, that although there were some differences between the open and square stance for both professionals and intermediate players, there was not sufficient evidence to suggest that the open stance would impose greater load on the players. This second example also illustrates the value of biomechanical analysis inbeing able to provide useful data on contemporary problems related to technique.

## 4 Force analysis studies

The force analysis of racket skills has received less attention from researchers. In relation to performance, the effect of grip forces on tennis racket-ball interaction has been of interest, but Elliott (1995) concluded that a high grip force is not the major factor in controlling post-impact ball velocity for centrally hit balls, although it is important if balls are hit off-centre.

In relation to injury, the way a racket is gripped is thought to be one factor influencing the onset of tennis elbow and it is generally found that novices are more likely to suffer from this condition than experts. Consequently researchers have looked closely at the racket arm technique demonstrated by novices in relation to experts. Knudson (1991) measured the contact forces between the hand and the racket as players performed backhand drives. The less experienced players held the racket with a lower grip force so at impact the racket would undergo a greater acceleration and thus displacement. Such a forced displacement of the racket results in an eccentric stretch of the wrist extensor muscles and is known to create high muscular stresses which Knudson suggested could be a causative factor in 'tennis elbow'.

This hypothesis has been supported by several recent studies. Blackwell and Cole (1994) investigated wrist motion during the performance of a backhand stroke by both novices and experts. The main difference between the two groups was that at impact, the novices held their wrist in a less extended position and as a result of impact the wrist was forced into flexion. The main muscle implicated in tennis elbow is the extensor carpi radialis brevis, and this action would cause an already extended muscle to extend further under eccentric contraction conditions. Their electromyographical data also supported the view that novices were unable to control the forced flexion of the wrist imposed by ball contact. Forced flexion will have the tendency to generate more force in the muscle-tendon complex and so apply more force to the origin of the muscle, the lateral epicondylitis, where tennis elbow manifests itself. Knudson and Blackwell (1997) reported a retrospective study of the one-handed backhand showing that players with a history of tennis elbow had significantly greater forced wrist extension after impact than tennis professionals without tennis elbow. A simulation study of the wrist extensors at impact in tennis backhand also supports the hypothesis of eccentric overload (Riek et al. 1999). Riek et al. used a Hill-type muscle model to predict the tension and length characteristics of the extensor carpi radialis brevis muscle based on goniometric wrist joint kinematic data. They found that novices were subjected to a large eccentric contraction when the muscle was at a greater length. The results of these studies provide strong evidence that tennis elbow in novices is implicated by poor technique that is observed in terms of wrist initial position and motion, and the muscular preparedness and reaction to the impact with the ball. These results also explain why certain racket characteristics have been identified as extrinsic risk factors such as racket weight, grip size, material stiffness and string type, all of which are likely to transmit impact shock and exacerbate the faulty wrist motions.

A second important area of injury in racket sport players is lower limb muscle injuries, particularly related to the Achilles tendon. Peak vertical ground reaction forces in the lateral movement of tennis players has been reported between 1.5 and 2.5 body weights (van Gheluwe and Deporte, 1992). For the badminton lunge, Lees and Hurley (1995) reported vertical and horizontal forces of 1.47 and 0.92 body weight respectively and noted that the less skilled players generated the higher forces. Simpson et al. (1992) found that the technique used to plant foot has a marked effect on loading and ankle movement and so it may be that less skilled players lack the movement skills to reduce the load they experience and as a result, would be more susceptible to injury. This interesting finding has never been followed up but it would be another example of where technique is important for reducing the load experienced by players.

## 5 Electromyographical (EMG) studies

Electromyography (EMG) has been used to detect patterns of muscle activation but there have been very few applications in racket sports. Those that have been conducted have given some insight into the way in which the muscles of the upper limb operate during selected strokes. van Gheluwe et al. (1986) reported the EMG profiles of nine shoulder and elbow muscles during the performance of a range of tennis strokes. Their general finding was that most muscles demonstrated their greatest activity during the active propulsion of the racket and during impact, and even moderate movements required strong levels of contraction. Buckley and Kerwin (1988) investigated the role of the triceps in rapid elbow extension during the slice serve in tennis as the extension angular velocities of the elbow during tennis serves and badminton smashes exceeds the maximum contractile capability of muscle. They found that the role of the triceps was to provide joint stabilisation, rather than to contribute to the extension velocity of the elbow joint. Sakurai and Ohtsuki (2000) reported EMG data on the muscles that control wrist actions (the extensor carpi radialis and flexor carpi radialis) in the 50 ms before impact in the badminton smash. They showed an extension-flexion-extension sequence of muscle activity which relates to the preparatory 'cocking' movements of forearm supination - wrist extension-radial flexion followed by the action movements of forearm pronation - wrist flexion-ulnar flexion which provide the power at impact and then finally a burst of muscle activity immediately after impact to slow the action during the follow through. In a comparison of skill level, they found that this sequence of muscle activity was well defined and consistent in skilled players, but small and inconsistent in unskilled players. The data suggested that the unskilled players had not been able to control the important final motions of the stroke before impact adequately so lost power in their shot. Knudson and Blackwell (2000) reported gender differences in abdominal muscle activation in the tennis forehand. A recent study of the serve showed a clear sequential activation of deltoid, pectoralis major, and triceps brachii in the serve.

These reports are helpful in establishing the general role of muscle activity in the performance of high-speed shots, and suggest some rather complex mechanisms operating. In addition there is some evidence that muscle activation patterns are sensitive to levels of skill and gender, areas which deserves more attention in the future.

## 6 Summary

Biomechanical methods have been used to investigate techniques used in a range of racket skills and have been interpreted in relation to both performance and injury. The general characteristics of racket skills and some underlying mechanisms of performance are well understood. Recent developments of quantitative analysis methods have enabled researchers to quantify the relative contribution that segments make to performance and to quantify joint torques and power production. These areas seem ripe for further research interest, particularly as they also have some relation to injury. It is evident that there needs to be further application of these methods to a range of racket skills and also across all of the racket sports.

## 7 References

Bahamonde, R.E. and Knudson, D. (2003). Kinetics of the upper extremity in the open and square stance tennis forehand. **Journal of Science and Medicine in Sport,** 6, 88-101.

Blackwell, J.R. and Cole, K.J. (1994). Wrist kinematics differ in expert and novice tennis players performing the backhand stroke: implications for tennis elbow. **Journal of Biomechanics,** 27, 509-516.

Buckley, J.P. and Kerwin, D.G. (1988). The role of the biceps and triceps brachii during tennis serving. **Ergonomics,** 31, 1621-1629.

Chow, J.W., Carlton, L.G., Lim, Y.-T., Chae, W.-S., Shim, J.-H., Kuenster, A.F. and Kokbun, K. (2003). Comparing pre-and post-impact ball and racket kinematics of elite tennis players' first and second serves. **Journal of Sports Sciences,** 21, 529-537.

Elliott, B.C. (1995). The biomechanics of tennis stroke production. In **Science and Racket Sports** (edited by T. Reilly, M. Hughes and A. Lees), London: E & FN Spon, pp. 89-97.

Elliott, B., Fleisig, G., Nicholls, R. and Escmilla, R. (2003) Technique effects on upper limb loading in the tennis serve. **Journal of Science and Medicine in Sport,** 6, 76-87.

Elliott, B.C., Marsh, A.P. and Overheu, P.R. (1989a). The topspin backhand drive in tennis: a biomechanical analysis. **Journal of Human Movement Studies,** 16, 1-16.

Elliott, B.C., Marsh, T. and Blanksby, B. (1986). A three dimensional cinematographic analysis of the tennis serve. **International Journal of Sports Biomechanics**, 2, 260-271.

Elliott, B.C., Marsh, T. and Overheu, P. (1989b). A biomechanical comparison of the multi-segment and single unit topspin forehand drives in tennis. **International Journal of Sports Biomechanics**, 5, 350-364.

Elliott, B.C., Marshall, R.N. and Noffal, G.J. (1995). Contributions of upper limb segment rotations during the power serve in tennis. **Journal of Applied Biomechanics**, 11, 433-442.

Elliott, B.C., Marshall, R.N. and Noffal, G.J. (1996). The role of the upper limb segment rotations in the development of racket-head speed in squash. **Journal of Sports Sciences**, 14, 159-165.

Elliott, B.C., Overheu, P.R. and Marsh, A.P. (1988). The service line and net volleys in tennis: a cinematographic analysis. **Australian Journal of Science and Medicine in Sport**, 20, 10-18.

Gowitzke, B.A. and Waddell, D.B. (1979). Technique of Badminton Stroke Production. In **Science in Racket Sports** (edited by J. Terauds), Del Mar, CA: Academic Publishers, pp. 17-41.

Gowitzke, B.A. and Waddell, D.B. (1986). The biomechanics of underarm power strokes in badminton. In **Sports Science** (edited by J. Watkins, T. Reilly and L. Burwitz), London: E & FN Spon, pp. 137-142.

Knudson, D. (1990). Intra-subject variability of upper extremity angular kinematics in the tennis forehand drive. **International Journal of Sport Biomechanics**, 6, 415-421.

Knudson, D. (1991). Forces on the hand in the tennis one handed backhand. **Journal of Applied Biomechanics**, 7, 182-292.

Knudson, D. (2003). **Fundamentals of Biomechanics**. New York: Kluwer Academic/Plenum Publishers.

Knudson, D. and Blackwell, J. (1997). Upper extremity angular kinematics of the one-handed backhand drive in tennis players with and without tennis elbow. **International Journal of Sports Medicine**, 18, 79-82.

Knudson. D. and Blackwell, J. (2000). Trunk muscle activation in open stance and square stance tennis forehands. **International Journal of Sports Medicine**, 21, 321-324.

Lees, A. and Hurley, C. (1995). Forces in a badminton lunge. In **Science and Racket Sports** (edited by T. Reilly, M. Hughes and A. Lees), London: E & FN Spon, pp.186-189.

Marshall, R.N. and Elliott, B.C. (2000). Long axis rotation: the missing link in proximal-to-distal sequencing. **Journal of Sports Sciences**, 18, 247-254.

Papadopoulis, C., Emmanouilidou, M., and Prassas, S. (2000). Kinematic analysis of the service stroke in tennis. In **Tennis Science and Technology** (edited by S. Haake and A.O. Coe), Oxford: Blackwell, pp. 383-388.

Plagenhoef, S. (1970). **Fundamentals of Tennis**. Prentice-Hall: Englewood Cliffs, NJ.

Plagenhoef, S. (1971). **Patterns of Human Motion: A cinematographic Analysis**. Prentice-Hall: Englewood Cliffs, NJ.

Riek, S., Chapman, A. and Milner, T. (1999). A simulation of muscle force and internal kinematics of extensor carpi radialis brevis during backhand tennis stroke: implications for injury. **Clinical Biomechanics**, 14, 477-483.

Sakurai, S. and Ohtsuki, T. (2000). Muscle activity and accuracy of performance of the smash stroke in badminton with reference to skill and practice. **Journal of Sports Sciences**, 18, 901-914.

Simpson, K.J., Shewokis, P.A., Alduwaisan, S. and Reeves, K.T. (1992). Factors influencing rearfoot kinematics during a rapid lateral braking movement. **Medicine and Science in Sports and Exercise**, 24, 586-594.

Sprigings, E., Marshall, R., Elliott, B. and Jennings, L. (1994). A 3-D kinematic method for determining the effectiveness of arm segment rotations in producing racket head speed. **Journal of Biomechanics**, 27, 245-254.

Tang, H.P., Abe, K., Katoh, K. and Ae, M. (1995). Three dimensional cinematographic analysis of the badminton forehand smash: movements of the forearm and hand. In **Science and Racket Sports** (edited by T. Reilly, M. Hughes and A. Lees), London: E & FN Spon, pp. 113-120.

van Gheluwe, B. and Deporte, E. (1992). Friction measurements in tennis on the field and in the laboratory. **International Journal of Sport Biomechanics**, 8, 48-61.

van Gheluwe, B., de Ruysscher, I. and Craenhals, J. (1987). Pronation and endorotation of the racket arm in a tennis serve. In **Biomechanics X-B** (edited by B. Jonsson), Human Kinetics: Champaign, IL., pp. 666-672.

van Gheluwe, B. and Hebbelinck, M. (1986). Muscle actions and ground reaction forces in tennis. **International Journal of Sport Biomechanics**, 2, 88-99.

# 16 Service in tennis: Speed and accuracy depending on the type of racket used

G. Ruiz Llamas and D.Cabrera Suarez
*Departamento de Educación Física, Universidad de Las Palmas de Gran Canaria Campus Universitario de Tafir, Gran Canaria, Spain.*

## 1 Introduction

In 1996, the ITF caused an uproar voting to outlaw rackets over 29 inches long for professional and organized amateur play, the ITF's contention was that these rackets would turn the game into nothing more than a fast service contest with few rallies. Many disagree arguing that the only source of serving speed in tennis isn't the racket but rather the server's technique and physical strength. So we decided to make a comparison of the results obtained by several groups of players, at different levels, in the performance of the first service, using several kinds of rackets. The aim was the observation of speed and accuracy, when carrying out the first service. Our intention was to determine the influence of materials, i.e. rackets, in this particular activity. We also tried to observe efficiency (number of good services in relation to the number of attempts to get them) in present day players when using the old type of rackets, since many consider they are the cause of a limitation in speed when performing the first service. Our main objectives were:

1. To analyse the speed in first service in relation to the type of racket used.
2. To analyse the speed and accuracy of the first service in relation to player level.
3. To compare several groups of players according to their level and the type of racket used.
4. To observe the efficiency of each type of racket used.
5. To analyse the efficiency of the first service and the speed obtained with the old metal and wood rackets by present day players.

## 2 Methods

### 2.1 Participants

The study was carried out using 4 groups of players, classified according to their player level as international, national, provincial, local club level (beginners). The sample included 40 male players (4 groups of 10) during 2001 and the first months of 2002. The groups were defined as follows:

LEVEL 1. Players possessing ATP points or frequently participating in ITF competitions. They were able to perform "whole tennis", i.e. all the combined hits with all the possible effects.

LEVEL 2. Advanced level players, performing all the possible hits and showing efficiency at play, usually processing to a high provincial ranking or else a low national one, similar to a ranking of 4.5-5.0 for USTA.
LEVEL 3. Intermediate players, showing limitations when hitting but practising regularly, with technical limitations but efficient at one type of service.
LEVEL 4. Beginners or regular players with fundamental technique limitations usually associated with a small swing.

## 2.2 Equipment

We used four different types of racket, according to their functions and features as given in Table 1. The Tennis ground used had a mixed surface (Tennisquick), and with a net placed according to official regulations, situated in Telde, Canary Islands, Spain. Radar was used for ball speed measurement (Speedcheck, T.M. TRIBAR, Tribar Inc., USA). The tennis balls used were pressurized and of standard size (model "Penn 1", made in USA by Penn Racquet Sports, Phoenix, Arizona).

Table 1. Types of rackets

| RACKET | MODEL | STRING TENSION | HITTING AREA |
|--------|-------|----------------|--------------|
| Wood | Dunlop Maxply | 21 kg | 541cm$^2$ |
| Metal | Wilson Force | 20 kg | 568 cm$^2$ |
| Fibre | Wilson Hammer 2.3. | 23 kg | 613 cm$^2$ |
| Super | Wilson Sledge Hammer 3.4 | 25 kg | 715 cm$^2$ |

## 2.3 Procedure

Each group was required to perform a series of first services, to determine both speed and accuracy. For speed the players had to get in at least five good serves (they could make more than five attempts until five good serves were obtained). The speed of these serves was measured by radar, and were repeated with each type of racket. For accuracy, the player had to perform only five first services directed at one of the three parts of the grounds which had been previously determined (Figure 1).

The player was allowed to use any type of service, flat, slice or spin according to his ability to develop speed and accuracy. Players were allowed to undertake some warming up exercises and a previous series of up to 10 first services with each of the rackets, so that they were able to get used to all the different types.

During the test itself, alternation between the players was allowed, since they had to perform a large number of first services but they were not allowed change the type of racket if they didn't finish the whole series. In the speed test they were required get five services into the service box, and five services correctly placed in the accuracy test.

We used the same ground, which was at sea level, for all the groups, in the same conditions and avoided windy days. The balls were also of the same type for all the players, each one using six of them. We changed them after being used by three players for levels 1 and 2, and after the performance of five players for levels 3 and 4.

This change was different between groups because the speed was higher in levels 1 and 2.

Data were recorded on a data sheet and were filled in by an external observer. These data were then analysed with a computer system (SPSS program), to determine mean and standard deviation.

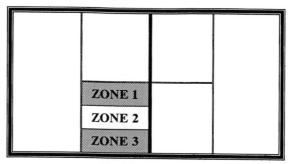

Figure 1. Parts of the court used for accuracy test.

## 3 Results

The results for the speed test are presented in the Table 2. In Table 3 we present the percentage efficiency (number of balls in service box/total number of attempts) for the speed test using the different types of rackets. Table 4 presents the results for the speed and accuracy results using the different types of racket.

Table 2. Speed test: maximum, mean and number of attempts used for each playing level and each racket used

|  | GROUP 1 | GROUP 2 | GROUP 3 | GROUP 4 |
|---|---|---|---|---|
| **WOOD** | | | | |
| *MAX. SPEED* (km.h$^{-1}$) | 178 | 159 | 110 | 78 |
| *MEAN SPEED* (km.h$^{-1}$) | 166 | 135 | 91 | 68 |
| *ATTEMPTS* | 12 | 15 | 19 | 24 |
| **METAL** | | | | |
| *MAX. SPEED* (km.h$^{-1}$) | 182 | 170 | 116 | 85 |
| *MEAN SPEED* (km.h$^{-1}$) | 170 | 140 | 101 | 72 |
| *ATTEMPTS* | 10 | 13 | 17 | 20 |
| **FIBRE** | | | | |
| *MAX. SPEED* (km.h$^{-1}$) | 189 | 176 | 136 | 113 |
| *MEAN SPEED* (km.h$^{-1}$) | 174 | 158 | 128 | 85 |
| *ATTEMPTS* | 8 | 9 | 14 | 14 |
| **SUPER** | | | | |
| *MAX. SPEED* (km.h$^{-1}$) | 184 | 173 | 148 | 120 |
| *MEAN SPEED* (km.h$^{-1}$) | 178 | 160 | 130 | 101 |
| *ATTEMPTS* | 7 | 8 | 9 | 10 |

Table 3. Efficiency using the different types of rackets (percentage)

|  | **LEVEL 1** | **LEVEL 2** | **LEVEL 3** | **LEVEL 4** |
|---|---|---|---|---|
| **WOOD** | 41.6 | 33.3 | 26.3 | 20.8 |
| **METAL** | 50 | 38.5 | 29.4 | 25 |
| **FIBRE** | 62 | 55.5 | 35.7 | 35.8 |
| **SUPER** | 71.4 | 62.5 | 55.5 | 50 |

Table 4. Speed and accuracy results using the different types of racket

|  | **GROUP 1** | **GROUP 2** | **GROUP 3** | **GROUP 4** |
|---|---|---|---|---|
| **WOOD** |  |  |  |  |
| *MAX. SPEED* (km.h$^{-1}$) | 170 | 139 | 93 | 60 |
| *MEAN SPEED* (km.h$^{-1}$) | 150 | 125 | 87 | 51 |
| IN ZONE | 3 | 2 | 4 | 1 |
| OUT OF ZONE | 2 | 3 | 1 | 4 |
| **METAL** |  |  |  |  |
| *MAX. SPEED* (km.h$^{-1}$) | 175 | 141 | 96 | 65 |
| *MEAN SPEED* (km.h$^{-1}$) | 156 | 130 | 89 | 60 |
| IN ZONE | 3 | 3 | 3 | 1 |
| OUT OF ZONE | 2 | 2 | 2 | 4 |
| **FIBRE** |  |  |  |  |
| *MAX. SPEED* (km.h$^{-1}$) | 185 | 169 | 106 | 89 |
| *MEAN SPEED* (km.h$^{-1}$) | 169 | 150 | 100 | 74 |
| *IN ZONE* | 4 | 4 | 3 | 3 |
| *OUT OF ZONE* | 1 | 1 | 2 | 2 |
| **SUPER** |  |  |  |  |
| *MAX. SPEED* (km.h$^{-1}$) | 178 | 158 | 136 | 112 |
| *MEAN SPEED* (km.h$^{-1}$) | 169 | 140 | 119 | 100 |
| *IN ZONE* | 4 | 4 | 4 | 4 |
| *OUT OF ZONE* | 1 | 1 | 1 | 1 |

## 4 Discussion

We can see from the tables above that an increase of service speed for every group is observed according to the type of racket used, beginning with the wood racket and finishing with the super racket, except for levels 1 and 2 which get more speed and precision with the fibre racket. This speed variation between groups 1 and 2 was 2% of the mean, smaller than in the other groups. This could be because the hitting area and the sweet point was bigger in the wood compared to the fibre racket. In group 3 the increment was 6% of the mean for the wood and metal racket, but increased to 10

% for group 4. Between the metal and fibre rackets group 3 obtained an 18 % increment while this was 30 % for group 4. Both levels increased by 10 % from fibre to super racket. So we can tell that the variation from metal to super racket is 30 % more speed for group 3 and 40% for group 4. The mean speed had the same variation from 2 – 3 % in level 1 and 2 with every racket, and 10 % with wood and metal for 3 and 4 level and 20 to 24% in the same groups for the fibre and super racket.

For all levels, accuracy increased between rackets. For level 1 there is a 20 % improvement from wood to metal and to fibre, and from fibre to super the increment in efficiency has a 12 %. The values for level 2 are the same except between fibre and super, with a 37% increment in efficiency with super racket.

Levels 3 and 4 have a greater increase in efficiency than levels 1 and 2. Level 3 increased efficiency by 12% from wood to metal, 20% using a fibre racket and 39% for super racket. Also for level 4, the increase inefficiency using a metal racket was 20% but 40% when using fibre and super racket.

It may also be noted that for the speed test, the fibre racket got the highest speed of 189 km.h$^{-1}$; for the accuracy test, the fibre racket and super racket, got the same score, 4 services in zone and 1 out of zone. Level 1 got the highest speed with each type of racket, and the same score in accuracy test as level 2 using metal, fibre and super racket. Levels 3 and 4 had a greater increase in both test using a super racket.

**5 Conclusions**

It was concluded that the super racket increased speed and accuracy serve only in levels 3 and 4; not for levels 1 and 2 in which the increase in speed and accuracy was obtained with the fibre racket. The accuracy and speed for all levels with the wood and metal rackets was poor compared to the standard and super racket.

# 17 An analysis of the relationship between the exit angle of the shuttlecock and the impact height of the clear, drop and smash strokes in badminton

A. Carazo[1], D. Cabello[2], F. Rivas[3] and A. Ferro[4]

[1]*Faculty of Exercise and Sport Sciences. University of Granada, Spain, and the Spanish Badminton Federation.* [2]*Faculty of Education. University of Granada, Spain, and the Spanish Badminton Federation.* [3]*Free University of Amsterdam (VU), Holland.* [4]*Biomechanics Department. Spanish Sport Council, Spain.*

## 1 Introduction

In an individual and competition sport such as badminton, where the spaces for game related activity are independent and separated by a net, the strokes and techniques that lead to winning points and, consequently matches, become crucial to study due to their importance as the means mostly used by the player to achieve the objective of the game. In fact, most of the scientific studies focus on the analysis of these kinds of strokes and, more specifically, on the overhead strokes called the clear, drop and smash. These analyses have mostly centered on the biomechanical study of the movements in each of the stroke's phases (Carazo et al., 2001; Gowitzke, 1979; Gowitzke and Waddell, 1986; Gowitzke and Waddell, 1991a; Gowitzke and Waddell, 1991b; Hong 1993; Luthanen and Blomqvist, 1996; Tang et al. 1995), but very few of them have studied the statistical influence of the clear, drop and smash strokes on the final result of a match.

The smash is the attacking stroke of choice. It is one of the most widely studied strokes from a biomechanical point of view because of its special characteristics and its spectacular execution and effectiveness. Authors such as Gowiztke and Waddell (1991a), Tang, et al. (1995), Breen (1975) and Hong (1993), among others, have highlighted the difficulties of the execution of this stroke, as well as the importance of the kinetic chain to achieve the maximum movement speed of the arm-racket segment and transfer it to the shuttle at the moment of the impact. Some of the most important characteristics of this stroke are: i) the execution of the stroke determines the exit speed of the shuttle; ii) the drop angle of the shuttle must have the largest inclination possible which depends on the height at which the shuttle is hit; iii) the best drop areas for the shuttle are those close to the side lines.

The clear is an overhead stroke executed from the back of the court, whose aim is to send the shuttle as close to the back line of the opponent's side of the court as possible. Certain authors such as Gowitzke and Waddell (1991a), Luhtanen and Blomqvist (1996) and Broer (1993) have established a few basic objectives of this stroke from the point of view of its execution: i) the trajectory and the speed of the stroke must leave the player enough time to go back to the center of his side of the court to protect the surrounding areas; ii) the aim of this stroke is to move the opponent away from the center of the court in order to create weak shuttle drop areas or angles.

The drop is an overhead stroke executed from the back of the court, the principal goal of which is to send the shuttle towards the net with a descending trajectory so as to make it drop near the net. Authors like Gowitzke and Waddell (1991a) and Broer (1993) have established other basic objectives for this stroke in connection with the players and their opponents. These objectives are: i) to send the shuttle as quickly and as closely possible to the net; ii) make the shuttle go over the net but as close to it as possible; iii) make the opponent move towards the center of the court in order to create weak areas.

Taking into account all the basic characteristics of the execution of these strokes, we can identify differences between them. A few examples of these differences are the exit angle of the shuttle to the horizontal at the moment of the impact, the maximum height of the participant's center of gravity and the height in the moment of the stroke and, finally, the shuttle's height at the moment of impact with the racket. The purpose of this study is to quantify these factors which constitute important performance characteristics related to the stroke played.

## 2 Method

### 2.1 Design
This is a descriptive study of three technical movements that have in common the fact that they are executed overhead. The striking area (back right and back left sides) has also been considered as a criterion for the selection.

We obtained the biomechanical variables characterizing the overhead strokes in three situations (A: clear, B: drop, C: smash) with two levels in each (1: Back right side, 2: Back left side), repeating each situation four times with the participants.

### 2.2 Participants
The test was made with four players (2 men and 2 women) of the Absolute Spanish Team. Six strokes executed from the back of the court were performed by each player: i) one clear from the back right side and one from the left side; ii) one drop from the back right side and one from the left side iii) one smash from the back right side and one from the left side. In all, 24 strokes were registered, of which 21 were finally processed because of the bad quality of the images of three movements obtained with one of the cameras. The most relevant characteristics of the players that took part in the analysis are displayed in Table 1.

Table 1. Characteristics of the participants in the study

| Player | Sex | Age | Height (cm) | Mass (kg) | Side | Best result |
|--------|-----|-----|-------------|-----------|------|-------------|
| S1 | M | 25 | 181 | 66 | Right-handed | Spanish Champion |
| S2 | M | 22 | 179 | 81 | Right-handed | 3$^{rd}$ Spanish Championship |
| S3 | F | 26 | 165 | 60 | Right-handed | Spanish Champion |
| S4 | F | 19 | 165 | 64 | Right-handed | Spanish Finalist |

### 2.3 Procedure
Images were registered with two Panasonic SVHS MS5 video cameras located at one of the court sides. This display allowed them to cover a specific area including the back of the court where the players were to execute their strokes. The first thing to be filmed was the reference system consisting of two cubes, the dimensions of which

were 157x314x157 cm, placed one on top of the other in the corresponding execution areas (back right side and back left side). The selection of the samples for analysis started once the images of the matches for each player in each take (camera 1 and camera 2) were captured. For each player, two clears, two drops and two smashes (one each from the back left back right sides) were chosen. The criteria used for the selection of the strokes were: i) they had to be executed in optimal conditions; ii) the player and their opponents actions had to be highly intense; iii) technically correct from the execution point of view; iv) with no contaminant variables. The selected samples were afterwards captured using a TV tuning card model AVER-TV at 50 Hz. For the digitization process, the software Cyborg v3.0® had to be adapted to the specific needs of our study, specially regarding the particular characteristics of the segment model used and of the implement characteristics (racket and shuttle). For each of the selected samples, we obtained a database with the 2D coordinates from camera 1 C1 ($u_1,v_1$) and camera 2 C2 ($u_2,v_2$), corresponding to the manual digitization of 30 points, of which 26 belong to the human body, 3 to the racket and 1 to the shuttle. The process of automatic synchronization required interpolating the samples up to 200 Hz without previously smoothing them, by applying a $5^{th}$ order spline. The subsequent synchronization of the interpolated flat images corresponding to each camera was made through a mathematical procedure based on the direct linear transformation (DLT). The data smoothing was achieved through the use of digital filters of low pass and variable level splines. The 3D reconstruction was made with the DLT algorithms (Abdel-Azir and Karara, 1971).

The final part of this process was obtaining the values regarding the exit angle of the shuttle referred to as the displacement angle of the center of gravity of the shuttle in the interval of the first three frames after the impact in the projection of the sagittal plane, the maximum height of the participant's center of gravity in the aerial phase, the height of the participant's center of gravity in the impact and the height of the shuttle at the moment of impact.

## 3  Results

### 3.1 Exit angle of the shuttle
In table 2 the mean displacement exit angle of the shuttle shows that in all the analyzed smashes, the trajectory was downwards. In the case of clear strokes we find the opposite situation: the trajectory was upwards as a consequence of having to displace the shuttle towards the bottom of the court, with an average angle of 15°, although variability is very high. In the execution of the drop stroke, the exit angle of the shuttle was more stable, the angles being negative.

### 3.2 Maximum height of the center of gravity during aerial phase
Table 3 gives the maximum height of the participant's center of gravity during the aerial phase for smash, clear and drop strokes. As expected, in the smash, the average height of the center of gravity is higher than in the rest of the strokes, bearing in mind that, in this case, there is really displacement of the center of gravity, with an average displacement of 0.11 m. (from the beginning of the jump until the maximum height of the center of gravity). On the contrary, in the cases of clear and drop, the average elevation of the center of gravity is highly reduced.

Table 2. Average displacement angle of the center of gravity of the shuttle projected in the sagittal plane between 1 and 3 frames after impact for the smash, clear and drop actions, where S1, S2...correspond to the analyzed participants, l to the left and r to the right (+ above horizontal, - below horizontal)

| SMASH (°) | | CLEAR(°) | | DROP(°) | |
|---|---|---|---|---|---|
| S1r | -12 | S1l | 30 | S1l | -6 |
| S1l | -10 | S1r | 6 | S1r | -5 |
| S2r | -3 | S2l | 22 | S2r | 1 |
| S2l | -12 | S2r | 12 | S3l | -2 |
| S3r | -6 | S3r | 20 | S3r | -5 |
| S4r | -5 | S3l | -1 | S4l | -5 |
| S4l | -9 | S4l | 18 | S4r | -9 |
| Mean | -8 | | 15 | | -4 |
| S.D. | 3 | | 10 | | 3 |

Table 3. Maximum height of the center of gravity during aerial phase for smash, clear and drop

| SMASH (m) | | CLEAR (m) | | DROP (m) | |
|---|---|---|---|---|---|
| S1r | 1.30 | S1l | 1.15 | S1l | 1.14 |
| S1l | 1.14 | S1r | 1.13 | S1r | 1.11 |
| S2r | 1.30 | S2l | 1.15 | S2r | 1.04 |
| S2l | 1.11 | S2r | 1.09 | S3l | 0.97 |
| S3r | 1.02 | S3r | 1.05 | S3r | 1.07 |
| S4r | 1.19 | S3l | 1.05 | S4l | 1.08 |
| S4l | 1.00 | S4l | 0.99 | S4r | 1.12 |
| Mean | 1.15 | | 1.09 | | 1.08 |
| S.D. | 0.12 | | 0.06 | | 0.06 |

## 3.3 Height of center of gravity during impact

Table 4 gives the values of the height of the players center of gravity at the moment of contact between shuttle and racket for smash, clear and drop strokes. The height is greater in the case of the smash, although the variability of samples should be noted: for example, smash in S1r executes the stroke maintaining the center of gravity relatively high in relation to S4l who has nearly no vertical displacement.

Table 4. Height of the center of gravity in the impact for smash, clear and drop strokes

| SMASH (m) | | CLEAR (m) | | DROP (m) | |
|---|---|---|---|---|---|
| S1r | 1.26 | S1l | 1.13 | S1l | 1.12 |
| S1l | 1.12 | S1r | 0.97 | S1r | 1.02 |
| S2r | 1.23 | S2l | 1.14 | S2r | 0.89 |
| S2l | 1.11 | S2r | 1.04 | S3l | 0.92 |
| S3r | 1.01 | S3r | 1.04 | S3r | 1.07 |
| S4r | 1.15 | S3l | 1.05 | S4l | 1.02 |
| S4l | 0.98 | S4l | 0.93 | S4r | 1.07 |
| Mean | 1.12 | | 1.04 | | 1.02 |
| S.D. | 0.10 | | 0.08 | | 0.08 |

### 3.4 Height of shuttle during impact

Finally, in Table 5, we present the values corresponding to the height of the shuttle at the instant of the contact between shuttle and racket. It has been stated that in the case of clear, despite the fact that the player's center of gravity was lower than in the smash (Table 4), the shuttle was hit at a greater height (0.10 m on average). This can be due to two reasons: a) the position of the player, which is more extended in the case of drop and b) the point of impact between shuttle and racket. The most extreme example of this is represented by smash S2r , whose vertical distance between his center of gravity and the shuttle in the moment of executing the smash was 1.11 m, whereas in the case of the left clear, it was 1.54m.

Table 5. Height of the shuttle at the moment of the impact

| SMASH (m) | | CLEAR (m) | | DROP (m) | |
|---|---|---|---|---|---|
| S1r | 2.60 | S1l | 3.14 | S1l | 2.49 |
| S1l | 2.37 | S1r | 2.18 | S1r | 2.38 |
| S2r | 2.34 | S2l | 2.71 | S2r | 2.04 |
| S2l | 2.52 | S2r | 2.49 | S3l | 2.20 |
| S3r | 2.27 | S3r | 2.32 | S3r | 2.39 |
| S4r | 2.40 | S3l | 2.36 | S4l | 2.32 |
| S4l | 2.30 | S4l | 2.29 | S4r | 2.39 |
| Mean | 2.40 | | 2.50 | | 2.32 |
| S.D. | 0.12 | | 0.33 | | 0.15 |

### 4 Discussion

In the smash the average height of the center of gravity is higher than in the case of the other strokes, but it cannot be asserted that a vertical jump to play the shot has taken place. More likely, players search for a shot that uses a backwards jump, rather than upwards. In the case of clear and drop, this vertical displacement is even smaller than in the case of smash, this is why the vertical jump to play the shot is even less significant. In spite of the fact that there is no real vertical shot, the shuttle is hit at an average height of 2.40 m in the smash, as a consequence of the player's shoulder elevation and the length of player and racket segments. This implies a height compared to that of the net, sufficient to enable the downwards displacement of the shuttle to follow the right trajectory without hitting the net. In the cases of the clear and the drop, given their upward initial trajectory, the stroke height is only relevant in anticipating the execution of the stroke in time, making it difficult for the opponent to react. Maybe the fact of not needing to hit the shuttle at an excessive height to reach the required shuttle trajectory further explains why no clearly vertical jumps were made in the execution of strokes from the base of the court.

### 5 Conclusions

It has been shown that in overhead strokes from the base of the court in real competition, the exit angle of the shuttle is determined by the type of stroke executed. Furthermore, players do not execute a real shot to hit the shuttle at the greatest height, but rather they show a slight displacement with a jump backwards with a low vertical elevation of the center of gravity. The lack of real jumps to play a shot is possibly due to four circumstances: a) arriving too late at the striking area, which implies having less time to locate the segments in the right position for the later execution of the stroke, b) being able to go back to the base position, in the middle of the court, in the shortest time possible, c) the articular stress caused by a change of direction forwards after a vertical jump, where the center of gravity reaches a relatively great height and d) the fact of not needing to hit the shuttle at an excessive height to reach the required shuttle trajectory.

# 6  References

Abdel-Aziz, Y.I. and Karara, H.M. (1971). Direct linear transformation for comparator coordinates into object space coordinates in close ranges photogrammetry. **Proceedings ASP/UI Symposium Close-Range Photogrammetry**, Illinois: Urbana, pp. 1-18.

Breen J.L. (1975). Biomechanics of batting techniques and badminton overhead shots (forehand and backhand). In **Proceedings XVIII International Congress of the International Council on Health, Physical Education and Recreation**, Rotterdam: ICHPER, pp. 114-121.

Broer, M. (1993). **Efficiency of Human Movement**. Philadelphia: W.B. Saunders.

Carazo, A., Rivas, F. and Cabello, D. (2001). A bi-dimensional study of the clear, drop and smash badminton strokes. **Biomecánica y deporte**, Valencia: Ayuntamiento de Valencia, pp. 123-129.

Gowitzke, B. (1979). Biomechanical principles applied to badminton strokes production. In **Proceedings of the International Congress of Sport Sciences**, California: Academia Publisher, pp. 7-16.

Gowitzke, B.A. and Waddell, D.B. (1986). The biomechanical of underarm power strokes in badminton. In **Sport Science** (edited by J. Watkins and T. Reilly), London: E&FN Spon, pp. 137-142

Gowitzke, B.A. and Waddell, D.B. (1991a). Biomechanical studies of badminton overhead power strokes - a review. In **IX International Symposium of biomechanics in Sports**, (edited by C. Tant et al.), Ames, Iowa: Iowa State University, pp. 103-109.

Gowitzke, B.A. and Waddell, D.B. (1991b). Biomechanical studies of badminton underarm power strokes, court movement, and flexibility - a review. In **IX International Symposium of Biomechanics in Sports**(edited by C. Tant et al.), Ames, Iowa: Iowa State University, pp. 273-274.

Hong, Y. (1993). The biomechanics of badminton smash technique. In **Proceedings XIV Symposium of Biomechanics in Sports**, París Société de Biomécanique, pp. 588-589.

Luhtanen, P.H. and Blomqvist, M.T. (1996). Kinematics of clear in junior badminton players. **XIV Symposium on Biomechanics in Sports**. Portugal: Universidade Técnica de Lisboa.

Tang, H.P., Abe, K., Katoh, K. and Ae, M. (1995). Three dimensional cinematographical analysis of the badminton forehand smash: movements of hand and forearm. In **Science and Racket Sports** (edited by T. Reilly, M. Hughes and A. Lees), London: E & FN Spon, pp. 51-54.

# 18 A descriptive study of the rotative topspin and of the striking topspin of expert table tennis players

G. Poizat, R. Thouvarecq and C. Sève
*CETAPS UPRES JE 2318, UFR STAPS University of Rouen, Bd Siegfried, 76821, Mont-St'Aignan, France.*

## 1 Introduction

Our study is a descriptive analysis of an essential stroke in table tennis: the topspin. The topspin is a discrete skill that combines speed and a forward rotation of the ball. Generally speaking two types of topspin strokes are distinguished according to the speed and rotation imparted to the ball: the striking-topspin (speed important and ball rotation less important), and the rotative-topspin (ball rotation important and speed less important). Sklorz et al. (1996) proposed a technical description of the topspin strokes. They clearly defined three stages which are (a) preparation, (b) execution, and (c) follow-through. The preparation-stage extends from the racket's neutral position in front of the player, until the end of the movement going backwards. The execution-stage extends from the beginning of the movement until the impact of ball-racket. The follow-through-stage takes place following the impact until the end of the movement.

The theoretical framework which dominates in the field of motor skill is the schema theory (Schmidt, 1993). This considers the movement to be centrally guided and predetermined by a generalized motor programme (GMP). A GMP covers a range of movements which are specified according to different parameters relative to the amplitude of the speed, strength and precision of the movement realized. These parameters are specified and assigned to the programme during the stage of programming. The movement is then prepared for its initiation and it is performed according to a rather rigid temporal structure, the superficial characteristics being adapted to the specific demands of the environment.

A GMP is the basis for a range of movements and is structured in the memory with a steady temporal organization. This temporal organization is characterized by its relative temporal structure which is rigid. This temporal structure is the fundamental structure of the movement as the organization and rhythm of a movement's pattern are independent from the global speed and the amplitude. This temporal organization is present in the memory and reflective of a GMP. These GMP's are being built progressively during practice and are the basis of the sportsmen's development. To our knowledge, no studies have analysed the temporal structure of the topspin strokes. The rare studies on the strokes' analysed have been conducted in a descriptive manner (e.g. Ramanantsoa et al., 1989) or have referred to the approach of the coupling perception – action (e.g. Bootsma and Van Wieringen, 1988, 1990; Savelsbergh and Bootsma, 1994). Our study was an analysis of the relative temporal structures of the both topspin strokes. The goal was to investigate two typical profiles and use a 2D reconstruction of the two strokes in order to establish if these two kinds of topspin strokes belong to the same GMP.

## 2 Methods

### 2.1 Participants
Eight French players (four right-handed/four left-handed) volunteered to participate in this study. Three were ranked among the best 100 table-tennis players in the world (ITTF ranking), five were ranked between the 100th and the 300th.

### 2.2 Materials
We used two video cameras (Panasonic type) with a 50 Hz sample rate. These two cameras were placed in such a way that they could film the player from two different angles (from above and side). The two cameras were synchronized with a video mixer (Panasonic Digital AV Mixer WJ – AVE 5 with a double entry). The latter was connected to a video tape recorder being connected to the monitor that transmitted the mixed images through the central board and the timer. The video data were then digitized at 25 Hz and studied frame by frame. The articulations (elbow and shoulder) of the playing arm and the tip of the racket were identified on each frame and were transformed into figures which were used in the 2D reconstruction and to define each stage (software programme 3Clic 2.0.0[©] Psy.Co, Rouen, France). Microsoft[©] Excel was used for the 2D reconstruction of the strokes and the study of each stage.

### 2.3 Procedures
One of the researchers (himself a table tennis player), having a ball basket, fed the balls with no spin. Between each throw, we announced the stroke the player was to perform, either a striking-topspin or a rotative-topspin. During this ball distribution exercise, the players produced a pseudo-random series of 20 rotative-topspins and 20 striking-topspins (each player performed the same pseudo-random series). The athletes played always along the same diagonal and each shot was recorded on video. The instructions were identical for each player.

### 2.4 Data processing
The data collected on video tapes were analysed frame by frame. The study consisted of: (1) representing the recorded coordinates (Microsoft[©]Excel and 3 Clic 2.0.0[©]) in order to study the coordinations and the reconstruction from shots, the positions and the movements of the different body segments in two dimensions, (2) analysing the temporal structures relative to three stages of the shot, (3) defining the range of movement along the anterior-posterior and vertical axe, (4) doing a global analysis on every player, of the differences according to the stroke, and (5) completing these results by a descriptive analysis.

### 2.5 Statistics processing
The information which needed a comparison was collated with Excel Software then transferred to STATVIEW for statistical analysis. We used a Wilcoxon test and the level of significance used was $P<0.05$.

## 3 Results

### 3.1 Global analysis
No significant differences were found between the temporal organization of striking-topspin and rotative-topspin.

### 3.1.1 Temporal organization of the strokes
Three stages in the topspin strokes were distinguished: preparation, execution, and follow-trough. The major results are that the relative temporal structure was identical, so it seems that these two strokes come from the same GMP (Table 1 and Figure 1).

Table 1. Relative duration of the three stages of the stroke (median percentage of total time of the stroke)

| | Rotative-topspin % | Striking topspin % | Difference between the two strokes P |
|---|---|---|---|
| **Preparation** | 66.27 ± 3.35 | 64.58 ± 4.77 | 0.161 (N.S) |
| **Execution** | 14.99 ± 3.48 | 14.74 ± 4.43 | 0.093 (N.S) |
| **Follow-trough** | 19.26 ± 2.62 | 22.45 ± 6.26 | 0.575 (N.S) |

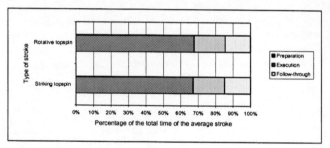

Figure 1. Relative temporal structures of the topspins for all players.

### 3.1.2 Vertical and horizontal ranges of movement
The two strokes had the same horizontal distance covered by the racket (backward to forward) (P = 0.093). However a topspin with a preparation positioned backward and a follow-through positioned less forward, can have the same horizontal range as when striking topspin with a preparation positioned less backward and a follow-through positioned more forward, so a descriptive analysis needs to be completed.

The difference in vertical range (the distance between the height of the racket at the end of the preparation-stage and the height at the end of the follow-through-stage) was significant (P = 0.012) with the position of the rotative-topspin ending higher than the striking-topspin. The vertical range distinguished these two strokes whereas the antero-posterior range was identical.

### 3.1.3 The two strokes' form
The two forms of movement differed from one other much later in the movement and did not seem to be the key factor of the differentiating the two strokes. The change in form between the two was often minimal and took place between the contact and the end of the movement.

## 3.2 Descriptive analysis

The comparison of the organization of the topspin strokes in terms of relative timing and vertical position of the racket enabled us to differentiate several profiles.

### 3.2.1 A dominating profile

Four players had identical organizations: (a) the preparation-stage was identical for both strokes and corresponded to 65% of the movement time, (b) the execution-stage was identical for both strokes, (c) the follow-through-stage was slightly greater for the striking-topspin than the rotative-topspin and (d) the horizontal and vertical ranges were not different between strokes (see Figure 2). Players who were not well classified (i.e. over 100th rank) represented this profile.

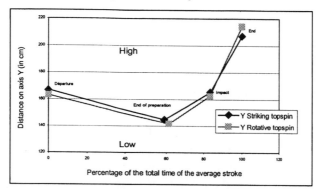

Figure 2. Average positions of the racket on the vertical axis (Y) according to the relative-timing of a player's movement.

### 3.2.2 Some specific and distinctive profiles

Two players had specific profiles: they were unusual and differed from the dominating profile above. All stages were different between strokes (see Figure 3) and players (for example the preparation-stage was longer for the striking-topspin for one player and longer for the rotative-topspin for the other). The vertical and horizontal ranges were also different for each stroke (Figure 4).

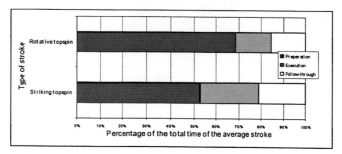

Figure 3. Relative temporal structures of the topspins for one player.

Two other players had a profile that was called distinctive: different from a dominating profile observed in several players (a) the preparation-stage was slightly longer for the rotative-topspin (b) the execution-stage was longer for the striking-topspin and (c) the follow-through-stage was identical for both strokes.

We noticed that three players having these specific or distinctive profiles were in the 100 top world table tennis players ("Top 100"), the fourth one was the best ranked among the players who didn't belong to this "Top 100".

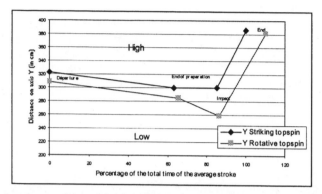

Figure 4. Average positions of the racket on the vertical axis (Y) according to the relative-timing of one player's movement.

### 3.3 Analysis of laterality

The left-handed players masked their strokes better (i.e. keeping the same form for a long time during the strokes) and differentiated their strokes later on. Concerning the horizontal range, the left-handed players had a difference between the strokes which took place between contact and the end of the movement, whereas the right-handed players made a difference in their movements before this. The left-handed players gave less information to the opponent concerning the stroke to be played.

### 4 Discussion

We can differentiate three groups of players: (a) the top-level players (ranked into the "Top 100") who have an unusual or distinctive organization, (b) the players not ranked in the "Top 100" who have a dominant profile (or accidentally a distinctive profile) allowing them to reach a high level without entering the "Top 100", (c) a player approaching the "Top 100" whose organizations are shared between unusual, distinctive and dominant which is maybe a sign of an evolution of technical skill. As a matter of fact, the dominant profile consists of the minimal modification of the movement and as a result there is a decreasing quantity of information given by the opponent but maybe at the expense of efficiency. It is worth observing that the most untypical in organization are the best players. These players belonging to the "Top 100" keep the same relative temporal structure when slightly modifying the form of the striking-topspin and the form of the rotative-topspin in order to preserve the highest efficiency (allowing the opponent to gain only limited information). We can then suggest that the dominant profile does not correspond to the most efficient organization. The top-level players, in order to be efficient concerning their motor control, keep the same temporal organization of the movement (which is different between the players), but adapt them slightly according to the topspin stroke produced. This change allows players to be more efficient with a limited source of information from the opponent. Our results confirm that the top-level players have, according to the opinion of the expert coach, a kind of "personal expression" : they adapt the traditional techniques (Sève, 2000). Of course, studies should analyse other strokes in order to confirm this fact -as far as we know there are no studies, in table tennis, having dealt with this aspect. We still have to ask about the dominant typical profile: does it come from constraints of a certain kind of practice level, or from training characteristics ? Is it necessary to reach a very high level? We cannot answer these questions from the results of this study. We would need to compare the players' organizations at different periods of time during their sport evolution. However, the profile of the "average player" (the one who is near to the "Top 100") makes us think that the "stage-typical profile" occurs before the more unusual profiles.

Moreover, our results make us think that the striking-topspin and the rotative-topspin come from the same GMP with superficial characteristics (vertical range) which are different. Indeed, the temporal structures relative to the topspin are identical for all the players and both strokes, whereas the amplitudes and the localisations of the key points (start, end of preparation, impact and end of movement) are different according to the players and the kinds of strokes (even if for a same player and a same stroke, these amplitudes and these localisations are steady).

## 5 Conclusion

If we consider the practical implications, this study shows the importance a) of combining the two topspins strokes as soon as possible while learning, and b) of focusing the player's attention on the action on the ball during the impact-stage (the form of the movement is less important than the type of contact ball-racket).

## 6 References

Bootsma R.J. and Van Wieringen P.C.W. (1988). Visual Control of an attacking forehand drive in table tennis. In **Complex Movement Behaviour: The Motor-Action Controversy,** (edited by O. G. Meijer and K. Roth), Amsterdam: North-Holland, pp. 189-199.

Bootsma R.J. and Van Wieringen P.C.W. (1990). Timing an Attacking Forehand Drive in Table Tennis. **Journal of Experimental Psychology: Human Perception and Performance,** 16, 21-29.

Ramanantsoa M.M., Ripoll H., Boissin C., Reine B., Durey A. and Varrin Ph. (1989). Mise en évidence des relations fonctionnelles entre information visuelle et efficience motrice en tennis de table: Les facteurs de la réussite et de l'échec [Revealing of the functional relations between visual information and motor efficiency in table tennis: The factors of the success and the failure]. **Rapport INSEP.** Paris: INSEP.

Savelsbergh G.J.P. and Bootsma R.J. (1994). Perception-Action coupling in hitting and catching. **International Journal of Sport Psychology,** 25, 331-343.

Schmidt R.A. (1993). **Motor Performance and Learning.** Champaign, IL: Human Kinetics.

Sève C. (2000). **Le Tennis de Table – Entraînement et Compétition** [Table Tennis – Training and Competition]. Aubenas: France Tennis de Table.

Sklorz M., Michaelis R. et Fédération Française de Tennis Table (1996). **Tennis de Table** [Table Tennis]. Paris: Hachette

# 19 The technique used to receive a rotating ball in table tennis

K. Yoshida, K. Sugiyama and S. Murakoshi
*Department of School Education, Faculty of Education, Shizuoka University, 836, Ohya, Shizuoka, 422-8529, Japan.*

## 1 Introduction

The flick stroke in table tennis is a returning technique with which a player returns a rotating ball quickly after the ball bounces on the court. Many coaches and players claim that it is one of the more important table tennis skills.

The dynamics of the flick stroke have been studied by several researchers (Yoshida et al., 1997; Kasai et al., 1999), but there have been very few kinesiological studies of the flick stroke. As a result, the muscular mechanism that enables the intended motions is not well understood.

In this work, the motion of joints and muscular activities of the upper limb were measured in one subject for forehand flick strokes. Returning techniques coping with service balls with different rotations were also examined.

## 2 Methods

Five university students and a coach participated in the present study. One was an elite player; a finalist of the All American Open U-22 (1999) and a member of the Japanese national team of the 2001 Universiade (participant A in this paper). The other four were members of a table tennis team but were average players (participants B, C, D and E). All participants used a shake-hand grip. Table 1 shows the characteristics of the participants.

Table 1. Characteristics of participants

| Subject | Age | Racket Arm | Rubber | Number of competitive years |
|---------|-----|------------|--------|------------------------------|
| A | 22 | right | reversed pimpled | 14 |
| B | 21 | right | reversed pimpled | 11 |
| C | 20 | right | reversed pimpled | 10 |
| D | 19 | right | reversed pimpled | 9 |
| E | 19 | right | reversed pimpled | 6 |

In the test, the coach acting as a server, sent a service ball and participants returned it with a forehand flick stroke. The service balls were controlled to touch a circle of radius 20 cm on the right half court of receiver, whose center was 50 cm from the end line and 40 cm from the side line. The service ball speed was approximately 4 m.s$^{-1}$. The receiver was required to return the ball in a 25 cm radius circle on the right half court of server, whose center was 95 cm from the net and 30 cm from the side line. Two cases, with and without back-spin, were examined. There was little variability in service ball speed and spin. The receiver was informed of whether the service ball had spin or not before the server hit. The tests were repeated for each case until the receiver succeeded in returning the ball more than 5 times as was required. In practice, about 10 trials were necessary for each case.

Concerning muscular activities in participant A, measurements were made for the following muscles: extensor carpi ulnaris, extensor digitorum communis, extensor pollicis longus and extensor pollicis brevis, flexor carpi radialis, pronator teres, biceps brachii, triceps lateral head. Muscular electric discharge was measured by a surface dipole dielectric method. After treatment to reduce skin resistance, miniature bio-electrodes of 12 mm diameter (NT-611U: Nihonkoden, Tokyo, Japan) were set at 20mm centers along the line of muscles following Zipp (1982).

Angles of the elbow joint and wrist joint were measured by goniometers (M110, M180: Penny and Giles, Gwent, UK). Flexion and extension as well as the rotation of joints were measured.

Acceleration sensors (AS-100HA: Kyowa Electronic Instruments, Tokyo, Japan) were installed on the table and racket to record the moment of bouncing.

Using a data analyzing system (MP100WS: Biopac Systems, California, USA) and PC (iMac: Apple Computer, California, USA), all the analog signals were sampled at a sampling frequency 1 kHz and converted to digital data for further processing.

Furthermore, the participant's motions in the test were recorded by a digital video camera (DCR-TRV10: Sony, Tokyo, Japan). EMG electrodes and the goniometers set on the racket arm are shown in Figure 1.

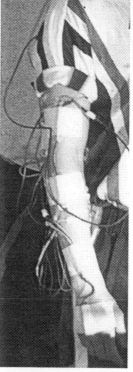

Figure 1. Setting of EMG and goniometer

## 3 Results and discussion

### 3.1 Timing of forehand flick stroke

Table 2 shows the time length between the moment when the ball bounces on the receiver's court and the moment when the receiver hits the ball. It is found from the table that the time length is about 0.2 s for all participants, regardless of the conditions of ball rotation and player quality. This time length was shorter than the values for elite players, 0.22 to 0.26 s, reported by Yoshida (1999). There is the possibility that this difference in the time length was caused by the difference in service speeds in experiments.

Table 2. Time (s) between the moment of ball bounce on the receiver's court and hitting the ball by forehand flick stroke

| Participant | Back-spin services | | No-spin services | |
|---|---|---|---|---|
| | N | Mean ± s | N | Mean ± s |
| A | 8 | 0.192 ± 0.013 | 7 | 0.185 ± 0.006 |
| B | 5 | 0.175 ± 0.011 | 5 | 0.185 ± 0.003 |
| C | 5 | 0.174 ± 0.022 | 6 | 0.181 ± 0.030 |
| D | 5 | 0.200 ± 0.009 | 6 | 0.212 ± 0.008 |
| E | 5 | 0.189 ± 0.006 | 5 | 0.191 ± 0.017 |

N: Number of the trials, s: Standard deviation

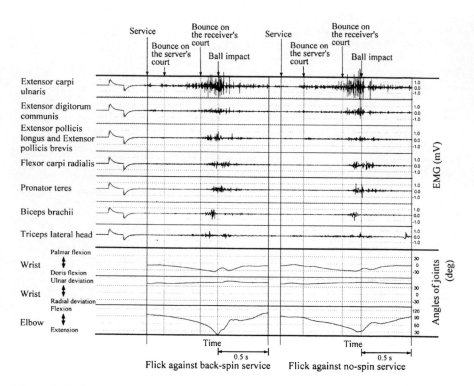

Figure 2. Variation of muscular discharge and angles of joints during forehand flick strokes (Participant A).

### 3.2 Motion of upper limb and patterns of electric discharge of muscles

Figure 2 shows the variation with time of muscular discharge and angles of joints. These results were obtained from the test on Participant A. Figure 2 is divided into two parts. The left hand side corresponds to the case of back-spin services and the right hand side to the case of no-spin services. In the present data arrangement, signal noise was removed by setting a threshold value, $20\mu V$, against the electric data.

The order of muscular electric discharge wasf extensor carpi ulnaris, extensor digitorum communis, extensor pollicis longus and extensor pollicis brevis, biceps brachii, flexor carpi radialis, pronator teres, triceps lateral head. This order was the same for both cases of back-spin and no-spin.

Figure 3 shows the time length between the starting time of muscular discharge and the moment when the receiver hits the ball.

No significant difference was observed between the two cases of back-spin and no-spin. This indicates that the muscular activities of the upper limb for Participant A were similar in the two cases. Muscular activities of the upper limb for the other four participants were different in the two cases, respectively.

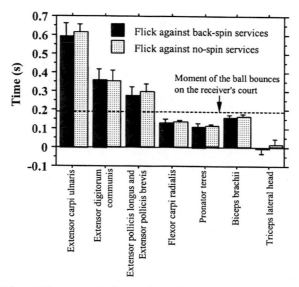

Figure 3. Time (s) between the beginning of muscular discharge and when the ball is hit during forehand flick strokes (Participant A). Values are mean $\pm$ s.

## 4 Conclusions

From the results and discussion above, there were no substantial differences in timing and muscular activation sequence during the forehand flick stroke for Participant A for the service ball with or without back-spin.

Nevertheless, as we watched the video record of the forehand flick stroke for Participant A, it was clear that the direction of the racket surface and the swing differed between the two cases of back-spin and no-spin.

Future studies are needed to investigate the muscular function of elite players in more detail in these two cases.

## 5 Acknowledgement

A part of this work was supported by a Grand-in-Aid for Scientific Research (C) (12680023) from the Japanese Ministry of Education, Culture, Sports, Science and Technology.

## 6 References

Kasai, J., Iino, Y. and Kojima, T. (1999) Three-dimensional analysis of a backhand flick stroke in table tennis. **Japanese Physical Fitness Society Sports Medical Sciences Annual Report NO.II   Research of Developing to Athlete Ability on Events**, 22, 171-173.

Yoshida, K., Murakoshi, S., Sugiyama, K., Kawai, M. and Minemura, S. (1997) Three-dimensional analysis of a forehand flick stroke in table tennis. **Biomechanics of Human Movement**, The 13th Japanese Society of Biomechanics Conference, 318-323.

Yoshida, K., Iimoto, Y., Hiruta, S., Ando, S., Takeuchi, T. and Yuza, N. (1999) Time analysis of In-table skills in table tennis. **Japanese Physical Fitness Society Sports Medical Sciences Annual Report NO.II Research of Developing to Athlete Ability on Events**, 22, 174-175.

Zipp, P. (1982) Recommendations for the standardization of lead positions in surface electromyography. **European Journal of Applied Physiology**, 50, 41-54.

# 20 Myoelectric and neuromuscular features of table tennis forehand stroke performance executed with balls of different sizes

M. Kondrič*, G. Furjan-Mandić** and V. Medved**
*Faculty of Sport, University of Ljubljana, Slovenia. **Faculty of Kinesiology, University of Zagreb, Croatia.

## 1 Introduction

Modern table tennis is a sports game that demands great speed, strength, power, endurance, flexibility, agility and good reflexes. The majority of top-level players prefer to concentrate on attacking or counter-attacking. Most international competitors favour the forehand spin stroke to produce high velocity and high rotation. However, the stroke angle used has changed since the circumference of the ball has been enlarged. The shoulder girdle muscles are today exposed to different loads than before because shoulder abduction should now be performed more quickly.

Physical conditioning and strength training, as well as modern physical fitness diagnostic procedures are becoming ever more important in the contemporary sports training process, including table tennis. In the course of table tennis history, systematic programmed training has become more important after attack strokes have been introduced. Numerous injuries to the shoulder girdle muscles compel us to investigate strains to which individual muscles are prone in the execution of certain table tennis strokes.

Sports preparation is aimed at improving efficacy of the various physiological systems of the body (cardio-vascular, respiratory, musculo-skeletal, etc.) in order to make them able to function efficiently at the higher levels required in competition. The primary goal of the best training system is the maximal performance in the shortest time with the least effort (Kondrič and Furjan-Mandić, 2002).

Grein (1953) developed a system of table tennis in which the training process was divided into six areas: physical, technical, tactical and theoretical preparation, then competition and development of athletic psychological profile. He was first to direct the attention of coaches to targeted strength training which focused on table tennis-specific or relevant muscle groups. Through a practical exercise programme he presented guidelines on how to enhance strength of individual muscle groups. The programme was based on functional features of activity of the recruited muscles.

The first functional classification of individual muscles for selected table tennis techniques was presented by Ogimura (1973). A multiple world champion with markedly attacking style, he assigned a great influence primarily to: *m. biceps brachii*, *m. deltoideus*, *m. pectoralis major* and stomach muscles. *M. biceps brachii* is especially important in his opinion because it is responsible for flexion of the arm in performance of quick forehand spin strokes. Performance of basic returns is based, according to him, on good functioning of *m. triceps brachii* and back muscles.

Ogimura's classification is, probably, based on his personal observations and self-observations and considerations, since no data are available on the systematic influence that particular muscles or muscle groups have on performance of strokes.

Trupković (1978) gave instructions on how to influence the performance of table tennis technical elements by strengthening exercises. He recommended precise exercises to be implemented in the preparation and competition period to strengthen certain muscles and muscle groups (e.g. push-ups for development of shoulder and arm muscles). He understands strength training as an execution of exercises the movement patterns of which are similar to the stroke performance techniques, but they are performed with a heavier racket or weights in order to strengthen particular muscles and improve their functioning.

In Kuala Lumpur, where the International Table Tennis Federation announced the replacement of the 38 mm ball with the 40 mm ball, it became evident that, due to the decreased ball speed and rotation, players would have to devote more time to physical preparation if they wanted to perform as well as before. The performance differences between the players in better physical condition and those less prepared became apparent at the World Championship in Osaka 2001. At the first world championship played with the larger ball, the number of strokes per rally increased, meaning that matches lasted longer and became more demanding. Taking into account rigours of a two-week competition, it turned out that physical preparation, and additional strengthening of the shoulder area in particular, would become a crucial factor to sport success.

The aim of our research was to find out if there are differences between top spin strokes with 38 mm and 40 mm ball. The data should facilitate planning of the training process of table tennis players and especially for promising young players.

## 2 Methods

### 2.1 Design
To design an optimal physical preparation for table tennis players, it is essential first to establish exactly which muscles of the shoulder area work harder due to the new ball. Therefore, we measured the magnitude of the difference in electromyographic (EMG) signals between the forehand strokes performed when using the 38 mm and 40 mm balls. The greater turn (as used in the 40 mm-ball strike) should ensure the greater angular velocity of the shoulders, which should also assist in generating higher linear velocities of the arm, forearm and hand segments. We analysed the muscles that are primarily involved in the forehand attack: *m. deltoideus, m. biceps brachii, m. pectoralis major, m. obliquus abdominis* and *m. latissimus dorsi*.

### 2.1 Participants
Intensity, as well as duration of contraction of the above mentioned muscles was measured on a professional table tennis player, a member of the national team. The data were collected and analysed both visually and quantitatively.

### 2.2 Materials
The EMG signal measurement technique used differential mode of detection, with two electrodes, positioned at a standardized distance of 3 cm between them at the midpoint of the measured muscle along the muscular fibres. The "Elite 2002" (BTS Bioengeneering, Milan, Italy) biomechanical system was used for motion data collection and analysis (Figure 1).

Figure 1. Measurement preparation.

## 2.3 Procedure

In the table tennis stroke a three-part pattern is obvious. The preparation phase is a predecessor to the main phase, in which the basic motor problem is solved – the impact of the ball and the racket, and then comes the follow through phase of the stroke performance.

The measurements were conducted during ten forehand spin strokes performed with the balls of two sizes: 38 mm and 40 mm. The participant was filmed as he executed the strokes. To ensure the same condition for all the ten performances (the same approaching ball trajectory), a table tennis machine was used. Electrodes were placed on the right side of the player's body due to his right-handedness.

## 3 Results and discussion

The measured muscles were hypothetically selected for the experiment, but after the visual analysis of the signals, the authors decide not to include data about *m. latissimus dorsi* and *m. obliquus abdominis* in the analysis because of technical errors that had occurred during the experiment. So, the further analysis will focus on the signals from just the first four channels: *m. deltoideus anterior*, *m. deltoideus posterior*, *m. biceps brachii*, and *m. pectoralis major*.

At first it looks as if there are no differences in the intensity of contraction of the observed muscles when striking the 38 mm (Figures 2a, 3a, 4a and 5a) and 40 mm (Figures 2b, 3b, 4b, and 5b) ball. A more thorough analysis of the amplitudes of the EMG signals though, reveals certain differences in the features of contraction in favour of the bigger ball strokes, as expected.

The peak EMG amplitude of the *m. deltoideus anterior* (Figure 2a) reached a value of 2.5 mV, for the 38mm ball stroke, but only for one out of the four registered strokes, whereas for the rest of the three registered strokes the value approximated 2 mV. With the 40mm ball (Figure 2b), nine strokes were registered, and in seven of them the peak EMG amplitude was higher than 2 mV, and in two it exceeded a value of 2.6 mV.

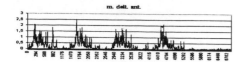

Figure 2a. EMG signal of m. deltoideus anterior with 38 mm ball.

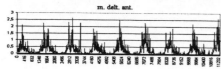

Figure 2b. EMG signal of m. deltoideus anterior with 40 mm ball.

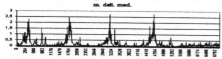

Figure 3a. EMG signal of m. deltoideus medialis with 38 mm ball.

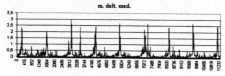

Figure 3b. EMG signal of m. deltoideus medialis with 40 mm ball.

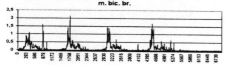

Figure 4a. EMG signal of m. biceps brachii with 38 mm ball.

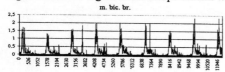

Figure 4b. EMG signal of m. biceps brachii with 40 mm ball.

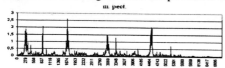

Figure 5a. EMG signal of m. pectoralis major with 38 mm ball.

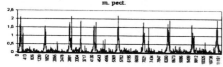

Figure 5b. EMG signal of m. pectoralis major with 40 mm ball.

The comparable contraction values in strokes with the balls of both sizes were obtained with the *m. deltoideus medialis*: the peak values ranged between 2 and 2.7 mV with 38 mm ball and between 2.1 and 3.0 mV with 40 mm ball.(Figure 3a and Figure 3b). However, *m. deltoideus* is not primarily involved in the stroke execution due to the fact that its primary function is upper arm abduction. In a forehand stroke, the upper arm moves from an adduction to a front raise diagonally inwards and so this muscle plays a secondary role.

Greater differences in the contraction intensities are obvious from the data obtained for the other two observed muscles. For the *m. biceps brachii* the peak EMG amplitude ranged from 1 to 2.2 mV (Figure 4a) and from 1.3 to 2.4 mV (Figure 4b) for the 38 mm and 40 mm ball strokes, respectively. The difference is by no means irrelevant when compared to the small differences in diameter between the old and the new ball.

A similar result was obtained for the *m. pectoralis major* contractions. Rather uneven intensities of contractions (Figure 5a) were obtained for the 38 mm ball strokes, ranging from 1.5 to 2.6 mV. More balanced values were obtained for the 40 mm ball strokes ranging from 1.6 to 2.2 mV (Figure 5b).

Another substantial difference existed in all the detected muscle contractions (Figures 2b, 3b, 4b, 5b). The 38 mm ball stroke contraction has only one peak (the maximal contraction), whereas in the 40 mm ball stroke two peaks frequently occurred. This peculiarity could be explained by the additional voluntary contraction (the so called, squeezing). It further means that muscle contraction in the 40 mm ball stroke lasts somewhat longer than in the 38 mm ball stroke.

Although the value of strength in table tennis is no longer an issue of debate, we should be careful not to work on development of massive strength exclusively. Our first concern should be to ensure all-round strengthening of the body and herewith to avoid injuries. When selecting exercises for the strengthening programme, an analysis of movements involved in a particular stroke, in terms of type, speed, direction, etc., should be done in order to be sure which groups of muscles are involved in these movements.

Special exercises should be designed to approximate as closely as possible the pattern and rate of movements of an actual table tennis stroke execution. This will recruit (activate) and train stroke-related groups of muscles thus enhancing their specific neuro-muscular functions needed for a particular performance.

Nevertheless, we must not forget that movement acceleration of a joint involved in a particular stroke will depend on the state of certain muscles which can influence the joint's degree of flexibility. From this point of view, it is obvious that both the ligamentous structures and muscular ability to contract and relax are important. Therefore, it is essential that table tennis players have good flexibility to assist movement and to control a particular stroke performance.

In our research we did not take into account the rubber gluing although it could have affected the measured parameters. Namely, several layers of glue can change the characteristic of rubber and consequently enhance the velocity of the ball.

## 4 Conclusions

The raw EMG data recorded from one player indicate that, there is a minor difference in operation of the studied muscles between forehand attack strike using 38 mm and 40 mm ball. Although there were no large differences in the amplitude of EMG signals, it seems that the player used more muscle activities in a stroke with the larger ball.

The contraction of m. deltoideus medialis seems to be more powerful when the player hits the larger ball. From this point of view more attention should be paid to develop this muscle in the physical preparation of the table tennis player. The qualified table tennis players should, therefore, develop those muscles and muscle groups that are needed for their specific style of play after they have established a broad foundation of physical fitness.

## 5 References

Grein, W. (1953). **Tischtennis** [Table tennis]. Hannover: Deutscher Tischtennis Sport.

Kondrič, M. and Furjan-Mandić, G. (2002). **Telesna priprava namiznoteniškega igralca** [Physical Conditioning of Table Tennis Players]. Ljubljana: Fakulteta za šport.

Ogimura, I. (1973). **Tischtennis** [Table tennis]. Sibeldingen: Joola.

Trupković, J. (1978). **Wege zum Leistungstischtennis** [Ways to the Top Table tennis]. Flensburg.

# Part Five

# Racket Equipment

# 21 Measuring the spin of a ball by digital image analysis

Y. Ushiyama[1], T. Tamaki[2], O. Hashimoto[1] and H. Igarashi[1]

*[1]Faculty of Education and Human Sciences, Niigata University. [2]Faculty of Engineering, Niigata University Ikarashi, Niigata 950-2181, Japan.*

## 1 Introduction

Ball spin is very influential on play in racket sports. In particular the effects of ball spin are important in tennis and table tennis, not only because of the motion in the air but also because of the motion associated with bouncing and hitting is largely affected by ball spin. It is important for players to know the effects of spin on the play quantitatively and so quantitative measurements should be done.

It is not easy to measure the ball spin in play and thus there are very few data of such measurements. It is laborious to obtain such data because an automatic data analysis method is not available for actual play in table tennis. A data analysis system for ball spin has been developed for golf balls. In that system, ball motion is recorded by a video camera and the spin is measured manually by recording marks on the ball.

The present work describes a digital image analysis system based on a high performance PC to measure the spin of flying balls automatically.

## 2 Method

In this work measurements were made for table tennis balls with top-spin. A high-speed digital camera (MotionMeter 500, Redlake, San Diego, USA) shown in Figure 1 was used to take sequential pictures of a ball at 500 Hz with an exposure time of 0.5 ms. A Canon 16-1.9 MACRO lens was used in the experiment.

The experiment was conducted in the gymnasium of Niigata University. Test players were two female students, one was an experienced player while the other was a beginner. Table 1 shows the characteristics of each player.

Figure 1. High-speed digital camera.

Table 1. Players characteristics

|  | Experienced Years | Dominant Hand | Grip & Rubber |
|---|---|---|---|
| Player A | 15 | Right | Pen-hold grip & reversed pimpled rubber |
| Player B | 0.5 | Right | Shake-hand grip & reversed pimpled rubber |

Figure 2. The experimental area.

Figure 3. Test ball with marks.

Figure 2 shows the experimental area. Four halogen lamps were used to light the test area on the side of the player's dominant hand where the camera was also placed. The test ball with top spin was thrown by a feeder. The player returned the ball with top spin.

Figure 3 shows a test ball (40 mm) with marks drawn randomly. The spin was measured from marks in sequential pictures taken by the camera (Figure 4). The camera was not suitable for storing many pictures. Thus, during the experiment, pictures were transferred to an ordinary camcorder. After the experiment, the images were transferred to PC through a video capture device.

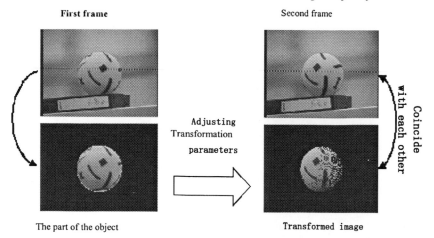

Figure 4. Principle of data analysis

## 3 Analysis on the PC

The principle of image analysis (Shum and Szeliski, 2000; Tamaki and Yamamoto, 2002; Tamaki and Yamamoto, 2003; Tamaki, et al., 2001) is shown in Figure 4. First, only the part of the object is extracted from the picture in the first frame. The other parts are not necessary for analysis. In the present case, the part of the object corresponds to the circle which is the projection of the sphere. Next, a part is extracted from the second picture in the same way as in the first picture. Two parts of both pictures are compared. When the ball spins, positions of marks in both pictures do not coincide. By adjusting transformation parameters, the position of marks can be made to coincide with each other. The spin is estimated from the change in these transformation parameters.

Figure 5 shows the transformation parameters. The center of the circle is taken as the origin. The horizontal axis passing through the origin is defined as the x-axis, where the right direction is positive. The downward vertical axis is defined as the y-axis. The direction normal to both x- and y-axis is defined as the z-axis. In general, the ball has 6 components of velocity: three components of translation and three components of rotation. Therefore, six transformation parameters should be considered to obtain coincidence of the two pictures. These are the rotation angles $\omega_x$, $\omega_y$, $\omega_z$ about the X, Y and Z axes, respectively and the translations $T_x$, $T_y$, $T_z$. The Gauss-Newton method was used to obtain the optimal values of the transformation parameters.

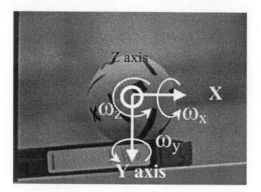

Figure 5. Variables measured.

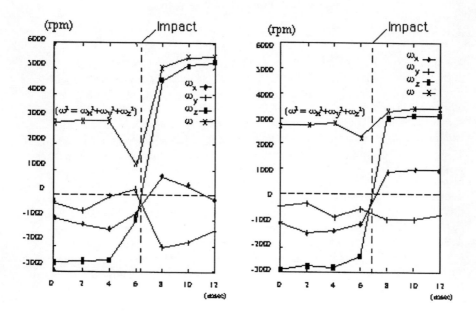

Figure 6. Spin velocity of Player A.          Figure 7. Spin velocity of Player B.

## 4 Results and discussion

Results are shown in Figures 6 and 7 where the spin is plotted against the time. Figure 6 is the experienced player, Player A while Figure 7 is the beginner, Player B. The ordinate represents the spin velocity (rotation) and the abscissa represents the time (ms). The moment of impact can be seen from the vertical line in the figures. The spin velocities before impact are nearly the same because the velocities before impact were given by the machine. It was found that the spin changed drastically around the Z-axis. The sign of spin around the Z-axis changed from a minus value (before impact) to a plus value (after impact). The spin velocities after impact are quite different in each figure. The absolute value of spin velocity of Player A changed from 2800 rpm to about 5500 rpm while the one of Player B changed from 2800 rpm to about 3300 rpm. This means that the top spin by the experienced player is much stronger than that by the beginner.

## 5 Concluding remarks

A system for digital image analysis has been developed to measure the ball spin in actual play. It is confirmed that reasonable results are obtained by this system. The spin velocity is expected to reach 8000 rpm in the case of elite players. To measure such high spin velocities, the speed of the present camera is not enough but another faster high-speed camera is needed.

## 6 References

Shum, H.-Y. and Szeliski, R. (2000). Systems and experiment paper: Construction of panoramic image mosaics with global and local alignment. **International Journal of Computer Vision**, 36, 101-130.

Tamaki, T. and Yamamoto, M. (2002). Camera Calibration Method by Image Registration. **Proceedings of the Forum on Information Technology**, 3, 11-12, (in Japanese).

Tamaki, T. and Yamamoto, M. (2003). Calibration Method by Image Registration with Synthetic Image of 3D Model, **IEICE Transactions on Information and Systems**, E86-D, No. 5, 981-985.

Tamaki, T., Yamamura, T. and Ohnishi, N. (2001). A Method for Compensation of Image Distortion with Image Registration Technique, **IEICE Transactions on Information and Systems**, E84-D, No. 8, 990-998.

# 22 Impact prediction between a ball and racket in table tennis

## Y. Kawazoe[1] and D. Suzuki[2]

[1]*Department of Mechanical Engineering, Saitama Institute of Technology 1690, Okabe, Saitama, 369-0293, Japan.* [2]*Hitachi Kodaira Semicon Ltd., Tokyo, Japan.*

## 1 Introduction

Currently, very specific designs for racket sport equipment are targeted to match the physical and technical levels of each player. However, the ball/racket impact is an instantaneous phenomenon, complicated by the involvement of a human. Many unknown factors are involved in the mechanisms that explain how the specifications and physical properties of the racket and the ball influence the racket capabilities (Kawazoe et al. 1998, 2000, 2002a,b).

This paper investigates the physical properties of the table tennis racket and ball, and predicts the impact force, the contact time, the deformation of ball and rubber, the coefficient of restitution and the racket rebound power associated with the frontal impact when the impact velocity and the impact location on the racket face are given. It is based on the experimental identification of the dynamic characteristics of the ball-racket-arm system and an approximate nonlinear impact analysis. Also considered are the vibrations at the grip portion of the racket handle. The diameter of the ball is 38 mm. The comparison of the 40 mm ball with the 38 mm ball is reported in a separate paper.

## 2 Main factors associated with frontal impact between ball and racket in table tennis

Figure 1 shows the test for obtaining the applied force-deformation curves schematically, where the ball was deformed between two flat surfaces as shown in (a) and the ball plus rubbers were deformed with a racket head clamped as shown in (b). Figure 2 shows the results of the force-deformation tests (38 mm ball, 2.5 g).

By assuming that a ball deforms only at the side in contact with the rubbers, we could obtain the curves of restoring force vs. ball deformation $X_B$, restoring force vs. rubber deformation $X_R$, and the restoring force vs. deformation $X_{RB}$ of the composed ball/rubber system from the results of deformation tests. These restoring characteristics are determined in order to satisfy a number of experimental data using the least squares method. The curve of the corresponding stiffness is derived by differentiation of the equations of restoring force with respect to deformation. The stiffness $K_{RB}$ of a composed ball/rubbers system exhibits strong non-linearity.

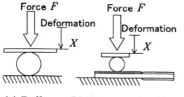
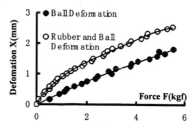

(a) Ball        (b) Composed rubber &
                     ball system

Figure 1. Illustrated applied force -
Deformation test.

Figure 2. Force-deformation of 38 mm
ball (1 kgf = 9.8 N).

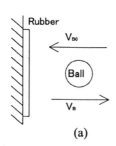

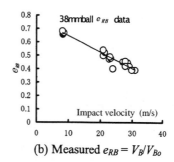

(a)                              (b) Measured $e_{RB} = V_B/V_{Bo}$

Figure 3. Coefficient of restitution between a ball and the clamped rubber (38 mm ball).

Figure 3 shows the coefficient of restitution $e_{RB} = V_B/V_{Bo}$ versus the incident velocity $V_{Bo}$ when a ball strikes the clamped rubbers used for estimating energy loss.

The reduced mass $M_r$ of a racket at the impact location on the racket face can be derived from the principle of the conservation of angular momentum if the moment of inertia and the distance between an impact location and a center of gravity are given. Figure 4 shows the single degree of freedom model of impact between a racket and a ball by introducing a reduced mass $M_r$ of a racket, where $m$ is the mass of a ball. Figure 5 shows the impact locations and the center of gravity of the tested racket made by Tamasu Co. Ltd. The mass of the racket (BISIDE) is 171 g including 79.5 g of two sheets rubbers (SRIVER). Figure 6 shows the comparison of the reduced mass at the locations along the longitudinal center line on the racket face between the freely-suspended racket and the handled racket (Kawazoe 2000a). The player's arm gives a remarkable effect on the reduced mass of racket.

## 3 Derivation of the impact force, contact time, coefficient of restitution and vibration

If we neglect the vibration of the racket frame as a first approximation, the momentum equation and the measured coefficient $e_{RB}$ give the approximate post-impact velocity $V_B$ of a ball and $V_R$ of a racket at the impact location. The impulse $\int F(t)dt$ could be described. Assuming the contact time $T_c$ to be half the natural period of a whole system composed of $m$, $K_{RB}$ and $M_r$, can be obtained according to vibration theory.

In order to make the analysis simpler, the approximate equivalent force $F_{mean}$ can be introduced during contact time $T_c$. Thus, the relationship between $F_{mean}$ and corresponding $K_{RB}$ against the pre-impact velocity $(V_{BO} - V_{Ro})$ is given by

$$F_{mean} = (V_{BO} - V_{Ro})(1 + e_{RB}) \, m_B^{1/2} \, K_{RB}^{1/2} \, / \, \pi (1 + m_B/M_r)^{1/2} \qquad (1)$$

On the other hand, the measured force curve can be expressed as the function of $K_{RB}$

$$F = f(K_{RB}) \qquad (2)$$

From equations (1) and (2), $K_{RB}$ and $F_{mean}$ against the pre-impact velocity can be obtained, accordingly $T_C$ can also be calculated against the pre-impact velocity. The force-time curve of impact is approximated as a half-sine pulse $F(t) = F_{max} \sin(\pi t/T_c)$ $(0 \le t \le T_c)$, where $F_{max} = \pi F_{mean}/2$. The Fourier spectrum of half-sine pulse is represented as $S(f)$ where $f$ is the frequency (Kawazoe 1992a).

The vibration characteristics of a racket can be identified using experimental modal analysis (Kawazoe 1989, 1992a, 1993, 1994, 1997) and the racket vibrations can be simulated by applying the impact force-time curve to the hitting portion on the racket face of the identified vibration model of a racket. When the impact force $S_j(f_k)$ is applied to the point $j$ on the racket face, the amplitude $X_{ijk}$ of $k$-th mode component at point $i$ is derived using the residue $r_{ijk}$ of $k$-th mode between arbitrary point $i$ and $j$.

The coefficient of restitution $e_r$ between a ball and a racket can be derived considering the energy loss due to rubber/ball deformation and the racket vibrations during impact. The coefficient of restitution $e_r$ corresponding to the total energy loss $E$ is

$$e_r = (V_R - V_B)/V_{BO} = [1 - 2E(m_B + M_r)/(m_B M_r V_{BO}^2)]^{1/2} \qquad (3)$$

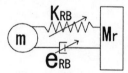

Figure 4. Single degree of freedom model of impact between a racket and a ball by introducing a reduced mass of a racket-arm system.

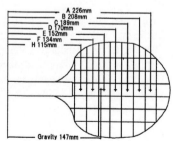

Figure 5. Impact and CG locations on the racket face of the tested racket (1.9 mm sponge).

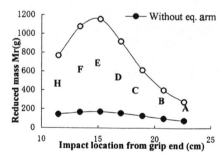

Figure 6. Reduced mass at along the longitudinal centerline on racket face. (eq.=equivalent).

The maximum shock acceleration $A_{grip}$ at the handgrip considering the equivalent mass $M_H$ of the arm can be derived using the distance $a$ between the center of mass of racket-arm system and the impact location of the racket, the distance between the center of mass of racket-arm system and the location of hand grip, the moment of inertia $I_G$ with respect to the center of mass of racket-arm system, the total mass $m_{racket}$ of the racket.

The initial vibration amplitude $A_{gripjk}$ of $k$-th mode acceleration component at the racket handle 50 mm from the grip end with the impact point $j$ is derived using the residue of $k$-th mode (Kawazoe 1989, 1992a, 1993, 1994, 1997).

## 4 Results and discussion

Figures 7-10 show the calculated impact force, contact time, deformation of the ball and deformation of the rubber against impact velocities respectively.

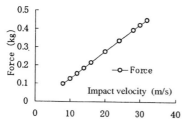

Figure 7. Calculated force vs. impact velocity (1 kgf = 9.8 N).

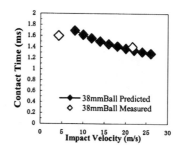

Figure 8. Predicted contact time vs. impact velocity compared to measured.

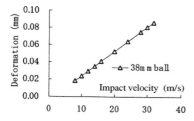

Figure 9. Calculated deformation of the ball vs. impact velocity.

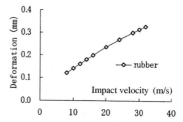

Figure 10. Calculated deformation of the rubber vs. impact velocity.

The ratio $e$ of rebound velocity $V_B$ against the incident velocity $V_{BO}$ of a ball when a ball strikes the standstill racket ($V_{Ro} = 0$) is

$$e = -V_B/V_{BO} = (e_r - m_B/M_r)/(1 + m_B/M_r) \qquad (4)$$

We define this coefficient $e$ the rebound power coefficient. The coefficient $e$ is often used to estimate the rebound power performance of a racket experimentally in the laboratory.

Figure 11 shows the effect of reduced mass on the rebound power coefficient. The player's arm has a remarkable effect on the reduced mass of racket but it does not have an effect on the rebound ball velocity because the mass of a ball is too small compared to the mass of a racket. Figure 12 shows the predicted rebound power coefficient $e$ of a racket when a ball strikes at the location of A (top side of racket face), comparing with racket board vibrations and without. There is no big effect of board vibrations on the rebound power coefficient. Figure 13 shows the predicted rebound power coefficient *e* vs. impact locations of longitudinal centre line on the racket face. Figure 14 shows the predicted rebound ball velocity vs. impact velocities when a ball strikes the location of D (center) and A (top side).

Figure 15 shows the main vibration modes of table tennis racket with rubbers (1st mode and 2nd mode). Figure 16 shows the predicted shock component and initial vibration amplitude component at the racket handle 50 mm from the grip end when a ball hits a racket at various impact locations with a velocity of 20 m.s$^{-1}$. The vibration component is much larger than the shock component at the racket handle.

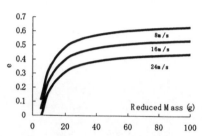

Figure 11. Effect of reduced mass on the rebound power coefficient.

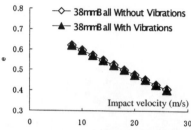

Figure 12. Predicted *e* of a racket when a ball strikes at the location of A (top side).

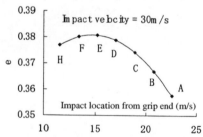

Figure 13. Predicted *e* along the longitudinal centerline.

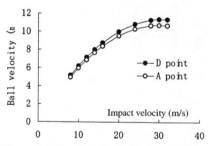

Figure 14. Predicted rebound velocity D(center) and A(top side).

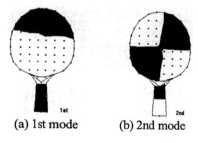

(a) 1st mode    (b) 2nd mode

Figure15. Vibration modes of table tennis racket with rubbers.

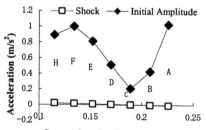

Figure 16. Shock and vibrations at the racket handle 50 mm from grip end with impact velocity 20 m.s$^{-1}$.

Furthermore, the sweet spot, in terms of vibration is easily located. It is possible that players might sense impact location on the racket face through the magnitude of vibrations at the grip portion. This might play an important role in table tennis.


## 5 Conclusions

The racket rebound power decreases remarkably with increasing impact velocity. Although the player's arm has a notable effect on the reduced mass of racket, it does not have an effect on the rebound ball velocity because of the relatively small ball mass.

The vibration component is much larger than the shock component at the racket handle. Furthermore, the sweet spot in terms of vibration is easily located with a possibility that players might sense impact location on the racket face through the magnitude of vibrations at the grip portion and could play an important role for a performance in table tennis.


## 6 References

Kawazoe, Y. (1989). Dynamics and computer aided design of tennis racket. **Proceedings of the International Symposium on Advanced Computers for Dynamics and Design'89** (edited by the Mechanical Dynamics Division of JSME), pp. 243-248.

Kawazoe, Y. (1992a). Impact phenomena between racket and ball during tennis stroke. **Theoretical and Applied Mechanics**, 41, 3-13.

Kawazoe, Y. (1992b). Ball/Racket Impact and Computer Aided Design of Rackets. **International Journal of Table Tennis Sciences**, 1, 9-18.

Kawazoe, Y. (1993). Coefficient of restitution between a ball and a tennis racket. **Theoretical and Applied Mechanics**, 42, 197-208.

Kawazoe, Y. (1994). Computer Aided Prediction of the Vibration and Rebound Velocity Characteristics of Tennis Rackets with Various Physical Properties. **Science and Racket Sports** (edited by T. Reilly, M. Hughes and A. Lees), London: E & FN Spon. pp. 134-139.

Kawazoe, Y. (1997). Experimental Identification of Hand-held Tennis Racket Characteristics and Prediction of Rebound Ball Velocity at Impact. **Theoretical and Applied Mechanics**, 46, 165-176.

Kawazoe, Y., Tomosue, R. and Yoshinari, K. (1998). Performance prediction of tennis rackets with different racket head size: impact shock vibrations of a racket grip and a player's wrist joint. In **The Engineering of Sport** (edited by S.Haake), Blackwell Science, Oxford. pp. 325-332.

Kawazoe, Y. and Yoshinari, K. (2000). Prediction of the Impact Shock Vibrations of the Player's Wrist Joint: Comparison between Two Super Large Sized Rackets with Different Frame Mass Distribution. In **Tennis Science & Technology** (edited by S. Haake and A. Coe), Blackwell Science, Oxford, pp. 91-99.

Kawazoe, Y. and Tanahashi, R. (2002a). Prediction of Various Factors Associated with Tennis Impact: Effects of Large Ball and Strings Tension. In **The Engineering of Sport** 4 (edited by S. Ujihashi and S. Haake) Blackwell Science, Oxford, pp. 176-184.

Kawazoe, Y., Tomosue, R., Muramatsu, T., Yoshinari, K. and Yanagi, H. (2002 b). Experimental Study of the Larger Tennis Ball Effects on the Comfort of the Wrist and the Elbow. In **The Engineering of Sport 4** (edited by S. Ujihashi and S. S.Haake), Blackwell Science, Oxford, pp. 192-199.

# 23 Comparison of the 40 and 38 mm table tennis balls in terms of impact with a racket based on predicted impact phenomena

Y. Kawazoe[1] and D. Suzuki[2]

[1]*Department of Mechanical Engineering, Saitama Institute of Technology 1690, Saitama, 369-0293.* [2]*Hitachi Kodaira Semicon Ltd., Tokyo, Japan.*

## 1 Introduction

Previous papers (Kawazoe, 1992; Kawazoe et al., 2002a,b; 2004) investigated the physical properties of the table tennis racket and the ball, and predicted the impact force, the contact time, the deformation of ball and rubber, the coefficient of restitution, the racket rebound power and the shock vibrations   associated with the frontal impact when the impact velocity and the impact location on the racket face are given. It is based on the experimental identification of the dynamic characteristics of the ball-racket-arm system and an approximate nonlinear impact analysis. Also considered are the shock vibrations at the grip portion of the racket handle. The results showed that the rebound power coefficient decreases remarkably with increasing impact velocity. Although a player's arm has a remarkable effect on the reduced mass of racket, it has almost no effect on the rebound ball velocity because the mass of a ball is too small compared to the mass of a racket itself.

This study compares the new larger 40 mm ball with the 38 mm ball in terms of the impact force, the contact time, the deformation of the ball and rubber, the coefficient of restitution and the rebound power coefficient associated with the impact between the table tennis racket and the ball when the impact velocity and the impact locations on the racket face are given. It is based on the predicted results using the experimentally identified dynamic characteristics of the ball-racket system and the approximate nonlinear impact analysis (Kawazoe, 2002a,b; 2004).

## 2 Nonlinear restoring force characteristics of balls and rubbers

The predicted performance of table tennis racket relating to the rebound power when using a 40 mm ball (2.7 g) is compared to that when using a 38 mm ball (2.5 g). The mass of a racket (BISIDE) is 171 g including 79.5 g of the rubbers (SRIVER). Table 1 shows the physical properties of the table tennis racket used in the study.

Figure 1 shows schematically the compression test for obtaining the applied force-deformation curves, where the ball was deformed between two flat surfaces as shown in (a) and the ball plus rubbers were deformed with a racket head clamped as shown in (b). Figure 2 shows the results of the compression test of balls. Figure 3 is the results of compression test of composed ball/rubbers systems with a 40 mm and a 38 mm ball.

Assuming that a ball deforms only at the side in contact with the rubbers, the curves of restoring force vs. ball deformation, vs. rubbers deformation, and vs. deformation of the composed ball/rubbers system are obtained from the results of applied force- deformation tests.

Figure 4 shows the deformation $X_B$ of a ball against the applied force assuming that a ball deforms only at the side in contact with the rubber. Figure 5 shows the deformations $X_R$ of rubbers for a 40 and 38 mm ball against the applied force. Figure 6 shows the restoring forces vs. deformations of the composed rubber/ball systems with a 40 and 38 mm ball. These restoring characteristics are determined in order to satisfy a number of experimental data using the least squares method.

Table 1. Physical properties of table tennis racket used in the study

| Racket | BISIDE with rubber | BISIDE without rubber |
|---|---|---|
| Face area | 185 cm$^2$ | 185 cm$^2$ |
| Mass | 171g | 91.5g |
| Center of gravity from grip end | 147 mm | 130 mm |
| Moment of inertia $I_{GY}$ about Y axis | 2.51gm$^2$ | 1.10 gm$^2$ |
| Moment of inertia $I_{GX}$ about X axis | 0.26 gm$^2$ | 0.16 gm$^2$ |
| 1st frequency | 253 Hz | 351 Hz |

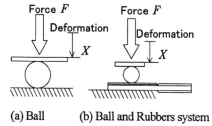

(a) Ball   (b) Ball and Rubbers system

Figure 1. Illustrated applied force - deformation test.

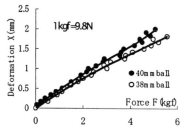

Figure 2. Results of the compression test of balls (1 kgf = 9.8 N).

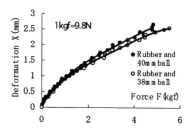

Figure 3. Results of compression test of composed rubbers & ball systems (1 kgf = 9.8 N).

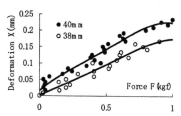

Figure 4. Deformations $X_B$ of ball s against applied force assuming balls deform only at the side in contact with the rubbers (1 kgf = 9.8 N).

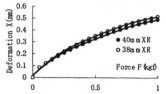

Figure 5. Deformations $X_R$ of rubbers with a 40 mm ball and a 38 mm ball against the applied force.

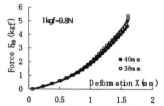

Figure 6. Restoring forces vs. deformations of the composed rubber/ball systems with a 40 and 38 mm ball.

The curves of the corresponding stiffness are derived by differentiation of the equations of restoring force with respect to deformation (Figures 7 and 8).

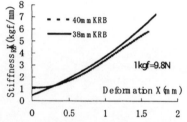

Figure 7. Stiffness vs. deformations of the composed ball/rubber systems with a 40 and 38 mm ball.

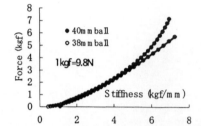

Figure 8. Restoring force vs. stiffness of the composed ball/rubber systems with a 40 and 38 mm ball .

## 3 Energy losses in a collision between a ball and rubbers

Figure 9 shows the illustrated collision test between a ball and clamped rubbers for estimation of energy loss of the ball and the rubbers. Figure 10 shows the measured coefficient of restitution $e_r$ $(= V_B/V_{Bo})$ vs. incident velocity $V_{Bo}$ of the 40 mm ball impacted to the clamped rubbers compared to that of the 38 mm ball. Figure 11 shows the computation of the velocities from recorded high-speed videos for the measurement of coefficient of restitution between ball and clamped rubber.

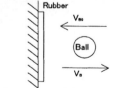

Figure 9. Collision test between ball and clamped rubbers for estimating energy loss.

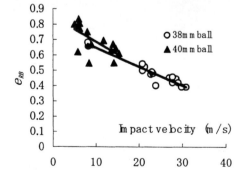

Figure 10. Coefficient of restitution of each ball impacted to the clamped rubbers.

## 4 Analytical results of factors associated with impact between a racket and a ball

According to the previous papers (Kawazoe et al., 2002a,b; 2004), we can predict the contact time $T_c$, the impact force $F(t) = F_{max} \sin(\pi t/T_c)$, $(0 \leq t \leq T_c)$, $F_{mean} = 2F_{max}/\pi$, the deformation $X_B$ of ball and $X_R$ of rubbers, the coefficient of restitution $e_r$, the racket rebound power coefficient $e$ associated with the frontal impact when the impact velocity and location on the racket face are given.

(a) Pre-impact: Initial position

(c) Post-impact: Initial position

(b) Pre-impact: position after 2 ms

(d) Post-impact: position after 2 ms

Figure 11. Computation of the velocities from recorded high-speed videos for the measurement of coefficient of restitution between ball and clamped rubber.

Figure 12. Tested racket BISIDE with rubber SRIVER (1.9 mm sponge).

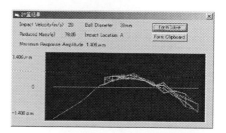

Figure 13. Predicted initial amplitude of table tennis racket vibration component.

Figure 12 shows the tested racket BISIDE with rubber SRIVER (1.9 mm sponge, Tamasu Co. Ltd., Tokyo, Japan). Figure 13 shows the predicted initial amplitude of table tennis racket vibration (1st mode component) when a ball hits a racket at impact location A (top side) with a velocity of 20 m.s$^{-1}$ using the performance prediction system developed in this study. Figure 14 shows the predicted impact force $F_{mean}$ vs. impact velocity when a ball strikes the center of racket face (impact location: D) and is slightly larger for the 40 mm ball.

The predicted contact time with 40 mm ball is shorter below, and longer above 15 m.s$^{-1}$ of impact velocity (Figure 15). The reason for this and that the rebound power coefficient is slightly larger below 20 m.s$^{-1}$ but smaller above 20 m.s$^{-1}$ of impact velocity with the 40 compared to the 38 mm ball is due to the larger stiffness of the composed rubber/ball system. The energy loss of the ball and the rubber during impact is also larger and the deformation of rubbers are larger at the lower impact velocities and smaller at the higher impact velocities with the 40 than with 38 mm ball.

The predicted deformation of the ball when striking the center of racket face is larger in the 40 mm ball (Figure 16) but the deformations of the rubbers are almost the same (Figure 17).

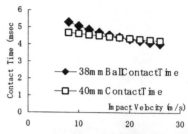

Figure 14. Predicted impact force vs. impact velocity when a ball strikes the center of racket face.

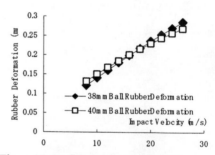

Figure 15. Predicted contact time vs. impact velocity when a ball strikes the center of racket face.

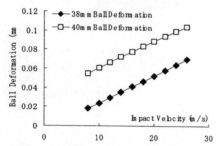

Figure 16. Predicted deformation of the ball vs. impact velocity when a ball strikes the center of racket face.

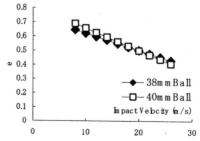

Figure 17. Predicted deformation of the rubber vs. impact velocity when a ball strikes the center of racket face.

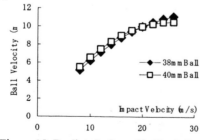

Figure 18. Predicted rebound ball velocity vs. impact velocity when a ball strikes the center on the racket face.

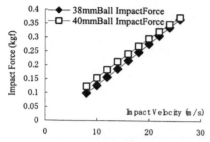

Figure 19. Predicted rebound power coefficient e when a ball strikes the center on the racket face.

Figure 18 shows the predicted rebound ball velocity vs. impact velocity when a ball strikes the center on the racket face. Figure 19 is the predicted rebound power coefficient $e$ when a ball strikes the center on the racket face at the velocity of 30 m.s$^{-1}$. The rebound power coefficient $e$ with 40 mm ball is slightly larger below but smaller above 20 m.s$^{-1}$ of impact velocity.

## 5 Conclusions

The predicted racket performances regarding the rebound power of a 40 mm ball (2.7 g) were compared to those of a 38 mm ball (2.5 g) using a racket with mass of 171 g including 79.5 g of rubbers. With the 40 mm ball compared to the 38 mm ball, the impact force is slightly larger, the contact time is shorter below 15 m.s$^{-1}$ and longer above 15 m.s$^{-1}$ of impact velocity, the deformation of the ball is much larger but that of the rubber is almost the same, and the rebound power coefficient is slightly larger below 20 m.s$^{-1}$ but smaller above 20 m.s$^{-1}$ of impact velocity. Accordingly, the post-impact velocity of the 40 mm ball is slightly faster below 20 m.s$^{-1}$ of impact velocity and slower above 20 m.s$^{-1}$ compared with those of the 38 mm ball. Since the drag force of 40 mm ball is larger than that of 38 mm ball, the velocity of 40 mm ball should be slower.

The reason that the contact time is shorter below 15 m$\cdot$s$^{-1}$ and longer above 15 m.s$^{-1}$ of impact velocity and the rebound power coefficient is slightly larger below 20 m.s$^{-1}$ but smaller above 20 m.s$^{-1}$ of impact velocity with the 40 mm ball than those with 38 mm ball is due to the fact that the stiffness of the composed ball/rubber systems is larger, the energy loss of the ball and the rubber during impact is also larger and the deformation of rubbers are larger at the lower impact velocities and smaller at the higher impact velocities with the 40 than with 38 mm ball.

## 6 Acknowledgments

The authors are grateful to Prof. Masuda of Saitama Institute of Technology and also to the research members at Tamasu Co. Ltd. (Tokyo, Japan). This study was also supported by the High-Tech Research Center of Saitama Institute of Technology.

## 7 References

Kawazoe, Y. (1992). Ball/Racket Impact and Computer Aided Design of Rackets. **International Journal of Table Tennis Sciences**, 1, 9-18.
Kawazoe, Y. and Suzuki, D. (2002a). Mechanism of Restitution Coefficient and Impact Factors between a Ball and a Racket in Table Tennis. In **The Book of the 4th International Conference on the Engineering of Sport** (edited by the Japanese Sports Engineering Association and Japan Society of Mechanical Engineers), pp.58-63.
Kawazoe, Y. and Suzuki, D. (2002b). Prediction of Rebound Velocity of the 40 mm New Ball Compared to the 38 mm Ball Impacted to the Table Tennis Racket. In **The 4th International Conference on the Engineering of Sport** (edited by Japanese Sports Engineering Ass. and Japan Society of Mechanical Engineers), pp. 64-69.
Kawazoe, Y. and Suzuki, D. (2004). Impact prediction between a ball and racket in table tennis. In **Science and Racket Sports III** (edited by A. Lees, J.-F. Kahn and I. Maynard), London: Routledge, in this volume.

# 24 Characterization of table tennis racket sandwich rubbers

Z. Major[1] and R.W. Lang[2]

[1]*Institute of Materials Science and Testing of Plastics, University of Leoben, Franz Josef Strasse 18, A-8700 Leoben, Austria.* [2]*Polymer Competence Center Leoben GmbH, Parkstrasse 11, A-8700 Leoben, Austria.*

## 1 Introduction

In table tennis recently, complex racket designs are used consisting of a wooden or glass or carbon fiber reinforced racket frame with multi-layer rubber/foam covers with special top surface properties. Various rubber compounds and glues (adhesives) are applied in the build up of the multi-layer rubber foam cover to impart greater spin or speed onto the celluloid ball. In terms of material characteristics, important aspects of a successful table tennis racket design are related to the elasticity and damping of the entire sandwich system and the specific surface properties that generate the spin of the celluloid ball upon the impact contact with the rubber surface. Despite the high interest of applying scientific concepts to table tennis, there is currently no widely accepted methodology available to characterize and to determine the performance profile of table tennis rackets as a whole or of individual or combined polymeric material layers in terms of their viscoelastic properties and property functions (Harrison and Gustavsen, 2002). On the other hand, materials science based concepts and criteria are necessary not only to objectively characterize the performance profile of new sandwich rubbers but also to study the change of materials properties over the playing time and to estimate the potential life-time of sandwich rubber sheets. In systematically characterizing table tennis racket materials, various aspects need to be considered. The commonly used subjective ranking parameters (i.e. control, speed, catapult and spin) are a complex combination of two basic material property groups. In general, both bulk and surface properties will play an important role in racket performance. Moreover, the sandwich rubber is highly anisotropic (i.e. properties depend on the loading direction), and the bulk material properties are affected by the behavior of the pimple-in or pimple-out rubber cover sheet and the cellular rubber (sponge). With similar bulk properites of rubber sheets, pimple-in and pimple-out rubbers reveal characteristicly different surface properties. For pimple-in rubbers the friction properties are of special importance, which are a complex product of the adhesion capability and the surface deformation behavior (Chamet et al., 1999).

The objective of this study was the systematic characterization of deformation behavior of table tennis sandwich rubbers consisting of specific rubber cover sheets (pimple-in) and sponge (cellular) rubbers under various loading conditions using polymer science based test methods.

## 2 Methods

### 2.1 Materials and specimens

The experimental work involved various table tennis sandwich rubber types from different producers with different thicknesses. Circular disc shaped specimens with a diameter of 34 mm were cut from new material sheets. Two manufacturers (Butterfly and Donic) and 4 products were selected for detailed investigations. Table 1 include ratings for performance variables of speed, control, spin and catapult (max =100).

Table 1. Characteristics of the commercial sandwich rubbers investigated (Contra, 2002)

| | | Speed | Control | Spin | Catapult |
|---|---|---|---|---|---|
| Product group 1 (Butterfly) | Tackiness, 1.9 mm | 85 | 96 | 96 | 82 |
| | Sriver L, 2mm | 95 | 94 | 94 | 94 |
| | Tackifire Soft, 2.2 mm | 95 | 95 | 97 | 94 |
| | Tackifire Special 2.2 mm | 93 | 96 | 98 | 92 |
| Product group 2 (Donic) | Vario, 2 mm | 96 | 95 | 95 | 94 |
| | Desto F3, 1.8 mm | 97 | 94 | 98 | 96 |
| | (DestoF2) | 98 | 93 | 98 | 97 |
| | Desto F1, 2 mm | 100 | 90 | 98 | 99 |

### 2.2 Test techniques

Monotonic uniaxial compression tests were performed over a wide loading rate range ($0.1$ to $100$ mm.s$^{-1}$) to characterize the bulk deformation behavior of the rubbers (Major, 2002). Cyclic (dynamic) characterization tests were performed under compression over a wide frequency range to determine the frequency dependence of the complex dynamic stiffness, $K^*$, the visco-elastic damping, $tan\delta$, the storage and the loss energy components and the frequency response functions (transmissibility). All of the above tests were performed at room temperature (23 °C) and at 50% relative humidity using a high rate servohydraulic polymer test system (MTS 831.59 Polymer Test System, MTS Systems Corp., MN, USA). During the cyclic experiments under compression loading the frequency was swept from 1 to 200 Hz, the mean load was force controlled having two values and the dynamic amplitude was displacement controlled also having two selected values (one represents smaller another larger deformations).

### 3 Results and discussion

The results of this investigation are discussed in terms of loading rate and frequency dependent material property functions.

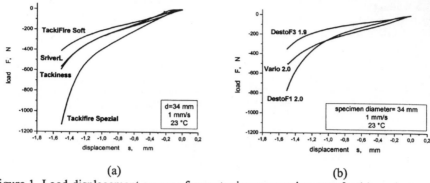

(a)                                                    (b)

Figure 1. Load-displacement curves of monotonic compression tests for (a) product
group 1 and (b) product group 2.

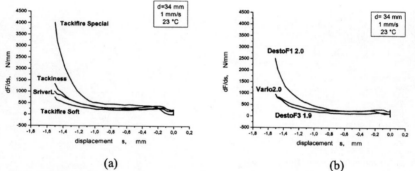

(a)                                                    (b)

Figure 2. Stiffness-displacement curves of monotonic compression tests for (a) product
group 1 and (b) product group 2.

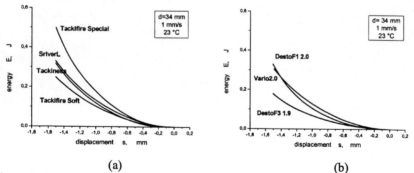

(a)                                                    (b)

Figure 3. Energy-displacement curves of monotonic compression tests for (a) product
group 1 and (b) product group 2.

### 3.1 Monotonic loading

Load-displacement curves of various sandwich rubbers are plotted in Figure 1 at a testing rate of 1 mms$^{-1}$. In general, distinct non-linear deformation behavior and rather moderate loading rate dependences were obtained for all materials investigated. Nevertheless, significant difference between the various products are also observed. Furthermore, to gain more insight into the monotonic deformation behavior of sandwich rubbers the continuous stiffness (dF/ds) and energy (integral of the F-s curves) were calculated in the deformation range up to 1.8 mm. The deformation dependence of the stiffness is plotted in Figure 2, the deformation dependence of the energy values is shown in Figure 3 for both product groups. Significant differences in both the stiffness and in the energy output level as well as in the deformation sensitivity of both quantities are observed.

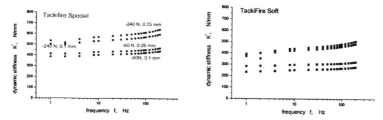

Figure 4. Frequency dependence of the dynamic stiffness for two rubber types selected from product group 1.

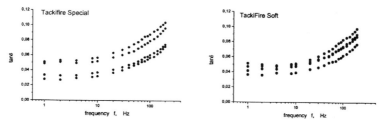

Figure 5. Frequency dependence of tanδ values for two rubber types selected from product group 1.

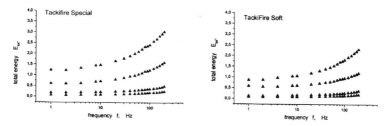

Figure 6. Frequency dependence of the total energy for two rubber types selected from product group 1.

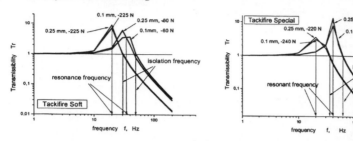

Figure 7. Frequency, mean load and dynamic amplitude dependence of transmissibility
values for two sandwich rubber types selected from product group 1.


## 3.2 Cyclic loading, dynamical characterization

The frequency and load level dependence of the following parameters are depicted in
Figures 4 to 7 and are subsequently discussed.

The stiffness (geometry dependent) is the ratio of change of force to the corresponding
change in deformation of an elastic element. The frequency dependence of the complex
dynamic stiffness is shown in Figure 4. Moderate frequency dependence and more
pronounced mean load and dynamic amplitude dependence were obtained. Tackifire
Special (TF) reveal about 20-25% higher stiffness in the frequency range than Tackifire
Soft (TFS). Moreover, TFS reveal more load dependence than TF. The stiffness of the
sandwich rubber should be correlated to the speed rating.

The **value of _tan δ_** is the tangent function of the phase angle difference between
load/stress and displacement/strain. The value of tanδ is a very important viscoelastic
parameter and proportional to the damping properties of a material. It is interesting to
note, that TF reveal a more pronounced load level dependence than TFS. Significant
frequency dependence of tanδ is observed for both materials (see Figure 5).The tanδ
should be correlated to the control characteristics of the sandwich rubber.

The total energy is stored in a sample per unit volume during a cycle period. Tackifire
Special reveal higher energy values than Tackifire Soft (see Figure 6). The total energy
should also be correlated to the speed and catapult characteristics of a sandwich rubber.

The transmissibility is the non-dimensional ratio of the response amplitude of a system
in steady forced vibration to the exication amplitude. The transmissibility (Tr) is a very
complex parameter to characterize frequency response of damping systems.
Transmissibility curves are shown in graphical form in Figure 7 for the two sandwich
rubber materials tested. The peak represents the resonant frequency of the system. A
higher peak means a lower tanδ value (lower damping) at the same excitation. The
isolation of input vibration begins at a frequency above which Tr is less than 1. The
frequency isolation at high frequencies decreases as the tanδ/damping of the materials
decreases. The actual isolation depends on the type of elastomer, the type and magnitude
of input (strike), the temperature and the amount of damping present. For a table tennis
sandwich rubber the Tr values characterizes the sensitivity of the rubber against various
inputs (strikes) both as an actuator (speed and catapult) as well as a damper (control).

# 4 Conclusions

The results of these characterization methods reveal more significant differences in the bulk mechanical behavior as the commercially used ranking parameters (compare figures and Table 1). The above findings are in good agreement with the subjective feeling of various players. In table tennis the rebound of the ball following an impact on the rubber is highly relevant to the character of the sport. The degree of rebound strongly depends on the value of tanδ. The rate of decay of vibration (related to the function of Tr) or the "magic sound" either "clang" or "bang" type of the racket is also closely related to this value. In addition, the impact force can be optimized (minimized for defensive and maximized for offensive player) by the value of tanδ.

Nevertheless, more detailed investigations are needed to characterize the effect of surface properties (wear, reduction of adhesion) and their relationship with the bulk properties on the overall performance of the sandwich rubbers. Increased attention should be devoted to the fatigue behavior and the influence of temperature and environmental conditions on all of the parameters mentioned above. What is also needed, is a thorough comparison between polymer science based properties and property functions and subjective performance evaluations by top players. In establishing correlations between subjective (player based) and objective (polymer science based) material rankings, a powerful tool may be made available to support future product development efforts.

Furthermore, the material science based methodology proposed can be applied for the ranking and classification of the sandwich rubbers, for ITTF product approval, for manufacturers product development, and for the selection of the optimum rubber for individual players.

# 5 Acknowledgments

Parts of this project were performed at the Polymer Competence Center Leoben GmbH within the K$_{plus}$-programme of the Austrian Ministry of Traffic, Innovation and Technology. The funding within this programme by the Governments of Austria, Styria and Upper Austria is gratefully acknowledged.

# 6 References

Charmet, J.C, Vallet, D., and Barquis, M. (1999). Surface and bulk properties in Adherence of Elastic-Viscoelastic Solids. In **Microstructure and Microtribology of Polymer Surfaces** (Eds. Tsukruk, V. and Wahl, K.J.) ACS Symposium Series 741, Washington, pp. 42-65.

**Contra Tischtennis Katalog** (2002). Contra-Sport GmbH., Henstedt-Ulzburg. Lakes, R.S (1999) **Viscoelastic Solids**, CRC Press, Boca Raton.

Harrison, R. and Gustavsen, O. (2002). The control of the racket coverings, **ITTF Equipment Committee**, Technical Paper, 23/07/2002, Lausanne.

Major, Z. (2002). A Fracture Mechanics Approach to Characterize Rate Dependent Fracture Behavior of Engineering Polymers, **Ph.D. Thesis**, University of Leoben.

**Part Six**

# Match Analysis of Racket Sports

# 25 Match analysis in racket sports

P. O'Donoghue

*School of Applied Medical Sciences and Sports Studies, University of Ulster, Jordanstown, County Antrim, Northern Ireland, BT37 0QB, UK.*

## 1 Introduction

Match analysis is an area of sports science that has matured over recent decades and has taken advantage of technological advances. Match analysis is a term used to describe the analysis of actual sports competition. Match analysis activities range from detailed technical analysis to qualitative analysis of performance. The analysis of competitive performance in sport has been described as being at the centre of sports science rather than at the periphery (Lyons, 1998). There are a number of terms used to describe the analysis of sport and closely related areas. Notational analysis (Downey, 1992) and computerised notational analysis (Hughes, 1995) are methods of analysing dynamic and complex situations which include competition and training in sport as well as having wider applications outside sport. Performance analysis is a term used exclusively for the analysis of performance in sport embracing notational analysis as well as biomechanical analysis (Hughes and Bartlett, 2002). Indeed, Bartlett (2002) has stated that notational analysis and biomechanics should be used within a unified approach to performance analysis. Performance analysis is not restricted to actual competition as the performance of closed skills, such as the tennis service, can be analysed in laboratory situations. Match analysis, on the other hand, is the analysis of performance within sport competition and often involves the application of performance analysis techniques.

The results of match analysis are used by coaches, the media, sports science and sports administrators to gain important match information and to inform decision making within these different fields. In each case, it is necessary to gather, analyse and summarise critical aspects of performance. The success of any match analysis depends to a large extent on the aspects of performance analysed and their validity in terms of association with successful performance. Therefore, match analysis uses a concise abstract view of competition in the form of a "finger print" of relevant performance indicators.

There are two broad types of match analysis activity; practical applied match analysis exercises and theoretical match analysis investigations. Practical applied match analysis exercises are relatively short term analysis tasks of individual matches. Most media and coaching applications of match analysis fall into this category. Theoretical match analysis investigations, on the other hand, are based on data from multiple matches and determine general properties of the nature of the sport. This paper commences with an outline of the performance indicators used in racket sports followed by a discussion of these two types of match analysis activity.

## 2 Performance indicators in racket sports

The use of performance indicators is essential within match analysis to allow the vast amount of match data to be reduced to a more concise manageable representation. Hughes and Bartlett (2002) describe the racket sports as net and wall games that are score dependent rather than time dependent.  Individual racket sports will have unique indicators as a result of different rules relating to the number of serves permitted, the number of bounces permitted and volleying.  However, common factors relating to all net and wall games are identified by Hughes and Bartlett (2002):

1.  Serving.
2.  Shot selection, shot execution and shot distribution.
3.  Winners and errors.
4.  Rally length.

Serving is an important aspect of racket sports, particularly in elite table tennis where there are generally fewer than 5 shots per rally (Drianovski and Otcheva, 2002) as well as in tennis where players are more successful when serving than receiving (Furlong, 1995).  The analysis of serving performance can include mechanical aspects (Drianovski and Otcheva, 2002), technical effectiveness (Croucher, 1998) as well as service strategy (King and Baker, 1979).  Shot selection and distribution has been analysed in table tennis (Drianovski and Otcheva, 2002), tennis (Hughes and Clarke, 1995), badminton (Liddle et al., 1996) and squash (Hughes and Robertson, 1998).  In table tennis, detailed aspects of shots including the application of spin has been analysed (Djokic, 2002).  Other research has concentrated on winners and errors rather than every shot in the rally (O'Donoghue and Liddle, 1998).  Rally times give an indication of the demands of different levels of competition within the different racket sports.  Rally times have been analysed for table tennis (Drianovski and Otcheva, 2002), badminton (Liddle and O'Donoghue, 1998), tennis (Collinson and Hughes, 2002) and squash (Docherty, 1982).  Other factors relevant to racket sports are positional play (Hughes and Clarke, 1995), distance covered (Underwood and McHeath, 1977) and point profiles (O'Donoghue and Liddle, 1998).

A performance indicator is a raw performance measures or synthetic combination of raw performance measures that defines some aspect of performance.  Performance indicators should be based on objective measurement rules and known reliability and validity.  The application of such measurement rules avoids match data being influenced by personal subjective judgement.  The reliability of any variable is the consistency with which it can be measured.  In match analysis, the variables are not properties of players but of performances.  Therefore, reliability studies will often use an intra-observer agreement study of the same performance rather than a test-retest design involving different performances by the subject.  Inter-observer agreement studies are used to establish objectivity, demonstrating whether or not the method is independent of an individual observer.  Therefore, inter- and intra-observer agreement studies have been used within the match analysis of racket sports (Wilson and Barnes, 1998; O'Donoghue and Ingram, 2001).

## 3 Practical match analysis exercises in racket sports

Practical match analysis exercises are used within media and coaching contexts to evaluate individual matches.  This type of match analysis activity is characterised by the need to produce rapid performance information which is used within a retrospective analysis of the match.

## 3.1 Media applications

Visual presentation of performance indicators is becoming increasingly common within newspapers, television coverage and the internet media. IBM provide a match analysis service at Grand Slam tennis tournaments where trained observers operate a tennis-specific keypad and a radar gun measures service speeds. The details provided for each player (or pair of players in doubles) on tournament internet sites includes:

1. The game score within sets as well as points score within any tie-breaks.
2. The total number of service points and the number of first serves that were in.
3. The number of service points won from first serve and second service.
4. The number of aces, double faults, winners (including serve winners) and unforced errors.
5. The number of net points played and the number of those that were won.
6. The number of break points earned and converted.
7. The total number of points won.
8. The speed of the fastest serve, average first serve and average second serve.

Detailed serve data are also provided, illustrating the number of times serves are played to the left, centre and right of the service box when serving to the deuce and advantage service boxes. The television media has used some very sophisticated image processing based systems to track player movements in tennis. This is periodically presented as a court graphic illustrating the areas of the court travelled by the players during rallies.

## 3.2 Coaching applications

The main purpose of match analysis within the coaching context is to provide feedback to players. Franks (1997) has described how match analysis can be used to provide feedback before (feed-forward), during and after competition. Tactical evaluation can provide valuable information regarding forthcoming opponents whereas technical evaluation can identify areas of a player's game that require attention during training. Bartlett (2002) recommends a unified approach incorporating biomechanical and notational analysis. Such an approach could use notational analysis to identify skills where the player needs to improve before more detailed biomechanical analysis can investigate problems with technique during the application of those skills.

Croucher (1998) has described the CompuTennis system which has been used by the USTA to monitor the progress of national tennis teams. The performance parameters entered and analysed using this system include details of key shots played during a rally as well as player locations at the end of the rally. Welsh squash squads have used hand notation of competition to provide feedback to players (Hughes, 1998). Players actually conduct the analysis of their team mates which has the added advantage of increased tactical awareness.

## 4 Theoretical match analysis research in racket sports

### 4.1 Match analysis as a research discipline

Match analysis is a research discipline within sport and exercise science because it can discover general properties of competitive sport rather than merely retrospectively analysing unique characteristics of matches for historical purposes.

O'Donoghue (2001b) undertook a repeated notational analysis investigation of tennis to compare results obtained from data sets from two separate years. This research confirmed that both gender and surface effect findings for 12 out of 13 dependent variables used in the study. Figure 1 shows that the profile of points played in ladies' and men's singles at the four Grand Slam tournaments was very similar between the two data sets despite the fact that totally different matches were analysed. However, O'Donoghue (2001b) stated that findings were only relevant to the era and level of the matches observed and there will always be a need to provide up-to-date performance profiles. Theoretical match analysis research is important for all five purposes of notational analysis described by Hughes (1998) and is covered below.

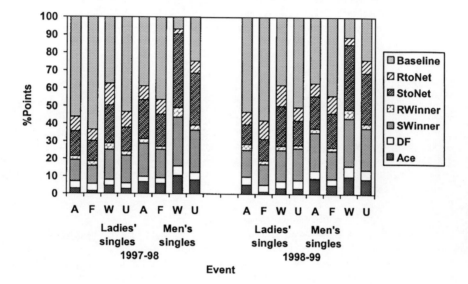

Figure 1. Distribution of point types in tennis discovered by a investigation. (A=Australian Open, F=French Open, W=Wimbledon, U-US Open; R=Return, S=Serve, DF=Double fault).

## 4.2 Technical evaluation

The purpose of analysing technical aspects of play in racket sports is to characterise the quality of play at different levels of competition. This can provide important information to aspiring players and their coaches about the standards needed at elite level. It is also important within matches at given levels to identify the factors that distinguish between the winning and losing players' performances. Such knowledge that is beyond the result of the match is very valuable in identifying critical aspects of the game for players to develop. Further important knowledge can come from comparing players with elite players; for example the comparison of higher and lower ranked players' stroke effectiveness in table tennis (Djokic, 2002).

## 4.3 Tactical evaluation

There is no gold standard measurement of strategy in racket sports but researchers have proposed using positional play (Underwood and McHeath, 1977) and point profiles (O'Donoghue and Liddle, 1998b). Service strategy is an important aspect of table tennis that has been analysed in detail (Drianovski and Otcheva, 2002). In comparing the distribution of serves played by Jinhao Guo (China) and Ryo Yuzawa (Japan), the following details of each serve were recorded and analysed:

1. forehand or backhand serve,
2. direction of the serve (diagonal, straight or reverse diagonal),
3. application of spin (back, top, side or some combination of these), and
4. depth of serve (short or long).

Another indicator of strategy is the proportion of non-service points (excluding aces, double faults, serve winners and serve return winners) where players attack the net. In tennis, court surface has been found to influence strategy with a serve-volley strategy more dominant on fast court surfaces and a baseline strategy more dominant on slow court surfaces (O'Donoghue and Ingram, 2001). Scoreline has also been found to influence the proportion of points where players attack the net in men's singles tennis. Scully and O'Donoghue (1999) found that in men's singles matches where both player had been level, ahead and trailing on service breaks during the match, the eventual loosing player attacked the net significantly less when leading on service breaks than when the score was level on service breaks. This research can be criticised for assuming that all players are effected by scoreline in the same way. Where there may be different types of players with respect to tactical or strategic aspects of the game, cluster analysis can be used to identify the different types of players (O'Donoghue, 2002b). O'Donoghue (2002b) discovered four main clusters of player; two of which were of particular interest. The first of these were players whose strategy was not effected when they were leading on service breaks but who attacked the net more when trailing on service breaks than when level. This indicates a tendency to experiment at the net when trailing on service breaks and needing to find a way of breaking back. This cluster contained a higher than expected number of female players as well as reputed clay court specialists. The other cluster of interest was a set of players who tended to attack the net less when trailing on service breaks but attack the net more when leading on service breaks. This cluster included a higher than expected number of male players, particularly reputed serve-volley players. The strategy of this cluster was not interpreted as being influenced by the score but rather by how the players got to the score.

**4.4 Analysis of movement**
The analysis of movement is important to gain an understanding of the demands of racket sports. Detailed analysis has provided important results concerning player movement within rallies. Richers (1995) has analysed sequences of footstep movements in tennis while Liddle et al. (1996) have estimated that male badminton players cover 18.6 m during a singles rally and 9.5 m during a men's doubles rally. This kind of theoretical research would clearly benefit from some of the image processing based automatic player tracking systems that have been used by the media.

**4.5 Performance modelling**
The ability to successfully produce a predictive model of any sport requires a great deal of knowledge and understanding of the sport. Probabilistic models have been produced to represent serving strategy (Gale, 1971) as well as analyse scoring systems within racket sports (Croucher, 1982). These models use the probability of the server winning a point. The models also assumed that the probability of winning a point was independent of the points score within a game; an assumption since validated by O'Donoghue (2001a). However, the probability of the server winning a point is an outcome measure and further work is needed to produce models in terms

of process indicators.  O'Donoghue (2002a) attempted to use correlation techniques to show the relationship between outcome indicators in tennis and process indicators such as service speed, percentage of points where players approached the net, shot types at the net and shot types at the baseline.  Another recent area of research within match analysis is perturbation analysis.  A rally can be modelled as an open system where a balance is maintained between the players involved in the rally until a perturbation occurs leading the rally to become unstable (McGarry et al., 1999). There are different types of perturbation which may have different impacts on rallies and their analysis can drastically cut down on the amount of match data that needs to be analysed.

### 4.6 Effectiveness of coach and player education
All of the first four purposes of notational analysis identified by Hughes (1998) discussed in the previous four sub-sections can be used within theoretical research investigations that indirectly provide information to coaches and players.  The fifth purpose of notational analysis identified by Hughes (1998) is coach and player education which is used predominantly within practical applied match analysis support for players and coaches.  However, there is still important theoretical research to be undertaken within this area relating to the effectiveness of such support.  Rather than assuming that supporting the coach with feedback based on match analysis will enhance performance, we need evidence to support this theory.  Early work to investigate the effectiveness of different types of feedback in tennis (Brown and Hughes, 1995) and squash (Murray et al., 1998) has provided a valuable insight into the difficulties of conducting such research due to the different training patterns of players and other extraneous variables.  More research is needed into the effectiveness of performance feedback, particularly in table tennis and badminton. Match analysis also has potential within quasi-experimental studies of the effectiveness of conditioning as well as psychological skills training programmes. These have traditionally been tested using fitness tests or skill tests in a controlled manner.  These tests are limited in terms of ecological validity but could be supported by observing player performance in a series of matches before and after the experimental period.


### 5 Conclusions

There are two broad classes of match analysis investigation, each of which include the areas identified by Hughes (1998).  Future directions for theoretical match analysis research include developing performance models that identify the contribution of different process indicators to match outcome. Practical applied match analysis exercises within coaching contexts can then analyse and provide valuable feedback to players in terms of these process indicators.  Analysing perturbations has the potential to improve the efficiency and effectiveness of match analysis. Theoretical research studies should apply cluster analysis where there are different types of players with respect to strategy used.  Match analysis should continue to follow technological advances with the systems used by the media being applied within coaching contexts.

# 6 References

Bartlett, R. (2002). Performance analysis: can bringing together biomechanics and notational analysis benefit coaches? **International Journal of Performance Analysis in Sport (electronic)**, 1, 122-126.

Brown, D. and Hughes, M. (1995). The effectiveness of quantitative and qualitative feedback on performance in squash. In **Science and Racket Sports** (edited by T. Reilly, M. Hughes and A. Lees), London: E & FN Spon, pp. 232-237.

Collinson, L. and Highes, M. (2002). Surface effect on strategy of elite female tennis players. **Proceedings of the 12ᵗʰ Commonwealth International Sport Conference**, Manchester, UK, 19ᵗʰ to 23ʳᵈ July 2002, p. 198.

Croucher, J.S. (1982). The effect of the tennis tie-breaker. **Research Quarterly for Exercise and Sport**, 53, 336-339.

Croucher, J.S. (1998). Developing strategies in tennis. In **Statistics in Sport** (edited by J. Bennett) London: Arnold, pp. 157-171.

Djokic, Z. (2002). Structure of competitors' activities of top table tennis players. In **Table Tennis Sciences 4 and 5** (edited by N. Yuza, S. Hiruta, Y. Iimoto, Y. Shibata, Y. Tsuji, J.R. Harrison, A. Sharara, J.F. Khan, K. Kimura, S.Araki), Lausanne: ITTF, pp. 74-90.

Docherty, D. (1982). A comparison of heart rate response in racket sports. **British Journal of Sports Medicine**, 16, 96-100.

Downey, J. (1992). The use of notational analysis in determining optimal strategies in sport In **Notational Analysis of Sport I and II** (edited by M. Hughes), Cardiff: UWIC, pp. 3-18.

Drianovski, Y. and Otcheva, G. (2002). Survey of the game styles of some of the best Asian players at the 12ᵗʰ World University Table Tennis Championships (Sofia, 1998). In **Table Tennis Sciences 4 and 5** (edited by N. Yuza, S. Hiruta, Y. Iimoto, Y. Shibata, Y. Tsuji, J.R. Harrison, A. Sharara, J.F. Khan, K. Kimura, S. Araki), Lausanne: ITTF, pp. 3-9.

Franks, I.M. (1997). Use of feedback by coaches and players. In **Science and Football III**, (edited by Reilly, T., Bangsbo, J. and Hughes, M.), London: E & FN Spon, pp. 267-278.

Furlong, J.D.G. (1995). The service in lawn tennis: how important is it? In **Science and Racket Sports** (edited by T. Reilly, M. Hughes, and A. Lees), London: E & FN Spon, pp. 266-271.

Gale, D. (1971). Optimal strategy for serving in tennis. **Mathematics Magazine**, 5, 197-9.

Hughes, M. (1995). Computerised Notation of Racket Sports. In **Science and Racket Sports** (edited by T. Reilly, M. Hughes and A. Lees,), London: E & FN Spon, pp. 249-256.

Hughes, M. (1998). The application of notational analysis to racket sports. In **Science and Racket Sports II** (edited by A. Lees, I. Maynard, M. Hughes and T. Reilly), London: E & FN Spon, pp. 211-220.

Hughes, M. and Bartlett, R. (2002). The use of performance indicators in performance analysis. **Journal of Sports Sciences**, 20, 739-754.

Hughes, M. and Clarke, S. (1995). Surface effect on elite tennis strategy. In **Science and Racket Sports** (edited by T. Reilly, M. Hughes and A. Lees), London: E & FN Spon, pp. 272-277.

Hughes, M. and Robertson, C. (1998). Using computerised notational analysis to create a template for elite squash and its subsequent use in designing hand notation systems for player development. In **Science and Racket Sports II** (edited by A. Lees, I. Maynard, M. Hughes and T. Reilly), London: E & FN Spon, pp. 227-234.

King, H.A. and Baker, J.A.W. (1979). Statistical analysis of service and match play strategies in tennis. **Canadian Journal of Applied Sports Science**, 4, 298-301.

Liddle, S.D. and O'Donoghue, P.G. (1998). Notational analysis of rallies in European circuit badminton. In **Science and Racket Sports II** (edited by A. Lees, I. Maynard, M. Hughes and T. Reilly), London: E & FN Spon, pp. 275-281.

Liddle, S.D, Murphy, M.H. and Bleakley, E.W. (1996). A comparison of the physiological demands of singles and doubles badminton: a heart rate and time/motion analysis. **Journal of Human Movement Studies**, 30, 159-176.

Lyons, K. (1998). Origins of notational analysis: Australian roots in sports coach. In **Proceedings of the World Congress of Notational Analysis of Sport IV**, 22nd-25th September 1998, Porto, Portugal, p. 59.

McGarry, T., Khan, M.A. and Franks, I.M. (1999). On the presence and absence of behavioural traits in sport: an example from championship squash match-play. **Journal of Sports Sciences**, 17, 297-311.

Murray, S., Maylor, D. and Hughes, M. (1998). A preliminary investigation into the provision of computerised analysis feedback to elite squash players. In **Science and Racket Sports II** (edited by A. Lees, I. Maynard, M. Hughes and T. Reilly), London: E & FN Spon, pp. 235-240.

O'Donoghue, P.G. (2001a). The most important points in Grand Slam singles tennis. **Research Quarterly for Exercise and Sport**, 72, 125-131.

O'Donoghue, P.G. (2001b). Is notational analysis research? A repeated investigation of tennis strategy. **Proceedings of the World Congress of Performance Analysis, Sports Science and Computers (PASS.COM)**, Cardiff, Wales, 26th to 29th June 2001, pp. 147-152.

O'Donoghue, P.G. (2002a). Performance models of ladies' and men's singles tennis at the Australian Open. **International Journal of Performance Analysis of Sport (e)**, 2, 73-84.

O'Donoghue, P.G. (2002b). The effect of scoreline on elite tennis strategy: a cluster analysis. **Proceedings of the 12th Commonwealth International Sport Conference**, Manchester, UK, 19th to 23rd July 2002, p. 264.

O'Donoghue, P.G. and Ingram, B. (2001). A notational analysis of elite tennis strategy. **Journal of Sports Sciences**, 19, 107-115.

O'Donoghue, P.G. and Liddle, S.D. (1998). A match analysis of elite tennis strategy for ladies' singles on clay and grass surfaces. In **Science and Racket Sports II** (edited by A. Lees, I. Maynard, M. Hughes and T. Reilly), London: E & FN Spon, pp. 247-253.

Richers, T.A. (1995). Time-motion analysis of the energy systems in elite and competitive singles tennis. **Journal of Human Movement Studies**, 28, 73-86.

Scully, D. and O'Donoghue, P.G. (1999). The effect of score line on tennis strategy in grand slam men's singles. **Journal of Sports Sciences**, 17, 64-65.

Underwood, G. and McHeath, J. (1977). Video analysis in tennis coaching. **British Journal of Physical Education**, 8, 136-138.

Wilson, K. and Barnes, C.A. (1998). Reliability and validity of a computer based notational analysis system for competitive table tennis. In **Science and Racket Sports II** (edited by A. Lees, I. Maynard, M. Hughes and T. Reilly), London: E & FN Spon, pp. 265-268.

# 26 Effect of gender and tennis court surface properties upon strategy in elite singles

M. Verlinden, J. Van Ruyskensvelde, B. Van Gorp,
S. De Decker, R. Goossens and J.-P. Clarijs
*Vrije Universiteit Brussel, Brussels, Faculty of Physical Education and Physiotherapy, Belgium.*

## 1 Introduction

Due to opponents' behaviour and own-strategic planning, tennis is a game during which players continuously take decisions about their position on the field and the implication upon their technique or tactical move for that specific location. As many professional tennis players travel thousands of kilometres, and as the four major Grand Slam tournaments are all played on different kinds of court-surfaces (see Table 1, based on Bollettieri; 1986 and O'Donoghue et al., 2000), any information on court properties might be useful during preparation as failure of a player in only one of the Grand Slam tournaments leads to missing the Grand Slam title. Intuitively the divergence of "court properties/type of player" is considered as an important area for study.

Therefore the aim of the study was to apply a reliable notational analysis method in order to determine the effect of gender and tennis court surface-properties upon the chosen strategies in elite singles tennis.

## 2 Method

### 2.1 Design

Since there is not a standard system available containing definitions of tennis specific motor behaviours and tactical components, the definitions used in this study were designed using following procedure:

1. Literature study
2. Identification of existing tennis specific motor behaviours
3. Design of provisional definitions of these existing behaviours
4. Questionnaire and expert rating for designing operational definitions.

The questionnaire had the purpose to test/try out the definitions for their criterion validity. They were sent to all tennis experts who have graduated and are recognised as experts by BLOSO (Commissariat-General for the Stimulation of Physical Development, Sport and Outbound Recreation) between 1995 and 2000 (n=24). The response quota was 33% (n=8). The experts were expected to "fully agree"/ "agree but remarks" / "reject but with adaptation suggestion" the written definitions, hence creating 3 groups (I,II,III) and a level of agreement (see example in Table 2 for selected defined items).

Table 1. Tennis Court properties and tactical behaviour

| Considered Properties | Type of court | Considered Tactics | Ball dynamics |
|---|---|---|---|
| Fast Courts (Wimbledon) | Grass, Concrete, Asphalt | Advantage to attacking player | Low bounce |
| Slow Courts (Roland Garros) | Clay, Artificial grass | Advantage to sliced and lifted balls, Advantage to player playing the least errors | High bounce, Slow after bounce, Unexpected bouncing variations |

Table 2. Example of expert rating (three definitions used as an illustration)

| Defined observational item | Expert 1 | Expert 2 | Expert 3 | Expert 4 | Expert 5 | Expert 6 | Expert 7 | Expert 8 | Freq Group I | Freq Group II | Freq Group III |
|---|---|---|---|---|---|---|---|---|---|---|---|
| Passing shot | I | I | I | II | II | I | I | III | 5 | 2 | 1 |
| Twist Service | I | I | I | II | II | I | I | I | 6 | 2 | 0 |
| Forehand | I | II | II | I | I | II | I | I | 5 | 3 | 0 |
| etc.... | | | | | | | | | ... | ... | ... |
| Agreement for all 77 items | | | | | | | | | 171 | 52 | 8 |

## 2.2 Materials

Computer Assisted Scouting and Match Analysis System-methodology (Dufour, 1993), which uses definitions based on observations and keyboard input, was used for post-match video-analysis. A digital tablet for x,y co-ordinates was used (MM1201 II, Summasketch®) as well as a BBC Concept Keyboard™ for entering codes representing 77 well-defined tennis specific motor behaviours and actions.

## 2.2 Games analysed

This study decided to compare 2 types of tennis court surfaces, namely the clay courts of Roland Garros and the grass courts of Wimbledon (Table 3). Of all 4 Grand Slam tournaments, the clay courts show the highest friction and restitution coefficients. Wimbledon on the other hand contains grass courts with the lowest friction and restitution coefficients. These parameters have a huge impact upon ball dynamics and thus on the tactical implications of the players and thus on their specific motor behaviours. All matches, except for one 1/8th final, were semi-finals and finals.

Table 3. Data analysed for two Grand Slam Tournaments

| | Time Period (hr:min) | Number of players | Number of sets | Number of games | Number of scores | Number of registrations |
|---|---|---|---|---|---|---|
| **Roland Garros 2000 (6 matches)** | | | | | | |
| Ladies | 3:31 | 4 | 5 | 45 | 334 | 5184 |
| Men | 6:06 | 4 | 9 | 75 | 511 | 7330 |
| **Wimbledon 2000 (5 matches)** | | | | | | |
| Ladies | 3:15 | 4 | 6 | 61 | 384 | 5065 |
| Men | 6:44 | 3 | 10 | 110 | 654 | 8154 |
| **Total** | 19:36 | 15 | 30 | 291 | 1883 | 25733 |

## 2.3 Processing of data

Many authors of previous tennis studies considered time factors, details of basic skills (Hughes and Clarke, 1995; O'Donoghue and Ingram, 2001), positioning, distances covered (Underwood and McHeadth, 1977) and score profiles (O'Donoghue and Liddle, 1998b). Taking into account these parameters of the game and based upon the expert rating and a mean observational reliability of the CASMAS Tennis Module of 83% (inter) and 84% (intra), 12 factors describing tennis strategy were considered to compare genders and court surface-properties:

| | |
|---|---|
| 1. the mean number of rallies per score | 2. the percentage forehand strokes |
| 3. the percentage services immediately followed by displacement towards the net/ typical net-attack | 4. the percentage of all observed motor behaviours executed very close to the net (typical net-play behaviour) |
| 5. the percentage of all observed motor behaviours executed from the baseline (baseline play) | 6. the percentage of aces |
| 7. the percentage of double service errors | 8. the percentage of winning services |
| 9. the percentage of winning returns | 10. the percentage of direct scores* won at the net |
| 11. the percentage of direct scores* won from the baseline | 12. the percentage of indirect scores** |

\* = a direct score is the collection of all passing shots and winners - ** = scores made by error of opposite player

To determine the significance of the first factor between different sets, a Mann-Whitney U-test was used. For comparison of the percentages, significance was determined by t-tests.

## 3 Results

For all results only significances are considered as indicated in Table 4.

Table 4. Comparison matrix

| Court surface comparison: Clay vs Grass | Gender comparison: Men vs Ladies |
|---|---|
| For Men's singles | On Clay |
| For Ladies Singles | On Grass |

A. Analyses of the techno-tactical profiles of the athletes:
1. Mean number of ball rallies per score: overall, women produce one more rally than men (P<0.01). Both ladies and men on the clay courts produce more ball changes than at grass courts (P<0.01).
2. Percentage forehand ground strokes: on clay, men produce more forehand ground strokes (as opposed to backhands) than women (P<0.05). On grass the opposite is true (P<0.05). Men produce more forehand ground strokes on the clay courts compared to their performances on grass (P<0.01).
3. Percentage services followed by immediate net-attack: grass conditions show that men more often use this strategy compared to women (P<0.01). Also both women (P<0.05) and men (P<0.01) use this typical net-attack-strategy as opposed to clay conditions.
4. Percentage typical net game behaviour: men play more often this style on grass when compared to women (P<0.01). Also men play more often close to the net on grass when compared to the clay performances (P<0.01).
5. Percentage typical baseline behaviour: complementary to net game behaviour: women play more often this style instead of men.

Table 5. Overview statistics techno-tactical profile

| | Roland Garros: Clay Courts | | Wimbledon: Grass Courts | |
|---|---|---|---|---|
| | Ladies | Men | Ladies | Men |
| 1. Mean number of ball rallies per score | 5.8*/** | 4.5*/** | 3.2*/** | 2.6*/** |
| 2. % Forehand strokes | 49.3*/** | 52.7*/** | 48.7*/** | 41.4*/** |
| 3. % services and net-attack | 1.3** | 3.5** | 4.2*/** | 29.1*/** |
| 4. % net play | 3.5 | 4.1** | 4.5* | 13.7*/** |
| 5. % baseline play | 96.5 | 95.9** | 95.5* | 86.1*/** |

\* = significant between gender - \*\* significant between court surfaces

B. Scoring behaviour:
6. % Aces: Both on grass (P<0.05) and clay (P<0.01) men produce more aces. Also both men (P<0.05) and women (P<0.01) produce more aces in Wimbledon when compared to Roland Garros.
7. % Double errors: no differences were found.

8. % Winning services: both on grass and clay, men produce more winning services than women (P<0.01). Grass conditions produce for both men and women more winning services as opposed to clay conditions (P<0.01).
9. % Winning returns: in Wimbledon men produce more than women (P<0.05).

Table 6. Overview statistics scoring behaviour

|  | Roland Garros: Clay Courts | | Wimbledon: Grass Courts | |
|---|---|---|---|---|
|  | Ladies | Men | Ladies | Men |
| 6. % aces | 1.50*/** | 5.69*/** | 5.21*/** | 9.23*/** |
| 7. % double errors | 4.49 | 3.92 | 7.29 | 5.08 |
| 8. % winning services | 10.82*/** | 26.62*/** | 39.64*/** | 52.28*/** |
| 9. % winning returns | 0.31** | 0.22** | 2.37*/** | 6.06*/** |

\* = significant between gender - ** = significant between court surfaces

C. Efficiency of chosen tactics (based upon number of scores):
10. % Direct scores from net position (passing shots and winners): on grass men produce more direct scores from the net position than women (P<0.01). Men also produce more in Wimbledon when compared to Roland Garros (P<0.01).
11. % Direct scores from baseline (passing shots and winners): no differences.
12. % Indirect scores (= scores made by error of opposite player): on grass men produce less indirect scores than women (P<0.01). Men also produced more errors in Roland Garros as opposed to Wimbledon-games.

Table 7. Overview statistics of efficiency

|  | Roland Garros: Clay Courts | | Wimbledon: Grass Courts | |
|---|---|---|---|---|
|  | Ladies | Men | Ladies | Men |
| 10. % net scores | 11.98*** | 10.98***/** | 9.38*/*** | 22.31*/**/*** |
| 12. % indirect scores | 72.75 | 70.59** | 72.91* | 61.23*/** |

\* = significant between gender   ** = significant between court surfaces
\*** = significant between baseline and net scores

## 4 Discussion and conclusions

The ladies played significantly more rallies on clay court and grass. According to Gunter (1973), ladies build up slower in order to determine the opponent's weakness. Also, only on grass courts, the men play the service-net-attack combination. Furthermore the higher bounce and the restricted speed of the ball on clay diminishes the level of difficulty to hit the ball back to the opponent, thus resulting in longer ball rallies. The combination of that information with the ball rallies statistics might also explain. Gender may not be the only influence upon typical net-play in grass conditions. The type of players (service-volley players) may play a role as well. Due to the larger number of typical net games in Wimbledon more direct scores are found (22.3%). It is clear that both gender and court-properties have an effect on the production of aces. Force might be one explanation, the larger mean height of men as opposed to women could be another one. This combination might explain the use of hard nearly-flat serves, resulting in more aces for men. Men produce more winning services in both court conditions but in Wimbledon they also produce more winning returns. On the other hand, there is no difference between genders nor for court-properties for double errors on service, because on the second serve the efficiency is greater. Although not given in the above description on clay conditions, our data also support the conclusions of Hughes and Clarke (1995) on the Australian open that players do not choose to run around the backhand, but position themselves in a suited location before the opponent hits the ball to automatically play the forehand. The point of view of Davies (1962) that game-properties of women and men will eventually equalize is still not true for the most important tennis games of 2000. Longer games (fatigue) may be the cause of augmented number of forced/unforced errors (Vergauwen, 1998). Clay conditions may provide more time for players to position themselves into a forehand ground stroke strategy. In grass conditions, elite male players show a preference towards net play strategy. A service-dominance strategy is found especially in grass conditions. Contrary to intuition, female players do not show the disadvantage of a smaller body height during service. We can support the conclusions of O'Donoghue and Ingram (2000), that ladies are more efficient at the net than men, but only for clay conditions.

## 6 References

Bollettieri, N. (1986). **Tennis leerplan voor de complete tennisser, Henk Schuurmans,** pp.138-139.

Davies, M. (1962). **Lawn Tennis.** London: Museum Press.

Dufour, W. (1993). Computer-assisted scouting in soccer. In **Science and Football II.** (edited by T. Reilly, J. Clarys and A. Stibbe), London: E & FN Spon, pp. 160-166.

Gunter, N.R. (1973). **Tennis for Women,** London: Agnus & Robertson, pp.11-19.

Jones, C. (1985). **Tennis,** Publiekboek/Baart, Soest/Deurne.

Newcombe, J.A. (1975). **Tennis,** In den Toren.

O'Donoghue, P.G. and Liddle, S.D. (1998a). A Match Analysis of Elite Tennis Strategy for Ladies Singles on Clay and Grass Surfaces. In **Science and Racket Sports II** (edited by A. Lees, I. Maynard, M. Hughes and T. Reilly), London: E & FN Spon, pp. 247-253.

O'Donoghue, P.G. and Liddle, S.D. (1998b). A Notational Analysis of Time Factors of Elite Mens and Ladies SinglesTennis on Clay and Grass Surfaces. In **Science and Racket Sports II** (edited by A. Lees, I. Maynard, M. Hughes and T. Reilly), London: E & FN Spon, pp. 241-247

O'Donoghue, P. and Ingram B. (2001). A notation analysis of elite tennis strategy, **Journal of Sport Sciences,** 19, 107-115.

Schönborn, R. (1983). **Praktisch Tennis Handboek,** Helmond – Helmond.

Underwood, G. and McHeadth J. (1977). Video analysis in tennis coaching, **British Journal of Physical Education,** 8, 136-138.

Vergauwen, L. (1998). Evaluation of stroke performance in tennis, **Medicine and Science in Sports and Exercises,** 30, 1281-1288.

# 27 Comparison of tactical solutions and game patterns in the finals of two grand slam tournaments in tennis

P. Unierzyski and A. Wieczorek
*University School of Physical Education, Tennis Department, Poznan, Poland.*

## 1 Introduction

Aggressive game style dominates modern tennis. Almost all professional players use every opportunity to open the court as soon as possible (usually with a serve or return) and put their opponents into a defensive position. Players who try "just to hit over the net" can hardly compete at a serious level. Despite the similarities between all players it is known that usually different players have won the most important tournaments played on fast (e.g. grass) and slow (e.g. red clay) surfaces.

Wimbledon and Roland Garros are considered as extremely prestigious events not only because of tradition and prize money but also because of their specific demands concerning technical ad tactical skills necessary to reach success on a certain surface. Both events represent two extremes of tennis competitions and, as different tactical and technical abilities are required to win on grass and clay courts, only very few players win both events during the same season in an era of open tennis.

The problem of game style, strategy tactics and game patterns used by players on slow and fast courts has already been analysed by various authors. They described, amongst others, time factors (Hughes and Clarke, 1995; O'Donoghue and Liddle, 1998a; Yoneyama, 1999), proportions of different strokes (Underwood and McHeath, 1977), point profiles (Lisson, 1996), effect of surface (Collinson and Hughes, 2002), patterns of play and movement (Taylor and Hughes, 1998; Hughes and Moore, 1998).

Despite these achievements there are not many publications relating the problem of stroke placement and its influence on result of a rally. In our opinion there is also a need to analyse the technique and the tactics used by players from the point of efficiency and shot precision. Describing which patterns should be used on diverse courts is important not only for better understanding of the game but also in helping the players to adapt their styles to various situations.

The purpose of this study was to describe game patterns used by world's best tennis players during final matches of two most important events played on the slowest (Roland Garros) and the fastest (Wimbledon). Special attention was given to serve and return widely (Bollettieri, 1995; Hedelund and Rasmusen, 1997; Schönborn, 1999; Kleinoder, 2001) considered as the most important shots in a modern game of tennis.

## 2  Materials and methods

Two finals of men's matches of the above-mentioned Grand Slam Tournaments in 2000 were analysed. For the purpose of notational analysis each half of the tennis court was divided into 16 equal rectangles (Figure 1). Four rectangles located in the middle of the court formed the "middle" zone, 12 other rectangles located close to side and base lines formed the external zone. In order to assess serve precision, each service box was divided into 3 zones (internal, middle, external). The placement of each shot was documented in a protocol which allowed an assessment of its precision, and was a basis for further analyses. The matches were compared according to the length of rallies, shot usage (shots proportions) and the placement of winning services and returns. The length of rallies was defined after Królak (1990) as: short (up to 5 shots); regular (6 to 9 shots); long (over 9 shots).

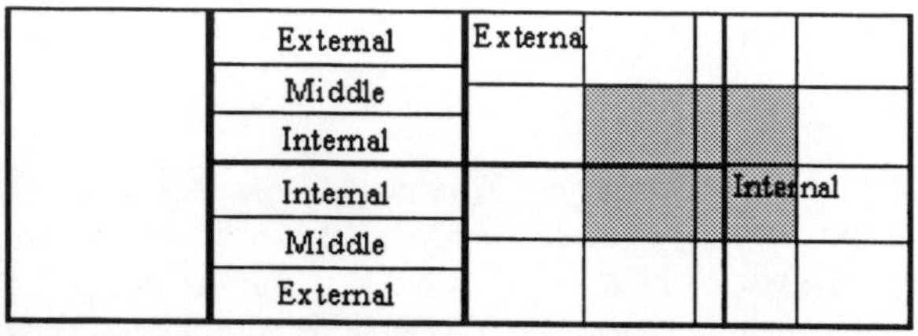

| | External | External | | | |
|---|---|---|---|---|---|
| | Middle | | | | |
| | Internal | | | | |
| | Internal | | | Internal | |
| | Middle | | | | |
| | External | | | | |

Figure 1. Division of tennis court for analysis purposes.

## 3  Results and discussion

The results of the current research (Table 1) show that the length of rallies, proportions between shots (game situations) vary according to the surface. The average number of shots per rally during Roland Garros final was to a large extent lower than during Wimbledon (Figure 2). Also 97% of all rallies at Wimbledon finished within 5 shots and only 3% ended within 9 shots (Figure 3). There were no rallies, which lasted over 10 shots. This suggests that serve and volley tactics were predominantly used during the final match of Wimbledon Championships, so the tactical patterns used by the players were similar to those described by O'Donoghue and Ingram (2001). At Roland Garros there were 61% of short rallies, next 22% lasted 6 to 9 shots and 17% had a long character lasting over 9 shots. These results are in the line with the previous studies.

Proportions between particular strokes also differ according to the surface (Figures 4 and 5). Proportionally, the usage of serves and returns was much higher during the Wimbledon final; in almost 70% of cases the players were in serve-return situations and only in 14% were all shots played from the baseline. The groundstrokes dominated at Roland Garros (65%) compared to 32% of serves and returns. Proportionally, at Wimbledon the players approached the net 6 times more often on (17% of all game situations to only 3% at Roland Garros) compared with Roland Garros final.

On both surfaces servers dominated over returners; but on the slow clay court players were winning proportionally their own service games less often. Servers won twice as many games as returners at Roland Garros but at Wimbledon these proportions were much higher (9/1). This data is similar to that of O'Donoghue and Ingram (2001). The players used different serve tactics depending on the surface.

Generally they served "wide" (into external zones) more often at Roland Garros while at Wimbledon they were serving almost equally into all corners of service boxes (Figure 6). It is interesting that more 2nd serves were placed in the middle zone (Figure 7).

Tactical solutions also varied according to the surface; the statistics show that at Roland Garros returning into the external zone of the court gave only a slightly better chance of winning a rally than returning to the middle of the court. Returning to the middle zone at Wimbledon decreased the chance of winning a rally. The percentage of winning rallies after an aggressive return into the external zone was higher, especially on fast courts (72%).

Table 1. Statistical data on two Grand Slam men's finals in 2000

| SURFACE | | ROLAND GARROS | WIMBLEDON |
|---|---|---|---|
| Strokes per rally | | 6.0 | 2.6 |
| Types of rallies (%) | Short | 60.7 | 96.7 |
| | Regular | 22.1 | 3.3 |
| | Long | 17.2 | 0 |
| Usage of particular strokes (%) | Serve | 17 | 38 |
| | Return | 15 | 31 |
| | On the net | 3 | 17 |
| | Ground strokes | 65 | 14 |
| Rallies (games) won when serving (%) | | 57 (68) | 68 (88) |
| 1st and (2nd) serve placement in winning rallies (%) | Internal zone | 31 (18) | 45 (44) |
| | Middle zone | 16 (49) | 4 (36) |
| | External zone | 53 (33) | 51 (20) |
| Returns' placement in winning rallies (%) | Internal zone | 43 | 28 |
| | External zone | 57 | 72 |

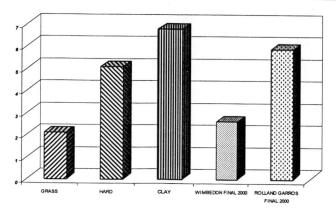

Figure 2. Average length of rallies (measured by number of shots) of Roland Garros and Wimbledon finals in 2000 in comparison with data for grass, hardcourt and clay published by Schönborn (1999).

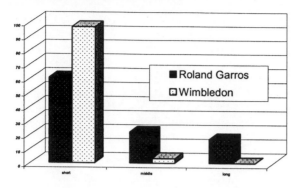

Figure. 3. Proportions between the lengths of rallies in two finals of
Grand Slam tournaments in 2000.

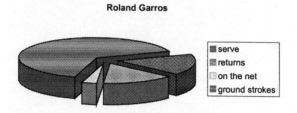

Figure 4. Proportions between particular kinds of strokes during Roland Garros
men's final in 2000.

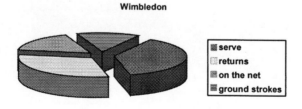

Figure 5. Proportions between particular kinds of strokes during Wimbledon men's
final in 2000.

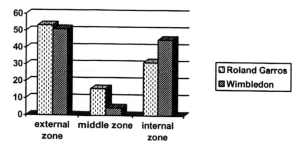

Figure 6. The 1st serve placement (in %) in winning rallies during finals of two Grand Slam tournaments in 2000.

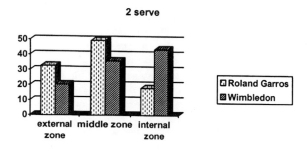

Figure 7. The 2$^{nd}$ serve placement (in %) in winning rallies during finals of two Grand Slam tournaments in 2000.

## 4 Conclusions

The aim of this project was to compare game patterns and tactical solutions used during two finals of Grand Slam tennis tournaments played on diverse surfaces. Generally, the research confirmed major differences between highest-level tennis matches played on fast and slow surfaces. The common belief that different styles and game patterns are used on various surfaces was also confirmed.

Fast courts, where the ball bounces low, benefit players using serve and volley tactics on serve and favour those who hit well-placed returns (close to the side lines). They also show that the placement of serve into the internal zone of the service box and return into the external zone gave a better chance of winning a rally on fast courts. Both strokes are decisive for winning matches on fast courts.

Slow clay courts at Roland Garros favour an aggressive baseline game and players who are able to open the court with a wide serve.

## 5  References

Bollettieri, N. (1995). Return of serve: My opinion. **ITF Coaches Review**, 6, pp. 1-2.

Collinson, L. and Hughes, M. (2002). Surface effect on strategy of elite female tennis players. In **Proceedings of the 12th Commonwealth International Sport Conference, Manchester, 19-23 July 2002**, London, Association of Commonwealth Universities, p. 198.

Hedelund, K.E. and Rasmusen, A. (1997). Serve and Return Tactics. **ITF Sport Science and Coaching Review**, 13, pp. 6-8.

Hughes, M. and Clarke, S. (1995). Surface effect on elite tennis strategy. In **Science and Racket Sports** (edited by T. Reilly, M. Hughes and A. Less), London: E & FN Spon, pp. 272-277.

Hughes, M. and Moore, P. (1998). Movement analysis of elite level male 'serve and volley' tennis players. In **Science and Racket Sports II** (edited by A. Lees, I. Maynard, M. Hughes and T. Reilly). London: E & FN Spon, pp. 254–259

Kleinoder, H. (2001). The return of serve, **ITF Sport Science and Coaching Review**, 24, 5-6.

Królak, A. (1990). **Introduction to modern tennis** (in Polish). Trening nr 2.UKFiS.

Lisson, H. (1996). **Analyse der Spielstruktur unterschiedlicher Leistungsklassen im Tennis-Einzel auf Sand durch systematische Spielerbeobachtung (Analysis of match structures of players of different performance levels in singles tennis)**. Ph. D.Thesis, Deutsche Sporthochschule, Cologne.

O'Donoghue, P. and Liddle, D. (1998a). A notational analysis of time factors of elite men's and ladies' singles tennis on clay and grass surfaces. In **Science and Racket Sports II,** (edited by A. Lees, I. Maynard, M. Hughes and T. Reilly), London: E & FN Spon, pp. 241-246.

O'Donoghue, P. and Liddle, D. (1998b). A match analysis of elite tennis strategy for ladies' singles on clay and grass surfaces. In **Science and Racket Sports II,** (edited by A. Lees, I. Maynard, M. Hughes and T. Reilly), London: Spon, pp. 247-253.

O'Donoghue, P. and Ingram, B. (2001). A Notational Analysis of Elite Tennis Strategy. **Journal of Sport Sciences**, 19, 107-115.

Schönborn, R. (1999). **Advanced techniques for competitive tennis**. Meyer & Meyer. Aachen.

Taylor, M. and Hughes, M. (1998). A comparison of patterns of play between the top under 18 junior tennis players in Britain and in the rest of the world. In **Science and Racket Sports II** (edited by A. Lees, I. Maynard, M. Hughes and T. Reilly), London: E & FN Spon, pp. 260-264.

Underwood, G. and McHeath, J. (1977). Video analysis in tennis coaching. **British Journal of Physical Education**, 8, 136-138.

Yoneyama, F., Watanabe, H. and Oda, Y. (1999). Game analysis of in-play-time and out-of-play-time in The Davis Cup. In **Proceedings of the Fifth IOC World Congress on Sport Sciences**. Sydney, Australia, p. 204.

# 28 The advantage of playing fewer sets than the opponent in the previous two rounds of Grand Slam tennis tournaments

P. O'Donoghue

*School of Applied Medical Sciences and Sports Studies, University of Ulster, Jordanstown, County Antrim, Northern Ireland, BT37 0QB, UK.*

## 1 Introduction

To win a singles event at a Grand Slam tennis tournament, a player must win seven singles matches within two weeks. Because tennis is a score-dependent rather than time-dependent sport, some matches may be longer than others resulting in fatigue and performance decrements. Long tennis matches played in hot environmental conditions can result in cramps and even heat stroke (Therminarias et al., 1995). Tennis can also cause elbow injuries (Renström, 1995) and other injuries that may result in reduced performance or even player withdrawal from tournaments. In Grand Slam tournaments, men's singles matches are the best of five sets whereas ladies' singles matches are the best of three. However, rallies are longer in ladies' singles than in men's singles (O'Donoghue and Ingram, 2001). Players in Grand Slam tournaments who win matches relatively quickly may have an advantage over opponents in subsequent rounds who have required more time on court during their early round matches. The purpose of the current investigation was to compare the performance of the higher and lower ranked player within Grand Slam singles matches where they had played different numbers of sets in the previous two rounds of the tournament.

## 2 Method

The result in sets of each of the 243 completed ladies' and men's singles matches played in the four Grand Slam tournaments in 2002 from the third round to the final were accessed from the tournaments' websites (Australian Open, 2002; French Open, 2002, Wimbledon, 2002; US Open, 2002). Each player within a match was defined as either the higher or lower ranked player based on their 52 week world ranking which was also available from the tournament website. For each of the matches, the difference in the number of sets the higher and lower ranked players played in the previous two rounds was also recorded.

The difference in number of sets played in the previous two rounds by the higher and lower ranked players within a match was cross-tabulated with the result of the match in sets with respect to the higher ranked player. The result in sets is an ordinal variable with a three sets to love victory in men's singles being the best result and a three sets to love defeat being the worst result. Therefore, two Kruskal Wallis H tests were used to compare the results achieved under different conditions based on the relative lengths of the matches in the previous two rounds. One of these tests was for the men's singles and the other was for the ladies' singles matches. Spearman's $\rho$ was used to determine the association between the difference in sets played in the previous two rounds and the set difference between the two players within a match.

## 3  Results

Table 1 shows the outcome of ladies' singles matches for a range of situations arising from the previous two rounds of the tournament. The higher ranked player's performance was significantly influenced by playing more sets than the opponent over the previous two rounds ($H_4 = 12.5$, $P < 0.05$). The mean rank for the higher ranked player's performance decreased as the difference between the player and her opponent for the number of sets played in the previous two rounds increased. There was also a significant negative association between playing more sets in the previous two rounds and set difference in the current match ($\rho = -0.284$, $P < 0.01$) in ladies' singles.

Table 1. Summary of analysis of ladies' matches with respect to higher ranked player

| Result in sets | How many more sets played in previous two matches than opponent | | | | | | | |
|---|---|---|---|---|---|---|---|---|
| | -3 or less | -2 | -1 | 0 | +1 | +2 | +3 or more | Total |
| Lost 0-2 | N/A | 0 | 3 | 5 | 6 | 1 | N/A | 15 |
| Lost 1-2 | N/A | 1 | 2 | 7 | 7 | 1 | N/A | 18 |
| Won 2-1 | N/A | 1 | 5 | 10 | 3 | 0 | N/A | 19 |
| Won 2-0 | N/A | 6 | 21 | 35 | 8 | 1 | N/A | 71 |
| Total | N/A | 8 | 31 | 57 | 24 | 3 | N/A | 123 |
| Mean Rank | N/A | 74.4 | 68.9 | 65.3 | 43.9 | 40.2 | N/A | |

Table 2 shows the proportion of matches won by the higher ranked player in ladies' singles matches at the four different Grand Slam tournaments under the different circumstances of interest. It is clear that the higher ranked player won a minority of matches (12 out of 27) where she had played more sets than the opponent in the previous two rounds. Overall, there was a higher proportion of upsets at the French Open (11 out of 31 matches) than at any of the other tournaments.

Table 2. Proportion of ladies' singles matches won by the higher ranked player

| Result in sets | How many more sets played in previous two matches than opponent | | | | | | | |
|---|---|---|---|---|---|---|---|---|
| | -3 or less | -2 | -1 | 0 | +1 | +2 | +3 or more | Total |
| Australian | N/A | 1/2 | 6/7 | 14/16 | 2/5 | 0/0 | N/A | 23/30 |
| French | N/A | 4/4 | 4/7 | 9/13 | 3/7 | 0/0 | N/A | 20/31 |
| Wimbledon | N/A | 1/1 | 4/4 | 14/17 | 4/8 | 0/1 | N/A | 23/31 |
| US | N/A | 1/1 | 12/13 | 8/11 | 2/4 | 1/2 | N/A | 24/31 |
| Total | N/A | 7/9 | 26/31 | 45/57 | 11/24 | 1/3 | N/A | 90/123 |

Table 3 shows the outcome of men's singles matches for a range of situations arising from the previous two rounds of the tournament. The higher ranked player's performance was not significantly influenced by playing more sets than the opponent over the previous two rounds ($H_6 = 3.6$, $P > 0.05$). Furthermore, there was no significant association between playing more sets in the previous two rounds and set difference in the current match ($\rho = -0.125$, $P > 0.05$) in men's singles.

Table 3. Summary of analysis of men's matches with respect to higher ranked player

| Result | How many more sets played in previous two matches than opponent | | | | | | | |
|---|---|---|---|---|---|---|---|---|
| In sets | -3 or less | -2 | -1 | 0 | +1 | +2 | +3 or more | Total |
| Lost 0-3 | 1 | 3 | 2 | 5 | 2 | 4 | 2 | 19 |
| Lost 1-3 | 2 | 2 | 2 | 3 | 2 | 1 | 1 | 13 |
| Lost 2-3 | 1 | 0 | 2 | 2 | 2 | 0 | 3 | 10 |
| Won 3-2 | 1 | 2 | 1 | 6 | 2 | 4 | 3 | 19 |
| Won 3-1 | 2 | 2 | 7 | 9 | 4 | 4 | 2 | 30 |
| Won 3-0 | 4 | 4 | 5 | 9 | 4 | 1 | 2 | 29 |
| Total | 11 | 13 | 19 | 34 | 16 | 14 | 13 | 120 |
| Mean Rank | 66.2 | 58.7 | 66.6 | 63.5 | 61.3 | 49.0 | 52.3 | |

Table 4 shows the proportion of matches won by the higher ranked player in men's singles matches at the four different Grand Slam tournaments under the different circumstances of interest. Despite a greater proportion of upsets occurring in men's singles than ladies' singles (42/120 against 33/123), the higher ranked player won the majority of matches under each situation in men's singles. There was a greater proportion of upsets at Wimbledon (13 out of 31 matches) than at the other tournaments but only three of these occurred in matches where the higher ranked player had played more sets in the previous two rounds than the lower ranked player.

Table 4. Proportion of men's singles matches won by the higher ranked player

| Result | How many more sets played in previous 2 matches than opponent | | | | | | | |
|---|---|---|---|---|---|---|---|---|
| In sets | -3 or less | -2 | -1 | 0 | +1 | +2 | +3 or more | Total |
| Australian | 2/4 | 1/1 | 2/3 | 6/8 | 3/4 | 3/5 | 3/5 | 20/30 |
| French | ½ | 1/4 | 3/4 | 6/8 | 5/5 | 3/4 | 1/3 | 20/30 |
| Wimbledon | ½ | 4/5 | 4/7 | 6/9 | 2/6 | 0/0 | 1/2 | 18/31 |
| US | 3/3 | 2/3 | 4/5 | 6/9 | 0/1 | 3/5 | 2/3 | 20/29 |
| Total | 7/11 | 8/13 | 13/19 | 24/34 | 10/16 | 9/14 | 7/13 | 78/120 |

## 4 Discussion

The current study provides evidence that requiring three sets to defeat an opponent in ladies' singles events at Grand Slam tournaments can increase the risk of losing subsequent matches. Indeed it is surprising that ladies' singles (where matches are the best of 3 sets) is associated with a detrimental effect of longer preceding matches rather than men's singles (where matches are the best of five sets). One possible explanation is that male players are fitter than female players and possess greater powers of recovery. An alternative explanation is that all completed men's singles matches at Grand Slam tournaments require at least three sets of strenuous effort and, therefore, it is difficult to gain a significant advantage over opponents in subsequent rounds of the tournament. Sets may be longer in men's singles as a greater proportion of sets in men's singles require tie breaks than in ladies' singles (Furlong, 1995). There is also a greater depth of quality in men's singles as indicated by the greater number of upsets. All of the finalists in the ladies' singles in the 2002 Grand Slam tournaments were all ranked in the World's top 4. With the exceptions of the Wimbledon champion (Leyton Hewitt ranked 1) and US Open runner up (Andre

Agassi ranked 6), the other six finalists in the men's singles events were all ranked outside the World's top 10.

The limitations of the current study need to be recognised. The analysis is based only on sets played. This does not necessarily reflect the number of points or total amount of time for a match. Indeed, one first round match at Wimbledon included in the current study required 22 games in the final set (Flavio Saretta's defeat of Thomas Johansson). A further factor that may influence performance in singles events at Grand Slam tournaments is whether or not players have also entered doubles events. Rain delays can cause matches to be played over several days. Although the analysis has distinguished between the higher and lower ranked players within each match, the gap in ability between the players has not been addressed. Within a match, one player may play longer service games than the opponent. This is important as heart rate has been found to be significantly higher during service games than when receiving serve (Reilly and Palmer, 1995).

## 5  Conclusions

The current study reveals that in elite ladies' singles, the outcome of a match is significantly influenced by the number of sets the players played in the previous two rounds. Female players aiming to win Grand Slam tournaments should defeat early round opponents in 2 sets if possible. Future work is recommended to further explore relationships between performances in matches and preceding matches within tournaments using process indicators as well as outcome indicators. Future work should also address relevant factors such as player world rankings, match durations and entry to doubles events.

## 6  References

Australian Open (2002). www.ausopen.org, accessed 28/1/02.

French Open (2002). www.frenchopen.org, accessed 10/6/02.

Furlong, J.D.G. (1995). The service in lawn tennis: how important is it? In **Science and Racket Sports** (Edited by T. Reilly, M. Hughes and A. Lees). London: E & FN Spon, pp. 266-271.

O'Donoghue, P.G. and Ingram, B. (2001). A notational analysis of elite tennis strategy. **Journal of Sports Sciences**, 19, 107-115.

Reilly, T. and Palmer, J. (1995). Investigation of exercise intensity in male singles lawn tennis. In **Science and Racket Sports** (Edited by T. Reilly, M. Hughes and A. Lees). London: E & FN Spon, pp. 10-13.

Renström, P.A.F.H. (1995). Elbow injuries in tennis, In **Science and Racket Sports** (Edited by T. Reilly, M. Hughes and A. Lees). London: E & FN Spon, pp. 155-180.

Therminarias, A., Dansou, P., Chirpaz, M.F., Eterradossi, J. and Favre-Juvin, A. (1995). Cramps, heat stroke and abnormal biological responses during a strenuous tennis match, In **Science and Racket Sports** (Edited by T. Reilly, M. Hughes and A. Lees). London: E & FN Spon, pp. 28-31.

US Open (2002) www.usopen.org, accessed 9/9/02.

Wimbledon (2002) www.wimbledon.org, accessed 8/7/02.

# 29 The impact of speed of service in Grand Slam singles tennis

P. O'Donoghue[1] and A. Ballantyne[2]

[1]*School of Applied Medical Sciences and Sports Studies, University of Ulster, Jordanstown, County Antrim, BT37 0QB, UK.* [2]*The School of Tourism, Leisure, and Sport, Fermanagh College, Enniskillen, Co. Fermanagh, BT74 6AE, UK.*

## 1 Introduction

Service has been recognised as an important part of Grand Slam tennis, especially at Wimbledon; O'Donoghue and Ingram (2001) found that there were more aces and serve winners played at Wimbledon than at any other Grand Slam tournament. Furlong (1995) found that more sets required tie breaks at Wimbledon than at the French Open indicating a greater importance of serve on grass courts. A mathematical model (Gale, 1971) has shown that the probability of the serving player winning a point in tennis, P, is given by $P = p1.q1 + (1 - p1).p2.q2$ where p1 and p2 are the probabilities of the first and second serves being in respectively and q1 and q2 are the conditional probabilities of the point being won given that the first and second serves are in respectively. The model considers serving strategy as a pair of serves to be used as the first and second serve respectively. The model still holds when p1 and p2 retrospectively represent the proportion of first and second serves that were in, and q1 and q2 retrospectively represent the proportion of points won when the first serve and second serve were in. Since Gale produced his model, it has been possible to measure the speed of the player's first serve, V1, and second serve, V2, during matches. This is done on selected courts at Grand Slam tournaments using the IBM radar gun (Wimbledon, 2003). Two specially designed radar sensors are positioned behind the baseline of each end of the court. Once the serving player strikes the ball during service, the radar guns detect its speed almost instantaneously utilising Doppler radar technology. The purpose of the current investigation was to analyse the relationship between service speed and Gale's model.

## 2 Methods

### 2.1 Data gathering and pre-processing
IBM provide a match statistics service at the four Grand Slam tournaments using a computerised data entry and analysis system (Wimbledon, 2003). Data is entered by trained operators using specifically designed tennis keypads. Match statistics for each match played in the 4 Grand Slam tournaments in 2002 were accessed from the tournaments' web sites (Australian Open, 2002; French Open, 2002, Wimbledon, 2002; US Open, 2002). Those 569 singles matches which were completed without player retirement and for which service speed data was provided were analysed; Table 1 summarises the matches. Each match was divided into the serving

performances of the two players involved. A player's service performance within a match comprises the variables of Gale's model, the percentage of aces and double faults served during those points where the player is serving. This meant that 1138 serving performances were analysed and the total number of points analysed in the study was 104,780.

Table 1. Matches used (Aus. = Australian; Fr. = French)

| Event | Aus. Open | Fr. Open | Wimbledon | US Open |
|---|---|---|---|---|
| Ladies'Singles | 83 | 66 | 65 | 68 |
| Men's Singles | 82 | 63 | 69 | 73 |

For each match, the gender of the players, the tournament and the players' world rankings at the time of the match were recorded. For male players, the ATP (Association of Tennis Professionals) 52 week world ranking was used and for female players the WTA (Women's Tennis Association) world ranking was used. The number of aces and double faults served by each player were recorded as percentages of the total number of service points. As well as mean speed of first and second service, elements of Gale's model were computed from the frequency data provided on the tournament web sites as follows:

- $p1$ = number of first serves in / number of service points.
- $q1$ = number of points won when first serve is in / number of first serves in.
- $p2$ = (number of service points - number of first serves in - number of double faults) / (number of service points - number of first serves in).
- $q2$ = number of points won when second serve is in / (number of service points - number of first serves in - number of double faults).
- $P = p1.q1 + (1 - p1).p2.q2$.

## 2.2 Data analysis

The proportion of points won by the serving player on both first and second serve is related to the gap in ability between the serving and receiving player, although there is variability due to many factors. It was decided to address the gap between the players by using the difference between their 52 week world rankings at the time of the match. Because, the serving performance of each player within each match was being considered separately, the difference between players 52 week world rankings was found to be symmetrical ($z_{Skew} = 0.0$). However, the variable was lepokurtic ($z_{Kurt} = +182.7$). When the magnitude of the difference between the two player's world rankings was raised to the power of 0.45, the variable became mesokurtic ($z_{Kurt} = +0.28$) and hence satisfied the assumption of normally. Therefore, the gap between the two players' abilities was represented by: ,

$$\text{Gap} = \pm(\text{absolute difference in players' 52 week world rankings})^{0.45}$$

where the negative value applied when the higher ranked player was serving and the positive value applied when the lower ranked player was serving.

A series of two-way analysis of covariance (ANCOVA) tests was applied to the performance variables including gender and tournament as between match effects and gap as a covariate. Bonferroni adjusted post hoc tests were employed to compare pairs of tournaments where tournament was found to be a significant factor. A series of partial correlations allowed elements of Gale's model to be correlated with service speed controlling for gap between the two players.

## 3 Results

### 3.1 The influence of gender and tournament on serving performance
Figure 1 shows the service speed of first and second serves during men's and ladies' singles matches at all 4 Grand Slam tournaments in 2002. This shows that men served faster than ladies and that, in both men's and ladies' singles, service was fastest at Wimbledon followed by the US Open.

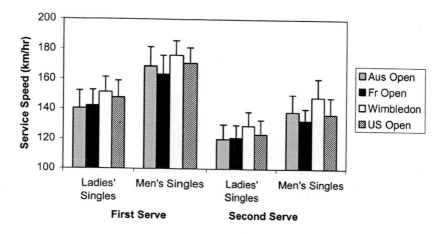

Figure 1. Service speed in singles events at Grand Slam tournaments.

Table 2 summarises the main dependent variables of interest in the 1138 serving performances within the 569 matches. Ladies' got their first serve in more often than their male counterparts but served fewer aces and more double faults than male players. At each tournament, men won a greater proportion of points than ladies when serving on both first and second service. The event with the lowest serving advantages was the ladies' singles at the French Open (54%) and the event with the highest serving advantage was the men's singles at Wimbledon (64%).

Table 2. Serving performance at different tournaments (mean $\pm s$)

| Variable | Ladies' Singles | | | | Men's Singles | | | |
|---|---|---|---|---|---|---|---|---|
| | Aus Open | Fr Open | Wimbledon | US Open | Aus Open | Fr Open | Wimbledon | US Open |
| P | 0.55±0.10 | 0.54±0.10 | 0.58±0.10 | 0.57±0.11 | 0.62±0.08 | 0.61±0.07 | 0.64±0.08 | 0.63±0.08 |
| p1 | 0.63±0.09 | 0.62±0.08 | 0.61±0.07 | 0.60±0.09 | 0.60±0.08 | 0.57±0.07 | 0.58±0.07 | 0.58±0.07 |
| q1 | 0.62±0.11 | 0.60±0.13 | 0.66±0.13 | 0.64±0.13 | 0.71±0.09 | 0.68±0.08 | 0.74±0.09 | 0.71±0.09 |
| p2 | 0.86±0.09 | 0.83±0.09 | 0.86±0.07 | 0.85±0.10 | 0.90±0.05 | 0.91±0.06 | 0.88±0.07 | 0.89±0.06 |
| q2 | 0.52±0.15 | 0.51±0.13 | 0.54±0.12 | 0.53±0.13 | 0.56±0.10 | 0.56±0.09 | 0.56±0.11 | 0.58±0.11 |
| Ace% | 2.3±2.6 | 2.5±3.2 | 4.1±3.9 | 4.1±5.1 | 7.6±5.5 | 4.9±3.9 | 8.5±6.5 | 8.4±5.5 |
| DF% | 5.1±3.6 | 6.1±3.1 | 5.4±3.1 | 6.1±4.3 | 3.9±2.2 | 3.8±2.5 | 5.1±3.0 | 4.8±2.5 |

Table 3 shows the results of the series of two-way ANCOVA tests as well as the results of Bonferonni adjusted post hoc tests to compare individual pairs of tournaments. These tests revealed that gender had a significant influence on each of the dependent variables ($F_{1,1129} > 32.9$, $P < 0.001$). Tournament had no significant influence on p2 or q2 ($F_{3,1129} < 2.3$, $P > 0.05$) but did have a significant influence on all other dependent variables ($F_{3,1129} > 5.4$, $P < 0.001$).

For both the speed of first service (V1) and second service (V2), there was a significant interaction between gender and tournament with slower services at the Australian Open than the French Open in ladies' singles but not in men's singles. Another significant interaction between gender and tournament was for the proportion of second serves that were in (p2). This was greatest at the French Open for men's singles but lowest at the French Open for ladies' singles. There were further interactions between gender and tournament for the percentage of aces and double faults served. In ladies' singles both of these values were lowest at the Australian Open where as they were lowest at the French Open in men's singles.

Table 3. ANCOVA results

| Variable | ANCOVA results | | | Bonferroni post hoc tests (Tournament) | | | | | |
|---|---|---|---|---|---|---|---|---|---|
| | Gender $F_{1,1129}$ | Tournament $F_{3,1129}$ | Gender X Tournament $F_{3,1129}$ | AvF | AvW | AvU | FvW | FvU | WvU |
| V1 | 133.4*** | 52.6*** | 5.5** | | *** | *** | *** | *** | *** |
| V2 | 659.2*** | 69.1*** | 9.1*** | * | *** | | *** | ** | *** |
| P | 182.0*** | 9.1*** | 0.6 | | * | | *** | ** | |
| p1 | 50.0*** | 6.6*** | 1.3 | ** | ** | ** | | | |
| q1 | 186.5*** | 14.7*** | 0.7 | | *** | | *** | *** | |
| p2 | 86.7*** | 1.7 | 8.0*** | | | | | | |
| q2 | 32.9*** | 2.3 | 0.3 | | | | | | |
| Ace% | 219.6*** | 18.6*** | 4.8** | ** | ** | ** | *** | *** | |
| DF% | 48.5*** | 5.4** | 4.8** | | * | ** | | | |

A (Australian Open), F (French Open), W (Wimbledon), U (US Open).
* $P < 0.05$, ** $P < 0.01$, *** $P < 0.001$

## 3.2 The relationship between service speed and service effectiveness

There were negative correlations between service speed and the probability of the serve being in on both first serve ($r = -0.384$, $P < 0.001$) and second serve ($r = -0.058$, $P > 0.05$). There was a positive correlation between service speed and the conditional probability of winning the point given that the serve was in on both first serve ($r = 0.552$, $P < 0.001$) and second serve ($r = 0.237$, $P < 0.001$). Overall the probability of winning a point on serve, P, was positively associated with V1 ($r = 0.472$, $P < 0.001$) and V2 ($r = 0.395$, $P < 0.001$).

Tables 4 and 5 show the partial correlations between service speed and aspects of service performance in ladies' and men's singles at the 4 Grand Slam tournaments for first serve and second serve respectively. In each case, service speed was negatively correlated with the proportion of serves that were in but positively correlated with the proportion of points won when the service was in. Female players had the highest correlations between first serve speed and proportion of points won when the first serve was in. However, male players had the highest correlations between second serve speed and proportion of points won when the second serve was in. The highest correlations between service speed and percentage of aces occurred at the US Open.

Table 4. Partial correlation results between first service speed (V1) and parameters of Gale's model (r)

| Variable | Ladies' Singles | | | | Men's Singles | | | |
|---|---|---|---|---|---|---|---|---|
| | Aus Open | Fr Open | Wimbledon | US Open | Aus Open | Fr Open | Wimbledon | US Open |
| p1 | -0.579*** | -0.376*** | -0.366*** | -0.305*** | -0.379*** | -0.423*** | -0.095 | -0.290*** |
| q1 | +0.383*** | +0.449*** | +0.484*** | +0.581*** | +0.365*** | +0.187* | +0.454*** | +0.446*** |
| P | +0.160* | +0.375*** | +0.365*** | +0.441*** | +0.303*** | -0.042 | +0.308*** | +0.376*** |
| Ace% | +0.462*** | +0.479*** | +0.412*** | +0.466*** | +0.511*** | +0.251** | +0.554*** | +0.618*** |
| DF% | +0.237* | +0.103 | +0.119 | +0.110 | +0.014 | +0.247** | +0.378*** | +0.230** |

* $P < 0.05$, ** $P < 0.01$, *** $P < 0.001$

Table 5. Partial correlation results between second service speed (V2) and parameters of Gale's model (r)

| Variable | Ladies' Singles | | | | Men's Singles | | | |
|---|---|---|---|---|---|---|---|---|
| | Aus Open | Fr Open | Wimbledon | US Open | Aus Open | Fr Open | Wimbledon | US Open |
| p2 | -0.196* | -0.089 | -0.290*** | -0.249** | -0.130 | -0.373*** | -0.537*** | -0.444*** |
| q2 | +0.066 | +0.072 | +0.077 | +0.221* | +0.237** | +0.108 | +0.244** | +0.361*** |
| P | +0.041 | +0.143 | -0.151 | +0.289** | +0.261** | +0.128 | +0.264** | +0.356*** |
| Ace% | +0.160* | +0.254** | +0.225* | +0.315*** | +0.405*** | +0.264** | +0.461*** | +0.492*** |
| DF% | +0.322*** | +0.264** | +0.324*** | +0.311*** | +0.183* | +0.414*** | +0.524*** | +0.421*** |

* $P < 0.05$, ** $P < 0.01$, *** $P < 0.001$

## 4 Discussion

The findings of this study fall into four categories; the influence of gender on service, the influence of tournament on service, aspects of service influenced by the interaction of gender and tournament and the relationship between service speed and Gale's (1971) model. With respect to gender, the current investigation agrees with the findings of Furlong (1995) that serve is of greater importance in men's singles than ladies' singles. On first serve, men serve faster getting a lower percentage of serves in but winning a greater percentage of points when the serve is in. On second serve, men not only serve faster and win more points when the serve is in, but they also get a greater proportion of serves in than ladies. The current study also found that men served significantly more aces than ladies, which agrees with the findings of O'Donoghue and Ingram (2001).

The proportion of points won when serving was significantly influenced by tournament, with serve being most important at Wimbledon followed by the US Open. The fastest first serves, fastest second serves and highest percentages of aces were also served at Wimbledon followed by the US Open. A fast service would be expected to be of most benefit on fast court surfaces where the receiving player has less time to return the service. Indeed, Hughes and Clarke (1995) found that in men's singles at Grand Slam tournaments, players on a grass court surface returned 11% fewer serves than players on synthetic courts. Collinson and Hughes (2002) also found that service was more difficult to return on faster surfaces in ladies' singles events at Grand Slam tournaments.

Gale's (1971) model assumed a negative relationship between p1 and q1 as well as between p2 and q2. This is confirmed by the current study where service speed was found to be negatively correlated with the proportion of serves that were in but positively correlated with the proportion of points won when the serve was in on both first and second serve in all 8 singles events. Although, there were many significant relationships between service speed and elements of Gale's model, the correlations were not strong enough to allow a predictive model incorporating service speed to be developed. There are other important factors that also contribute to the proportion of points won on first and second serve. These include aspects of service strategy such as placement of serve (Croucher, 1998) and types of serve used. Other factors also include player strategy and performance within rallies that are not won or lost on service. Where rallies go beyond 2 shots, players will either attack the net or remain at the baseline. Ability to win points at the net as well as winner to error ratio at the baseline will contribute to the outcome of the match (O'Donoghue and Ingram, 2001; O'Donoghue and Liddle, 1998).

## 5  Conclusions

Gale's model assumed a negative relationship between the probability of a serve being in and the conditional probability of the point being won when the serve is in. In the current study, the proportion of serves that were in has been found to be negatively related to the speed of service on first and second serve in all 8 Grand Slam singles tennis events. Furthermore, the proportion of points won when the serve was in was found to be positively related to the speed of service on first and second serve in all 8 Grand Slam singles events. However, the coefficients of determination ($r^2$) were too small for service speed to be incorporated into Gale's model. This is because the proportion of points depends on many factors as well as service speed.

## 6  References

Australian Open (2002). www.ausopen.org, accessed 28/1/02.

Collinson, L. and Hughes, M. (2002). Surface effect on strategy of elite female tennis players. In **Proceedings of the 12th Commonwealth International Sport Conference** (19th-23rd July 2002, Manchester, UK), p. 198.

Croucher, J.S. (1998). Developing strategies in tennis. In **Statistics in Sport** (edited by J. Bennett), New York: Arnold, pp. 157-171.

French Open (2002). www.frenchopen.org, accessed 10/6/02.

Furlong, J.D.G. (1995). The service in lawn tennis: how important is it? In **Science and Racket Sports** (Edited by T. Reilly, M. Hughes and A. Lees), London: E & FN Spon, pp. 266-271.

Gale, D. (1971). Optimal strategy for serving in tennis. **Mathematics Magazine**, 5, pp. 197-199.

Hughes, M. and Clarke, S. (1995). Surface effect on elite tennis strategy. In **Science and Racket Sports** (Edited by T. Reilly, M. Hughes and A. Lees), London: E & FN Spon, pp. 272-277.

O'Donoghue, P.G. and Ingram, B. (2001). A notational analysis of elite tennis strategy. **Journal of Sports Sciences**, 19, 107-115.

O'Donoghue, P.G. and Liddle, S.D. (1998). A match analysis of elite tennis strategy for ladies' singles on clay and grass surfaces. In **Science and Racket Sports II** (Edited by A. Lees, I. Maynard, M. Hughes and T. Reilly), London: E & FN Spon, pp. 247-253.

US Open (2002). www.usopen.org, accessed 9/9/02.

Wimbledon (2002). www.wimbledon.org, accessed 8/7/02.

Wimbledon (2003). www.wimbledon.org/guide/technology.stm, accessed 5/3/03.

# 30 Functional differences between tennis and badminton in young sportsmen

G. Torres[1], D. Cabello[2] and L. Carrasco[3]
[1]*Faculty of Health and Sport Sciences, University of Zaragoza.*
[2]*Faculty of Education, University of Granada.* [3]*Faculty of Exercise and Sport Sciences, University of Murcia, Spain.*

## 1 Introduction

Both tennis and badminton share similar characteristics with regard to the use of an implement, an objective, a net that separates the opponents, and so on. Both has a similar game structure with different parts (service, attack strokes, defence strokes, net game, and so on).

Tennis and badminton have been studied independently as a consequence of which several similarities have been observed. Different studies have focused on the assessment of the anthropometric profile (Elliott et al., 1989; Fernández del Prado, 1991; Centeno et al., 1999); game structure and execution in different matches (Reilly and Palmer, 1995; Cabello, 2000; Smekal et al., 2001); and heart rate changes during a match (Bergeron et al., 1991; Liddle et al., 1996; Ferrauti et al., 2001; Cabello and González-Badillo, 2003). However, very few of these studies refer exclusively to young players; normally, these studies have covered very different ages and levels.

Due to the great specialization in sport nowadays and the efforts made to find talents in sport, it becomes especially interesting to determine the differences and similarities in teenage players as regards two sports which are *a priori* very similar (i.e. tennis and badminton). The goal of this study was to determine specific functional differences in some anthropometric properties of the players and general match play actions between these two racket sports.

## 2 Method

### 2.1 Participants
The study was conducted on 28 participants aged 16-18 years, 14 were tennis players and 14 were badminton players, all of them specialized in their respective sport competed at regional and national levels. All these participants gave their informed consent (in the case of minors, parental consent was also required) before participating voluntarily in this study.

### 2.2 Procedure and materials
All players attended the laboratory at the same time in the morning. Once there, they underwent a medical examination, carried out by the same doctor in all cases. A medical history, a cardio-respiratory auscultation and an electrocardiogram were made in order to reject those participants with possible health problems. The

following anthropometric measures were taken to establish the percentage of body fat, mass, height and skin folds (tricipital, sub-scapular, supra-spinal, abdominal, middle thigh and medial leg). Measures were taken following the recommendations of the Spanish Group of Kinanthropometry (Esparza, 1993). The average temperature of the facility was 21°C with a relative humidity (RH) of 40%.

After the anthropometric measurements, the participants took part in an official competition, each in his/her own speciality. Badminton players competed indoors, on a badminton court (22°C and 50% RH) and tennis players competed outdoors, on a fast court (21°C ± 2 and 40% RH). Each match started out with the bouncing of new balls or shuttles and was recorded on video with a Sony Handycam, in order to estimate afterwards the total playing time (TT), real playing time (RT) and pause time (PT). These estimations were made by the same four observers, all of whom had experience in the use of the same analysis system. Each player wore a heart rate monitor Polar Accurex Plus™ (Polar Electro Oy, Kempele, Finland), that recorded the heart rate (HR) every 5 s. This record was then assessed on a laptop computer by the program Training Advisor through the Polar Interface Plus encoder, and immediately converted into a graphical profile. The highest HR obtained during the match, the total average HR and the percentage of the last as opposed to the first HR were then calculated.

The statistical assessment of data was made using SPSS for Windows (version 11.0). After examining the frequency distributions shown by the variables recorded for this study with the Kolmogorov – Smirnov test, and although a few of them showed a normal distribution, it was decided to apply non-parametric methods for the analysis due to the small size of the sample. The comparison of the different variables between all groups was made with the Mann-Whitney tests. In all cases, the level of significance was set at $P < 0.05$.

## 3 Results

Tables 1-3 show significant differences ($P < 0.05$) in TT, RT and PT. Bearing in mind the fact that the rules of each sport clearly influence the absolute value of these data, if we translate RT and PT into a percentage of TT, we obtain an average of 30% (RT) and 70% (PT) in tennis, compared with 36% (RT) and 64% (PT) in badminton.

Table 1. Comparison of anthropometric parameters between tennis and badminton players

| Tennis Players | | | Badminton Players | | |
|---|---|---|---|---|---|
| Mass (kg) | Height (cm) | Fat % | Mass (kg) | Height (cm) | Fat % |
| 61.69 ± 6.87 | 169.80 ± 7.47 | 13.09 ± 3.19 | 64.14 ± 4.10 | 171.20 ± 4.92 | 13.30 ± 2.35 |

Table 2. Comparison of game characteristics between tennis and badminton players

| Tennis Players | | | Badminton Players | | |
|---|---|---|---|---|---|
| TT (min) | RT (min) | PT (min) | TT (min) | RT (min) | PT (min) |
| 105.0** ± 28.7 | 31.5** ± 5.8 | 73.5** ± 8.5 | 26.4 ± 12.1 | 9.5 ± 4.0 | 16.9 ± 5.2 |

*Significant difference between sports ($P < 0.05$)

Table 3. Comparison of tennis and badminton players Heart Rate (IIR) during the competition

| Tennis Players | | | Badminton Plàyers | | |
|---|---|---|---|---|---|
| Max HR (bpm) | Aver.HR (bpm) | HR % aver/max | Max HR (bpm) | Aver.HR (bpm) | HR %aver/max |
| 193.6 ± 4.9 | 158.4 ± 8.5 | 80.3 ± 4.4 | 196.1* ± 8.0 | 179.5** ± 8.0 | 91.5* ± 2.0 |

* (P < 0.05),  ** (P < 0.01)

## 4 Discussion

The anthropometric characteristics of tennis and badminton players show similar values to those obtained in young sportsmen and women of the same age (Esparza, 1993). An important parameter in racket sports is the percentage of body fat: in our study both had a value of 13% . These results agree with the values expressed by other authors, who found this between 11 and 16% for young people (Fernández del Prado, 1991; Unierzyski, 1995; Centeno et al., 1999). Although during adolescence the organisms suffer many changes, no significant differences between these two racket sports have been found in our study. This is evidence of the similarity of the anthropometrical profile of these players at this age.

With reference to the analysis of the game characteristics, we find certain differences between tennis and badminton regarding their rules and structure. While in tennis the game is divided in 3 sets of the first to 6 games (with a possible tie break at 6-6) each and it is possible to rest for 90 s during the change of ends (when the number of games is odd), in badminton, the game is structured in 3 sets of 15 points with a pause of 90 s between sets and 5 min in the case of a tiebreak set (IBF, 1999; ITF, 2000). Bearing this in mind and taking into account the significant differences found during this study, we can state that TT, RT and PT are higher in tennis players than in badminton players. However, and given the differences when applying the rules, it is interesting to note the percentage of RT and PT of the match's TT are 30% and 70% in tennis and 36% and 64% in badminton, respectively (P < 0.05). These sports have not been widely and independently studied by other authors as regards to game dynamics in adolescents, although the data obtained contrasts with those obtained for other categories and levels (Cabello and Serrano, 1997; Cabello et al., 2000; Elliott et al., 1985; FAT, 2001; Reilly and Palmer, 1995; Smekal et al., 2001). Despite the fact that the Real Playing Time and the Pause Time structure is quite similar in both sports, the specialization at these early ages becomes clearly important if we are to introduce players to high performance sport.

By analysing the heart rate (HR), we are able to assess the intensity required in these sports and its relation with the dynamics of the game. It is important to take into account the changes regarding this parameter in tennis and badminton players, since they are intermittent: HR can easily pass from low to high (Pujol, 1997). We observe significant differences as regards to the maximum HR, which is 193 beats·min$^{-1}$ for tennis players and 196 beats·min$^{-1}$ for badminton players (P < 0.05); and an average HR close to 158 and 179 beats·min$^{-1}$ respectively (P < 0.01). These results show that the intensity of the game is significantly higher in badminton than in tennis at young ages. This corroborates the findings of other studies (Bangsbo, 1996; Bergeron et al., 1991; Ferrauti et al. 2001; Liddle et al., 1996). In badminton, because there is no resting time between points, the HR cannot recover and, as a result, the cardiovascular effort is much higher. This has been also scientifically stated by other authors (Cabello, 2000; Tabata et al., 1997). In tennis, the fact of having a rest of 20 s between points reduces this cardiovascular effort, as observed by other studies (Smekal et al., 2001; Therminarias et al., 1990; 1995). This distinction between both sports is even more clearly defined when observing the percentage of the average HR as opposed to the maximum HR, approximately 80% in tennis and 91% in badminton. This confirms that there is higher intensity in one modality compared with the other.

These results define a great functional difference between these two sports, because in badminton there is less total playing time but the cardiovascular intensity is much higher; whereas tennis is characterised by longer duration and lower intensity. This clearly highlights the importance of specialization in both sports.

## 5 Conclusion

Although tennis and badminton players have similar anthropometric profiles, the differences regarding game dynamics and cardiovascular intensity required in each of them, show a distinction between both sports from a functional point of view and highlight the importance of specialization in young sportsmen in order to achieve higher performance in the future.

## 6 References

Bangsbo, J. (1996). Physiological factors associated with efficiency in high intensity exercise. **Sports Medicine**, 22,  299-305.
Bergeron, M., Maresh, C., Kraemer, W., Abraham, A, Conroy, B. and Gabaree, C. (1991). Tennis: A physiological profile during match play. **International Journal of Sports Medicine**, 12,  474-479.
Cabello, D. (2000). **Analysis of the characteristics of competitive badminton. Its application to training. (in Spanish)** Doctoral Thesis. University of Granada.
Cabello, D. and González-Badillo, J.J. (2003). **British Journal of Sport Medicine**, 37, 18-25 .
Cabello, D. and Serrano, D. (1997). **Complete analysis of Badminton.** (in Spanish) Granada Badminton Association. Granada.
Cabello, D., Serrano, D. and González, J.J. (2000). Energy demands and temporal structure in competitive badminton. Relationship with game performance indicators and the result (in Spanish). **INFOCOES** – High Studies Olympic Center Information, 4(2), pp. 71-83.
Centeno, R.A., Naranjo, J. and Guerra, V. (1999). Estudio cineantropométrico del jugador de badminton de élite juvenil. **Sport Medicine Reports**, 70, 115–119.
Elliott, B., Ackland, T., Blansky, B., Hood, K. and Bloomfield, J. (1989). Profiling junior tennis players Part 1: morphological, physiological and psychological normative data. **Australian Journal of  Science and Medicine in Sport**, 21, 14-21.
Esparza, F. (1993). **Manual de cineantropometría.** (Kinanthopometric Dossier). Spanish Federation of Sport Medicine Monograph.
Federación Andaluza de Tenis (2001). **Valoración de tenistas adolescentes,** (Evaluation of the young tennis players). Andalusia Tennis Federation.

Fernández del Prado, J., Ceberio, F., Usoz, B. and Aragonés, M.T. (1991). Somatotipo y pliegues cutáneos en mujeres tensitas (Body profile and cutaneous pleats in women's tennis players). **Sport Medicine Reports**, 31, pp. 21-25.

Ferrauti, A., Bergeron, M., Pluim, B. and Weber, K. (2001). Physiological responses in tennis and running with similar oxygen uptake. **European Journal of Applied Physiology**, 85, 27–33.

IBF (1999). **Status Book**. Gloucestershire. International Badminton Federation

ITF (2000). **Rules of Tennis**. London. International Tennis Federation.

Liddle, S.D., Murphy, M.H. and Bleakley, W. (1996). A comparison of the physiological demands of singles and doubles badminton: a heart rate and time/motion analysis. **Journal of Human Movement Studies**, 30, 159-176.

Pujol, P. (1997). **Rendimiento físico y la salud en la práctica del tenis** (Fitness performance and health in tennis practice). San Cugat High Performance Center. Barcelona.

Reilly, T. and Palmer, J. (1995). Investigation of exercise intensity in male singles lawn tennis. In **Science and Racket Sports** (edited by T. Reilly, M. Hughes and A. Lees), London: E & FN Spon, pp. 10-13.

Smekal, G., Von Duvillard, S., Rihacek, C., Pokan, R., Hofmann, P., Baron, R., Tschan, H. and Bachl, N. (2001). A physiological profile of tennis match play. **Medicine and Science in Sports and Exercise**, 33, 999-1005.

Tabata, I., Irisawa, K., Kouzaki, M., Nishimura, K., Ogita, F. and Miyachi, M. (1997). Metabolic profile of high intensity intermittent exercises. **Medicine and Sciences in Sports and Exercise**, 29, 390-395.

Therminarias, A., Dansou, P., Chirpaz-Oddou, M. and Quirino, A. (1990). Effects of age on heart rate response during a strenuous match of tennis. **Journal of Sports Medicine Physical Fitness**, 30, 389-396.

Therminarias, A., Dansou, P., Chirpaz, M., Eterradossi, J. and Favre – Juvin, A. (1995). Cramps, heat stroke and abnormal biological responses during a strenuous tennis match. In **Science and Racket Sports** (edited by T. Reilly, M. Hughes and A. Lees), London: E & FN Spon, pp. 28-31.

Unierzyski, P. (1995). Influence of physical fitness specific to the game of tennis, morphological and psychological factors on performance level in tennis in different age groups. In **Science and Racket Sports** (edited by T. Reilly, M. Hughes and A. Lees), London: E & FN Spon, pp. 61-68.

# 31 Patterns of play of elite female badminton players

M. Hughes and A. Tutton
*Centre for Performance Analysis, UWIC, Cardiff CF23 6XD, UK.*

## 1 Introduction

Studying the difference in play patterns from recreational to elite players can provide useful data/information that can be used to help developing players to improve their game.

Hughes (1985) set an empirical model template for analysing patterns of play, by examining elite men's squash at different competitive levels. Hughes et al. (2000) extended this work to women, they considered the following questions:

1. What are the patterns of play at elite, county and recreational standards?
2. What are the training needs with respect to periodicity and intensity, (length of rally/game).
3. What comparisons can be made to the men's game?

The study concluded that there were many differences in playing patterns between each standard including the number of shots per rally and shots per match. This was due to the fact that recreational players were found to have not developed a normal playing pattern whereas county players had the basis of a pattern forming and elite had an established normal playing pattern. The results also showed evident similarities with the men's game. It may be assumed that similar analysis might produce similar templates of performance profiles or elite women badminton players.

The purpose of this study was to compare patterns of play between elite, county and recreational badminton players.

## 2 Method

A hand-notation system was used to collect the data which was analysed post-event. The court was divided into eighteen cells (nine cells each side of the net) to analyse the position of each shot. The shots were identified as two types of serve and nine shots that occurred in open play. Rally and match lengths, and winners and errors were also examined. For the reliability study, a game from an elite match was analysed 3 times with more than a week between each set of data gathering. The data was collected of ladies singles badminton players from the 1997 Bath Open and 1999 Welsh Open, South Wales county competitions and local known recreational players. This gave a data population of elite (n=10 matches), county (n=10) and recreational (n=10) badminton players.

The establishment of normative profiles was carefully explored. For example, a normative profile, within a 5% limit of error, was established for elite players after 7 matches when analysing mean error values, and 4 matches when studying mean winner values. It was found that after 4 matches the mean error values for county players stabilised with a normative profile set within 10% limits of error but for mean winner values a normative profile was established after 6 matches with a 5% limit of error. There was no normalisation of the recreational data for mean winner and error values.

The data sets were compared using Kruskal-Wallis and $\chi^2$ tests, differences being accepted as significant if P < 0.05.

## 3 Results and discussion

### 3.1 Reliability
Percentage error calculations and $\chi^2$ tests for comparisons of distributions showed that the largest differences were less than 2%, and that there were no significant differences ($\chi^2 = 0.15$; P < 0.001). Unlike the findings by Hughes et al. (2000), this investigation found that as the standard of play decreased it became increasingly difficult to define shots accurately. This was thought to be due to the recreational players not possessing the skill or ability to produce technically and consistently well defined shots. Ideally to increase the level of reliability, a match from each standard of play could have been notated and examined in the same way.

### 3.2 Profiles of performance
Ideally, a normative profile study should be performed for all the levels of the analysed data, but as this is generally not possible due to the time it would take, a wide and representative  selection of the variables should be examined, as was the case in this study. The cumulative mean was calculated for the normative profiles using the matches in the order in which they were analysed, and also in their reverse order. These two separate methods were used in an attempt to establish whether the data had provided a normative profile. The advantage of using two methods to establish a normative profile allows for a more reliable and true comparison of the data and has extended the previous research of Hughes et al. (2001). Evans (1998) found that for each standard there was a different number of matches to constitute a normative template, this study agreed with these findings. The elite players were found to form a normative profile after 6-8 matches (5% limit of error), for the majority of the variables analysed. Within the county standards of play a normative profile (5% limit of error) was only established for the variables: shots per rally and winners and shots in position E (see Figure 1 for definition of positions). This was observed after 5-7 matches. The variables: rallies per match, errors, and shots in position D only stabilised as a normative profile within the limits of 10% error for the county matches. This, therefore, indicated that for county matches more performances had to be analysed to establish a true normative profile, set within 5% limits of error.

For the recreational standards of play only the variable shots per rally produced a sound stable profile, which emerged after 4 matches. The remaining variables found no normalisation amongst the data collected. These results reflected those of Hughes et al. (2001) with reference to squash players. They also found that the higher the playing standard the quicker the patterns of play became stable whereas recreational players were found to never achieve a stable profile due to their erratic playing performances.

### 3.3 Patterns of play

A significant difference (P < 0.01) was found between all standards of play for the frequency of shots per match. A chi-square test found elite players to have a significantly higher number of shots per match than county and recreational players. The elite players had an average total of nearly 1.75 times as many shots per match than county players, and almost double the frequency of shots per match than recreational players. Although the values of shots per match for county players and recreational players are substantially closer than when compared with those of elite payers, a significant difference was still found between their frequencies. These results relate closely to the findings of Hughes et al. (2000) and Hughes (1985), when the performance profiles and patterns of play of squash at different competitive levels were investigated. The increased difference between elite players and the other playing standards was attributed by Hughes (1985) to the 'far greater fitness, covering ability and speed and skill level' of elite players. Hughes et al. (2000) also found a significant difference between county and recreational standards and concluded that this difference was due to 'the tactical game of the county players and their better skills than the recreational players.' These findings in the games of squash are comparable to the games of badminton analysed within this study, as both are similarly skilled racket sports.

Table 1. A comparison of match data (n=10 matches) for elite, county and recreational women badminton players

|  | Elite | County | Recreational |
|---|---|---|---|
| Mean no. of shots/match | 439 (±113) | 253.5 (±74.7) | 222.1 (±94.8) |
| Mean no. shots/rally | 5.76 (±0.85) | 4.18 (±1.01) | 4.4 (±0.70) |
| Mean rallies per match | 76.5 (±17.5) | 62.2 (±16.1) | 49 (±18.9) |
| Mean winners per match | 31.7 (±9.0) | 28.4 (±7.1) | 29.7 (±12.3) |
| Mean errors per match | 44.2 (±9.4) | 35.8 (±12.0) | 19.2 (±7.8) |
| Winner to error ratio | 1:1.4 | 1:1.3 | 1.5:1 |

A Kruskal-Wallis test found there to be no significance difference between the average frequencies of shots per rally for all three standards of play. Hong and Tong (2000) found that for elite top singles male badminton players the average shots per rally was 7.37. This difference is most probably due to the difference in gender, but another factor could have been that Hong and Tong (2000) used data from the world's top players at the 1996 Hong Kong Badminton Open whereas this study used elite players ranked generally between 20-50 worldwide.

A chi-square test was performed to establish whether a significant difference was found between the frequencies of rallies per match for each standard of play. There was no significant difference (P < 0.01) found between the county and recreational frequency of rallies per match. These findings could be attributed to the small differences between players at elite level. It could be assumed that each elite player would have a similar level of technical development; therefore weakness within the game at a tactical level would have to be sought. Technical flaws made by the recreational players resulted in their inability to produce a tactical all-court game.

Table 2. Frequencies of shot type winners for elite, county and recreational
players (n=10 matches)

| Shot | Frequency of winners | | |
|---|---|---|---|
| | Elite | County | Recreational |
| block | 12 | 7 | 4 |
| clear | 24 | 24 | 48 |
| drive | 4 | 2 | 4 |
| drop shot | 81 | 52 | 60 |
| hit | 15 | 31 | 13 |
| lift | 20 | 18 | 26 |
| net | 40 | 49 | 30 |
| push | 7 | 12 | 12 |
| serve high | 15 | 5 | 20 |
| smash | 66 | 117 | 73 |

Winning shots could be caused through the skill and tactics applied by the player but could also be due to luck or chance (e.g. a player may leave the shuttle thinking that it will go out but when it doesn't the opposition will win the rally). For the purpose of this study it was decided to classify all winners as the same regardless of how the rally was won. When comparing the mean winners per match using a statistical chi-square test it was found that elite players produced a significantly higher ($P < 0.01$) number of winning shots than any other standard (Table 1). This may be attributed to their increased accuracy and variety of shots (Table 2), or their diverse placements of these shots around the court (Figure 1). The elite players also displayed an increased percentage of hit and smash shots in order to win a rally. Evans (1998) stated that in elite men's singles a winner to error ratio of 2.2:1 should be apparent for the smash shot. This was also found to be true for the elite players (n=10 matches) within this study, 36% of winners (Table 2) were caused by the smash shot, whereas only 16% of the total errors were caused by the smash. This suggests tactical similarities between males and females. Future research could be performed to discover further comparisons between genders.

It was also noted that there were no significant differences found between the winning shots played at county and recreational levels. A possible explanation for this may be due to the relatively low skill level of the Welsh county players. The winning shots used by both standards were similar in their total percentage frequencies (Table 2) It was also found though that county players used an increased frequency of drop shots (30%) and recreational players used an increased proportion of clears (16%) in order to produce a winning outcome. The elite players were also found to have a significantly higher ($P < 0.01$) frequency of errors, with a mean of 44.2 ($\pm$9.4) per match. The shots that caused the most errors were the net (18%), dropshot (17%), smash (16%) and clear (15%). Evans (1998) found in a study of the ladies singles final of the All England Championship 1998 that the clear shot produced the highest frequencies of error and that it is usually expected for the clear to produce a low winner to error ratio. This study agrees with the study by Evans (1998) as, although the clear was not the highest producing error shot, it was shown to produce nearly double the number of errors (15%) than winners (8%) for elite players. County players also had a low winner to error ratio of 1:1.6 for the clear shot. Recreational players however produced nearly three times as many winning clears than errors. Recreational players were found to be the only standard of play analysed that produced a greater number of winners than errors. Both elite and county players had higher frequencies of errors than winners.

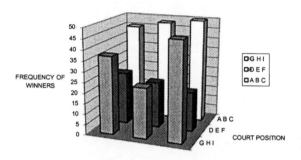

Figure 1. Distribution of elite winners around the court (front of court is to the left of the figure).

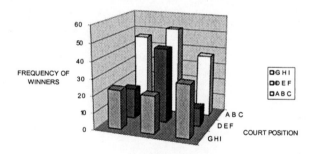

Figure 2. Distribution of county winners around the court.

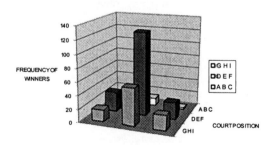

Figure 3. Distribution of recreational winners around the court.

These findings correspond with the study by Evans (1998), of the All England Championship ladies singles final 1998 where both players analysed produced low winner to error ratios. The increased pressure of the competitive environment was given as possible reason for the results attained. Within this study the data collected for elite and county standards were taken from within competitive environments, the recreational players however were not performing in such surroundings. The recreational players therefore were unlikely to produce any errors due to extra extrinsic pressure.

## 4 Conclusions

It was found that that there was no significant difference between all three playing standards for the variable 'shots per rally'. Significant differences ($P < 0.01$) were found amongst the variables, 'frequency of shots per match', 'frequency of rallies per match', 'frequency of winners per match' and 'frequency of errors per match' when elite players were compared with county and recreational players. With the exception of the variable 'frequency of shots per match', there were no significant differences found for the above stated variables when county players were compared with recreational players.

It was concluded that the elite players used their tactical knowledge, technical ability and physical fitness as a means of employing the most effective playing patterns. The county players displayed developing playing patterns whereas the recreational players lacked the tactical knowledge and technical ability to produce a skilled performance.

## 5 References

Evans, S. (1998). Winners and errors. **The Badminton Association of England Limited: Coaches Bulletin "Courtside"**, 108, 8-9.

Hong, Y. and Tong, Y.M. (2000). The playing pattern of the world's top single badminton players in competition – a notation analysis. **Journal of Human Movement Studies**, 38, 185-200.

Hughes, M. (1985). A comparison of the patterns of play of squash. In **International Ergonomics** (edited by Brown, I., Goldsmith, R., Coombes, K. and Sinclair, M.). London: Taylor & Francis, pp. 139-141.

Hughes, M., Evans, S. and Wells, J. (2001). Establishing normative profiles in performance analysis. **International Journal of Performance Analysis of Sport** (electronic), 1, 4–27.

Hughes, M., Wells, J. and Matthews, K. (2000). Performance profiles at recreational, county, and elite levels of women's squash. **Journal of Human Movement Studies**, 39, 85-104.

# 32 Performance profiles of elite men's squash doubles match play

J. Wells[1], C. Robertson[2], M. Hughes[1] and D. Howe[1]
[1]*Centre for Performance Analysis, U.W.I.C., Cyncoed, Cardiff, CF23 6XD.* [2]*National Coach, Squash Wales, St. Mellons Squash Club, St. Mellons, Cardiff, UK.*

## 1 Introduction

Hughes (1986) created a large database on different standards of play and modelled their patterns of play, defining the patterns of play that were characteristic of elite, county and recreational squash players. Ten years later similar research was carried out by Hong, et al. (1996). Hughes and Robertson (1998) used computerised notational analysis to create a template for elite male squash and its subsequent use in designing hand notation systems for player development. The modelling of competitive sport is an informative analytic technique because it directs attention to the critical aspects of data that delineate successful performance (McGarry and Franks, 1996). Murray and Hughes (2001) reviewed the development, methodology and application of tactical performance profiles used with elite level squash players.

It is important to investigate the reliability of the data gathering processes. Hughes, et al. (2002) found that 70% of papers presented in Notational Analysis at previous World Conferences did not present any mention of reliability studies. The raw data for each reliability test (intra and/or inter) should be scanned and any discrepancies discussed and clarified in detail between the analyst(s).

A major area also within performance analysis is the definition of a "profile" of a performance (team, individual, playing standard). The analyst must provide coaches and players with accurate information in the quickest time possible. Therefore to achieve this they should notate the minimum number of matches necessary to create a reliable profile. Hughes et al. (2000) established performance profiles for women squash players at different playing standards. Questions were raised regarding the research process in terms of the consistency of the means of the measured variables from match to match. Large variation in the frequencies of the individual variables between matches gives no credibility to the presentation of this data as a performance profile. It is an implicit assumption in notational analysis that in presenting a performance profile of a team, or an individual that a 'normative profile' has been achieved. Inherently this implies that all the means' of the variables that are to be analysed and compared have all stabilised. Most researchers assume that this will have happened if they analyse enough performances (Hughes et al., 2001).

The need for analysis of squash doubles has grown over the past 4 years since its inclusion in the Commonwealth Games (1998 and 2002). The coaches and players are realising that these analyses are necessary to define the successful tactical patterns. The aim of this work was to produce performance profiles of elite men's doubles in squash.

## 2 Method

Doubles matches of elite male squash players (N = 5) were analysed using the Sports Code computerised software system. The elite men's matches were recorded during the 2002 World Invitation Doubles Championships. Performance indicators were identified between the Welsh National coach and the analyst and then coded into Sports Code. The matches were analysed post-event due to the detailed information that was notated. An intra-observer reliability test was performed on the data input, which resulted in no significant differences – percentage error differences showed less than 5% error on all categories of variables. To ensure that a performance profile has reached stable mean, a calculation of percentage difference was determined, between the cumulative mean and the final mean of all the games in the matches analysed.

## 3 Results and discussion

### 3.1 Reliability of the data

From this study the data input were analysed using intra-observer reliability tests. One hundred pieces of data for each variable were analysed three times to test for any differences that may occur while notating the matches. The results were displayed using a percentage error plot (See Figure 1). No significant differences (less than 5% error) were found between the sets of data, therefore, the data input was accepted as reliable.

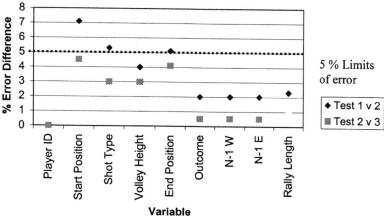

Figure 1. Intra-reliability of the data gathering process. (N-1W, N-1E = number of shots that precede winner, error)

### 3.2 Establishing normative profiles

The tests involved investigating the cumulative mean values of different variables from the analysis of each ensuring game. Each variable has its own individual representation for where it stabilises, i.e. remains within 10% of the final mean (example, Figures 2 and 3). This clearly demonstrated the pattern of stabilisation towards the mean. The danger with using this percentage error method is that the data will naturally move towards the mean.

Therefore a second plot was created which involved changing the order of the games within the profile calculation (calculation 1 and 2). Is important to try and understand the nature of the data, as extreme scores will affect the data, depending upon the order in the sequence. The results clearly showed similarities and differences of variability between the different types of data. An overall average was calculated for a percentage error below 10. This showed that an average of eight games would be sufficient to reach a profile for elite men's squash doubles play.

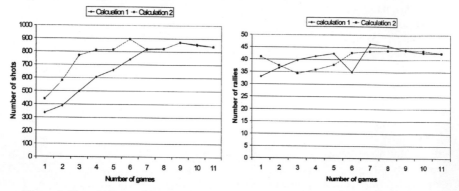

Figure 2. Cumulative mean values/game for number of shots per game.

Figure 3. Cumulative mean values/game or no. rallies per game.

### 3.3 Patterns of play

The winner/error ratios clearly demonstrated the "weaker link" in each pairing (Table 1). From this it identified that players were forcing errors, rather than hitting winners. This type of data highlights a simple tactical plan for future matches to overload and expose the weaker player and force errors.

Table 1. Winner and error ratios for each pairing

|  | Pairing 1 | | Pairing 2 | | Pairing 3 | | Pairing 4 | | Pairing 5 | | Pairing 6 | |
|---|---|---|---|---|---|---|---|---|---|---|---|---|
| Player | 1 | 2 | 3 | 4 | 5 | 6 | 7 | 8 | 9 | 10 | 11 | 12 |
| Winner | 6 | 3 | 16 | 18 | 9 | 19 | 14 | 10 | 14 | 15 | 3 | 11 |
| Error | 6 | 7 | 20 | 1 | 29 | 7 | 13 | 18 | 16 | 20 | 14 | 10 |

▓ = Weaker link

The overall rally length was an average 21 shots/rally (the elite men's singles game has reduced from 20 to 14 shots/rally over the last 20 years), the majority of rallies fell between 1-30 shots. However there were many drawn out rallies, which resulted in 'Let' situations (over 40% of the rally outcomes). This requires patience and composure in concentration levels from the players that want to be successful. It is also extremely frustrating for the spectator and clearly demonstrates why it would struggle as a television sport. A shot analysis (Tables 2 and 3) showed that positive winner/error ratios were achieved when playing a cross-court drive, a cross-volley or volley drop, but that poor ratios were incurred when playing a boast or drive.

Table 2. Successful Shots

| Xdrive | XVolley | Volley Drop |
|--------|---------|-------------|
| W/E Ratio | W/E Ratio | W/E Ratio |
| 30/13 | 21/14 | 23/17 |

W/E = winner/error ratio

Table 3.   Unsuccessful Shots

| Boast | Volley |
|-------|--------|
| W/E Ratio | W/E Ratio |
| 4/35 | 4/21 |

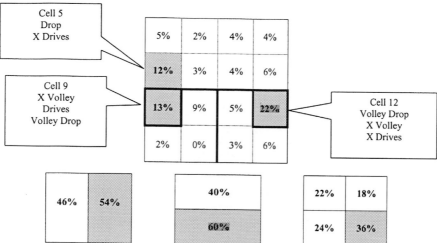

Figure 4. Distribution of winners around the court, including the shot type.

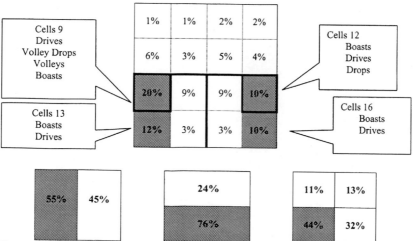

Figure 5. Distribution of errors around the court, including the shot type.

Court representations clearly demonstrated (Figures 4 and 5) where these winners and errors were played from on the court. The successful players would push up the court, hunting for the volley opportunities around the service box areas of the court. Once the players were in a strong position they would force their opposition into the back of court, pressurising for the errors to occur.

Further analysis into the volley demonstrated some tactical conclusions for the elite standard of player. The results showed that players produced a winner to error ratio (12:30) below unity when volleying a low ball (below waist level), whereas volleys played above waist height produced a higher success rate (58:53), Figure 6. This clearly demonstrates that player's should tactically exploit this low height level. High frequencies of winners were played off a boast from their opponent.

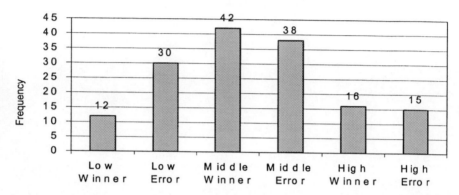

Figure 6.  Number of volleys at differing heights producing either a winner or error.

The boast shows how it can be used negatively to open up the court for winning opportunities and should be used selectively by the players. However, the use of straight drives and cross-court drives produced large frequencies of errors on the next shot (Figure 7). The game of doubles produces a variety of cross-court drives due to the dimensions of the court, such as drives that are hit across the court and down the middle of the court. Further research into these types of shots need to be investigated in order to determine their success in match play.

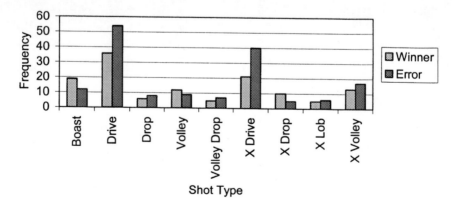

Figure 7. Type of shot preceding a winner and an error.

## 5 Conclusion

It was concluded an average of eight games would be sufficient to reach a profile for elite men's squash doubles play. A general definition of the playing patterns of elite men's doubles in squash has been identified, which opens up the possibilities to further develop these analyses in more depth. In order to make doubles squash more interesting, these results demonstrate the need to make dramatic changes to heighten the game as a spectator sport. It is recommended that these methodologies be used in "profiling" performance in the other doubles events (women's and mixed) in squash rackets, and in other sports that have similar demands.

## 6 References

Hong, Y., C.-M. Chang, T. and W.-K. Chan, D. (1996). A comparison of the game strategies employed by national and international squash players in competitive situation by notational analysis. **Journal of Human Movement Studies**, 31, 89-104.

Hughes, M.D. (1986). A review of patterns of play in squash. In **Science and Racket Sports** (edited by T. Reilly, M. Hughes and A. Lees), London: E & FN Spon, pp. 363-368.

Hughes, M.D., Cooper, S.M. and Nevill, A. (2002). Analysis procedures for non-parametric data from performance analysis. **International Journal of Performance Analysis of Sport** (electronic), 1, 6-20.

Hughes, M.D., Evans, S. and Wells, J. (2001). Establishing normative profiles in performance analysis. **International Journal of Performance Analysis of Sport** (electronic), 1, 4-27.

Hughes, M. and Robertson, C. (1998). Using computerised notational analysis to create a template for elite squash and its subsequent use in designing hand notation systems for player development. In **Science and Racket Sports II** (edited by A. Lees, I. Maynard, M. Hughes and T. Reilly), London: E & FN Spon, pp. 227-234.

Hughes, M.D., Wells, J. and Matthews, K. (2000). Performance profiles at recreational, county and elite levels of women's squash. **Journal of Human Movement Studies**, 39, 85-104.

McGarry, T. and Franks, I.M. (1996). Analysing championship squash match play: In search of a system description. In **The Engineering of Sport** (edited by S. Haake), Rotterdam: Balkema, pp. 263-269.

Murray, S. and Hughes, M. (2001). Tactical performance profiling in elite level senior squash. In **pass.com** (edited by M. Hughes and I.M. Franks), Cardiff: CPA, UWIC, pp. 185-194.

# 33 Differences between the winning and the losing players in a squash game in terms of distance covered

G. Vučković[1], B. Dežman[1], F. Erčulj[1], S. Kovačič[2] and J. Perš[2]
[1] Faculty of Sport, University of Ljubljana, Slovenia. [2] Faculty of
Electrical Engineering, University of Ljubljana, Slovenia.

## 1 Introduction

In squash, each player tries to force his/her opponent to move all over the playing area during the game, which results in them covering a longer distance and being subjected to a higher loading. Player's loading during a match is his/her activity on the court which is expressed in physical units and has two components: quantity and intensity of movements. The quantity of cyclic movements is measured in terms of distance covered by the player (m), while that of acyclic movements is measured in terms of number (frequency) of executions of certain movements (turn, jump, lunge, side-step) and others activities (particularly strokes). Intensity of cyclic movements is measured in terms of velocity of movement (m.s$^{-1}$), while that of acyclic movements in terms of number of repeated movements in a time unit (s$^{-1}$). Players' loading during a match or training encompasses all cyclic and acyclic movements executed by the player. Cyclic movements combine the same elements, repeating over a certain period of time, including walking and various ways of running (forwards, sideways, backwards). In squash, a movement in one direction is very short, thus cyclic movements mostly occur before and after acyclic movements and activities. As the playing area is small, acyclic movements are very frequent, characteristically brisk, and unique and their structure varies. Among them are different ways of stopping and positioning, changing direction, turning, jumping, lunging, side-stepping and various strokes.

A squash match consists of three to five games. In a game there are active (rallies) and passive phases (interruptions). In terms of loading the active part of play is much more interesting. In the elite players' game active part accounts for over 60% of total time of play (Mercier et al., 1987). Each rally starts with a service and ends at the moment one of the players play a winning shot or make a mistake or the game is interrupted for any other reason (players obstruct each other). Good club players on average cover a distance of 12 m during a rally (Hughes, 1998).

Information on squash players' loading is highly important in view of the training activity. Based on such data the trainers may adequately plan and dose loading during trainings, which indirectly influences the efficacy of the training process.

There is some research in squash aimed at defining various aspects of players' loading in a match. Hughes and Franks (1994) established some statistically significant differences between the winning and the losing player in terms of the distance covered during lateral and longitudinal movements as well as the average velocity of movement in four groups of squash players of greater or lesser ability.

According to the research of Eubank and Messenger (2000) the players make 2,866 steps throughout the match (580 steps per game). As much as 74.4% of movements consisted of the "flying phase", which in the authors' opinion was due to the dynamic nature of squash. None of the above research revealed any information on total distance covered by the player during a game or match. We assume that distance covered is mostly affected by total time of game or match and in this framework also by the percentage of active part of play. Both of them depend on a player's ability, ranking, fitness, importance of the match and are strongly influenced by the players' technical and tactical skills and knowledge. All this reflects in a player's correct set-up and movements as well as the right choice of strokes. In this way they exert pressure on their opponents (forcing them to move in all court area) and force them to run greater distances. Based on the above we assume distance covered by the winning side of a game to be lower than that of the losing side.

The purpose of this research was to measure distances covered by squash players during acyclic movements in a game and match as well as to establish any statistically significant differences between the winner and the loser of a game in terms of the loading indicator (distance covered).

## 2 Methods

### 2.1 Design
Data were collected in 6 matches featuring 24 games in total. Three of them took place in the Slovenian National Championship finals (April 2001) and three in the Austrian International Championship finals (October 2001). The sample of variables included distance covered by the winning and losing sides of a game and the number of strokes.

### 2.1 Participants
The sample consisted of eight top-ranked Slovenian, Austrian and Bavarian squash players with experience in the major European competitions and professional tournaments.

### 2.2 Materials
All matches were recorded with a fixed SVHS video camera (Ultrak CCD Color KC 7501 CP) with the frequency of capturing input images of 25 Hz. The camera was fastened to the ceiling in the centre of the squash court and its wide-angled lens (Ultrak KL2814IS 2.8 mm, Japan) covered the entire court. The camera did not interfere with the play and could not be hit by the ball. The video-recordings were digitized using the Video DC30+ video digitizer hardware (Miro, Germany) with the resolution of 384x576 at 2 MB.s$^{-1}$ data rate, while the processing was carried out at a resolution of 384x288 pixels.

### 2.3 Procedure
Digital images were processed by the SAGIT/SQUASH tracking system (Perš et al., 2001). We tracked both players' movements in terms of space and time.

Figure 1. Left is the image of players, right is the binary image *S*.

Conversion into numerical data was carried out by the following steps. ***Step 1 –*** *System calibration based on the court markings.* ***Step 2 –*** *Determination of the processing point.* The image of the empty court is subtracted, pixelwise, from the current image, yielding the greyscale image, on which players are visible and the court is not. The greyscale image is binarized, assigning values of "one" to the pixels that are brighter than the predetermined threshold and "zero" to pixels darker than the threshold. The result of the binarisation is a new image, showing only two values. The first value (in this case "zero") determines the points representing the *background* (black points on the right side of Figure 1), while the second value (in this case "one") determines the points representing the moving objects – *players* (white points on the right side of Figure 1). The actual position of the players in an image is obtained by calculating the centres of gravity for each of two blobs, corresponding to each of the players. Their positions in the court coordinate system are calculated from the calibration equations, obtained in Step 1. ***Step 3 –*** *Potential re-setting, in case the computer software "loses track"* (manual redefining of the player's position). ***Step 4 –*** *Reduction of measurement errors* in the calculation of velocity and distance separately by the means of Gaussian filtering of player trajectories, as described by Perš et al. (2002). The results stated herein are based on the following kernel width: 2Nf+1 = 11 samples, which on a time scale equals 0.5 s. For explanation of Nf see Perš et al., (2002). ***Step 5 –*** *Final data processing.* Calculation of velocity for the each moment of the match, and calculation of total distance covered by the player based on the following equations:

$$v_x(k) = \frac{\Delta x(k)}{\Delta t(k)} = \frac{x(k) - x(k-1)}{\Delta t(k)}, \ v_y(k) = \frac{\Delta y(k)}{\Delta t(k)} = \frac{y(k) - y(k-1)}{\Delta t(k)} \text{ and } v(k) = \sqrt{v_x(k)^2 + v_y(k)^2}, \text{ as}$$

well as the distance covered: $s(k) = \sum_{j=1}^{k} v(j) \cdot \Delta t(k)$, where $\Delta t(k) = t(k) - t(k-1)$, and is determined by the frequency of capturing input images, which in this case is 40 ms (1/25 s). ***Step 6 –*** *Numerical and graphical presentation of movements* (Figure 2).

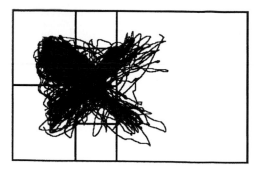

Figure 2. Diagram of player's movements in active part of the game.

## 3 Results

### 3.1 Average indicators of players' loading in a match

Results in Table 1 show some statistical indicators in all games and matches. On average the players made 1,130 strokes per match, which is slightly more than the number of strokes Hughes and Robertson (1998) recorded in their research (i.e. 1,089). The reason probably lies in higher average number of games per match, as the average number of stokes per game (282.6) was lower than that established in the above-mentioned research (351.2).

Table 1. Average indicators of players' loading in individual games

| Variable | Mean (±SD) |
|---|---|
| Average time of a game | 700.0 (±246.0) s |
| Average number of rallies in a game | 25.0 (±7.5) |
| Average time of a rally | 16.4 (±13.2) s |
| Average time of a passive phase | 11.6 (±5.4) s |
| Percentage of active part of play in matches | 59.5 (±5.7)% |
| Average distance covered during a rally | 26.1 (±22.4) m |
| Average distance covered during a passive phase of a game | 10.6 (±5.3) m |
| Average number of strokes per game | 282.6 (±109.7) |
| Average number of strokes per match | 1130.0 (±336.4) |

### 3.2 Distance covered by the winning and losing sides in games and matches

The results in Table 2 show great differences in the distance covered by players during acyclic movements in games and matches. Differences are also seen in the distance covered by winners and losers during the above mentioned movements in individual game and its active part. Statistical significance of these differences (at the level of 0.05) between both sub-samples of players was established with paired samples t-test. We found out that the differences in distance covered between winners and losers of the games were statistically significant only in active parts of games (df = 23, t = 2.199, P < 0.038).

Table 2. Distance covered (m) by winners (W) and losers (L) during cyclic movements in individual game and in the active part of a game (in brackets)

| players | 1st game | 2nd game | 3rd game | 4th game | 5th game | total - match | mean- game |
|---------|----------|----------|----------|----------|----------|---------------|------------|
| W1 | 1297 (925) | 762 (508) | 776 (496) | 347 (249) | / | 3182 | 796 |
| L1 | 1308 (923) | 747 (504) | 690 (464) | 332 (236) | / | 3077 | 769 |
| W2 | 524 (391) | 1298 (1020) | 1241 (915) | 1449 (1063) | 655 (455) | 5167 | 1033 |
| L2 | 583 (434) | 1378 (1042) | 1132 (881) | 1389 (1036) | 619 (452) | 5101 | 1020 |
| W3 | 825 (716) | 972 /741) | 905 (678) | / | / | 2702 | 900 |
| L3 | 793 (681) | 1018 (780) | 946 (718) | / | / | 2757 | 919 |
| W4 | 1207 (876) | 834 (641) | 1368 (983) | / | / | 3418 | 1139 |
| L4 | 1130 (807) | 811 (583) | 1350 (949) | / | / | 3291 | 1097 |
| W5 | 850 (583) | 744 (548) | 606 (396) | 637 (432) | / | 2837 | 709 |
| L5 | 875 (614) | 680 (495) | 603 (375) | 591 (378) | / | 2749 | 687 |
| W6 | 872 (659) | 1303 (966) | 1200 (862) | 292 (193) | 1183 (836) | 4850 | 970 |
| L6 | 827 (641) | 1325 (993) | 1187 (830) | 254 (179) | 1090 (754) | 4683 | 937 |

Table 3. Average distance (m) covered by winners and losers in the game (total distance and distance in active part of the game)

| Players | Mean (±SD) |
|---------|-----------|
| Winners (total distance) | 922.0 (±328.1) m |
| Winners (distance in active part of the game) | 672.0 (±250.3) m |
| Losers (total distance) | 902.0 (±329.8) m |
| Losers (distance in active part of the game) | 656.0 (±250.3) m |

## 4 Discussion

The average distance covered by players during acyclic movements in rallies in games was 26 m and passive phases were approximately 10 m. The longest distance covered in a rally was 152 m, with 40.9 m the passive phase. In our research, average distance covered was much greater than the relevant result in Hughes' research (1998), i.e. 12 m. These differences probably stem from different quality of the sampled players and different methodology used in tracking players' acyclic movements.

The results in Table 3 show that distance covered by winners of games during acyclic movements was on average 20 m longer than that of losers. In the active parts of games losers covered statistically significant shorter distance than winners ($P < 0.05$). On average these differences were approximately 16 m (W = 672 m > L = 656 m). These differences probably arise due to the fact that the winner makes more services and winning returns in a game. Immediately after servicing the player reaches their basic position in two or three steps. Meanwhile, the receiving player is already in position enabling them to make a good return and so does not move a lot. Minor differences in distance covered by both sub-samples during acyclic movements also show very similar playing quality in these matches, resulting in fairly equal play. The results showing time and distance covered in individual games prove that players cover a distance of 1,000 m in approximately 13 min. In view of the fact that individual top-level games last for at least 25 min, it may be concluded that top squash players cover up to 2 km in a game.

## 5 Conclusions

The results of our research are somewhat surprising, as the previous squash theories (McKenzie, 1994) and research findings (Hughes and Franks, 1994) led us to believe that the distance covered by losers of individual games during cyclic movements would be significantly greater than that of winners. In view of these results it would be reasonable to examine in further research the distance covered during cyclic movements in a rally of a game and identify winners and losers of individual rallies. We have also established that the applied technology can help us track cyclic movements of squash players and record their acyclic movements in time and space in a match or training. This enables close examination of players' loading and indirectly facilitates planning and implementation, of the training process for squash players.

## 6 References

Eubank, C. and Messenger, N. (2000). Dynamic Moves and Stepping Patterns Typical to the Game of Squash. **Journal of Sports Sciences**, 18, 471-472.

Hughes, M. (1998). The Application of Notational Analysis to Racket Sports. In **Science and Racket Sports II** (edited by A. Lees, I. Maynard, M. Hughes and T. Reilly), London: E & FN Spon, pp. 211-220.

Hughes, M. and Franks, I.M. (1994). Dynamic Patterns of Movement of Squash Players of Different Standards in Winning and Losing Rallies. **Ergonomics**, 37, 23-29.

Hughes, M. and Robertson, C. (1998). Using Computerised Notational Analysis to Create a Template for Elite Squash and Its Subsequent Use in Designing Hand Notation Systems for Player Development. In **Science and Racket Sports II** (edited by A. Lees, I. Maynard, M. Hughes and T. Reilly), London: E & FN Spon, pp. 227-234.

McKenzie, I. (1994). **Excelling at Squash.** London: Hodder & Stoughton.

Mercier, M., Beillot, J., Gratas, A., Rochcongar, P., Lessard, Y., Andre, A.M. and Dassonville, J. (1987). Adaptation to Work Load in Squash Players: Laboratory Tests and on Court Recordings. **The Journal of Sports Medicine and Physical Fitness**, 27, 98-104.

Perš, J., Vučković, G., Kovačič, S. and Dežman, B. (2001). A low-cost real-time tracker of live sport events. In **Proceedings of the 2nd International Symposium on Image and Signal Processing and Analysis in conjunction with 23rd International Conference on Information Technology Interfaces** (edited by S. Lončarić, H. Babić), Pula, Croatia, pp. 362-365.

Perš, J., Bon, M., Kovačič, S., Šibila, M. and Dežman, B. (2002). Observation and Analysis of Large-scale Human Motion. **Human Movement Science**, 21, 295-311.

# 34 Monitoring the time and frequency of players staying on the basic T-position in squash

G. Vučković[1], B. Dežman[1], F. Erčulj[1], S. Kovačič[2] and J. Perš[2]
[1] *Faculty of Sport, University of Ljubljana, Slovenia.* [2] *Faculty of Electrical Engineering, University of Ljubljana, Slovenia.*

## 1 Introduction

Squash is a game in which technical and tactical skills, knowledge and experience play a substantial role. This is clearly reflected in correct execution and adequate choice of different strokes. Nevertheless, victory does not only depend on a larger number of winning shots whereby the striking side scores a point, it also depends on the constancy of good play (Hong et al., 1996a). Studies of squash tactics are most often concerned with the number of different strokes executed by players in each part of the court (McGarry and Franks, 1994) based on which various ways of playing may be identified (Hughes and Robertson, 1998). Hong et al. (1996b) studied the efficiency of individual strokes and established that playing tactics change with the quality of play. From his own experience, Sanderson (1983) found out that the players use the same playing tactics whether they are winning or losing. The results McGarry and Franks (1996) presented in their research were slightly different. They pointed out that the playing tactics strongly depended on the interaction between the players and/or on the opponent's play. They also established that players changed their tactics less frequently when playing against the same opponent than against different opponents.

Good tactics include not only the right choice of stroke but also the most effective way of moving and positioning during play (co-ordination of the above mentioned activities in terms of time and space) and/or in the situations when players find themselves either in a superior, equal or inferior position.

Performance in squash is strongly linked to players' correct positioning on the basic position (T-position). The basic position is not limited only to the point where the short line and the half court line intersect but covers a specific area in that segment of the court (Figure 1). The basic position optimises the players' chances of making the right move, positioning properly and then striking the ball. It is the best position from which players run and cover all opponents' shots and for that reason enables good control over the play. In their research McGarry, et al., (1998) examined the radial distance between the players and the T as well as the absolute distance between the players. They established that during a rally the players alternately took the T-position in an anti-phase relation. This means that in a given moment one of the players is at T and the other at a certain distance from the T.

Our research was aimed at establishing the time and frequency of players' staying on the basic T-position during the rallies of individual games as well as identifying the statistically significant differences between the winning and losing sides of games in terms of time and frequency of staying on this position.

## 2 Methods

### 2.1 Design

Data were collected from 6 matches. Three of them took place in the Slovenian National Championship finals (April 2001) and three in the Austrian International Championship finals (October 2001). The sample of variables included the time during which the winners and losers of games (24 games in total) stayed on the basic (T) position as well as the number of times (frequency) the players took this position at the moment the opponent struck the ball. In the latter case it is possible to examine how many times players covered opponent's shot from the best position. Both variables were measured only in active parts of the games.

### 2.2 Participants

The sample consisted of eight top-ranked Slovenian, Austrian and Bavarian squash players with experience in the major European competitions and professional tournaments.

### 2.3 Materials

All matches were recorded with a fixed SVHS video camera (Ultrak CCD Color KC 7501 CP) with the frequency of capturing input pictures of 25 Hz. The camera was fastened to the ceiling in the centre of the squash court and its wide-angled lens (Ultrak KL2814IS 2.8 mm, Japan) covered the entire court. The wide-angle lens did not affect the measurements (Pers et al., 2002). The camera did not interfere with the play and could not be hit by the ball. The video-recordings were digitized using the Video DC30+ video digitizer hardware (Miro, Germany) with the resolution of 384*576 at 2 MB.s$^{-1}$ data rate, while the processing was carried out at a resolution of 384*288 pixels.

### 2.4 Procedure

Digital images were processed by the SAGIT/SQUASH tracking system, based on the technology of computer vision (Perš et al., 2001) in which the segment of the court that the authors defined as the basic position was marked (Vučković, 2002). The testing of statistically significant differences between the winning and the losing sides of games in terms of time of staying on the basic position was based on the paired samples t-test. The differences between the winning and losing sides of games in terms of frequency of positioning on T at the moment the opponent struck the ball was established by Chi-Square, while Pearson's correlation coefficient was used to establish correlation between time and frequency of positioning on the T with a level of significance set at $P < 0.05$.

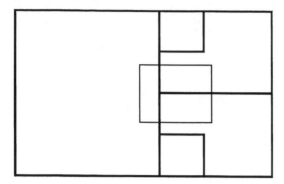

Figure 1. The segment of the court defined as the basic position (T-position).

## 3 Results

### 3.1 Times and percentage of times players stayed on the T-position
The times during which the players stayed on the basic position were recorded only during the active part of play. The results are given in the Table 1 and Figure 2.

Table 1. Mean values (±s) showing the time (s) and percentage of time during which the winning and losing players stayed on the T-position

| Players | Time (s) | Percentage time |
|---|---|---|
| Winners | 171.11 (±67.37) | 40.95 (±7.04) |
| Losers | 170.47 (±74.86) | 40.53 (±7.15) |

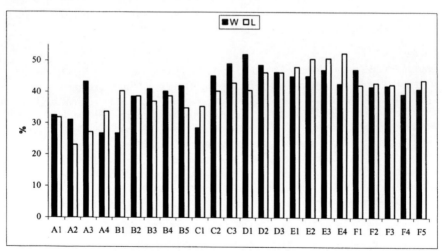

Figure 2. Chart showing percentage of time during which the winners (W) and losers (L) of individual games (over all matches) stayed on the basic position. Different matches are labelled from A to F and different games in the same match from 1-5.

The results show that the players on average stayed on the basic position more than 40% of time in the active part of the play and there was no difference between winning and loosing players.

## 3.2 Frequency of players' positioning on the basic position

The frequency of players' positioning on the T position at the moment the opponent struck the ball is given in Table 2 and Figure 3. The winners of a game took the basic position statistically more frequently ($P < 0.05$) than the losers at the moment the ball was struck by the opponent. The correlation between the time and the frequency of players' staying on the T- position was not significant ($r=0.103$, $P=0.489$)

Table 2. Mean values (±s) showing frequency of players' positioning on the T position at the moment the opponent struck the ball

| Players | frequency |
|---------|-----------|
| Winners | 93.79 (±39.67) |
| Losers | 88.79 (±38.44) |

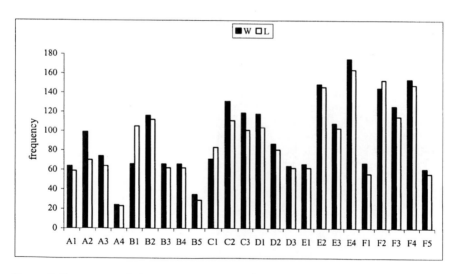

Figure 3. Frequency of players' positioning on the basic position during a game at the moment the opponent struck the ball. Different matches are labelled from A to F and different games in the same match from 1 to 5.

## 4 Discussion

The results in Table 1 show great variability in the times during which the players stayed on the basic position. Similar variability was also observed in the percentage of times during which the players stayed on the basic position (Figure 2). The results in Figure 2 show that the losing player stayed longer on the basic position in as many as twelve games, which is exactly one half of the total number of games. The lowest percent measured was that of the losing player of the second game in the first match (only 23%). It is interesting that the highest percentage was also that of a losing player, namely, in the last game in the fifth match player stayed on the basic position in the active part of play for more than 52% of total time. The differences in times and percentage of times are quite striking even between the winners and losers of games in the same match, with maximum differences accounting for about 17%. It is difficult to confirm whether these results indicate that the tactics of the winners and losers of games differ, as the differences in time and percentage of time may also stem from technically improperly employed tactics and not from the differences in the tactics as such.

Despite the fact that the differences between the winning and the losing sides of a game were quite large in terms of time and percentage of staying on the basic position (up to 16% of the total), the percentages of time were almost the same at the level of total games played.

As some of the above results showed that the losers stayed longer on the basic position, it may be concluded that longer time does not necessarily give the player the advantage that decides the winner. Therefore, our goal was to find out whether the success in playing squash depends more strongly on the frequency of players' taking the basic position at the very moment the opponent strikes the ball. The results in Table 3 and Figure 3 shows that the winners of games took the basic position at the moment the opponent struck the ball many more times than the losers i.e. in twenty-one games. These differences are statistically significant ($P < 0.05$).

The results in the first game in the second match (B1, Figure 2 and Figure 3) are somewhat surprising, as the losing player stayed longer on the basic position and positioned more frequently in this segment of the court at the moment the opponent struck the ball. It was concluded that the losing player had greater chances of winning that game but probably failed to accomplish that.

## 5 Conclusions

Based on these results we have concluded that success in a play does not depend that much on the time the player spends on the basic position, as it does on how often this position is taken at the right time. Our findings have brought about new ideas in the theory of squash which will have to be confirmed by further research. In the future we will aim at establishing whether the time and frequency of players' staying on the basic position differ in squash played by top, club and recreation players and whether these two parameters are susceptible to the players' tactics. Moreover, it would be useful to monitor the players' velocity of movement at the time they are on the basic position. We assume that a player whose velocity on the basic position is high is not in control of play.

# 6 References

Hong, Y., Robinson, P.D., Chan, W. K., Clark, C.R. and Choi, T. (1996). National Analysis on Game Strategy used by the World's Top Male Squash Players in International Competition. **The Australian Journal of Science and Medicine in Sport**, 28, 18-23.

Hong, Y., Chang, T.C. and Chan, D.W. (1996). A Comparison of the Game Strategies Employed by National and International Squash Players in Competitive Situation by Notational Analysis. **Journal of Human Movement Studies**, 31, 89-104.

Hughes, M. and Robertson, C. (1998). Using Computerised Notational Analysis to Create a Template for Elite Squash and its Subsequent Use in Designing Hand Notation Systems for Player Development. In **Science and Racket Sports II** (edited by A. Lees, I. Maynard, M. Hughes and T. Reilly), London: E & FN Spon, pp. 227-234.

McGarry, T. and Franks, I.M. (1994). A Stochastic Approach to Predicting Competition Squash Match-play. **Journal of Sports Sciences**, 12, 573-584.

McGarry, T. and Franks, I.M. (1996). In Search of Invariant Athletic Behaviour in Sport: An Example from Championship Squash Match-play. **Journal of Sports Sciences**, 14, 445-456.

McGarry, T., Khan, M.A. and Franks, I.M. (1998). Analysing Championship Squash Match-play as a Dynamical System. In **Science and Racket Sports II** (edited by A. Lees, I. Maynard, M. Hughes and T. Reilly), London: E & FN Spon, pp. 221-226.

Perš, J., Vučković, G., Kovačič, S. and Dežman, B. (2001). A low-cost real-time tracker of live sport events. In **Proceedings of the 2nd International Symposium on Image and Signal Processing and Analysis in conjunction with 23[nd] International Conference on Information Technology Interfaces** (edited by S. Lončarić, H. Babić), Pula, Croatia, pp.362-365.

Perš, J., Bon, M., Kovačič, S., Šibila, M. and Dežman, B. (2002). Observation and Analysis of Large-scale Human Motion. **Human Movement Science**, 21, 295-311.

Sanderson, F.H. (1983) A Notation System for Analysing Squash. **Physical Education Review**, 6, 19-33.

Vučković, G. (2002). Measurement characteristics and applicability of the player tracking system during a squash match. **Unpublished Master's thesis**, Faculty of Sport, Ljubljana, Slovenia.

# 35 A process oriented approach for match analysis in table tennis

A. Baca, R. Baron, R. Leser and H. Kain
*Institute of Sport Science, University of Vienna, Auf der Schmelz 6, A-1150 Wien, Austria.*

## 1 Introduction

In order to identify strengths and weaknesses in the technical and tactical behaviour of racket sports players and to find out possible reasons for these, structure and process oriented models of the match have been constructed (Hughes, 1998). These models have shown to be effective tools in providing feedback on performance to coaches and athletes. If process oriented models are used, the temporal evolution of the match may be described.

This approach has also been applied to table tennis. Boguschewski et al. (1994) describe one of the few systems developed for use in table tennis. Wilson and Barnes (1998) investigate the inter- and intra-observer reliability when notating the events of a game. They conclude that in the design of a computer based notation system care should be taken to minimize subjective interpretation on the part of the observer.

A process oriented approach has also been chosen to analyse and improve the behaviour of players of the Austrian national team. The primary aim was to introduce a method for a detailed quantitative performance analysis in order to establish a data base containing numerical and video informations on the behaviour of players.

The second aim was to develop a computerised system for providing information for the competing players during a tournament. The computer assisted presentation of selected video sequences should help coaches and players to realize technical and tactical peculiarities and to confirm or disprove assumptions. A qualitative method, similar to that described by Lames and Hansen (2001) was selected for the latter purpose.

## 2 Methods

According to the goals and objectives of the project two different strategies have been followed: a very detailed analysis is performed for gathering information for the data base, and a coarse but rapid analysis is applied when immediate feedback and/or information is required.

## 2.1 Detailed quantitative analysis

### 2.1.1 Model

In cooperation with trainers and players of the Austrian national team a model has been developed for a process oriented description of the match. In addition to grip (shakehand/penhold), left/right handed and type of player (offensive/defensive), the model comprises information on

- the positions of the players
- when the bat hits the ball
- the position of the bat with respect to the player, when the bat hits the ball
- the impact position of the ball on the table
- the times when the ball hits the table
- strokes (forehand/backhand, topspin, block, flip, smash, chop, push, etc.)
- ball speed, spin speed and height over net
- service technique
- special remarks (it is most probable that the opponent will make the point because of this stroke; the player tries to make the point with this stroke)
- result, errors and special events.

### 2.1.2 Data collection and presentation

Matches were recorded by a digital video camcorder and evaluated afterwards. The camera was set up on a solid tripod near the ceiling, allowing an extension the field of view to a minimum of 3 m behind the end lines of the table and to detect the impact points of the ball on the table from the video image. The times when the ball hit the table were registered by using the timecode information from the digitized video.

The possibility of recording heart rates synchronized to the video was also available. Heart rates can therefore be analysed in relation to observable actions of the match. In a subsequent step the time histories of the heart rates may be superimposed to the video recorded.

A commercial game analysis software package (SIMI Scout®) was used for data input. The software allows the free definition of categories and attributes. Video images can be overlaid on the computer monitor. Impact positions of the ball on the table can be obtained by either clicking on the estimated position in a graphic representation of the table or directly on the respective position in the video image. The latter method requires a calibration procedure to be performed and assumes that the position of the recording camera does not change.

Twenty categories for the single and twenty two categories for the double (two more for the positions of the additional players) were defined.

Although SIMI Scout® allows the use of filter functions to display selected scenes, an alternative procedure is used. A table tennis specific software based on a SQL (Structured Query Language) data base has been developed which allows us to

- import data files generated with SIMI Scout®
- calculate additional parameters from those imported (e.g. if a stroke results in a point or error at the end of the rally)
- use predefined filter functions based on imported and calculated parameters
- define additional complex filter functions utilizing the potential of Microsoft Access as a front end
- calculate descriptive statistics
- display selected scenes based on these filter functions.

A wide range of presentation modes has been provided. Selected scenes (e.g. related actions found by using filter functions) may be displayed repeatedly and/or sequentially. The user may freely select (in percent of the normal speed) the speed of presentation of the video sequences.

Nine singles and two doubles matches from international championships have already been evaluated. Digital video was captured (excluding pauses between sets) and stored direct from the camcorder via IEEE-1394 (firewire) interface. In a subsequent step the video was compressed using MPEG-4 codec. Two observers were trained in the operation of the data collection system. Both were experienced players at a national standard.

The service technique was not input by these evaluators, because it was assumed that a valid observation of this parameter was restricted to the player himself or to his coach. This complies with the findings of Wilson and Barnes (1998). If the performance of different service techniques is to be analysed, the player or coach may input this parameter later.

Objectivity measures were calculated for the data collected by both observers from two matches. From these it was concluded that it was difficult for the evaluators to assess the parameters ball speed, spin speed and height over net. These parameters will therefore not be included in subsequent statistical analyses.

## 2.2  Qualitative analysis

A hardware and software system was designed and developed to assist players and coaches during a competition (e.g. an International Championship). An overall system was not aimed for in order to analyse all aspects of playing behaviour of a player or potential opponent. Only that information was collected from which the possibility of an efficient and rapid diagnosis and presentation of strengths and weaknesses of players and opponents was expected.

### 2.2.1 Model

In addition to frame data (grip, left/right handed, etc.) the following attributes have therefore been included into the model:

- strokes (forehand/backhand, topspin, block, flip, smash, chop, push, etc.)
- approximate impact position of the ball on table (forehand side, backhand side, …)
- errors and results·
- special remark: obvious when opponent makes the point because of this stroke
- service technique (optional).

### 2.2.2 Data collection and presentation

Matches were recorded by a digital video camcorder and evaluated (at least partly) in parallel. Beginning and end of rallies were marked by registering the respective time code.

Selected sequences are presented to coaches and players applying filter functions based on the attributes recorded. The filters used are rather wide (e.g. all services of player A) than restricted in order to result in representative and not too specific scenes. Presentation speed and mode may be varied. Evaluators, coaches and player all together try to interpret the displayed scenes and to find out strengths and weaknesses.

# 3 Results

## 3.1 Detailed quantitative analysis
The method was applicable to answer questions from practice, such as
- How effective was a particular stroke?
- How to play to make a topspin attack possible?
- Which service was most successful?
- Which return on a specific service was most successful?

As an example one result of a single match is presented (A vs B). The return of player B on the service of player A has been investigated. Only rallies with less than 6 strokes were considered. Figure 1 illustrates the impact positions of the serviced ball on the table – forehand, backhand side or middle of the table (± 381.25 mm of the middle line).

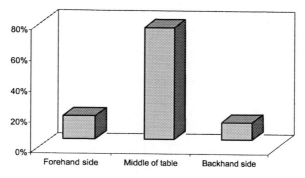

Figure 1. Impact positions of serviced balls.

The percentages of rallies won and lost when returning the service with a forehand (N = 12) or backhand (N = 14) stroke are shown in Figure 2.

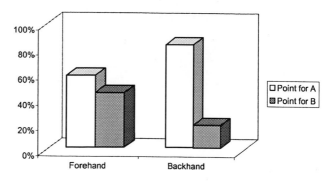

Figure 2. Percentages of rallies won and lost: Forehand/backhand return on service.

Special emphasis was therefore given to the analysis of backhand returns on services with impact position in the middle of the table. Player B returned 58% of these services with a backhand stroke. Figure 3 demonstrates that 89% of these returns resulted in a loss of the rally.

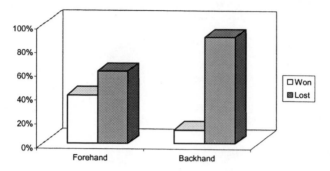

Figure 3. Percentages of rallies won and lost with impact position of service in the middle of the table: Forehand/backhand return.

From the results it was concluded that player B might be more successful when making increased use of the forehand to return services with impact position in the middle of the table. The corresponding video sequences were selected for a presentation to player and coach.

### 3.2 Qualitative analysis
The system was already utilised at the International Croatian Championships. Future opponents' matches were recorded and evaluated. Different sequences were selected and presented to the players prior to the match against these opponents. The following filter functions were applied for this purpose:
- all rallies without pauses
- all rallies with service of player X
- all rallies with service of player X resulting in a point of player X/team X-Y
- all rallies with service of player X resulting in an error of player X/team X-Y
- short rallies (less than 6 strokes).

Players and evaluators discussed and analysed the scenes presented and drew their conclusions. They found out, for example, that when playing against one particular opponent, the ball should be served in the middle of the table and not in the wide forehand or backhand side.

### 4  Discussion

Combining digital video technology, a commercial game analysis software for data acquisition and a self-developed software for data analysis and presentation, systems for quantitative and qualitative analyses of table tennis matches have been developed. Coaches and athletes participated in the construction of the process oriented models underlying these systems. It is assumed that this is an important prerequisite for a better acceptance of the systems as a coaching aid in practice.

From the results obtained so far it is found that both the quantitative and qualitative methods are applicable to assist coaches and athletes to answer questions of a practical relevance. Hidden information could be found using the quantitative approach, immediate information and feedback could be given by presenting selected video scenes during a tournament as a preparation aid.

The quantitative approach may be applied to undertake longitudinal studies for obtaining information on temporal changes in a player's behaviour or for investigating tactics and strategies of a player against different opponents. Qualitative feedback may not only be helpful during competition. Coaches have expressed great interest for an application in training in order to be able to analyse and demonstrate to what extent tactical instructions from the coach are carried out by the player.

Objectivity measures of some of the parameters collected during the quantitative analysis (ball speed, spin speed and height over net) were low. These parameters have therefore not been included into statistical analyses. They may, however, be considered when applying filter functions to select scenes to be presented, because coaches and athletes will be able to draw certain conclusions even though.

The detection of impact points coordinates and impact times turned out to be timely extensive. Methods for detecting the impact point of the ball on the table automatically are therefore under investigation. One approach is to fix accelerometers onto the underside of the table and to determine the impact point from the vibration signals. From first experiments it is expected that the method will be accurate enough (Kornfeind et al., 2003).

For future use of the systems a software extension is under development in order to further simplify data input for the qualitative analysis.


## 5  Conclusions

Quantitative and qualitative information systems were developed to assist coaches and players in elite table tennis. It is expected that unknown, new and potentially useful information will be found if larger data sets are available.


## 6  References

Boguschewski, J., Meiberth, T. and Perl, J. (1994). Das Tischtennis-Simulations-System TiSSy. (A Table Tennis Simulation System), **Tischtennis Lehre**, 8, 5-8.
Hughes, M. (1998). The application of notational analysis to racket sports. In **Science and Racket Sports II** (edited by A. Lees, I. Maynard, M. Hughes and T. Reilly), London: E & FN Spon,  pp. 211-220.
Kornfeind, P., Baca, A. and Tutz, M. (2003). A method for detecting the impact position in table tennis. **Proceedings of the 4th International Conference of Computer Science in Sport**, Barcelona, Spain, p. 95.
Lames, M. and Hansen, G. (2002). Designing observational systems to support top-level teams in game sports. **International Journal of Performance Analysis in Sport**, 1, 83-90.
Wilson, K. and Barnes, C.A. (1998). Reliability and validity of a computer based notational analysis system for competitive table tennis. In **Science and Racket Sports II** (edited by A. Lees, I. Maynard, M. Hughes and T. Reilly), London: E & FN Spon,  pp. 265-268.

# 36 Performance diagnosis through mathematical simulation in table tennis in left and right handed shakehand and penholder players

A. Hohmann[1], H. Zhang[1] and A. Koth[2]

[1]Institute of Sport Science, University of Potsdam, Am Neuen Palais 10, 14469 Potsdam, Germany. [2]Armstrong Atlantic State University, Savannah, Georgia, USA.

## 1 Introduction

The purpose of this paper is to show how the concept of match-play analysis and performance diagnosis through mathematical simulation by means of the Markov chain model (Schutz, 1970; Hannan, 1976; Parlebas, 1988; Lames, 1991; McGarry and Franks, 1994) can be transformed and applied to table tennis.

Markov chains are special cases of stochastic processes, that are used to describe systems, which move stepwise through defined conditions. In sport games such conditions are represented by the different game actions. In addition to the game actions, in table tennis also the stroke positions, stroke directions, and stroke techniques can be defined as states of the game. The transitions between the successive states of the game are described by probabilities. If the number of the conditions of the system is limited, this process can be described by a transition matrix. According to that concept, the series of interactive game actions (Serve, receive, offense, defense and so on) can be described by means of a statistical transition matrix between the different strokes (game actions). After the series of the defined conditions are modeled by a Markov chain, the relevance of each condition for the final win or loss of the game can be mathematically simulated. In the Markov model the game performance is understood as the result of a dialogic process, so that the point probability (PP) of each opponent is explicitly influenced by their mutual interaction in the game.

## 2 Methods

### 2.1 Participants
In this study, 152 matches of the top 50 male world class players were assessed during a time span of 3 years (1997-2000). For the match analysis the sample of matches was divided into four groups: shakehand vs. shakehand player (SH-SH, n = 78), shakehand vs. penholder player (SH-PH, n = 25), penholder vs. shakehand player (PH-SH, n = 28), and penholder vs. penholder player (PH-PH, n = 21).

### 2.2 Design
A table tennis match was studied by means of four observation systems: game action, stroke position, stroke direction and stroke technique (Table 1; see also Zhang and

Hohmann, 2004). It is common for all four observation systems that they start off with a serve and end with game action points of player A or player B. The objectivity of the match observation systems is determined by the common variance between the results of two independent observers, and Cohen's kappa.

Table 1. Observation systems in table tennis game analysis

| Game action | Stroke position | Stroke direction | Stroke technique |
|---|---|---|---|
| Serve | Forehand (FH) | Short Forehand | Service |
| Receive | Backhand (BH) | Long Forehand | Topspin |
| Neutral | Pivot (PI) | Short Backhand | Quick attack |
| Offense | Backhand turn (BHT) | Long Backhand | Smash |
| Defense | | Close to the Body | Flip |
| Control | | Net or Edge Ball | Chop |
| | | | Chopping short |
| | | | Block |
| | | | Cut |
| | | | Push |

**Definitions of game actions: Neutral**: If both players strike with attack techniques; **Offense**: When a player strikes back with attack technique from opponents control or defense shot. **Defense**: When a player strikes back with defense technique from opponents attack shot. **Control**: When both players strike with control techniques or one with defense technique and other with control technique.

## 3  Results

### 3.1 Objectivity of the game observation systems and model validity

The common variance between the results of two observers varied between 91.9% ($r = 0.96$) for the stroke technique and 97.4% ($r = 0.99$) for the stroke position. Cohen's kappa varied between $\kappa = 0.91$ (stroke technique) and $\kappa = 0.97$ (stroke position). All four observation systems led to sufficiently objective data.

The observed and the mathematically modeled point probabilities showed no systematic deviation, so that the correlation was high. Correlation coefficients for the four game observation systems varied between $r = 0.995$ and $r = 0.999$ ($P < 0.001$), which proved the validity of the Markov model.

### 3.2 Performance relevance of the categories of the game observation systems
### 3.2.1 Game action

The matrix in Table 2 shows that the direct point rate of each game action was smaller than the corresponding fault rate. The direct point rate of the offense action was highest, followed by the neutral action. The direct point rates of the other game actions were very low. The fault rate of the defense action was over 50%. The fault rate of the neutral action amounted to 24.97% and the fault rate of the offensive action was 17.31%. This result shows that offense leads to a higher point rate and a comparingly lower fault rate. In order to determine the performance relevance of a specific game action, the original transition probability between the action of interest and one of the following game actions was changed virtually in each observed match and by the same fixed percentage[1]. The mutual statistical dependence of the various game actions within the Markov chain contributes to the fact that due to the existing manipulation of one game action all other transition probabilities between the following game actions will also change step by step[2]. After the simulation procedure, the average difference in the resulting point probabilities in the 152 games indicates the level of performance relevance of the investigated game action.

Table 2. Mean transition percentage between different game actions in 152 observed table tennis matches of the top 50 male world class players

| Game action | Receive | Neutral | Offense | Defense | Control | Point | Fault |
|---|---|---|---|---|---|---|---|
| Serve | 98.23 | | | | | 0.47 | 1.30 |
| Receive | | 23.21 | 43.19 | 4.10 | 12.89 | 2.39 | 14.22 |
| Neutral | | 56.22 | | 12.77 | | 6.04 | 24.97 |
| Offense | | 38.85 | | 32.05 | | 11.79 | 17.31 |
| Defense | | | 39.61 | | 6.24 | 2.19 | 51.96 |
| Control | | | 62.09 | | 20.21 | 1.72 | 15.98 |

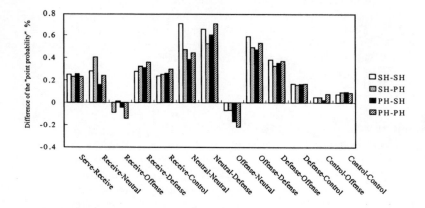

Figure 1. The performance relevance of each game action of different play types of the men's world class (top 50) in table tennis.

---

[1] According to Lames (1991, p. 96) the model function of deflection is described as:
$$\delta TP (TP) = C + B \bullet 4 \bullet TP \bullet ( 1 - TP )$$
Legend:
TP    is the transition probability of the investigated game action,
$\delta TP$    is the change of the transition probability of the investigated game action,
C    is a constant, which describes the deflection in the border probabilities,
B    is a constant, which determines the maximum value of the relative portion of deflection,
4    is a standardizing factor, so that the constant B is equal to the maximum value of deflection.

[2] Since the sum in each row of the transition matrix must equal 1.00, e.g. an increase of one transition probability (TP) must be compensated by a decrease of all other transition probabilities of the game actions in this row. In this study each compensation procedure was based on a proportional compensation of all other transition probabilities $(1 - TP_x)$:
$$\delta TP_{yi} = - ( TP_{yi} / (1-TP_x) ) \bullet \delta TP_x$$

High performance relevance was detected in the transition neutral to defense, neutral to neutral, and offense to defense (Figure 1). In the 152 matches the mean difference of the observed and simulated point probabilities (PPD) of the transition neutral to neutral amounted to 0.57%, which was a little lower than that of neutral to defense.

The performance relevance of the transition neutral to neutral depended on the various play types: for example, the performance relevance was higher in matches of shakehand vs shakehand players. The mean values of the other play types were significantly lower ($\chi^2 = 24.64$, P < 0.001). When a shakehand player competes with another shakehand player, an increase in the rate of the transition neutral to neutral has a greater influence on the match win. The average values of other game actions were below 0.50%.

### 3.2.2 Stroke position

The direct point rate of the pivot position was 9.29% which was much higher than those of the other stroke positions, and therefore produced a better striking effect in the pivot position. Forehand position followed with 5.84%, whereas the direct point rate of the backhand was relatively lower (3.55%).

The transitions forehand to backhand and backhand to backhand showed a higher performance relevance than other transitions (Figure 2). The PPD of the transition backhand to backhand was 0.81%, and in the play type SH-SH it was significantly higher than those of other three play types (F = 8.83, df = 3; n = 152; P < 0.001).

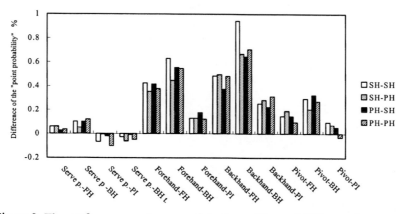

Figure 2. The performance relevance of stroke positions of different play types of the men's world class (top 50) in table tennis.

### 3.2.3 Stroke direction

The direct point rates were nearly the same in the long forehand and backhand zone (7.43% vs 6.38%), and the fault rate was a little higher in the long forehand zone compared to the long backhand. The fault rate was very high in the close to the body zone (40.18%), which indicates that the close to the body is an effective stroke direction in table tennis.

The stroke direction long backhand to long backhand showed a very high performance relevance (Figure 3). The average PPD amounted to 0.95% in that transition, and was the most significant in the different stroke directions. An increase in the rate of this specific transition had a significantly higher influence on the match result than those of the transitions long forehand to long forehand, long forehand to long backhand, and long backhand to long forehand.

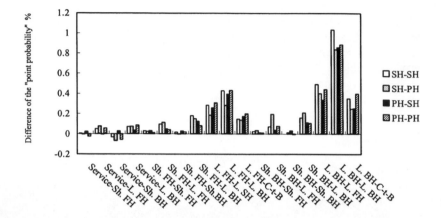

Figure 3. The performance relevance of stroke directions of different player types in table tennis (world top 50) (Sh=short; L=long; C-t-B=Close to the body).

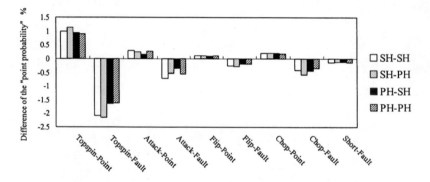

Figure 4. The performance relevance of direct point or fault in the stroke techniques of different play types of the men's world class (top 50) in table tennis.

### 3.2.4 Stroke technique

The direct point rate was the highest for the very effective smash with 17.55%, followed by the topspin with 8.78%. In addition, both techniques lead to smaller fault rates than the other attack techniques quick attack and flip. The defense technique block had by far the highest fault rate with 55.64%.

PPD of the transition topspin to fault was the greatest among all observed transitions between stroke techniques (Figure 4). The mean values of the play type SH-SH and SH-PH were clearly higher than those of the play type PH-SH and PH-PH ($\chi^2 = 17.09$, P = 0.001). In summary, the topspin stroke showed the highest relevance of all techniques for winning a table tennis match, especially for shakehand players.

## 4 Discussion

In this study, performance diagnosis in table tennis by mathematical simulation was used for the first time. In comparison with traditional methods, for example the "3-phases-method" (Wu et al., 1989), or the "10-norms-method" (Li and Su, 1996), the main advantage of the mathematical simulation method is that it delivers not only a statistical description of the observed game actions, but is also able to: (a) analyze the performance relevance of the different game actions, and (b) to provide a prognosis on the probable effects of certain modifications of strategic behavior, based on mathematical simulation of the interactive game process.

Neutral and offence are the two most important game actions in table tennis. In regard to the transition rates, the offensive action is still more important than the neutral action, because of its better stroke effect. Looking at the calculated values of the PPD, the neutral action is more important than the offensive action, because the frequency of the neutral action exceeds that of the offensive action. Therefore, an increase in the frequency of the offensive action and the effect of neutral action are the main winning strategies in table tennis.

In general, the long backhand zone is a very important stroke direction. It shows a very clear advantage compared to the other stroke directions. An increase in the rate of strokes to the opponent's backhand position has a great impact on winning the game.

With regard to the stroke techniques, the topspin has an outstanding importance, especially for shakehand players. All other techniques seem to have little effect on the outcome of a match.

## 5 Conclusion

The performance diagnosis through mathematical simulation of the point probability by means of the Markov chain model is a worthwhile procedure in table tennis. In world class competitions between shakehand players neutral game actions, strokes from backhand to backhand, especially when played long, and topspin faults were most important. In the matches of penholder players neutral actions that forced the opponent into defense, strokes from (long) backhand to (long) backhand, and also the topspin faults proved to be decisive.

## 6 References

Hannan, E.L. (1976). An Analysis of Different Serving Strategies in Tennis. In **Management Science in Sport** (edited by R.E. Machol, S.P. Ladany and D.G. Morrison), pp. 125-135. Amsterdam.

Lames, M. (1991). **Leistungsdiagnostik durch Computersimulation. Ein Beitrag zur Theorie der Sportspiele** [Performance diagnosis by computer simulation]. Frankfurt/Main, Harri Deutsch.

Li, J. and Su, P. (1996). Evaluation of Technique Strength of Some World Class Men's Elite Table Tennis Attacking Players. **Journal of Beijing University of Physical Education**, 71-76.

McGarry, T. & Franks, I.M. (1994). A stochastic approach to predicting competition squash match-play. **Journal of Sport Science**, 12, 573-584.

Parlebas, S. (1988). Analyse et modélisation du volley-ball de haute compétition [Analysis and modeling of elite volleyball competition], **Science et Motricité**, 2(4), 3-22.

Schutz, R.W. (1970). Stochastic Processes: Their nature and use in the study of sport and physical activity. **Research Quarterly for Exercise and Sport**, 41(2), 205-213.

Wu, H., Li, Z., Tao, Z., Ding, W. and Zhou, J. (1989). Methods of actual strength evaluation and technical diagnosis in table tennis match. **Journal of National Research Institute of Sports Science**, 32-41.

# 37  Table tennis after the introduction of the 40 mm ball and the 11 point format

H. Zhang and A. Hohmann
*Institute of Sport Science, University of Potsdam, Am Neuen Palais 10, 14469 Potsdam, Germany.*

## 1  Introduction

In order to increase the attractiveness of table tennis and to win more people for this sport, the ITTF changed the table tennis rules in recent years. Since October 1st, 2000, the ball with a diameter of 40 mm is used and replaced the 38 mm ball. From September 1st, 2001 a new scoring system was introduced with the game ending with 11 instead of 21 points. The differences between a 40 mm and a 38 mm ball (Zhang and Wu, 2000; Tsuji and Muguruma, 2002; Iimoto, Yoshida and Yuza, 2002; Ishigaki, 2002; Takeuchi, Kobayasji, Hirua and Yuza, 2002) as well as between an 11 and a 21-point game format (Hammer, 2001) have been extensively studied. Possible differences in playing techniques and game tactics have not yet been evaluated.

In this study, 40 mm ball/11 point match and 38 mm ball/21-point match were systematically compared with the help of statistical transition rates (in percent) between the different game actions. As was demonstrated by Schutz (1970), Hannan (1976), Parlebas (1988), Lames (1991), as well as McGarry and Franks (1994) the analysis of transition rates by means of the mathematical model Markov chain can be used to analyze the game process and to evaluate tactical behavior in match-play. In this study, the Markov chain model was used to calculate the transition rates between certain game actions and strokes (Hohmann, Zhang and Koth, 2004), and, in a second step, to compare the performance relevance of the game actions and strokes in the two game formats.

## 2  Methods

### 2.1 Participants

In the present study, 38 singles matches played with a 38 mm ball and a 21-point format (top 50 male table tennis players 1997-2000), and another 38 singles matches played with a 40 mm ball and an 11 point format were assessed. Differences between games were analyzed by t-tests, significance was indicated by P < 0.05.

### 2.2 Design

Table tennis game observation was conducted by means of four observation systems: game action, stroke position, stroke direction and stroke technique (see Table 1 in Hohmann, Zhang and Koth, 2004). The objectivity of the match observation systems is determined by the common variance between the results of two independent observers, and Cohen's kappa.

# 3  Results

## 3.1 Objectivity of the game observation system and model validity

All four observation systems led to sufficiently objective data, as was reported by Hohmann, Zhang, and Koth (2004). The validation procedure was also part of the general performance diagnosis project in elite table tennis and proved the validity of the Markov model data in general (see Hohmann, Zhang and Koth, 2004). In this study, it was assumed that there are no substantial differences in the validity of the Markov models that were used to compare the two sub-samples of 38 mm ball and 40 mm ball matches.

In the context of model validity it is more difficult to defend two basic assumptions of the Markov chain model: (1) each state of the process, that is the table tennis rally, is only dependent on the last former state of the process and independent of all the other earlier states in the process, (2) the transitions between the different states are stable all over the match. Both assumptions are taken for granted here, but have to be investigated in further studies.

## 3.2 The comparison and the performance relevance of the game strategies
## 3.2.1 Game action

In the observed matches, the average transition rates (in percent) between the different game actions show that there is only one significant difference between the 40 mm ball/11 point and the 38 mm ball/21-point format. The mean percentage of the transition "receive to defense" amounted to 1.91% in the 40 mm ball/11 point format, which was significantly less than the 3.49% in the 38 mm ball/21-point format (Table 1). This result expresses that the effect of the receive action is relatively weaker in the 40 mm ball game. One possible reason is that the players return more conservatively because of the change of the right to serve every two points in the 11 point format. The mathematical simulation is based on a standardized manipulation of the observed game behavior of each player. The standardized change in one specific transition rate is followed by a difference in the point probability of that specific game action, stroke position, stroke direction, or stroke technique. The results of the simulations shown in figure 1 enhance the fact that the performance relevance of the receive action is decreased in the 40 mm ball/11 point format. In the analyzed 38 matches, the mean difference in the point probability of the transition "receive to defense" was significantly lower in the 40 mm ball/11 point format than in the 38 mm ball/21-point format ($t=-3.050$, $P=0.003$).

## 3.2.2 Stroke position

In the transition rates between the stroke positions, there are two significant differences between the 40 mm ball/11 point and the 38 mm ball/21-point format (Table 1). The percentage of the transition "forehand to backhand" was significantly smaller in the 40 mm ball/11 point format. That means that after a player strikes on the forehand side, the opponent hits the next ball less often in the backhand side.

In contrast, the average percentage of the transition "backhand to pivot" was significantly higher in the 40 mm ball/11 point format. After a player strikes on the backhand side, the opponent has more chance to attack with forehand technique in the pivot position (Table 1).

Table 1. The significant differences of the statistical transition rates (in percent) in the four observation systems (1) game actions, (2) stroke position, (3) stroke direction, and (4) stroke technique between 40 mm ball/11 point and 38 mm ball/21-point format in men's world class table tennis

| Transitions in the four observation systems | | 40 mm ball / 11 point format | | | 38 mm ball / 21-point format | | | t | P |
|---|---|---|---|---|---|---|---|---|---|
| | | Mean | ± s | N | Mean | ± s | N | | |
| (1) Receive | Defense | 1.91 | ± 2.05 | 38 | 3.49 | ± 3.53 | 38 | -2.39 | .019 |
| (2) Forehand | Backhand | 26.92 | ± 10.2 | 38 | 32.40 | ± 8.50 | 38 | -2.54 | .013 |
| (2) Backhand | Pivot | 18.75 | ± 9.19 | 38 | 14.46 | ± 7.28 | 38 | 2.25 | .027 |
| (3) Service | Long backhand | 7.83 | ± 5.81 | 38 | 14.07 | ± 9.53 | 38 | -3.44 | .001 |
| (3) Long forehand | Long forehand | 32.39 | ± 16.9 | 38 | 24.84 | ± 12.5 | 38 | 2.20 | .031 |
| (3) Long forehand | Close to body | 2.06 | ± 3.04 | 38 | 4.51 | ± 4.47 | 38 | -2.79 | .007 |
| (4) Topspin | Topspin | 34.01 | ± 9.57 | 38 | 25.32 | ± 10.4 | 38 | 3.78 | <.001 |
| (4) Attack | Topspin | 45.84 | ± 16.5 | 28 | 34.51 | ± 17.1 | 32 | 2.60 | .012 |

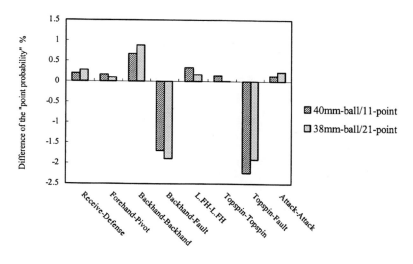

Figure 1. The significant differences in the point probability of the items in the four observation systems (1) game actions, (2) stroke position, (3) stroke direction, and (4) stroke technique as measure of the performance relevance of the observed game behavior between 40 mm ball/11 point format and 38 mm ball/21-point match in men's world class table tennis (L=long; FH=Forehand).

The performance relevance of the transition "forehand to pivot" was increased in the 40 mm ball/11 point format (Figure 1). The mean difference in the point probabilities of the transition "forehand to pivot" was significantly greater in the 40 mm ball/11 point matches than in the 38 mm ball/21-point matches ($t = 2.000$, $P = 0.049$). Also, the performance relevance of the transition "backhand to backhand" was lower in the 40 mm ball/11 point format (Figure 1), because the mean difference of the point probabilities of the transition "backhand to backhand" was significantly smaller ($t = -2.695$, $P = 0.009$).

The mean difference in the point probability of the fault in the stroke position backhand was significant smaller in the 40 mm ball/11 point match than in the 38 mm ball/21-point format (Figure 1; $t = -2.016$, $P = 0.047$). This result shows that the performance relevance of the stroke position backhand is reduced in the 40 mm ball/11 point match.

### 3.2.3 Stroke direction

In the transition rates between the observed stroke directions, differences between 40 mm ball/11 point format and 38mm ball/21-point format occurred in service and in long forehand. In the 40 mm ball/11 point format, 6.24% less "service to long backhand" were observed (Table 1). The most possible reasons might be that the effect of the long-ball-service is weaker, because the speed of the 40 mm ball is reduced, and players seem to serve more conservatively in the 11 point match.

The mean percentage of the transition "long forehand to long forehand" was 7.55% higher in the 40 mm ball/11 point format than in the 38 mm ball/21-point format (Table 1). In contrast, the average rate of the transition "long forehand to body" was significantly lower in the 40 mm ball/11 point format. Furthermore, these results reveal that on the one hand, the players have more occasions to interact with forehand attack techniques, because the speed and rotation of the ball is reduced, and on the other hand, the effect of the stroke direction "close-to-the body" might be weaker in the 40 mm ball/11 point match.

As Figure 1 illustrates, the performance relevance of the stroke direction "long forehand to long forehand" is clearly increased in the 40 mm ball/11 point format. The mean difference in the point probabilities of the transition "long forehand to long forehand" was significantly greater in the 40 mm ball/11 point format ($t = 2.243$, $P = 0.028$).

### 3.2.4 Stroke technique

In the transition rates between the main stroke techniques, there are two striking differences between the 40 mm ball/11 point and the 38 mm ball/21-point format. The average percentage of the transition "topspin to topspin" was 8.69% higher in the 40 mm ball/11 point format (Table 1). Furthermore, the mean percentage of the transition "attack to topspin" was 11.33% higher in the 40 mm ball/11 point format. Both show that topspin was used more often in the 40 mm ball/11 point format.

The performance relevance of the topspin was increased in the 40mm ball/11 point format, but the performance relevance of the transition "attack to attack" was decreased (Figure 1). In addition to that, the mean differences in the point probabilities of the transitions "topspin to topspin" and "topspin to fault" were significantly higher in the 40 mm ball/11 point format ($t = 1.992$, $P = 0.050$, and $t = 1.996$, $P = 0.050$, respectively). The mean difference in the point probability of the transition "attack to attack" was significantly lower in the 40 mm ball/11 point format than in the 38 mm ball/21-point match ($t = -2.098$, $P = 0.040$).

## 4 Discussion

Among 62 transition rates compared, only 8 showed significant differences after the change of the rules from 38 mm ball/21-point format to 40 mm ball/11 point format. The mathematical simulations suggest that the change of the rules had only minor consequences for the strategy of the game. Again, only eight of the analyzed transitions led to significant differences in the outcome of a game in men's world class table tennis.

Despite the fact that the 40 mm ball lowers the speed and the rotation of the ball, and the 11 point match shortens the total game time and accelerates the game rhythm, the results demonstrate that the changes in game strategy with respect to the game actions, and the positions, directions and techniques of the strokes are relatively small. That result might be contradictory to the impressions of many coaches and players. Possible reasons for that could be seen in two aspects. On the one hand, the more frequent change of the right to serve in the 11 point format might have led to the consequence that also the tactical situations change more often. Another reason might be the risk of losing the game due to shorter games. This could lead to a higher psychological pressure, especially for elite players.

## 5 Conclusions

The study showed that the introduction of the 40 mm ball and the 11 point format had only minor consequences for the tactical and technical strategies of the game.

After the change of the rules, players serve and receive more conservatively. The performance relevance of the stroke in the position backhand is lower, but strokes in the direction from the long forehand to the long forehand side of the opponent are of increased importance. With regard to stroke techniques, topspin will play a more important role in the future.

## 6 References

Hammer, H. (2001). Sätze bis 11 – Versuch einer Analyse [Games up to 11 – attempt of an analysis]. **Tischtennis Lehre**, 3, 26-29.

Hannan, E.L. (1976). An Analysis of Different Serving Strategies in Tennis. In R.E. Machol and S.P. Ladany and D.G. Morrison (eds.), **Management Science in Sport**, Amsterdam, pp. 125-135.

Hohmann; A., Zhang, H. and Koth, A. (2004). Performance Diagnosis through Mathematical Simulation in Table Tennis. In **Science and Racket Sports, III,** (edited by A. Lees, J-F. Kahn and I. Maynard), London: Routledge, in this volume.

Iimoto, Y., Yoshida, K. and Yuza, N. (2002). Rebound characteristics of the new table tennis ball. Differences between the 40 mm (2.7 g) and 38 mm (2.5 g) balls. In **Table Tennis Sciences 4&5** (edited by N. Yuza, S. Hiruta, Y. Iimoto, Y. Shibata, Y. Tsuji, and J.R. Harrison), Lausanne: ITTF, pp. 233-243.

Ishigaki, H. (2002). Distribution of contact points on the racket when hitting 40mm balls. In **Table Tennis Sciences 4&5** (edited by N. Yuza, S. Hiruta, Y. Iimoto, Y. Shibata, Y. Tsuji and J.R. Harrison), Lausanne: ITTF, pp. 244-250.

Lames, M. (1991). **Leistungsdiagnostik durch Computersimulation** [Performance diagnosis by computer simulation]. Harri Deutsch, Frankfurt/Main.

McGarry, T. and Franks, I.M. (1994). A stochastic approach to predicting competition squash match-play. **Journal of Sport Science**, 12, 573-584.

Parlebas, S. (1988). Analyse et modélisation du volley-ball de haute compétition. [Analysis and modeling of elite volleyball competition], **Science et motricité**, 2 (4), 3-22.

Schutz, R.W. (1970). Stochastic Processes: Their nature and use in the study of sport and physical activity. **Research Quarterly for Exercise and Sport**, 41 (2), 205-213.

Takeuchi, T., Kobayasji, Y., Hirua, S. and Yuza, N. (2002). The effect of the 40mm diameter ball on table tennis rallies by elite players. In **Table Tennis Sciences 4&5.** (edited by N. Yuza, S. Hiruta, Y. Iimoto, Y. Shibata, Y. Tsiúji and J.R. Harrison), Lausanne: ITTF, pp. 267-277.

Tsuji, Y. and Muguruma, Y. (2002). Numerical simulation of motion of table tennis ball; Effect of ball diameter. In **Table Tennis Sciences 4&5,** (edited by N. Yuza, S. Hiruta, Y. Iimoto, Y. Shibata, Y. Tsiúji and J.R. Harrison), Lausanne: ITTF, pp. 38-53.

Zhang, X. and Wu, H. (2000). Effect of 40 Millimetre Ball on Competition State in Table Tennis Athletes. **Journal of Tianjin Institute of Physical Education**, 3, 65-66.

# Part Seven

# Psychology of Racket Sports

# 38 The sources of stress for junior table tennis players who attend the English National Training Academy

M.A.K. Bawden, B.J. Chell and I.W. Maynard
*Centre for Sport and Exercise Science, Sheffield Hallam University, Collegiate Crescent Campus, Sheffield, S10 2BP, UK.*

## 1 Introduction

The English National Table Tennis Training Academy was set up in 1998. One year into the programme players started to show signs of stress whilst living at the academy, which seemed to be having a negative effect on motivation and performance. This required the sources of stress to be identified. It is important to note that this study was not empirically-based, but an applied tool used to identify sources of stress at the academy that could be targeted for applied intervention.

An integral part of competing in sport is the capability to cope with intense pressure, stress and anxiety (Jones and Hardy, 1990). This is reflected by the amount of documented research in the academic literature relating to pressure and stress in elite athletes (Jones and Hardy, 1990). Pressure refers to the increased demands of performing well, whereas stress is the perception as to whether those demands can be successfully met (Hardy, Jones, and Gould, 1998).

A perceived inability to cope with stress will almost certainly influence an athlete's psychological state, which can lead to a decrement in performance (Jones and Hardy, 1990). Current research has highlighted pressure and stress as being fundamental antecedents associated with decrements in motor performance (Mullen and Hardy, 2000). Apprehension and doubt relating to an athlete's perceived ability to cope with a stressful situation is likely to be reflected in heightened levels of anxiety (Hardy, et al., 1998). Mullen and Hardy (2000) proposed anxiety to be a contributing factor to the demise of performance under stress.

Jones and Hardy (1990) interviewed several athletes from a cross-section of sports regarding their perceived sources of stress. The main sources of stress for these athletes were: uncertainty of conditions, performing in front of an audience, injury / physical weaknesses, high self-expectation, responsibilities of being part of a team, negative comments from coaches and parents and the outcome of performance. An investigation by Gould, Jackson and Finch (1993) examined the sources of stress experienced by U.S. national champion figure skaters. The main sources of stress experienced by the skaters were: relationship issues (partner / familial stress; coach conflict), expectations and pressure to perform (e.g. pressure to be better than previous performance; self-imposed perfectionist standards), psychological demands on skater resources (self-doubt, competitive anxiety, social comparison anxiety), physical demands on skater resources (e.g. physical demands on the body, attain / maintain weight; injury), environmental demands on skater resources (e.g. too much media coverage; financial stress, skating politics) and life direction concerns.

Although the primary sources of stress have been identified in some elite sports, a new development in contemporary sport has been the emergence of national training academies, which have not received attention in the academic literature. When attending a national academy many young sports performers are required to live and train within a highly intense and potentially stressful environment. The young athlete is required to adapt to many lifestyle changes in order to try and reach an elite standard in their sport. These adaptations often involve being exposed to many extra stressors that contribute to the pressure that athletes perceive themselves to be under, in their quest to reach their goals.

The primary aim of the present research was to identify the sources of stress for the England Junior table tennis players at the national training academy from both a player and coach perspective. A further aim was to establish strategies to help players not only cope with their stress, but promote a positive attitude in order to create the right psychological state for them to perform optimally whilst training and competing at the academy. The findings are discussed with reference to recommendations to help young players cope with and positively use stress when living, training and competing in a national academy environment.

## 2 Method

### 2.1 Participants
Participants (male n = 11; female n = 9) were comprised of elite table tennis players (age range = 13-18 years; mean = 15.2 yrs) and senior coaches (male n = 4) based at the England National Table Tennis Academy.

### 2.2 Procedure
Prior to players being interviewed, consent to be involved in the research was obtained from the national governing body (England Table Tennis Association) and players' parents. Participation within the study was voluntary and interviewees were advised that all data would be kept strictly confidential.

*Interview Format:* A Semi-structured interview format was used to ensure a consistent protocol was used during the data collection procedure as recommended by Scanlan, Stein and Ravizza, (1991). Prior to each interview participants were briefed as to the nature of the survey and the format of the interview. Once the players were happy with the interview environment the following open ended question was asked: "What are the main sources of stress, related to living at the training academy that you believe negatively influence your table tennis performance?". Once the players had recounted their initial thoughts, they were asked general probe questions (Patton, 1990) to elicit further sources of stress. This was then followed by elaboration probe questions in order to generate further information regarding these sources of stress (Scanlan et al., 1991). The coaches followed the same protocol, however the initial question that they were asked was: "What are the main sources of stress, related to living at the training academy that you as a coach believe negatively influence players' performance?".

*Follow-up Interview:* Subsequent to all participants being interviewed, players and coaches were then asked, independently, to rank the ten most commonly cited sources of stress from most stressful to least stressful. The top ten most commonly cited sources of stress were then placed into a hierarchy for both players and coaches.

# 3 Results

The top ten most commonly cited sources of stress as perceived by the players and the coaches were placed into an overall hierarchical table (see Table 1). The results indicated that the coaches identified many of the dominant sources of stress for players at the training academy. Major differences in perception between players and coaches were that the coaches highlighted the need to improve, selection, school and the demands of training as factors that they considered to be stressful for the players that were not identified by the players themselves. Sources of stress that were only highlighted by the players included personal expectation, the need to reach goals, playing players of lesser ability and the perception of people outside the centre.

Table 1. The stress source hierarchy for players as perceived by players and coaches

| Players Perception | Coaches Perception |
| --- | --- |
| 1. Critical eye of the coach | 1. Parents |
| 2. Personal expectation | 2. Coaches |
| 3. The constant need to win | 3. Lack of social activities |
| 4. Living at the academy | 4. The need to win |
| 5. Other players' perception of their ability | 5. The need to improve |
| 6. Parents | 6. Evaluation from peers |
| 7. The need to reach goals | 7. Selection |
| 8. Playing players of lesser ability | 8. School |
| 9. Perception of people outside the academy | 9. Living away from home |
| 10. Lack of freedom to socialise | 10. Demands of training |

# 4 Discussion

The findings of the present study show some similarity to those of Gould et al. (1993) who found that 'expectations' and 'pressure to perform' were major sources of stress for senior elite figure skaters. However, there are a number of stressors established in the present study which are more specific to junior performers and also specific to training and living at a national academy.

The main findings clearly show that players believe that the coaches were the number one source of stress at the academy. This was primarily due to the fact that they felt that the coaches were constantly evaluating their performance in both practice and in competition. One player stated "always being watched by the coaches is stressful as I always feel like I'm being analysed". This is a factor that is acknowledged by the coaches as they rated themselves to be the second biggest source of stress.

The coaches perceived that parents were the number one source of stress for the players. They perceived that the parents had extremely high expectations for their son or daughter, based on the fact that they had been selected for a National Academy. They perceived that the players' parents were becoming more 'outcome' oriented with a far greater focus on the results, with this perception also manifesting itself amongst the players. In addition, coaches asserted that this change in focus away from 'improvement' and onto results had become a major source of pressure.

Players also perceived their parents to be a stressor, however not to the same extent as the coaches (ranking = 6/10). Many of the players commented about "not wanting to let their parents down", and made reference to the increased pressure they felt from their parents, not only to get results in table tennis, but also to maintain good school grades whilst living at the academy.

The sources of stress that were identified by the players as specifically related to academy life were; living at the academy, other players' perception of their ability, the perception of people outside the centre and lack of freedom to socialise. The players identified that the fact they were 'living at the academy' (ranking = 4/10) was a major source of stress for them. This was largely due to the fact that they were having to live away from home and that they were required to leave behind many close friends and family to pursue their goals in table tennis. One player reported "I have friends here, but it's not the same. I miss doing normal stuff like going out and having fun with my friends back home." This factor was also identified by the coaches as a source of stress (ranking = 9/10). A further factor that players perceived to be stressful was how their peers within the centre rated their ability. The players felt that there was a constant need to improve their standard. Consequently, by training with the best players and coaches in the country the players felt that they were being continuously evaluated by each other. This was primarily associated with results from foreign tournaments and also their daily training routine at the academy. 'Evaluation from peers' (ranking = 6/10) and 'the need to improve' (ranking = 5/10) were also identified by the coaches as stressors on the players.

As with any sport there were a limited number of places available at the academy. Consequently, many players were unsuccessful in being selected. It is for this reason, players were concerned as to what non-academy players thought of them and the pressure they felt when competing domestically. The final factor relating to stress at the academy was' the lack of freedom to socialise'(ranking = 10/10). As the players practiced table tennis every day after school this did not leave them much time to socialise with friends or leave the training centre environment. They perceived this continuous cycle of school and table tennis to be stressful as it gave them very few opportunities to relax or 'switch off'. Interestingly school itself was not cited as a major source of stress. The coaches identified the 'lack of social activities' as being a major source of stress (ranking 3/10). Thus, the coaches recognised that the players were not getting enough time to 'switch off' from table tennis. A further factor identified by coaches related to life at the centre was 'selection' (ranking 7/10). The coaches felt that the players perceived that they were under pressure to be selected for the foreign competitions and felt increased levels of stress if they failed to be selected.

Both the players (ranking = 3/10) and the coaches (ranking = 4 /10) identified 'the need to win' as a source of stress. The players were aware that they needed to obtain good results when playing in foreign competitions. The focus of the players changed from 'how to win' to 'the need to win'. This simply meant that when players' perceived an increase in pressure, this would result in a direct decrease in competitive performance. This point was also identified by the players who recognised that there was a 'need to reach goals' (ranking = 7/10). These were not only their own personal goals but also the goals by the performance director. Athletes also highlighted 'playing players of lesser ability' (ranking = 8/10) as a source of stress. In this situation the players perceived themselves to be in a lose / lose situation. Thus, if they won it was assumed that they should win anyway and if they lost it was perceived to be a poor defeat. It was evident from this finding that the players had changed their focus away from a 'need to achieve' towards a 'fear of failure' (Hardy et al., 1998).

The coaches perceived the 'demands of training' (ranking = 10/10) to have been a stressor on the players. The academy training programme required the players to have on-table training sessions each day after school, to have regular fitness sessions and to be involved in education sessions in sport psychology, tactical awareness and nutrition. The coaches perceived this change of lifestyle to be a stressor, however this was not highlighted by the players as a source of stress.

Players reported their own personal expectations as a major source of stress (ranking = 2/10). All the players had high expectations of themselves and had a strong personal desire to achieve their goals and 'make it' in table tennis. However, it was evident from the findings that living and training in an academy environment created a number of extra stressors that were not evident in the players' game before they came to the national training centre.

There are a number of recognised skills to help individuals cope with stress induced anxiety at both a cognitive and a somatic level (Jones and Hardy, 1990). Techniques such as progressive muscular relaxation, breathing techniques, positive self talk and cognitive restructuring are all skills that can be individually refined to best suit the needs of each player. However, based on the findings from the present study it was thought that a number of environmental changes could be made at the academy to help create the appropriate attitude and behaviour required for players to cope with the pressure of competing and the stressors of everyday life (Martens, 1987). It was thought that these changes in the environment could then compliment the individual work that was being carried out with the players at a cognitive or somatic level.

To manipulate the environment at the academy two basic principles were followed. Firstly, to develop the players' mental toughness it was felt that pressure in the training hall needed to increase (Jones, Hanton and Connaughton, 2002). The reason for this was to allow the players to become desensitised to playing under pressure, to help them to develop their own strategies and refine their preparation and routines. A further goal of these sessions was to encourage the players to become independent thinkers. Thus, enabling players to develop problem solving skills and greater tactical awareness on the table, rather than being reliant upon the coach to make such decisions.   Secondly, the stress experienced outside the training hall needed to decrease so that the players felt like they could 'switch off' from table tennis.

The first strategy was to design pressure practice sessions. During these sessions conditions would be set up to simulate a competition environment. The objective of this simulation was to establish a more competitive match play environment, which was ego-involving for the players. Other stressors were incorporated into this environment, such as spectators, video cameras, an academy ranking list and an outcome attached to the results of the match (e.g. selection). The matches were often designed so that players had to play opponents of lesser ability, so they could develop strategies to 'play to win' rather than 'playing not to lose'. To supplement this intervention, players were required to play more domestic competitions. This was to help players to become desensitised to the pressure and expectation of playing lesser players and learn to win in a lose/lose situation.

For reducing stress outside the training hall it was proposed that players should have one night off a week to do a social activity unrelated to table tennis. It was also proposed that this activity should take place away from the training academy. It had become evident that the players needed a change of environment to break the monotony of their usual routine. A further suggestion was that players should have greater freedom to leave the academy as long as they were under supervision. More social facilities were also to be included in the common room so that the players could 'switch off' from table tennis. The coaches were also encouraged to carry out more individual and group educational sessions so that players could have an opportunity to discuss aspects of their game via the use of video analysis. It was felt that this would help educate the players and develop the communication between coach and player. Finally, it was proposed that parent education seminars should be established. These sessions were designed to make parents aware of the stressors that their son/daughter are under at the academy and how best to support them.


## 5 Conclusion

There are many benefits of centralised training academies. The athlete has access to excellent facilities, coaching, training, sport science support and education. However, the findings from this study suggest that training at a national academy creates a number of additional stressors that need to be considered in order to help players to maximise their potential. Many of these stressors can be manipulated or appeased to create a more suitable environment that will best facilitate the growth of the athletes. This can be achieved by increasing pressure inside the training hall to help develop mental toughness (Jones et al., 2002), whilst keeping stress to a minimum outside the training hall to help promote a more balanced lifestyle. If this environment is coupled with good provision from the support team (parents, coach and sport science team) then the player can grow to be stronger mentally and also experience a more balanced approach to every day life as an elite performer.


## 6 References

Gould, D., Jackson, S.A. and Finch, L. (1993). Sources of stress in national champion figure skaters. **Journal of Sport and Exercise Psychology**, 15, 134-159.

Hardy, L., Jones, G. and Gould, D. (1998). **Understanding psychological preparation for sport: Theory and practice of elite performers**. Chichester: John Wiley and Sons.

Jones, G. and Hardy, L. (1990). **Stress and performance in Sport**. Chichester: John Wiley and Sons.

Jones, G., Hanton, S., and Connaughton, D. (2002). What is this thing called mental toughness? An investigation of elite performers. **Journal of Applied Sport Psychology**, 14, 205-218.

Martens, R. (1987). **Coaches guide to sport psychology**. Human Kinetics Publishers, Inc. Champaign, Illinois.

Mullen, R., and Hardy, L. (2000). State anxiety and motor performance: Testing the conscious processing hypothesis. **Journal of Sports Science**, 18, 785-799.

Patton, M.Q. (1990). **Qualitative evaluation and research methods** (2nd ed). Newbury Park: Sage.

Scanlan, T.K., Stein, G.L., and Ravizza, K. (1991). An in-depth study of former elite figure skaters: III. Sources of stress. **Journal of Sport and Exercise Psychology**, 13, 103-120.

# 39 The effectiveness of repetitive practice on the neuromuscular pathways in elite badminton athletes

A.J. Pearce[1,2], G.W. Thickbroom[1], M.L. Byrnes[1] and F.L. Mastaglia[1]

[1]Clinical Neurophysiology Laboratory, Australian Neuromuscular Research Institute, Nedlands, Western Australia, 6009. [2]Director of Coaching, Tennis Australia, Australia.

## 1 Introduction

To be an elite badminton athlete requires many years of constant training and refinement of specific skills. Although widely acknowledge as the "fastest" racket sport (in terms of the speed of the shuttle hit as compared to speed of the ball in other racket sports), it is the fine touch skills (particularly around the net) that differentiate badminton from other racket sports. Elite athletes will dedicate daily practice refining net skills which include "tumbling and spinning" the shuttle.

By the nature of their training, badminton players have developed strong neuromuscular patterning through repetition. However, no study has investigated the underlying neurophysiological mechanisms, such as motor cortex excitability and representation that contribute to highly skilled movement.

Transcranial Magnetic Stimulation (TMS) is a tool commonly used in clinical neurology. TMS is non-invasive and causes no pain (Barker et al., 1985). More recently, TMS has become widely used as a research tool investigating many areas of human neuromuscular physiology including the effects of motor control and skill acquisition. However, to date, studies have been limited to simple, short-term learning tasks such as five-fingered tapping tasks (see a review by Hallett, 2000).

The aim of this study to use TMS to measure the neuromuscular excitability and motor representation of a hand muscle used extensively in badminton in a group of highly skilled elite badminton athletes.

## 2 Methods

### 2.1 Participants

The investigation focussed on three groups. The elite group consisted of five athletes (4 male, 1 female; 22-28 years). All athletes participated in regular international standard competition and, apart from one, played right handed. On-court training averaged 16 hours per week (total average training of 22 hours per week), which included match play, drill-practice and technical skill training. All athletes had suspended their training program for two weeks prior to testing. Five social-competition level participants (3 male, 2 female; 22-50 years, all right handed) who play regularly (up to 3 times per week) but who did not actually train their skills, and 10 normal right handed participants (5 male, 5 female; 23-40 years) who did not participate in any form of racket sport served as controls. All participants gave written informed consent, and the study had the approval of the Human Rights Committee of the University of Western Australia.

## 2.2 Materials

TMS was delivered using a Magstim 200 stimulator (Whitland, Dyfed, UK) with a 5cm diameter figure-eight coil. A snugly fitting cap (Figures 1a and b), with pre-marked sites at 1cm spacing was placed over the participant's head and positioned with reference to the nasion-inion (NIL) and inter-aural lines (IAL).

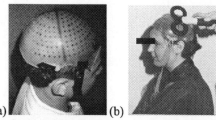

(a)                      (b)

Figure 1. (a) Fitted cap for identification of sites for mapping, and (b) Antero-
          posterior orientation of coil held during studies.

Skilled badminton strokes (e.g. precise net shots) require racket manoeuvres involving muscles of the hand. Electromyographic (EMG) activity was recorded from surface electrodes (4mm, Grass-Telefactor, USA) placed over the motor point and the insertion of the first dorsal interosseous (FDI) muscle of the hand. EMG signals were amplified (x1000) and digitised at 200 Hz for 500 ms after a stimulus.

## 2.3 Procedure

Prior to testing participants answered a written questionnaire on handedness, and training schedule including training time on-court and off-court.

Participants in each group were tested individually in the laboratory, and sat relaxed in a comfortable chair during the testing session. Testing consisted of concentrating on one half of the scalp, being the participant's non-dominant hemisphere, then after a short rest period, the other half of the scalp (participant's dominant hemisphere).

With the coil held tangential to the skull in an antero-posterior orientation, (Figure 1b), sites near the estimated centre of the hand area (4-7 cm lateral to the vertex) were first explored to determine neuromuscular excitability, that is, the site at which the largest motor evoked potential (MEP) could be obtained. This site was defined as the centre site. At centre site, input/output curves were measured by increasing stimulus intensity in 5% steps from a level below the participant's motor threshold until the MEP amplitude became saturated. Motor threshold was defined as the intensity at which a MEP could be obtained with at least two from a series of four stimuli. Following input/output curve measurement, stimulus intensity was set at 20% of stimulator output above motor threshold for mapping each hemisphere.

For motor representation mapping, four stimuli were delivered at the first site, and then at increasingly anterior, and then posterior sites (2 cm steps) until a MEP could no longer be elicited. This pattern was repeated for lateral and then medial sites (1 cm steps) until all map borders had been determined. Stimuli were a minimum of 5 s apart and participants rested briefly between stimulation at each site.

MEP latency (from stimulus to onset of MEP), amplitude (peak-to-peak) and silent period (SP) duration (from MEP onset to return of uninterrupted EMG activity) were measured off-line for the four stimuli at the first site (Figure 2). A complete map of

MEP amplitude vs. scalp position was generated by calculating mean peak-to-peak MEP amplitude at each stimulus site and interpolating these values between stimulus sites. The peak of the maps was determined from the position of the greatest value. This position was expressed in millimetres from the vertex and from the IAL (Figure 3). For a detailed description of the cortical mapping protocol, see Thickbroom et al. (1999). Neuromuscular and mapping parameters from participants in the elite and social groups were compared to normal range at a significance level of $P < 0.05$.

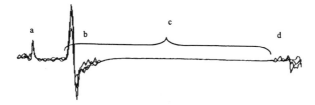

Figure 2. An example of Motor Evoked Potential. MEP latency is measured from stimulus onset (a) to deflection defining the MEP (b). The silent period (SP) determined from the onset deflection of the MEP (c, highlighted with bracket) until return of EMG signal (d). This example shows an overlay of 20 MEPs illustrating the reliability of TMS and the MEP.

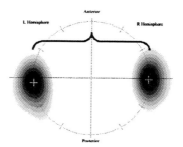

Figure 3. MEP map viewed from superior for control and social players. Vertex divides left/right hemisphere. White cross represents peak value of maps.

## 3 Results

### 3.1 Control participants
Control participants' showed small, but non-significant differences in motor threshold between dominant and non-dominant sides, being equal to or less than 5% for all control participants.

MEP parameters also showed no differences. MEP latency for the dominant and non-dominant sides was $21.3 \pm 2.2$ ms and $21.4 \pm 2.1$ ms respectively. MEP amplitude between dominant and non-dominant sides was $6.0 \pm 4.9$ mV and 5.8 mV $\pm 3.4$ mV respectively. SP duration was also similar on both dominant and non-dominant sides ($175 \pm 35$ ms and $182 \pm 42$ ms respectively).

A typical symmetrical map observed in participants in both control and social player groups is shown in Figure 3. Medio-lateral interside difference (dominant/non-dominant map centre calculation) from the vertex was less than 3 mm and antero-posterior difference from the IAL was less than 7 mm (Figure 5, for all participants).

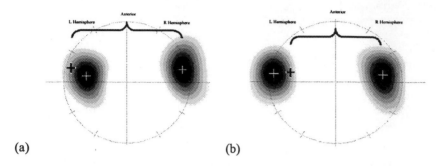

(a)                                                      (b)

Figure 4. Typical MEP maps for two elite athletes showing (a)medial and (b)lateral shifts in MEP maps. Black cross is where a symmetrical map would be.

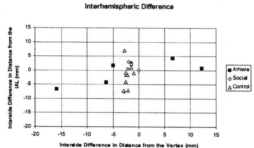

Figure 5. Inter-side difference in map position in the mediolateral and anteroposterior axis for all participants in all groups.

### 3.2 Social players

Interhemispheric results in motor threshold, MEP latency, MEP amplitude and SP duration were non-significant for all social players.

There were no significant interside differences in the centre of the maps between the playing and non-playing sides (Figure 3) with less than 3 mm difference in medio-lateral and less than 7 mm difference in antero-posterior maps (Figure 5).

### 3.3 Elite athletes

MEP latency was similar on both sides in the elite athlete group (mean 20.6 ms for the non-playing side, 21.2 ms for the playing side).

Comparisons of motor thresholds between dominant and non-dominant hemispheres were similar to controls and social players in 3 of the 5 participants (participants 1, 2, and 5). However, for two participants, the motor threshold was 10% lower in the hemisphere controlling the playing side compared to the non-playing side ($P < 0.05$).

MEP amplitude was higher on the playing side for all participants in the athlete group (mean playing amplitude 10.5 mV vs. mean non-playing amplitude 5.7 mV; $P < 0.05$). SP duration was similar on each side ($168 \pm 31$ ms vs. $162 \pm 38$ ms).

MEP maps on the athletes' non-playing side ranged from 45 mm to 58 mm (mean 54 mm) from the vertex and from 13 mm anterior to 3 mm posterior to the IAL (mean 6 mm anterior). Map centre on the athlete's playing side ranged from 39 mm to 59 mm lateral (mean 52 mm) to the vertex and from 17 mm anterior to 5 mm posterior to the IAL (mean 5 mm anterior). Maps on the athletes playing side were displaced 7 to 16 mm medially in 3 participants (Figure 4a), and 6 mm to 12 mm laterally in 2 participants (Figure 4b) with respect to the maps on the non-playing side. No significant differences where found in the antero-posterior position of the maps on the two sides.

There was no association between MEP changes, or degree of map shift and the overall time the athlete had been playing badminton.

## 4 Discussion

Results showing no differences between social players and control participants suggest that reorganisation in the athletes may be influenced by structured, effective motor practice. These results concur with the studies of Grafton et al. (1992) and Plautz et al. (1995) who demonstrated neuromuscular changes associated with dexterous motor skill compared with elementary motor use. Plautz et al. (1995) demonstrated reorganisation in the representation of digit and wrist muscles in the monkey following structured motor training compared to simple motor use, similarly, Grafton et al. (1992), demonstrated neuro-anatomical differences between motor learning and general motor execution. Although skilful in their own right, social players do not undertake skilled practice sessions as the elite athlete group, further supporting the contribution of repetitive motor training in neuromuscular alteration and motor representation.

The changes found in 4 of the 5 elite athletes, suggest changes in the neuromuscular excitability to the playing hand. A change in motor threshold may arise from a shift in the balance between inhibitory and excitatory inputs to cortical or spinal motoneurons. A change in MEP amplitude in the absence of a change in motor threshold could arise from an increase in the number of descending volleys generated by the cortical stimulus, or from an increase in the number of cells activated. Mechanisms that have been suggested to explain such changes include the establishment of new motoneuron connections, and/or alterations in the effectiveness of previously existing motoneuron connections (Kaas, 1991; Pascual-Leone et al., 1994).

The variances of asymmetry found in all of the maps in the elite athletes suggest that there has been a functional reorganisation in the cortical hemisphere controlling the playing side in the elite athlete group. Such reorganisations may be a consequence of a change in the pattern of sensory inputs to the motor cortex, such as grip and stroke technique changes, or a reflection of task-related changes in the functional organisation of the primary motor cortex itself. Evidence of sensory influence on reorganisation in primary sensory cortex has been demonstrated on the playing side of highly trained musicians (Elbert et al., 1995), and it has been suggested that enhanced afferent input from increased use of a body part can produce reorganisation in the motor cortex (Kaas, 1991). Changes within primary motor cortex may be a result of repetitious motor training of complex skills from an early age and for long periods of time. Although, no correlation was found between the degree of map shift and the age at onset and duration of formal training, or success of the athlete; the presence of map shifts in all of the elite athletes suggests that there has been modulation of the motor representation as a result of reinforced, continuous, skill training.

The range in the magnitude and direction of the map shifts maybe due to individual changes in the excitability of sub-sets of motor neurones within the cortical representation of the target muscle. Monkey studies (Schieber and Hibbard, 1993) have shown that the neuromuscular projection to individual hand muscles utilise a population of neurones dispersed throughout the motor cortex rather than a clearly defined segregated population, and that the pattern of modulation seems to be movement and task influenced. Again, the direction and magnitude in map shifts could not be correlated to playing history or success of the athlete.

## 5 Conclusion

This study aimed to investigate the effect of repetitive training on neuromuscular excitability and representation in the motor cortex.

It is clear that further study should investigate elite athletes from other racket sports. Moreover, study into elite athlete's who have retired would provide further insight into neuromuscular and brain plasticity, particularly when retired champions are still capable of producing excellent technique many years after ceasing formal training.

## 6 References

Barker, A.T., Jalinous, R. and Freeston, I.L. (1985). Non-invasive magnetic stimulation of the human motor cortex. **Lancet, 2**, 1106-1107.

Elbert, T., Pantev, C., Wienbruch, C., Rockstroh, B., and Taub, E. (1995). Increased cortical representation of the fingers of the left hand in string players. **Science**, 270, 305-307.

Grafton, S.T., Mazziotta, J.C., Presty, S., Friston, K.J., Frackowiak, R.S.J. and Phelps, M.E. (1992). Functional anatomy of human procedural learning determined with regional cerebral blood flow and PET. **Journal of Neuroscience**, 12, 2542-2548.

Hallett, M. (2000). Transcranial magnetic stimulation and the human brain. **Nature**, 406, 147-150.

Kaas, J.H. (1991). Plasticity of sensory and motor maps in adult mammals. **Annual Review of Neuroscience**, 14, 137-167.

Pascual-Leone, A., Grafman, J. and Hallett, M. (1994). Modulation of cortical motor output maps during development of implicit and explicit knowledge. **Science**, 263, 1287-1289.

Plautz, E.J., Milliken, G.W. and Nudo, R.J. (1995). Differential effects of skill acquisition and motor use on the reorganisation of motor representations in area 4 of adult squirrel monkeys. **Society of Neuroscience**, San Diego, CA.

Schieber, M.H. and Hibbard, L.S. (1993). How somatotopic is the motor cortex hand area? **Science**, 261, 489-491.

Thickbroom, G.W., Byrnes, M.L. and Mastaglia, F.L. (1999). Methodology and application of TMS mapping. **Electroencephalography and Clinical Neurophysiology**, suppl. 51, 48-54.

# 40 Disguising ones intentions: The availability of visual cues and situational probabilities when playing against an international level squash player

N. James and C. Bradley

*Department of Sports Science, University of Wales Swansea, Vivian Tower, Singleton Park, Swansea SA2 8PP, UK.*

## 1 Introduction

It has been suggested that it is important to be able to anticipate ball trajectories in racket sports such as tennis (Féry and Crognier, 2001), squash (Abernethy, 1990a), and badminton (Abernethy and Russell, 1987). Experts have consistently been shown to possess a significant advantage over less skilled players in utilising advance visual cues (e.g. racket and arm), thought to enable superior performance in anticipating ball trajectories (Abernethy, et al., 2001; Buckolz, et al., 1988; Williams, et al., 2002). The large set of published work suggesting an expert advantage have utilised a range of experimental methodologies with the majority having been conducted within artificial environments. This typically involves participants watching a video recording of a performance taken from the perspective of a performer. This visual representation is then either stopped at set times prior to and after the ball (or shuttlecock) is hit (temporal occlusion) or sections of the display are hidden from view (spatial occlusion).

The findings from the temporal occlusion studies suggest that when the occlusion takes place before or around ball contact, performance is related to the skill level of the participant with experts having a significant advantage over less skilled players (e.g. Abernethy, 1990a; Buckolz et al. 1988). Whilst these findings have been reasonably robust they have offered no insight with regard to the nature of the cues thought to be used. Abernethy et al. (2001), using a comparison of film and point-light displays, demonstrated that it was the display kinematics as opposed to figural or textural information that was useful. Also Abernethy and Russell (1987) demonstrated a decrement in the experts' prediction accuracy, down to a similar level of the novices in the study, when the racket and arm were spatially occluded in a badminton study. This was the only occlusion that had this effect and led to the conclusion that the racket and arm were a critical cue used by experts resulting in their superior task performance. This finding was not supported in a similar squash study (Abernethy, 1990b) where no selective occlusion of any body part resulted in a decrement of performance. It was suggested, however, that the latter finding may have been due to the occlusion technique having been ineffective.

The previous studies have been criticised on a number of points. Firstly, watching a film representation is not the same as actually playing in a game (i.e. they lack ecological validity). For example, the time demands in the artificial setting may not replicate the real situation and introduce memory distortions. Secondly, many of these studies use only one or two performers in the presented film clips and thus idiosyncrasies in the performer's technique may aid or constrain participants' predictions. There was no contextual information (i.e. related to what happened previously, such as a player's tendency to play a particular shot) present in these film representations. Consequently, efforts have been made to investigate advance cues in more naturalistic settings.

Féry and Crognier (2001) had tennis experts view passing shots both *in situ* whilst on court wearing liquid crystal occlusion glasses and on a video presentation. Their findings suggested that the *in situ* experience allowed more precise and consistent spatial and temporal estimations than the video presentations. Since it appeared that the participants could still demonstrate their perceptual expertise in the more artificial environment (see also Abernethy, 1990a) the study supported the use of film based studies.

Howarth et al. (1984) recorded actual squash matches with a high speed camera. Visual cue usage was calculated on the basis of the first movement to intercept the ball, hypothesised to take place once a player had sufficient information to determine ball trajectory. A simple calculation to account for reaction time (based on Mcleod's (1987) suggestion of 200 ms) allowed an estimate of the moment when the player had collected enough information to make this movement. Bakker, Whiting and van der Brug (1990) have criticised this suggesting delays may be less than 200 ms. Although this study was based on a small sample size (12 events for each of two levels of squash player) the differences appeared marked. Grade A players had enough information 87.5 ms prior to the ball being hit compared to the grade D players 163 ms after the ball was hit. Methodological concerns are raised regarding the accuracy of judging the first movement towards the ball however. Furthermore, it was unsure whether first movement reflected the use of visual cues or whether other information sources intervened. Situational information such as knowledge of the opponent's weaknesses or preferences (Buckolz et al. 1988) or the difficulty of the shot attempted may have provided additional predictive information (Alain and Sarrazin, 1988).

Abernethy et al. (2001) recently had expert and novice squash players attempt to return a shot played by an intermediate standard opponent whilst wearing liquid occlusion glasses (Milgram, 1987) that were turned opaque at quasi-random intervals. Realistic match conditions were applied ensuring that situational probabilities varied. Expert players were shown to perform better than novices in recognising ball trajectories, selecting either short or long and straight or crosscourt. However, this finding needs to be interpreted with caution because the expert players (playing opponents less skilled than themselves) would have put their opponent under significantly more pressure than the novices could have achieved (against more skilled opponents). Indeed, the experts' performance was significantly better than chance when vision had been removed before the opponent had even moved into position to play the stroke. Both of these observations suggest the experts made use of situational probability information.

Previous studies therefore suggest that both situational probabilities and visual cues seem to be used to anticipate ball trajectories but the extent of their use in actual matches is unclear. Little emphasis has been placed on trying to control for different shot difficulties which must impact on the availability of these cues. Also no studies seem to consider whether expert players attempt to hide the suggested visual cues to prevent anticipatory behaviour. Therefore the aim of this study was to assess expert players' visual cue usage whilst playing against a similarly ranked opponent but only when the opponent was about to play an easy shot. This situation enabled the opponent to disguise his/her intentions if he/she so wished and also meant that the estimation of situational probabilities was of maximum difficulty.

## 2 Methods

### 2.1 Participants
A male world ranked squash player (number 15 during data capture, but previously ranked in the top 5 for 1 year, mainly in 2001) was filmed playing matches against three opponents (4, 61, 76 their highest world rankings in the previous two years). He was also filmed in a training situation where the ball was fed to selected areas of the court.

### 2.2 Apparatus
A high speed camera (Motionscope PCI 1000S, Redlake Imaging Corporation, Morgan Hill, USA) captured real event and training scenarios at 250 Hz. The camera operates through a PCI card in a PC such that just over 4 s of play (1024 frames) were continuously recorded. The trigger to transfer the images from memory to hard disk was set to record the 4 s of play prior to trigger activation (so that the desired shot could be viewed before deciding to record it). The focal length was set to allow near full coverage of the court without the need of moving the camera. This enabled virtually all shots to be in view (the back corners were partially restricted). A Panasonic NV-MX300B digital video camera also continuously recorded the matches.

### 2.3 Procedure
In the match situations (conducted under World Squash Federation rules) participants prepared and were asked to play as they normally would. Each four second clip was selected on the basis of the *a priori* criteria that only relatively easy shots (ball at contact was away from the side wall and the player not overly stretching to make the shot) were to be analysed. This was to limit the use of situational probabilities (suggested as a confounding variable in the study by Abernethy et al., 2001) and enhance the likelihood of disguise or deception being used. Following a suitable event the trigger was activated resulting in a clip containing the selected shot and the movement sequence made by the opponent in response to the shot. In the training situation the ball was hit to the player (short to the forehand from deep) who was instructed to play different shots, as he would during a match, but to actively try to disguise his intentions. This data was analysed using biomechanical video analysis software (Quintic Consultancy Ltd., Coventry, UK). For the stroke analysis accurate timings of ball bounce, racket swing and point of ball contact as well as synchronised images (to ball contact and ball bounce on floor) of the player hitting different strokes were produced (to aid qualitative analysis). For the movement analysis, timings of foot movements were made with respect to the ball being played by the opponent. Inter- and intra-reliability tests revealed maximum discrepancy between two timings of 0.016 s and 0.012 s respectively. A further analysis of movement times (taken from the Panasonic recording) was carried out using the Observer Pro (Noldus Information Technology, Wageningen, The Netherlands).

# 3 Results

## 3.1 Disguise and deception

Analyses showed that the ball was hit between 0.24 s and 0.63 s after the ball bounced on the floor (across both conditions, Figure 1). This was in part due to the previous shot (i.e. pace of ball in the match situation) but was also under the control of the player. There was no significant difference (P=0.19) between the time of the ball bounce and the ball being hit when comparing straight shots 0.38 s (±0.03) and cross court shots 0.47 s (±0.14). When similar shots were played during the training scenario (off similar ball velocities) the ball was struck at very consistent time delays after the ball bounce (e.g. straight drop shots were between 0.2 s and 0.24 s). This very small variation may have been indicative of the player intentionally hitting the ball early or late. The swing characteristics (kinematics) of the racket (when playing either straight, crosscourt or short) was judged to be remarkably similar (the first author is a Level 4 squash coach and previous National squad coach). Clear differences only became apparent between 0.07 s and 0.03 s before ball contact. This difference was as a result of differing wrist angles employed to play the shot of choice at the last moment and corresponded to swing times (initiation of forward travel of racket to ball contact) of 0.20 s (±0.09).

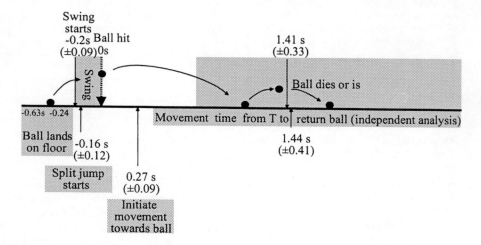

Figure 1. Scaled representation of events relative to ball contact.
* Shaded areas represent the range of values from minimum to maximum recorded

## 3.2 Movement and ball travel times

The three opponents responded to the main participant's shots in a very predictable manner by initiating a split-step jump (one foot take-off to spread legs so that on landing either foot can initiate the directional response, see also Singer et al. 1994) -0.16 s (±0.12) relative to the racket ball contact (Figure 1). These times appeared quite normally distributed (skewness = -0.22, SE $^-$ 0.32) with one outlier (-0.49 s) occurring when returning a straight drop shot played from the front of the court. This jump was followed by an initiation of a movement towards the ball destination occurring 0.27 s (±0.09) relative to the racket ball contact again normally distributed (skewness = -0.17, SE = 0.32).

The time taken for the ball to reach its intended destination and become un-returnable was calculated for a range of shots played from different court areas. The overall mean 1.41 s (±0.33) included the relatively short time of 1.27 s (±0.33) for straight drop shots. This compared very similarly with the Observer Pro analysis of the time taken to move from the T area (near the centre of the court) to return the opponent's shot 1.44 s (±0.41).

## 4 Discussion

Many previous studies show that experts in racket sports are able to use early visual cues to anticipate ball direction but seldom have these studies involved similarly ranked opponents, controlled for shot difficulty or considered the intentional deceptive actions likely to be present in expert players. Qualitative assessment of a player of exceptional ability revealed minor kinematic differences in the wrist area for relatively easy shots, only apparent a maximum of 0.07s prior to the ball being struck. The usefulness of this information was assessed by measurements of the opponent's movements in relation to similarly easy shots in match situations. This analysis suggested that the first movement in the direction of the ball's finishing location was predominately over 0.2 s after ball contact. Given that reaction times are likely to be less, not greater than 0.2 s, this suggests that this player, in this situation, is able to disguise his intentions sufficiently to prevent the opponent using visual cues to anticipate relatively easy shots. This was contrary to the findings of Howarth et al. (1984) where their experts moved towards the ball far earlier (0.11 s). However, it is likely that the sampled shots in the Howarth et al. study were more difficult (i.e. the player making the shot was under pressure). This would have resulted in greater situational information available allowing earlier anticipatory movements compared with this study. Also a methodological difference was observed where Howarth et al. did not mention the split jump technique used by all of the players in this study, perhaps indicative of skill level differences in the participants or a possible source of measurement error. The split jump technique was remarkably robust temporally in relation to ball contact with qualitative assessments suggesting that positioning on or around the 'T' was more indicative of anticipation strategy. For example players positioned themselves nearer the front wall in response to a shot played from the front of the court but movement times remained similar to other shots. This positioning was subjectively rated as probabilistic (because of its early nature) and not visual cue driven. Incidentally, this was identified as a training objective by the main participant (i.e. to rationalise possible shot alternatives in certain circumstances). Further analysis of the time taken for shots to reach their intended destinations and independent analyses of the movement times for players to run from the T area to retrieve the ball confirmed that in the majority of instances players hit the return shot around 1.44 s after the ball was struck. Given the court dimensions this is easily achievable at elite player's fitness levels confirming that seldom do these players need to utilise risky anticipatory behaviour.

## 5 Conclusions

Expert squash players viewed another expert playing relatively easy shots in real match situations. This was thought to minimise the use of situational information because the player hitting the ball was not restricted or more likely to play any particular shot. It was found that in this situation the majority of first movements towards the intended ball location required some ball flight information in addition to any anticipatory information available. This supported the kinematic analysis which suggested the expert player was able to disguise his intentions until at least 0.07 s before ball contact. Evidence was found for movements to be made to slightly different areas around the T area (spatial adaptation) rather than to be temporally related to the opponent's shot. This is indicative of using situational information as opposed to visual cues.

## 6 References

Abernethy, B. (1990a). Expertise, visual search and information pick-up in squash. **Perception**, 19, 63-77.

Abernethy, B. (1990b). Anticipation in squash: Differences in advance cue utilization between expert and novice players. **Journal of Sports Sciences**, 8, 17-34.

Abernethy, B. and Russell, D.G. (1987). Expert-Novice differences in an applied selective attention task. **Journal of Sport Psychology**, 9, 326-345.

Abernethy, B., Gill, D.P., Parks, S.L. and Packer, S.T. (2001). Expertise and the perception of kinematic and situational probability information. **Perception**, 30, 233-252.

Alain, C. and Sarrazin, C. (1988). Study of decision-making in squash competition: A computer simulation approach. **Canadian Journal of Sports Science**, 15, 193-200.

Bakker, F.C., Whiting, H.T.A. and van der Brug, H. (1990). **Sport Psychology: Concepts and Applications**. Chichester: John Wiley.

Buckolz, E., Prapavesis, H. and Fairs, J. (1988). Advance cues and their use in predicting tennis passing shots. **Canadian Journal of Sports Science**, 13, 20-30.

Féry, Y. and Crognier, L. (2001). On the tactical significance of game situations in anticipating ball trajectories in tennis. **Research Quarterly for Exercise and Sport**, 72, 143-149.

Howarth, C., Walsh, W.D. and Abernethy, B. (1984). A field examination of anticipation in squash: Some preliminary data. **The Australian Journal of Science and Medicine in Sport**, 16, 7-11.

McLeod, P. (1987). Visual reaction time and high-speed ball games. **Perception**, 16, 49-59.

Milgram, P. (1987). A spectacle-mounted liquid crystal tachistoscope. **Behavior Research Methods, Instruments and Computers**, 19, 449-456.

Singer, R.N., Cauraugh, J.H., Chen, D., Steinberg, G.M., Frehlich, S.G. and Wang, L. (1994). Training mental quickness in beginning/intermediate tennis players. **The Sport Psychologist**, 8, 305-318.

Williams, A.M., Ward, P., Knowles, J.M. and Smeeton, N.J. (2002). Anticipation skill in a real-world task: Measurement, training and transfer in tennis. **Journal of Experimental Psychology: Applied**, 8, 259-270.

# 41 Tennis as a dynamical self-organizing system

Y. Palut and P.G. Zanone
*EA 2044 "Acquisition et Transmission des Habiletés Motrices",
UFR STAPS, Université Paul Sabatier, Toulouse, France.*

## 1 Introduction

Behavioural studies in sports have mostly used analytical methods. Racket sports are no exception. Notably, a detailed scrutiny of squash players revealed a relationship between the types of shot and its outcome (win or loss) (McGarry et al., 1994, 1996). Results showed that some shot sequences were adopted most frequently and tended to lead to a winning point. These sequences defined a behavioral invariant repertoire for an individual player, which coaches should take into account to optimize the tactical preparation. Such invariance, however, was only relevant in reference to one single pair of players, a clear shortcoming as players are known to change their playing style as a function of their opponent. Moreover, the huge amount of data that has to be processed in studies using these kinds of procedures renders any medium or long term prediction quite unlikely. By and large, analytic methods appear then to be inept for addressing the complexity of dual sports.

To circumvent such a limitation, some authors proposed to adopt a framework drawn from self-organization theories in order to study the behavior of dual sports players in a (more) systemic fashion (Hodges et al., 1998; McGarry et al., 2002). Dual sports are no longer considered to be the sum of two individual behaviors but rather a complex system composed of many interacting components. From such an interaction may emerge a coherent collective behaviour from the players, which may show, for instance, through their relative displacement on the court. From that perspective, dual sports may be studied as a dynamical system, the evolution of which captures the invariance and the change in the players' collective behavior.

In line with the above perspective, the present study investigates tennis as a self-organized dynamical system. A first step is to identify a so-called collective variable (Haken, 1983) that sums up the invariant features and the changes occurring in the players' behaviour. In tennis, the game requires that the players go back to the middle of the baseline after they have moved away from it in order to return the ball. Thus, tennis players exhibit continual to-and-fro displacements about a central "home position" on the baseline. Therefore, such periodic motion may be ascribed theoretically to that of an oscillator. Moreover, in order to move in a proper fashion, the players must take into account their own position, as well as those of their opponent and of the ball. This reciprocal attending constitutes an informational linkage, so that theoretically, the two players constitute a system formed by two coupled oscillators. A well-established property of coupled oscillators, whatever their nature and their scale, is phase synchronization (Pikovsky et al., 2001). Thus, the collective behaviour of coupled oscillators is adeptly captured by their relative phase, a measure of their lead-lag relationship. Therefore, we hypothesize that phase lag or relative phase is a pertinent collective variable to characterize the modes of displacements exhibited by two tennis players during the game.

## 2 Methods

### 2.1 Participants
Four male students at the Sports Faculty in Toulouse (age: mean $= 21.3$, $s = 0.95$ years) volunteered for the experiment. They have practiced tennis at least for fifteen years and had attained a national level.

### 2.2 Apparatus
The experiment took place on an indoor clay tennis court. A digital camera was fixed on the top of a ten-meter high scaffold placed in an adjacent court. The camera recorded the players' displacements on the entire court at 25 Hz.

### 2.3 Protocol
After an initial warm-up lasting 15 min, the participants were instructed to play each other under the specific requirement that before the seventh shot of the rally, only indirect winning points were permitted, that is, following a mistake from their opponent; from the eighth shot on, direct winning was allowed. This was intended to induce longer games, so stable displacement modes might emerge and be analyzed.

### 2.4 Data processing
Trials with more than seven rallies were selected ($N = 40$). They lasted 20 s on average. A motion analysis system tracked the x-y position of both players on the video and reconstructed their 2D displacements with a precision of 40 cm. The reference was set in the middle of the court. The x-axis and y-axis corresponded to a horizontal and a vertical motion on the screen, respectively. Two positional time series were obtained for each player corresponding to their longitudinal displacements, forward and backwards, and to lateral displacements, to the left or right, respectively. The data were smoothed through a second-order low-pass Butterworth filter with a 1 Hz cut-off. The longitudinal displacements were mostly of very small amplitude (actually less than 200 cm) or, when they were of larger scale, they preceded the end of a trial, as the player was smashing close to the net or running for a drop shot. Thus, longitudinal displacements were too scarce or did not exhibit an amplitude large enough to be included in the subsequent analyses. Therefore, this study will present data pertaining only to the lateral motion of the players.

### 2.5 Relative phase calculation
In order to determine the phase synchronization in the players' displacements, we carried out a windowed cross-correlation for every trial. A standard cross-correlation computes successive correlation measures to assess how and how much two time series covary. Initially, a standard correlation was computed (lag = 0). Then, one series was shifted by one sample (lag = 1), that is, in our case by 40 ms, and another correlation was computed. The same procedure was repeated until the shifted series had been entirely shoved with respect to the other (lag = number of samples − 1). The outcome was then a correlation value for each lag. By definition, a positive

correlation means that both series increase or decrease simultaneously, whereas a negative value means that when one series increases, the other decreases, and conversely. The value of the correlation indexes the strength of such a direct or inverse covariation of the time series. Of course, such covariation may well be non significant. Now, the lag for which the correlation is larger in absolute value informs the time shift to be inserted to maximize covariation. Hence, relative phase between the time series is that time shift divided by the average period of the series (phase relative = (lag/period) * 360).

In order to reveal the development of the synchronization of the players' displacements over one single trial, cross-correlations were calculated within successive windows. As the leading frequency for the time series was about 0.25 Hz, the width of the windows was set to the compatible period, namely, 5 s. Trials were thus divided into 3 to 6 consecutive windows, depending on their total duration. For each window, a cross-correlation was computed, yielding the leading period, the lag maximizing correlation, hence relative phase.

## 3 Results

### 3.1 Relative phase evolution
By simply eyeballing all trials, three types of relative phase evolution within a trial were identified. The first category, comprising 40% of the trials, consisted of trials in which no change was observed, relative phase remaining stable about 180° (Figures 1 and 2). In a second category, also including 40%, relative phase exhibited a sharp transition from 180° to 0° (Figures 3 and 4). In the remaining trials, no clear trend could be detected. For each category, mean relative phase and the associated variability were computed within each successive window.

### 3.2 Stable trials
Figure 1 presents the evolution of the average relative phase for the stable category. The abscissa represents time, rendered by the widow number. The ordinate represents the mean relative phase for each window, lasting 5 s. Vertical bars represent the associated between-trial standard deviation. Relative phase seemed to hover about 180°, irrespective of the window number. An analysis of variance with repeated measure failed to detect any effect of the window number on relative phase ($F_{5, 5} = 0.98$, $P > .05$). This finding indicates that for the stable category, relative phase did not change significantly from the initial 180° value. In other words, players exhibited a stable synchronization of their displacements with a 180° phase lag, that is, an anti-phase pattern of relative motion. Moreover, vertical bars in Figure 1 show that variability remained fairly constant over time, standard deviation being limited with a 30° range. This suggests that the players adopted the anti-phase mode quite consistently over the trials.

Figure 2 displays an example of the players' displacements typical of the stable category illustrated in Figure 1. The ordinate represents the lateral motion of the players in cm, with the origin set in the middle of the court baseline. Comparison of the two curves shows that in the anti-phase mode, when a curve goes up, the other goes down, that is, in fact, both players moved on their left or right simultaneously.

These first findings corroborate our hypothesis that in tennis, the players' relative displacement exhibits coherent modes of synchronization, and that such modes may be captured by a pertinent collective variable, relative phase. Here, the anti-phase mode of synchronization is rendered by a relative phase of 180°.

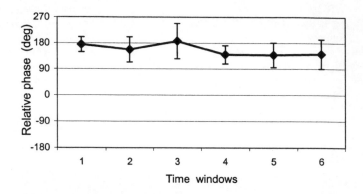

Figure 1. Relative phase development in the stable trials category.

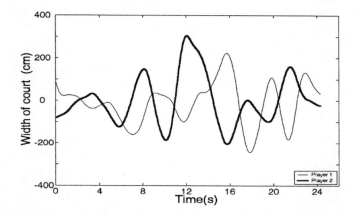

Figure 2. Typical displacement of players in the stable trials category.

### 3.3 Transition trials

Figure 3 presents the development of average relative phase for the transition category, on a similar display as for Figure 1. For the first two windows, relative phase remained stable about 180°. During the next two windows, it appeared to destabilize and switch in the direction of 0°. Finally, relative phase stayed about 0° value for the last two windows. An ANOVA with repeated measure revealed a significant effect of window number on relative phase ($F5, 5 = 20.03$, $P < 0.01$). This finding indicates that for this transition category, players exhibited first a stable synchronization of their displacements with a 180° phase lag, and then switched to a 0° synchronization, that is, a in-phase mode if displacement . Moreover, vertical bars in Figure 3 show that for 0° and 180° (viz. windows 1 and 6), the standard deviation was small (4°), indicating that these two modes were performed in a fairly regular fashion. In contrast, for the other windows, variability was substantially larger (40°, 86°, 121°, and 70° for the windows 2, 3, 4, and 5, respectively ). This means that as relative phase switches from 180° to 0°, it underwent a marked increase in variability. This suggests that the change in the observed relative displacement results from a loss of stability of the initial mode.

Figure 4 displays a typical example of the transition category described in Figure 3. For the first third of the trial (for about 8 s), the players were synchronized in the anti-phase mode illustrated in Figure 2 (when one curve goes up, the other goes down, and inversely). In a second phase (from 8 to 14 s), such a coherent mode disappears to give rise, in a third phase (after 15 s), to the in-phase mode of relative displacement, in which both curves move in the same direction.

The above results substantiate the idea that the players resort to only a few modes of relative displacement, actually two, in-phase and anti-phase, assessed by a value of relative phase of 0° and 180°, respectively.

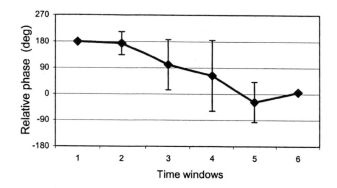

Figure 3. Relative phase development for the transition trials category.

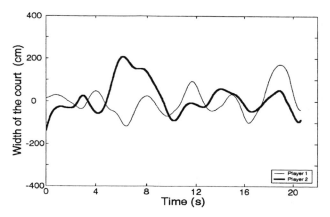

Figure 4. Typical displacement of players for the transition trials category.

## 4 Discussion and conclusion

This experiment investigated tennis from a dynamical system perspective. Our hypothesis is that relative phase was a relevant variable to capture the displacements of the two players. The findings indicate, on the one hand, that relative phase stays about 180° when players happen not to change the synchronization mode between their displacements. On the other hand, relative phase undergoes a transition from 180° to 0° when there is a change of mode. Therefore, relative phase is quite adept to characterize both invariance and change in the relative motion of the two players.

In self-organizing complex systems, fluctuations of the collective variable are a direct measure of the system's stability. Results show that only two values of relative phase are exhibited with a low variability, 0° and 180°, suggesting that theoretically these values are stable states of underlying dynamics. In other words, among all possible modes of synchronization between their displacements, tennis players adopt only two, in-phase and anti-phase. Results also demonstrate that transition between the anti-phase and in-phase modes are concomitant with an enhancement of the relative phase variability, a clear sign of loss of stability. This phenomenon is a typical feature of self-organized systems, so-called 'critical phenomena', as they switch from one stable state to another. This finding further supports the contention that tennis players do behave like a coupled oscillator dynamical system.

In conclusion, identifying stable states through preferred, more frequent modes of collective behavior is a primordial step to a complete understanding of what the underlying dynamics might be. The present study provides some initial evidence for such stable displacement modes in tennis players necessary to unravel the complete dynamics and to relate such dynamics to the perceptual, physical or tactical aspects of the game.

## 5 References

Haken, H. (1983). **Synergetics, an introduction: Non-equilibrium phase transitions and self-organization in physics, chemistry and biology.** Berlin: Springer.

Hodges, N.J., McGarry, T. and Franks, I.M. (1998). A dynamical system's approach to the examination of sport behavior. **Avante**, 4, 16-38.

McGarry, T. and Franks, I.M. (1994). A stochastic approach to predicting competition squash match-play. **Journal of Sports Sciences**, 12, 573-584.

McGarry, T. and Franks, I.M. (1995). Modelling competitive squash performance from quantitative analysis. **Human Performance**, 8, 113-129.

McGarry, T. and Franks, I.M. (1996). Development, application, and limitation of a Stochastic Markov model in explaining championship squash performance. **Research Quarterly for Exercise and Sport**, 67, 406-415.

McGarry, T., Anderson, D., Wallace, S., Hughes, M. and Franks, I.M. (2002). Sport competition as a dynamical self-organizing system. **Journal of Sports Sciences**, 20, 771-781.

Pikovsky, A., Rosenblum, M. and Kurths, J. (2001). **Synchronization: A universal concept in nonlinear sciences**. Cambridge University Press. University of Potsdam, Germany.

# 42 Self-controlled learning of the forehand topspin stroke in table tennis

A. Bund
*Tecnical University of Darmstadt, Magdalenenstr. 27, Darmstadt, Germany.*

## 1 Introduction

The effectiveness of self-controlled learning has been discussed in the verbal or cognitive learning domain for a number of years (for an overview see Boekaerts et al., 2000). The consensus seems to be that self-controlled learning has a beneficial effect on the learning process.

The term 'self-controlled learning' is not well defined. Normally, during practicing a new skill, the practice schedule is controlled by a teacher or instructor. For example, he or she provides instructions and feedback, deciding how many trials the learner performs, and selecting the tasks to practice. In contrast to this, self-controlled learning implies, that the learner has some control over the practice situation, so that he or she is able to use individual cognitive or behavioural strategies. That is, the learner takes charge of and is responsible for his or her own learning. However, it is important to note that on the one hand every learning process is realized in a social environment and on the other hand needs the participation of the learner. For this reason, the learning of new skills always includes elements of external influence and self-control at the same time but to various extent (see Kraft, 1999).

Recently, researchers have begun to examine the influence of self-control on motor skill learning. In those studies an experimental group, in which the participants have control over some aspects of the practice schedule is compared with a so called yoked group, in which the participants don't have the option to self-select their practice activities. Each subject in the yoked group is matched with a subject in the self-control group and receive the same practice schedule chosen by this counterpart. In general, the findings of these studies indicate, that self-controlled practice enhances the learning of complex movements, as shown by the retention results. For example, Janelle and colleagues (Janelle et al., 1997; Janelle et al., 1995) found that learners who could decide when they wanted to receive feedback outperformed (yoked) learners in retention tests who had no control over the provision of feedback. Wulf and Toole (1999) showed that participants who could self-control the use of ski-poles while practicing a ski-simulator task performed larger movement amplitudes in retention than their yoked counterparts. Finally, Wulf et al. (2001) examined how self-control versus no self-control affects the learning of the same task under dyad practice conditions. Interestingly, they found no group differences in movement features that can be easily observed (amplitude and frequency), but the self-control participants were more effective than the yoked participants with respect to force onset, which is a feature that can not be observed by other performers. This suggests that self-control learning interacts with observational learning.

Nevertheless, the research is still in its infancy and the studies are limited in several aspects. For example, as a result of psychological studies, it is well known, that the effectiveness of self-controlled learning is considerably influenced by personal and task-related factors (Boekaerts et al., 2000; Schunk and Zimmerman, 1994). Because of the interdependent structure of these relationships, the relative influence of personal factors (cognitive and affective processes) on self-controlled learning depends on the learning task and vice versa. However, previous research on self-controlled motor learning has totally ignored these complex relationships.

The purpose of this study was to include the learner-task interaction in the context of self-controlled learning. One important aspect of this interaction might be which part of the practice situation the learner has control over. It is probable that learners have different preferences regarding this point. Therefore, before the beginning of the experimental sessions, participants filled out a questionnaire and indicated which practice conditions they would prefer to self-control while practicing the forehand topspin stroke in table tennis and which not. In summary, we examined the effects of a learner-controlled practice schedule regarding a preferred practice condition versus a non-preferred practice condition. We hypothesized that giving learners the control over a preferred part of the practice schedule is more beneficial for learning the forehand topspin than giving control over a non-preferred condition of practice.

## 2  Methods

### 2.1 Participants
Fifty-two students  (32 male, 20 female, age: mean = 24.5, s =3.4 years, range 20-32 years) participated in this study.  None of them had considerable experience with the task, and all were informed about the purpose of the study. The students participated voluntarily, they were not paid for their services, and confidentiality was assured throughout the research.

### 2.2 Equipment and task
The equipment consisted of a regular-sized table-tennis table, high-quality white balls (40 mm), a ball firing machine, and a target area. The ball firing machine was set to deliver balls about every 3 s and so that the balls bounced about 20 cm before the edge of the table-tennis table. On a dial from 1 to 9, the ball velocity was set at 1, that is the ball velocity was about 15 $km.h^{-1}$. The target area was on the same side but crosscourt from the participant. Made of cardboard, the target consisted of seven rectangles (zones) with different colours, so that the participant could easily see the target. Each of the zones were 10 x 65 cm. Balls landing in the middle target zone were given 4 points, balls landing in the zones next to this field received 3 points, and so forth. During all experimental sessions the target area was videotaped in order to measure the hitting point of the balls accurately. For balls that were missed or did not land in any of the zones, 0 point was recorded. All participants used the same racket, an all-round composite racket with a conic handle, and preferred the shake-hands grip.

The participants' task was to learn the forehand topspin stroke. They were told that the goal was (1) to hit the ball as accurately as possible to the target area (movement accuracy), and (2) to perform the stroke technique correctly (movement form).

## 2.3 Procedure

Before the beginning of the experiment, participants were asked to fill out a questionnaire regarding their preferences for the self-control of practice conditions while learning the topspin stroke. The questionnaire included 16 items, in which different aspects of a practice schedule were described (e.g. type of movement instruction, frequency of feedback, number of acquisition trials). All items were introduced with the phrase "I would like to self-control...", and the participants responded on a scale from 1 (not true) to 4 (very true). The results showed that the instruction schedule was the most preferred practice condition to self-control ($M = 3.5$), whereas the option to self-determine the variability of practice was the less preferred condition ($M = 1.6$).

Based on these results, participants were randomly assigned to one of four experimental groups. Those in the *SC+* group had control over a preferred practice condition, that is they determined how often the video instruction was repeated during the practice phase. Participants in the *SC-* group had control over a non-preferred practice condition, that is they were allowed to choose the variability of practice (e.g. direction and length of the balls delivered by the machine). The experimenter recorded the schedules generated in the self-control groups. In contrast, participants in the yoked groups had no control over the practice situation. Rather, each in the *YO+* group was yoked to a participant in the *SC+* group and received the same schedule of movement instruction as his or her counterpart. Also, participants in the *YO-* group were matched with those in the *SC-* group. Thus, a 2 (self-control: yes vs. no) by 2 (practice condition: preferred vs. non-preferred) design was used.

Participants were tested individually. After some preliminary instructions about the procedure, participants watched a videotaped model of a highly skilled female table tennis player. They were told to focus on the model's movement form and it was stressed that correct form would eventually result in increased accuracy of the stroke. Altogether, participants saw eight repetitions of the model stroke from four different perspectives, partly in slow motion. Participants were then randomly assigned to the experimental groups as described above. The practice session consisted of 100 trials which were divided into 10 blocks of 10 trials per block. Each participant in one of the self-control groups had the option to see the videotape again whenever he or she wants (*SC+*) respectively to select a block of 10 trials, in which the balls varied in length and direction (*SC-*). Finally, all participants performed two retention tests after a break of five minutes (early retention) and two days (late retention) respectively. No augmented feedback regarding the technique was provided during practice or retention.

## 2.4 Dependent measures and data analysis

The dependent measures included movement accuracy and movement form. A target zone recorded by a video camera was used to assess the accuracy of balls (see above). The accuracy scores were averaged across blocks of 10 trials. For the practice phase, those scores were analysed in a 2 (self-control) x 2 (practice condition) x 10 (block) analysis of variance (ANOVA) with repeated measures on the last factor. The retention scores were analysed in a 2 (self-control) x 2 (practice condition) ANOVA.

Movement form was measured on the basis of a number of criteria (e.g., Gross and Huber, 2000; Hudetz, 2000). Those criteria referred to the position, swing, stroke, point of impact, and end of the stroke. Two independent raters assessed the quality of the third, fifth, and eighth strokes of each block and awarded a score between 0 and 26, with the highest score indicating perfect performance. The correlation between the scores of the two raters was 0.89. The form scores for the practice phase were analysed in a 2 (self-control) x 2 (practice condition) x 10 (block) repeated-measures ANOVA. For the retentions tests, the form scores were analysed in a 2 (self-control) x 2 (practice condition) ANOVA. The level of significance was set at an alpha level of $P < 0.05$.

## 3  Results

### 3.1 Practice schedules of self-control groups

Participants of the *SC+* group requested 21 repetitions of the video instruction during the practice phase. Relating to the total number of practice blocks (10) this indicated a relative frequency of 16.15%. Participants of the *SC-* group used the option to self-control their practice variability 16 times, indicating a relative frequency of 12.30%.

### 3.2 Practice

*Accuracy scores*

The scores achieved by each of the four groups during the practice phase can be seen in Figure 1. All groups demonstrated a consistent increase in the accuracy of the strokes; the main effect of block was significant ($F_{9,432} = 7.42$, $P < 0.001$). The main effects of self-control and practice condition failed to reach significance ($F_{1,48} = 0.18$, $P > 0.05$; $F_{1,48} = 2.29$, $P > 0.05$). Also, none of the interactions was significant.

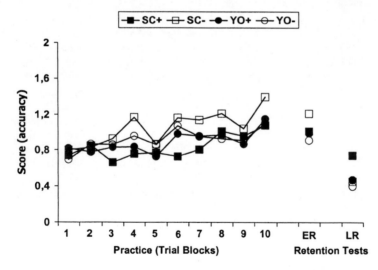

Figure 1. Accuracy scores of the experimental groups during practice and retention. ER=Early retention; LR=Late retention.

*Form scores*

In terms of movement quality, the analysis yielded a significant main effect of block ($F_{9,432} = 19.19$, $P < 0.001$), exhibiting a general improvement in form scores across practice trials (Figure 2). The self-control effect fell short of significance ($F_{1,48} = 7.42$, $P = 0.08$). The main effect of practice condition ($F_{9,432} = 0.50$, $P > 0.05$) and all interaction effects were not significant.

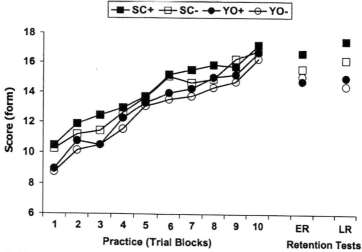

Figure 2. Form scores of the experimental groups during practice and retention. ER = Early retention; LR = Late retention.

### 3.3 Retention

*Accuracy scores*

The accuracy scores of the early and late retention tests can be seen in Figure 1 (right panel). Neither during early retention nor during late retention significant main or interaction effects were found (e.g., effect of self-control in early retention: $F_{1,48} = 0.73$, P > 0.05), indicating similar performance rates for all participants.

*Form scores*

With regard to movement form, no significant group differences were observed during early retention (self-control: $F_{1,48} = 1.51$, P > 0.05; practice condition: $F_{1,48} = 0.78$, P > 0.05). However, as can be seen in Figure 2 (right panel), there were differences between groups in the late retention test. The self-control main effect was significant, with $F_{1,48} = 5.95$, P < 0.01. Whereas the self-control groups continued to increase their form scores from the performance level they had reached during early retention, the yoked groups demonstrated a drop in performance, relative to the early retention test. Again, the main effect of practice condition was not significant ($F_{1,48} = 1.13$, P > 0.05).

### 4 Discussion and conclusion

The purpose of the present study was to examine the role of individual preferences in the context of self-controlled learning of the forehand topspin stroke in table tennis. Participants were given the option to self-control either a preferred practice condition (schedule of video instruction) or a non-preferred practice condition (variability of practice). Participants in two yoked groups were matched with and received the same practice schedule chosen by their self-controlled partners. We assumed that self-controlled learning is more effective when it refers to a part of the practice situation which is important for the learner than to a part which is not.

Results did not support this hypothesis, neither for the practice phase nor for one of the retentions tests where the effect of self-controlling a preferred vs. a non-preferred practice condition was significant. That is, participants who had control over a preferred part of the practice situation did not execute the stroke more accurately or show better technique than participants who only could self-select a non-preferred condition. Rather, we found small (during practice) respectively clear (during late retention) advantages for the self-controlled groups as compared with the yoked groups. Participants who could self-control a part of their practice (unimportant whether it was a preferred or a non-preferred part) demonstrated better learning with regard to movement form than participants who could not.

Thus, giving the learners some control over the practice situation seems to be more important than the question which aspect of the practice schedule it should be. This suggests that the benefits of self-controlled practice are not restricted on certain aspects of the situation, rather the benefits appear to be a result of the self-control process itself. Interestingly, the benefits were found for movement form but not for movement accuracy, which confirms a recent finding of Chiviacowsky and Wulf (2002). It will be a challenge for future research to identify the exact mechanisms responsible for the advantages of self-controlled practice regimes.

# 5 References

Boekaerts, M., Pintrich, P.R. and Zeidner, M. (2000). **Handbook of self-regulation.** San Diego: Academic Press.

Chiviakowsky, S. and Wulf, G. (2002). Self-controlled feedback: Does it enhance learning because performers get feedback when they need it? **Research Quarterly for Exercise and Sport**, 73, 408-415.

Gross, B.-U. and Huber, D. (1995). **Tischtennis: Moderne Technik für Anfänger und Könner** [Table Tennis: Modern technique for novices and experts]. Hamburg: Rowohlt.

Hudetz, R. (2000). **Table Tennis 2000. Technique with Vladimir Samsonov.** Zagreb: Huno Sport.

Janelle, C.M., Kim, J. and Singer, R.N. (1995). Subject-controlled performance feedback and learning of a closed motor skill. **Perceptual and Motor Skills**, 81, 627-634.

Janelle, C.M., Barba, D.A., Frehlich, S.G., Tennant, L.K. and Cauraugh, J.H. (1997). Maximizing performance feedback effectiveness through videotape replay and a self-controlled learning environment. **Research Quarterly for Exercise and Sport**, 68, 269-279.

Kraft, S. (1999). Selbstgesteuertes Lernen. Problembereiche in Theorie und Praxis [Self-regulated learning. Issues in theory and practice]. **Zeitschrift für Pädagogik**, 45, 833-845.

Schunk, D.H. and Zimmerman, B.J. (1994). **Self-regulation of learning and performance: Issues and educational applications.** Erlbaum, Hillsdale.

Wulf, G. and Toole, T. (1999). Physical assistance devices in complex motor skill learning: Benefits of a self-controlled practice schedule. **Research Quarterly for Exercise and Sport**, 70, 265-272.

Wulf, G., Clauss, A., Shea, C.H. and Whitacre, C.A. (2001). Benefits of self-control in dyad practice. **Research Quarterly for Exercise and Sport**, 72, 299-303.

# 43 Anticipating serve direction: Implicit sequence learning in tennis

R.C. Jackson and M. Gudgeon
*Department of Sport Sciences, Brunel University, Uxbridge, Middlesex, UB8 3PH, UK.*

## 1 Introduction

Expert performance in many racket sports is characterised by athletes reacting extremely quickly to key events such as the direction of an opponent's shot. Returning the serve in tennis is no exception and with men and women now serving at speeds of up to 240 km.h$^{-1}$ and 205 km.h$^{-1}$ respectively it is perhaps unsurprising that the first serve is such a dominant factor in the game. For example, Magnus and Klaassen (1999) collated statistics from four years of singles matches at the Wimbledon championship and found that men won 73.3% of points when their first serve was 'in'. Nevertheless, elite players are able to make many successful returns and much research over the past 20 years has focused on establishing the means by which they are able to be successful. This research has centred on the comparison of expert and novice players, and evidence points towards the expert's superior ability to anticipate the likely direction of the serve before the ball has actually been struck.

A variety of research paradigms have been used to study this ability. One of the most commonly used methods is the temporal occlusion paradigm in which players observe video clips of serves that are occluded at a number of specific points, typically several frames either side of the moment at which the server strikes the ball. After the video clip is occluded, the participant indicates the type of serve and/or the direction in which they felt the ball would go. This research has revealed that experts perform significantly better than chance level with expert-novice differences most prominent at the pre-contact occlusion points (Farrow and Abernethy, 2002; Jones and Miles, 1978). Additional research using 'event' or 'spatial' occlusion paradigms to mask a variety of postural cues as well as that using eye-tracking equipment (e.g., Goulet et al., 1989) has yielded information regarding the visual cues upon which expert anticipation is based (see Williams and Grant, 1999, for a review).

Currently, there is a debate over how such skills are learned together with the related question of how they should be coached. Specifically, it has been suggested that the ability to anticipate may be acquired implicitly, that is, experts may become sensitive to subtle postural cues or situational probabilities without necessarily intending to do so and in such a way that the resulting knowledge is difficult to express (Berry and Dienes, 1993). For example, Jackson (2003a) has argued that the subtle nature of the postural cues distinguishing different types and directions of serve might negate the utility of explicit instructions, particularly at the higher ability levels. In support of this argument, Jackson points to the limited success of the small number of perceptual training programmes in which explicit instruction has played a prominent role. For example, Farrow et al. (1998) instructed novice tennis players to attend to the server's stance, ball toss, racket position and racket speed. After eight 15-minute training sessions, these players became significantly faster at responding to the serve, however, this was offset by a 22% decrease in the accuracy of judgments. Further, Jackson noted that interventions that have resulted in improved anticipation (e.g. Abernethy et al., 1999) have incorporated many components, making it difficult to determine whether the effective components are those that promote explicit learning, those that promote implicit learning, or a combination of the two.

Recently, Farrow and Abernethy (2002) addressed this issue by conducting a perceptual training experiment in which they compared the effectiveness of explicit and implicit learning paradigms. In order to promote implicit learning, players were distracted from focusing explicitly on potential sources of information by being given the task of estimating the speed of each serve. Farrow and Abernethy argued that their results indicated that the implicit learning paradigm was more effective than the explicit instructions. Although their analyses and interpretations have recently been questioned (Jackson, 2003b) other recent research supports the view that less explicit modes of instruction, such as guided discovery, may be an effective means of training sensitivity to key postural cues (Williams, 2003).

In the implicit learning literature, one of the most frequently used paradigms is the serial reaction time task. In this task, the participant attempts to respond as quickly as possible to a visual stimulus appearing in one of several possible locations. Unbeknownst to the participant, the order in which the stimulus appears follows a complex sequence. In terms of implicit learning the key finding from this research is that reaction times gradually decrease but then increase when the sequence of locations is changed even when subsequent questioning of participants reveals an absence of explicit knowledge that trials followed a sequence. Recently, Howard and Howard (1997) devised an alternating serial reaction time task in which trials alternate between those following a pre-determined sequence and those in which location is randomly determined. Using this paradigm, a difference between reaction times in the random and sequence trials in the absence of explicit knowledge of the existence of a repeating sequence constitutes evidence for implicit learning. An additional advantage of this task is that it enables one to see when as well as whether implicit learning occurs by comparing reaction times on the random and sequenced trials at all stages of the experiment.

In men's tennis matches of the best of five sets, an average of approximately 230 points are played (Magnus and Klaassen, 1999). This provides ample opportunity for servers to develop sequences (with or without explicit knowledge that they are doing so) and the primary aim of the present study was to investigate whether implicit sequence learning could occur in tennis. In particular, it was of interest to see whether (a) reaction times would improve on serves following a sequence and (b) whether this would be independent of explicit knowledge that such a sequence existed.

## 2 Method

### 2.1 Design
The study utilised a mixed design in which two groups of players (coaches and club players) each received 9 blocks of 12 serves directed to one of three locations (down the centre, into the body, out wide). In line with the alternating serial reaction time paradigm, the location of serves alternated between those following a pre-determined sequence and those directed randomly to one of the three locations. The reaction time

of the receiver served as the dependent variable, determined by counting the number of frames from when the server struck the ball to the moment the receiver first initiated a lateral movement in order to facilitate a return. Inter-rater agreement in a random sample of 100 serve clips was acceptable (92%).

## 2.2 Participants

Eleven male right-handed tennis players (n = 5 coaches, n = 6 club players) took part in the study. The coaches had a mean age of 24.60 years (±5.86) and a mean of 17.60 years playing experience (±6.88) and had competed at a higher level than the club players who had a mean age of 31.00 years (±13.67) and a mean of 12.42 years playing experience (±9.15).

## 2.3 Materials

Prior to the study, each player filled out a brief questionnaire assessing general background information and also containing two questions about what advice they would give to a player wishing to anticipate the direction and type of serve. A post-test questionnaire asked the same questions in relation to the specific player they had just faced. In addition, an open-ended question about whether or not they had noticed any "sequence or pattern" to the direction of serves just faced was used to assess explicit knowledge. Finally, a free-generate test was used in which participants were informed of the presence of a sequence and then attempted to write down the order of the repeating sequence.

## 2.4 Procedure

All players were informed that the study was about the serve and return of serve in tennis and that they would play a series of 'points' in which only these two shots would be played. After giving informed consent and filling in the pre-study questionnaire, the players were given up to 10 minutes to warm-up. During the study, each player served a total of 108 serves in 9 blocks of 12 directed to one of three locations in the 'deuce' service box. Each block contained a repeating sequence of 6 serves (e.g. centre, body, wide, body, centre, wide) interspersed with serves randomly directed to one of the three locations. After each block, the players swapped ends so that the server became the receiver and the receiver became the server. A 50 Hz Panasonic NV-MS4 S-VHS video camera was positioned behind the receiver to enable subsequent determination of the reaction time of the receiver to the nearest 20 ms. Each player was given a folder containing the required serve directions for each block. In each pair of players both the repeating and random sequences were different as was the first or second serve containing the sequence. Data were analysed by a 9 x 2 x 2 (block x sequence x ability) analysis of variance (ANOVA) with repeated measures on the block and sequence factors. Alpha level was set at 0.05.

# 3 Results

## 3.1 Reaction times

As can be seen in Figure 1, differences between the mean reaction time on random and sequenced serves quickly appeared in the club players so that in blocks 4, 5, and 6 a difference of approximately 40ms was apparent; however, there was no evidence of sequence learning in the coaches. This was reflected in the results of the ANOVA which revealed a significant interaction between sequence and ability ($F_{1,8} = 8.57$,

P < 0.05, $\eta_p^2 = 0.49$). Figure 1 also indicates that the reaction time of the coaches was faster than that of the club players, reflected in a significant main effect for ability ($F_{1,9} = 31.79$, P < 0.01, $\eta_p^2 = 0.78$). Finally, neither the three-way interaction nor the two-way interactions involving the block factor reached significance.

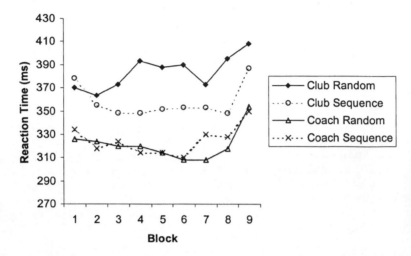

Figure 1. Mean of median reaction times for the coaches and club players in each block of 12 serves when facing the random and sequenced serve directions.

## 3.2 Explicit knowledge

In response to the open-ended questions, no player reported noticing a repeating sequence. Additional evidence for the lack of explicit knowledge was apparent in the free generate task in which club players correctly reported a mean of 1.5 out of 6 locations, which is slightly less than would be expected by chance. Coaches correctly reported a mean of 2.4 out of 6 locations.

## 4  Discussion

The results revealed a significant difference in reaction time between random and sequenced serves in the club players but not the coaches. Evidence for sequence learning being implicit in the club players was apparent in their lack of explicit knowledge regarding the presence of a sequence and chance performance on the free-generate test. Overall, coaches were faster in responding to their opponents' serves than their club playing counterparts, concurring with recent tennis research focusing on response latencies to shots played during rallies (Rowe and McKenna, 2001).

   Previous research has made extensive use of the serial reaction time task in order to demonstrate implicit learning. Although there is continuing debate over the extent to which implicit learning can and/or has been shown in humans (see Shanks and St. John, 1994 for a critique), the present study capitalised on tennis players' use of postural cues and the ball toss to promote implicit sequence learning. To explain, Shanks and St. John (1994) argued that any test of explicit knowledge needs to be sensitive enough to pick up all the explicit rules generated by the performer (the sensitivity criterion), and also needs to probe all appropriate information (the information criterion). With respect to the latter a potential problem is that participants generate rules that are correlated with the "correct" rules. In such cases, it may be incorrectly concluded that participants are learning the task implicitly. In satisfying these criteria, some of the strongest evidence for implicit learning has come from studies in which participants are led to believe that their success is contingent upon one feature of a task (e.g. tapping out the number of tones they hear) when it is in fact contingent upon a different feature (e.g., the force with which they press the button to indicate the number of tones they heard). In such experiments, it has been found that participants' responding becomes sensitive to the implicit contingency even though their attention is directed towards a contingency that is unrelated to success (e.g. Svartdal, 1992). In the present experiment, tennis players tended to focus their attention on postural cues and/or the ball toss, strengthening the case for sequence learning being implicit.

A key question emanating from this research is why implicit sequence learning did not occur in the higher-level players (i.e. the coaches). First, it should be noted that the small sample size limited the power of the present analysis and replication is required before the null finding in higher-level players can be confirmed. Assuming the finding proves robust, one possibility is that there was a floor effect, below which reaction times cannot be improved, in which case the practical implications for expert players are limited. Alternatively, competing explicit cues may prevent the expression of implicit sequence learning that is subsequently revealed when competing explicit cues are suppressed or withdrawn (Cleeremans, 1997). Thus, it is possible that high-level tennis players base their anticipation upon a small number of indicative cues that 'override' the expression of implicit sequence learning. Should the cues prove poor predictors of serve direction then one would expect differences in reaction times for random and sequenced serves to emerge.

From a practical point of view, the results suggest that a sequence can be learned implicitly, resulting in faster reaction times and, assuming this is advantageous for the receiver, reducing the inherent advantage of the server. Further, the advantage on sequenced serves emerged by the third block of 12 serves, suggesting that reaction time changes might occur fairly rapidly during a match. Although it could be argued that the results were due to receivers emphasising the speed rather than accuracy of their responses on the sequenced trials, we argue that this is unlikely due to the alternating nature of the random and sequenced trials. Specifically, the receiver would similarly have to have an alternating strategy, which seems unlikely in the absence of explicit knowledge regarding the sequence.

## 5 Conclusions

The focus of much anticipation research in tennis and other racket sports has been on identifying the visual cues that may help players predict the likely outcome of key events. Previously unconsidered, the present study found evidence for implicit sequence learning that resulted in faster reaction times to serves in male club tennis players. This adds to the growing body of research into anticipation, a skill that most likely involves a subtle combination of explicit and implicit processes. Having established reliable differences between expert and novice performers, determining the precise manner in which explicit and implicit processes interact represents a significant challenge for those conducting research in this area.


## 6  References

Abernethy, B., Wood, J.M. and Parks, S. (1999). Can the anticipatory skills of experts be learned by novices? **Research Quarterly for Exercise and Sport,** 70, 313-318.

Berry, D.C. and Dienes, Z. (1993). **Implicit learning: Theoretical and empirical issues.** Hove, England: Lawrence Erlbaum Associates.

Cleeremans, A. (1997). Sequence learning in a dual-stimulus setting. **Psychological Research,** 60, 72-86.

Farrow, D. and Abernethy, B. (2002). Can anticipatory skills be learned through implicit video-based perceptual training? **Journal of Sports Sciences,** 20, 471-485.

Farrow, D., Chivers, P., Hardingham, C. and Sasche, S. (1998). The effect of video based perceptual training on the tennis return of serve. **International Journal of Sport Psychology,** 29, 231-242.

Goulet, C., Bard, C. and Fleury, M. (1989). Expertise differences in preparing to return a tennis serve: A visual information processing approach. **Journal of Sport and Exercise Psychology,** 11, 382-398.

Howard, J.H. and Howard, D.V. (1997). Age differences in implicit learning of higher order dependencies in serial patterns. **Psychology and Aging,** 12, 634-656.

Jackson, R.C. (2003a). New directions in the development of concentration skills: A behavioural perspective. In **Concentration Skills Training in Sport** (edited by I.P. Greenlees and A.P. Moran), Leicester, UK: British Psychological Society. pp. 33-42.

Jackson, R.C. (2003b). Evaluating the evidence for implicit perceptual learning: A re-analysis of Farrow and Abernethy (2002). **Journal of Sports Sciences,** 21, 503-509.

Jones, C.M. and Miles, T.R. (1978). Use of advance cues in predicting the flight of a lawn tennis ball. **Journal of Human Movement Studies,** 4, 231-235.

Magnus, J.R. and Klaassen, J.G.M. (1999). On the advantage of serving first in a tennis set: Four years at Wimbledon. **The Statistician,** 48, 247-256.

Rowe, R.M. and McKenna, F.P. (2001). Skilled anticipation in real-world tasks: Measurement of attentional demands in the domain of tennis. **Journal of Experimental Psychology: Applied,** 7, 60-67.

Shanks, D.R. and St. John, M.F. (1994). Characteristics of dissociable human learning systems. **Behavioral and Brain Sciences,** 17, 367-395.

Svartdal, F. (1992). Sensitivity to nonverbal operant contingencies: Do limited processing resources affect operant conditioning in humans? **Learning and Motivation,** 23, 383-405.

Williams, A.M. and Grant, A. (1999). Training perceptual skill in sport. **International Journal of Sport Psychology,** 30, 194-220.

Williams, A. M. (2003). Developing selective attention skill in fast ball sports. In **Concentration Skills Training in Sport** (edited by I.P. Greenlees and A.P. Moran), Leicester, UK: British Psychological Society, pp. 20-32.

# 44 Impact of the new scoring system on expert table tennis players' activity

C. Sève

*French Table Tennis Association, CETAPS UPRES JE 2318, University of Rouen, France.*

## 1 Introduction

The activity of expert table tennis players during matches under the old scoring system was studied within the French Table Tennis Federation. These studies were conducted from the theoretical framework of the course-of-action (Theureau, 1992) used in ergonomics research. A course of action is a chain of elementary units of meaning (EUMs) or activity units that are meaningful for the actor. When actors are asked to describe their activity, they spontaneously break down the continuous stream of actions into discrete units that are meaningful to them. These discrete units may be physical actions, communicative exchanges, interpretations, or feelings: they constitute the EUMs of the course of action. The course of action reflects the temporal organization of the activity and is analysed in relation to situational variables. This methodology relies on videotaped recordings collected in real situations, and then self-confrontation interviews in which the actors viewing the videotapes are urged to recall and explain what they were experiencing at the time (von Cranach and Harré, 1982). This methodological framework provides a means for describing and finely analyzing a person's activity in accordance with its temporal dynamics, and for grasping the meaning each actor gives to his/her own activity. The results of our previous studies showed that the players' actions were organized to form sequences dividing each match into phases of exploration and execution (Sève, 2000; Sève et al., 2003). Matches began with an inquiry period during which the players looked for strokes that impinged upon the opponent's play. Regardless of the outcome of the inquiry phase, however, it had to come to an end when the players felt they could no longer afford to sacrifice points for fear of losing the match. The activity of table tennis players during a match could not be reduced to the mere performance of skills acquired during practice and the application of predefined plans: it included exploration, learning, and disguise. During games, players constructed and validated new knowledge about the current interactive situation by testing hypotheses, which were necessarily limited in number due to the risk of losing points and the game (Sève et al., 2002).

On September 1, 2001, the scoring system changed, and the goal of the present study was thus to evaluate the impact of this new system on elite table tennis players' activity during matches. To facilitate the comparison of results between this study and earlier ones, the same theoretical and methodological framework was used. Based on the content of previous interviews (about the new scoring system) with expert table tennis players (Sève and Birocheau, 2002), it was predicted that the new system would disturb the exploratory phase.

## 2  Methods

### 2.1 Participants and procedure
Four top-level table tennis players from the French Men's Table Tennis Team
volunteered to participate in the study. The players' activity was studied in four
matches (Table 1). These matches took place during the French Championships in
2002.

Table 1. Characteristics of matches

| Match | Player's name | Age | International experience (in years) | Player's world ranking | Opponent's world ranking | Result |
|---|---|---|---|---|---|---|
| A | CH | 30 | 11 | 33 | 24 | Won 4 sets to 1 |
| B | PA | 33 | 15 | 24 | 33 | Lost 4 sets to 1 |
| C | PH | 34 | 17 | 32 | 143 | Won 4 sets to 0 |
| D | SE | 27 | 7 | 143 | 32 | Lost 4 sets to 0 |

*Note.* The players' world rankings were the ones held at the time of the competition.

### 2.2 Data collection
Two types of data were gathered: (a) recording of the match, and (b) verbalizations
during a post-match interview. The match was recorded with an 8-mm video camera.
The camera was positioned above and behind the table, and was set for a wide-angle,
top view that framed the table and the movement area of both players. This setup
allowed for continuous recording of the players' moves during the match.

The verbalization data was collected via an interview with the players conducted
after the match. During the interview the searcher and the player viewed the
videotape of the match together. The player was asked to describe and comment upon
his activity during the match. Either person could stop the tape and backtrack at any
time. The interviewer's prompts were related to descriptions of the actions and events
as experienced by the player; requests for interpretations and generalizations were
avoided. The entire interview was recorded using an 8-mm video camera and a tape
recorder.

### 2.3 Data processing
The data was processed in three steps: (a) construct chronicles of matches, (b) label
the elementary units of meaning and compile condensed narratives, and (c) label the
series.

*Constructing chronicles of matches*
The descriptions of the players' actions and the player's verbalizations during the
interview were mapped to each other by constructing tables called chronicles of
matches. The first column gave the score and the server's name. The second column
listed the actions of the two opponents. The third column contained the verbatim
transcription of the prompted verbalizations (see Table 2).

Table 2. Excerpt from the chronicle of match of game 1, Match A

| Score | Players' actions | PA's verbalizations |
|---|---|---|
| PA 0-0 | PA serves long to CH's backhand side. CH attacks to PA's backhand side. PA blocks to CH's backhand side and scores the point. | So here I'm testing a long serve. He's attacking but I'm doing a stroke I like: a sideway backhand block on his backhand. I know the ball will come back to my forehand side. It's a game configuration that I know and like. |
| 1-0 2-0 | PA serves short and sidespin to CH's backhand side. CH returns a short ball. PA attacks and scores the point. | Here I'm testing a short sidespin serve. That forces him to play short on my forehand and I do a stroke I don't often do: smash when he returns a short ball. Attacking the ball like that gives me confidence. I don't often pull off strokes like that. |

*Labelling the elementary units of meaning and compiling condensed narratives*
This step involved drawing up a summary presentation or condensed narrative of each course of action. A narrative was made up of a chain of elementary units of meaning (EUMs). The narratives were delineated by breaking the chronicle matches down into EUMs. The EUMs were labelled by simultaneously analyzing the chronicles of matches and the videotapes while systematically asking questions about the player's actions (What is he doing?), his interpretations (What is he thinking?), and his feelings (What is he feeling?) as they appeared in the log. This analysis was done step by step for each instant in each course of action, and allowed us to reconstruct a chain of EUMs for each match (Table 3). Two experienced investigators (one of whom was the researcher who conducted the interviews) separately coded the data into EUMs. The initial agreement rate was 90%. Initial disagreements were resolved by discussion between the researchers until a consensus was reached. The name of the EUM was a phrase that expressed the player's concern and specified his physical action, interpretation, and/or feeling.

Table 3. Excerpt from the condensed narrative of Match A, Set 1

| Score | Elementary Units of Meaning |
|---|---|
| 0-0 | EUM 1. Tests effect on the opponent of serving long to his backhand side |
| 1-0 | EUM 2. Tries to win point by blocking sideway to Chris's backhand side |
| | EUM 3. Tests effect on the opponent of serving short and sidespin to his backhand side |
| 2-0 | EUM 4. Tries to win the point by attacking |
| | EUM 5. Confident that he's made a difficult stroke |

*Labelling the series*
EUMs are linked together and nested within larger units that correspond to higher-level meaningful structures. Among these, we shall focus in the present analysis on so-called series. Series account for similarities between concerns during the match. Series were identified and labelled by finding relationships between the elementary units. Each series was made up of elementary units that formed a coherent chain

around a meaningful theme for the player. The EUMs were grouped into series on the basis of three criteria: (a) the meaning of the statements, (b) a comparable level of generality across series, and (c) the use of series definitions that were discriminating enough to avoid overlapping. In illustration, EUMs 1 and 3 of Match A were grouped together into a series called "Look for effective serves" and EUMs 2 and 4 into a series called "Reproduce effective game configurations". Two experienced investigators separately grouped the EUMs into series. The initial agreement rate was 95%. Initial disagreements were resolved by discussion between the researchers until a consensus was reached.

## 3 Results

### 3.1 Exploration series and execution series

The analysis pointed out nine series that could be classified into two categories: exploration series and execution series (Table 4).

Table 4. Series in the players' courses of action, classified into two categories

| Exploration series | Execution series |
|---|---|
| 1. Look for effective serves | 1. Reproduce effective serves |
| 2. Look for effective serve returns | 2. Reproduce effective serve returns |
| 3. Look for effective first attacks | 3. Reproduce effective first attacks |
| 4. Look for effective game configurations | 4. Reproduce effective game configurations |
| | 5. Perturb the opponent |

These two categories expressed the two characteristic types of concerns the players had in the situation: determining what type of opposition there was, and scoring points. During the exploration series, the players mainly tried to build and validate knowledge likely to help them win. They did not seek immediate effectiveness but gave themselves time to test the opponent's response to different strokes. They placed priority on testing the effectiveness of their favourite serves, returns, first attacks, and game configurations, and strokes likely to jeopardize the opponent's game. They strove to identify the strokes that hindered or bothered the opponent at the current time, based on the assumption that his particular way of playing would vary across matches and moments within a match.

During the execution series, the players tried to make points. They reproduced strokes judged effective based on the outcome of earlier matches or games, and they varied these strokes to avoid counterattacks. They sought immediate effectiveness.

### 3.2 Temporal arrangement of series in the matches

We have constructed graphs in order to present the temporal organization of the exploration and execution series during the four matches (Figure 1). These graphs pointed out that the structure of the series evolved during the matches. At match onset, the players were mainly involved in interpreting the opposition; in the later stages of the match, they were attempting to reproduce effective actions in order to score.

The four matches began with an inquiry period during which the players looked for strokes that impinged upon the opponent's play. This lasted about one or two games. They tested the effectiveness of different strokes: serves, serve returns, initial attacks, and game configurations (i.e. chains of different strokes). As soon as they had identified the effective strokes, the players started reproducing them. This began at different points in the match, depending on when identification took place. Certain effective strokes were detected very early whereas others were identified later.

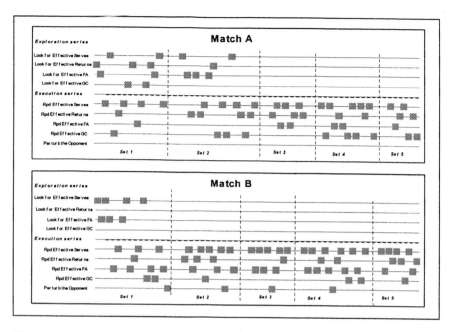

Figure 1. Arrangement of series in Matches A and B.
        Legend: Rpd = reproduce. GC = game configuration. FA = first attack.

## 4 Discussion and conclusions

Our results must be generalized with caution because of the small number of participants, but they do show that the new scoring system has had an impact on expert table tennis players activity' during matches. Although the series composing this activity have remained the same, their organization has changed and the relative duration of the exploration phase is now shorter in comparison with the execution phase (see Figure 2). Under the old system, players divided the 21-point game into three characteristic periods related to the successions of five serves: the beginning of the game (the first four successions of serves), the middle of the game (the following two successions), and the end of the game (the last two successions) (Sève, 2000). They assumed that they could perform exploratory actions in the beginning of a game without risking their chances of winning (Sève et al., 2003). With the new 11-point game, the players now find that these early exploratory actions pose a threat to winning (Sève and Birocheau, 2002), and they therefore place greater emphasis on maximal effectiveness from the very beginning of play and have correspondingly shortened the exploration phase, during which they increase the risks of losing points.

Unsurprisingly, analysis also showed greater difficulty in identifying effective serves and serve returns under the new scoring system. Under the old system, the players took advantage of the five successive serves (or serve returns) to limit the number of plays needed to determine which serves (or serve returns) were effective. The players looked for effective serves by producing five serves (or returns) of different lengths (short, long, two-bounce), directions (to the opponent's forehand or backhand side, to the middle of the table), spins (backspin, topspin, no spin, sidespin), and speeds (slow, fast). In each case, they tried to determine what aspects of the stroke's trajectory perturbed the opponent's play. This was achieved by retaining one or more characteristics of the trajectory—i.e. the one(s) thought to be likely to hinder the opponent—while varying the others (Sève et al., 2003). Under the new system, the status of server or receiver changes every two points and players can no longer implement such successions of serves and serve returns to gather here-and-now information on their opponent's play.

It is concluded that the new scoring system disturbs the strategies habitually employed by expert table tennis players to determine effective strokes.

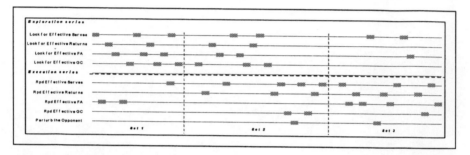

Figure 2. Example of the arrangement of series in a match (old scoring system).

## 5 References

von Cranach, M. and Harré, R. (Eds.). (1982). **The Analysis of Action. Recent Theoretical and Empirical Advances**. Cambridge: Cambridge University Press.

Sève, C. (2000). **Tennis de table: entraînement et compétition** [Table tennis: Training and competition]. Paris: Fédération Française de Tennis de table.

Sève, C. and Birocheau, P. (2002). Le nouveau système de comptage [The new scoring system]. **France Tennis de Table Magazine**, 766, 10-11.

Sève, C., Saury, J., Ria, L. and Durand, M. (2003). Structure of expert table tennis players' activity during competitive interaction. **Research Quarterly for Exercise and Sport**, 74, 71-83.

Sève, C., Saury, J., Theureau, J. and Durand, M. (2002). La construction de connaissances chez les sportifs au cours d'une interaction compétitive [Knowledge construction by athletes during competitive interaction]. **Le Travail Humain**, 65, 159-190.

Theureau, J. (1992). **Le cours d'action: Analyse sémiologique. Essai d'une anthropologie cognitive située.** [The course of action: semiological analysis. Essay on situated cognitive anthropology]. Berne: Peter Lang.

# Index